Robert Lowery: Radical and Chartist

Robert Lowery (1809-1863)

Robert Lowery

Radical and Chartist

Edited by Brian Harrison and Patricia Hollis

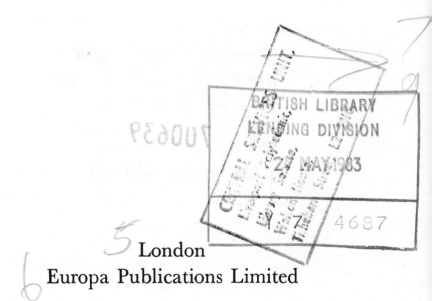
London
Europa Publications Limited

Europa Publications Limited
18 Bedford Square, London, WC1B 3JN

© Brian Harrison and Patricia Hollis, 1979

British Library Cataloguing in Publication Data

Lowery, Robert
    1. Lowery, Robert   2. Trade unions—Great Britain—Biography
    3. Radicals—Great Britain—Biography   4. Chartism
    322.4′4′0924   HD8393.L/

ISBN 0-905118-31-6

Printed and bound in England by
Staples Printers Rochester Limited
at the Stanhope Press

Contents

Foreword

Robert Lowery: Radical and Chartist is the third in a series of republications of working men's autobiographies from the nineteenth century. As with the works contained in the first volume, *Testaments of Radicalism*, it is primarily a political autobiography; its author's main concern is to present, and attempt to understand, his career as an activist in a series of working class political movements, particularly Chartism. Patricia Hollis and Brian Harrison have performed a great service in rescuing the text from the columns of the *Weekly Record of the Temperance Movement*, for whilst the memoirs of working class politicians are so scanty as to make any addition to their number an important event, Lowery's preoccupation with the practical details of the life of an organizer and travelling "missionary", renders his work in some respects more valuable than the better known but more generalized accounts of William Lovett and Thomas Cooper.

The autobiography was published at almost the same time as the second of the republished autobiographies, James Dawson Burn's *The Autobiography of a Beggar Boy*, and by the same publisher, William Tweedie. Both Lowery and Burn spent their formative years in Northumberland before moving further afield, and throughout their lives and their autobiographies both men were centrally concerned with the relationship between working class respectability and working class radicalism. Respectability stood as both the justification for and the goal of entry into national political life, yet in practice it often seemed to be the victim of the form and content of the political organizations in which the working class was involved. For these men, Chartism at first appeared as the triumphant statement of working class pride and independence, and then, as its hostility towards the middle class became more entrenched and talk of violence more widespread, they began to fear that the movement would betray the values of sobriety and rationality to which they attached such significance. There was no simple answer to the problem, but the historian can only understand both its nature and the efforts that were made to resolve it, by studying the way in which a man like Robert Lowery wrestled with it both in his life and in his attempt to record it.

DAVID VINCENT
University of Keele

Introduction

Brian Harrison and Patricia Hollis

Robert Lowery's autobiography is so well written, so detailed and so early in its date, that one might have expected it to become a major historical source. R. G. Gammage consulted Lowery when compiling his *History of the Chartist Movement*, and William Lovett's famous *Life and Struggles* (1876) relies on "a series of articles written by Mr. Robert Lowery, one of our convention, and published in the *Temperance Weekly Record*" for the origins of the Chartist newspaper the *Northern Star*.[1] Lovett may have misled historians by abbreviating the title of the journal, *The Weekly Record of the Temperance Movement*; and by failing to state the date of publication, he condemned historians to forage about in a periodical which ran for many years. But a much more likely explanation for the neglect of Lowery's autobiography is simply that historians of nineteenth-century England have only recently interested themselves in the Victorian Liberal Party's popular base, and in the many reforming movements which enabled Liberals to develop links with working men. Only recently, then, could *The Weekly Record of the Temperance Movement* have found readers interested in both the Chartist and temperance movements.

Lowery's memoir, some 80,000 words in all, consists of 33 articles published in the *Weekly Record* at irregular intervals between 15 April 1856 and 23 May 1857.[2] It is reprinted here in full, together with some of his other writing, letters, reports of his speeches, and a pamphlet. Obvious printer's errors have been removed, but the original spelling and punctuation have been retained. Lowery (whose name was quite often spelt "Lowry" or "Lowrey" by others, but always "Lowery" by himself) never publicly put his name to the autobiography, but it is quite clear that he wrote it. Three aspects of the autobiography seem worth discussing here: its contribution to our understanding of working class history; its status as autobiographical literature; and its

---

[1] W. Lovett, *Life and Struggles* (1876), p. 173; Lovett's quotation from Lowery has minor inaccuracies, but it is clear that Lovett was consulting Lowery's articles. See also R. G. Gammage, *History of the Chartist Movement 1837–1854* (1969 ed.), p. 267.
[2] The final page is in fact dated 30 May, but nonetheless comes from the number for 23 May.

1

purpose in, and illumination of, Lowery's own career. But as Lowery has not hitherto featured prominently in Chartist historiography, it may first be useful to say something about his life.[3]

I

Robert Lowery was born in North Shields in 1809, the eldest of four boys. He left school at nine and a year later was working at a colliery mouth near Newcastle. His father, a sailor, died when the boy was thirteen, and Robert got himself apprenticed to a brig in the North American timber trade. Sea life damaged his health: within a year he was recuperating in a Quebec nunnery from a serious illness which lamed him for life. He obviously could not return to sea, so he was apprenticed to a Newcastle tailor, and joined a trade eminently compatible with self-education. He married young, had two daughters, and began lecturing and debating on universal suffrage and the new poor law. By moving between masters he took only two years to qualify as a journeyman. This led to somewhat ambiguous relations with the older men, and Lowery found himself reluctantly leading the younger and more radical journeymen tailors into a less exclusive general union at the time when the Grand National Consolidated Trades Union (GNCTU) was making federated trade unionism the issue of the hour. His radical connexions were reinforced when his employers gave him the "silent sack", for he began selling unstamped radical newspapers in Newcastle. During 1837 local political unionism (on the Birmingham model) revived; the poor law commissioners moved north; and after a brief interval managing a wine and spirit merchant's shop and then running a public-house, when he published a lecture on *State Churches Destructive of Christianity and Subversive to the Liberties of Man* (1837), Lowery joined the newly-founded and highly radical *Northern Liberator*.

Soon afterwards he was elected Newcastle delegate to the London Chartists' Palace Yard meeting of 17 September 1838; from then onwards, Chartism absorbed all his time. In the next two years he undertook eight major lecture-tours—usually with his fellow Chartist Abram Duncan—and carried Chartism to much of the Celtic Fringe: to Cumberland, Durham and Scotland, where he was introduced to Christian Chartism; to Cornwall, where he was sponsored by the convention only to find his good work impeded by Methodist revivalism; and to Ireland, where local Chartists bungled the arrangements and where O'Connell's followers refused him a

---

[3] For a fuller summary, see our memoir of Lowery in *Dictionary of Labour Biography* (Ed. J. Bellamy & J. Saville), IV (1977), pp. 112–7 and also our "Chartism, Liberalism and the Life of Robert Lowery", *English Historical Review*, July 1967, pp. 507–11. This introduction reproduces only a small quantity of the material in the latter article, to which we refer readers who seek an assessment of Lowery's place in nineteenth-century political and labour history.

public hearing. He was prominent in the 1839 Chartist convention as one of its younger and more extravagant members. He was rebuked for his violence, ironically by John Frost, but behind the scenes Lowery was relatively moderate.

After the convention was dissolved he wrote his pamphlet on exclusive dealing (pp. 195 ff.) and tried bookselling and journalism, only to find that this got him into trouble with O'Connor. He returned to lecturing, and extended his range by publicly criticizing the Anti-Corn Law Leaguers, pondering on the drink question, and studying foreign policy under Urquhart's Russophobic guidance. In 1839 the Frost rising led to the arrest of many Chartist leaders, but Lowery kept clear of trouble and continued lecturing in Scotland. Late in 1839 he participated in a second convention, which met in London to plan Frost's defence. Before the repercussions of Frost's trial had died away, Lowery again fell seriously ill, and was helped to recovery by Urquhart's friends. It was his Urquhart connexion which took him to France in autumn 1840 on a delegation seeking an Anglo-French *entente* which would frustrate Palmerston's new-fangled friendship with Russia. But unlike some Chartist Urquhartites, Lowery did not fall out with his old Chartist friends; nor did he stay with Urquhart's movement for very long.[4] His autobiography speaks of Urquhart almost as a voice from the past, despite Urquhart's continued political activity in the 1850s. Shaken into political prudence by the demonstration of Chartist weakness during 1839–40, by his Urquhartite connexions and by his illness, Lowery now supported Lovett's New Move, and gravitated towards the temperance movement and Chartist moral self-help in all its aspects.

At this point, rather more detail is needed because Lowery's autobiography stops at 1841; this terminal date is the more unfortunate because no periodical thereafter reports his activities in detail. With Lowery, as with the whole Chartist movement, "the full story of the 'Chartist aftermath' will never be written, for it depends on the accumulation of a large mass of local material".[5] Lowery was never as prominent in the teetotal as in the Chartist movement, and no temperance periodical resembled the Chartist press in printing his speeches at length.

A reading of the autobiography alone might suggest that Lowery abandoned Chartism after the 1841 general election; yet he remained an active Chartist, particularly in Scotland, for at least another eighteen months. Scottish Chartists were not attracted by O'Connor's National Charter Association, which reorganized Chartism in 1840; they argued that English Chartism and its conventions drained Scotland of its funds. They preferred to retain their own Glasgow-based central committee and their own *Chartist Circular*. Lowery and Duncan were among their most able lecturers and missionaries. But by 1842 the *Circular* was heavily in debt; when it collapsed,

[4] Gertrude Robinson, *David Urquhart* (Oxford, 1920), pp. 95–6.
[5] Asa Briggs (Ed.), *Chartist Studies* (1959), p. 293.

Scottish regional organization collapsed with it. Some months later during autumn 1842, Edinburgh Chartists tried to reconstruct Scottish Chartism along the lines of the National Charter Association, with corresponding secretaries in each of the large towns. Lowery was to be both their paid secretary and editor of their projected *Scottish Chartist Pioneer*. But local funds seem to have dried up in sending delegates to Birmingham for the Complete Suffrage conference in December 1842, and Lowery seems gradually to have withdrawn from what remained of Scottish Chartism. Only in 1848 did Chartism in Scotland briefly revive.[6]

Lowery aimed at diverting Chartist energies away from squabbles with the middle class radicals. He signed Joseph Sturge's complete suffrage declaration in 1842, and told O'Connorite critics that "he had acted honestly and he would rather cut off his hand than retract his signature".[7] At the Chartist convention in April 1842 he was active in committee work; he helped devise ways of extending Chartist influence and tried to restrain Chartists from quarrelling amongst themselves and with middle class radicals. He wanted the name Chartist retained, but "did not wish to see the two parties [i.e. Chartists and Sturgeites] amalgamated . . . If a union was effected it would be one of outward appearance, and not of the heart". No doubt the memory of summer 1839 was in his mind when in May he "trusted they would act calmly, and not allow their zeal to outstep their prudence" if the House of Commons rejected the Chartist petition for a second time.[8]

He was still trying to get Edinburgh Chartists to work with the CSU in winter 1842, but by December he had clearly antagonized a section of them, for his election to the CSU conference was disputed. At a fractious local meeting, he quibbled when asked whether he supported the Charter in its entirety, and "ridiculed the idea of sticking to the past, as obstructive and detrimental to the political advancement of the people". Mr. Cumming, a disgusted local Chartist, concluded that "the best thing they could do was to make a present of Mr. Lowery to Joseph Sturge".[9] By contrast, the *Nonconformist* on 14 December praised "the manly and honest manner in which Mr. Lowrey [*sic*] repelled the silly and ill-natured attacks made upon him". At the CSU conference in December 1842, Lowery kept silent. He seems to have been absent from the later Chartist and Land Plan conventions, and played no further role in Chartism. But like Lovett he had not forsaken the original Chartist objectives; in 1848 he was first secretary of the "People's League"—an organization campaigning for franchise extension

---

[6] A. Wilson, *The Chartist Movement in Scotland* (Manchester, 1970), pp. 186, 196–7.

[7] Quotation from *Northern Star*, 23 April, 1842, p. 7; see also *Nonconformist*, 13 April 1842, p. 231.

[8] Quotations from *Northern Star*, 23 April, 1842, p. 8; 14 May, 1842, p. 7.

[9] *ibid.* 17 December, 1842, p. 6; compare Gammage's recollection in *Newcastle Weekly Chronicle*, 8 November 1884; we are most grateful to Professor W. H. Maehl for making photostats of Gammage's articles available to us.

and tax reform, which was supported by Lovett but strongly opposed by O'Connor and Ernest Jones.

During the 1840s Lowery developed further links with parliamentary radicalism by joining Sturge and former Chartists like Arthur O'Neill and Henry Vincent in the peace congresses.[10] But from 1842 onwards, his activities can be charted only from a few brief references in temperance periodicals. The transition from Chartism to temperance lecturing could not have been difficult. Both movements aimed to develop the integrity and intelligence of working men, and by the early 1840s teetotalism was well-rooted in Scotland and on relatively good terms with Chartism. At the Chartist convention in 1842 Lowery supported the motion for total abstinence from all intoxicating drinks, tobacco, snuff, and as far as possible from all exciseable articles. The political motive remained uppermost in Teetotal Chartism, whereas temperance reformers favoured abstinence primarily for reasons of health and morality; nonetheless, a healthy and independent working class could hardly diminish in political influence. In 1849 we find Lowery still urging working men to "arise and work out their own elevation, as had been done by the Birmingham freeholders" and urging them to remember "that a people at once political and wise never could be kept in bondage".[11]

His energies were now channelled into semi-religious rather than overtly-political organizations. By 1845 he was keeping a temperance hotel in Aberdeen, and we find him arranging to debate Christianity with the secularist Emma Martin at Arbroath. In 1846 he lectured for the Scottish Temperance League, in 1848 for the Central Temperance Association, and in 1851–2 for other temperance organizations. In 1852 the British Association for the Promotion of Temperance passed a resolution expressing "its high estimate of his [i.e. Lowery's] character and ability as an agent, and the uprightness and integrity which have marked his conduct while employed by this Association". In the same year he went as domestic missionary to West Bromwich—hence the reference to religious activity there in the autobiography (p. 101). By October 1854 he was again giving temperance lectures in Scotland.[12]

Like Samuel Bamford before him, and like his contemporaries Henry Vincent, Thomas Cooper and William Lovett, as well as the lesser known James Burn—Lowery had come to believe that social reform could never be effective unless supplemented and even preceded by moral reform. At a

---

[10] A. Tyrrell, "Making the Millennium: the Mid-Nineteenth Century Peace Movement", *Historical Journal*, Vol. 21 (1978), p. 85.

[11] Quotation from *National Temperance Advocate*, 1 November, 1849, p. 131; see also *Northern Star*, 30 April 1842, p. 6 and B. Harrison, "Teetotal Chartism", *History*, June 1973, pp. 193–217; D. Jones, *Chartism and the Chartists* (1975), pp. 45–9.

[12] Quotation from *British Temperance Advocate*, 1 March 1852, p. 33. See also *Scottish Temperance Review*, May 1847, p. 201; *British League*, May 1847, p. 118; *Abstainers Journal*, October 1854, p. 246; November 1854, p. 269; December 1854, p. 289. For Emma Martin, see E. Royle, *Victorian Infidels* (Manchester, 1974), p. 86.

conference of the London Temperance League in 1855 he favoured the Sunday closing of public-houses and suggested that had the Sunday question been presented as part of "the rights of labour", sabbatarians would have found strong working class support: "hundreds of mechanics would have signed the petition for the entire closing". The National Temperance League was equally pleased with Lowery as temperance lecturer in the late 1850s: on 4 March 1859 its minute-book reports "that the engagement of Mr. Lowery had given general satisfaction to the Societies visited". But by 1862 he was in bad health, and a public subscription had to be raised for him; in September he left for Canada to spend the rest of his life with a married daughter at Woodstock, but his bad health continued and he died there on 4 August 1863.[13]

II

Autobiographies can be deceptive. The writer has often an almost fictional sense of his own self. He has smoothed out the unpredictability of his experience, tidied up the litter and debris of passing causes and commitments. He has turned his life into an art form. He contrives a coherence, presents an evolution. Earlier views and positions, where they diverge from those he now holds, are seen as immature and in need of explanation; they were the stance of the moment, ephemeral; it is his present views that are truly timeless and eternal. On the other hand, significance is attributed in retrospect to events which at the time were experienced as random—there is a process of what E. H. Carr calls backing horses that have already won. Lowery avoids many of these pitfalls: his very lack of egoism, odd in an autobiographer, is both his strength and his weakness. His strength, in that he recognizes both the ambivalence and the authenticity of positions he comes later to disavow; he realizes that both his past and his present views are equally in need of explanation. But his weakness also, because he is most reticent where autobiographies are usually at their strongest, on the development of the individual personality.[14]

An autobiography of this quality sheds much light on Chartism and early Victorian radicalism, even though its early date created difficulties for Lowery. He himself says that "many facts and events will be better understood by those persons who came later than I into these movements, or who at the time were not acquainted with the springs of action which moved the movers of the masses" (p. 39). When he is puzzled, for example, by the

---

[13] Quotations from *Proceedings at the Annual Conference of the .... London Temperance League .... September 11th, 1855* (1855), p. 17; National Temperance League, *MS Minutes 1856–61*, at Livesey-Clegg House, Sheffield. See also *Weekly Record [of the Temperance Movement]*, 16 October 1858, p. 358; 23 October 1858, p. 366; 3 March 1860, p. 106; 15 February 1862, p. 52; 5 September 1863, p. 397.

[14] cf. D. Vincent (Ed.), *Testaments of Radicalism. Memoirs of Working Class Politicians 1790–1885* (1977), pp. 19–21.

apparently violent conduct of the moderate John Frost, he says so (p. 137). At the time the autobiography was published, O'Connor had only just died, Frost had only just returned from exile, and Urquhart had only just published his Chartist correspondence of 1839 in the *Free Press* for 19 and 26 January 1856. It was by no means clear in 1856–7 that the mid-Victorian "equipoise" was secure, and Lowery may have wished to protect his former friends from victimization; not until the 1880s were old Chartists to be petted and fêted in that classless union of hearts which was Gladstonian Liberalism. The vagueness of "a person who had been a member in the Convention" (p. 155), "a person resident in London" (p. 92), "the man who kept the New-castle shop" (p. 94) may have been deliberate.[15] Nor does he ever clarify his relationships with present or former members of the Chartist movement after 1841. It is almost as though that mid-Victorian insulation of Chartism from the mainstream of nineteenth-century history—which is one of the peculiar features of Chartist historiography—was already standing between Lowery the Chartist and Lowery the autobiographer. Lowery's own views on controversial issues were perhaps intentionally left unclear, and he occasionally takes cover by slipping unobtrusively into the third person. He is reticent on the extent of his early Owenite connections, refrains from mentioning his pamphlet on exclusive dealing (pp. 195–204), is uninformative on his role in the first Chartist convention, opaque on his role in the second, and downright obscure on his ties with Urquhart. His recollections were written almost entirely from memory, it is true, but his memory served him very well when it came to describing the scenery around Banff.

A more important criticism of the autobiography is that its author, a former Chartist, was interpreting Chartism rather than merely recollecting it.[16] There is no evidence that any other Chartist apart from Lovett ever saw Lowery's account: the *Weekly Record* carried no letters on it even from tee-totallers. But several Chartists disliked the history of the movement which Lowery helped Gammage to prepare. Ernest Jones's *People's Paper* uncompromisingly dismissed it in February 1855: "this disgusting trash Mr. Gammage calls 'History'. It is an insult to the Chartist body to associate the name with such a production."[17] On the other hand, Lowery was not a Chartist leader of national stature, and could perhaps claim to be more detached than either Lovett or Cooper. He was in any case instinctively independent and almost as instinctively charitable. His autobiography includes fine descriptions of leading Chartists, usually his opponents rather than his allies—O'Connor, Taylor and Beaumont, rather than Lovett, Vincent or Cooper. While Lowery is open in his criticism of them, his comments are sufficiently qualified to carry conviction. In a crusade riddled

---

[15] For other instances, see pp. 120, 145, 147, 159, 162 below.
[16] cf. D. Vincent, *op. cit.*, p. 2.
[17] *People's Paper*, 17 February 1855, p. 5; cf. Thomas Cooper, *The Life of Thomas Cooper* (1872), p. 277.

with bitter quarrels and personal feuds, Lowery is remarkably unresentful, cheerfully detached, and shrewd without being cynical.

An interpretative autobiography has virtues of its own. Lowery often diverges from narrating his own life into analytic comment, personality-sketches and general reflection of a fascinating kind. For long sections (sometimes for a complete article in the *Weekly Record*) the author disappears entirely from view; over a third of the text consists of contextual discussion. Lowery is quite prepared to make comparative generalizations about social movements—on speaking styles, for example; he also makes suggestions on current policy for the 1850s at several points—on interdenominational education, for example (p. 43), sabbath observance (p. 45), and the need for removing trade restrictions (p. 59). These suggestions are made only in passing, and seldom spoil the flow of the narrative. By embarking on general discussion of the poor law, regional contrasts, Chartist leadership, Owenism, or changes in social class relations, he aims to do more than merely set the scene for his own activities. Indeed, his intention is precisely the reverse; the sole reason for discussing his own career is to shed light on these general problems, and his analytic passages can therefore only on a narrow view be seen as digressions.

Lowery's autobiography is important for the information it provides on Chartism, particularly on the second 1839 convention. But it is at least as important for its threefold perspective on the movement—distinctively provincial, inevitably artisan and (as communicator) decidedly professional. Lowery vividly describes the mounting activity in the months preceding the 1839 convention, the travelling of delegates, the snowballing of open air meetings, the tension heightened by Oastler and Stephens. As he was already an experienced public speaker, he was sent as missionary to Cornwall, Scotland and Ireland in turn. He was therefore absent from some of the key debates on ulterior measures, and also from some of its crises, such as the arrest of Lovett and Collins after the Bull Ring riots (p. 138). But this did give him a real sense of the regional response to national policy; his judgement matured accordingly.

He came to the convention in 1839 thinking that the people had only to "demand and receive" their rights, that the petition was self-evidently just and its prayer totally compelling. "If men once knew their rights", he had said in 1834, "—if they once knew their power—there would soon be an end to the present system of misgovernment".[18] Yet in 1839 the government rejected a Chartist petition with over a million signatures. Lowery naively concluded that this was simply because the petition lacked adequate pressure from without. So he became an advocate of missionaries and lecture-tours to stir up the "unawakened districts". Exclusive dealing, a three-day national holiday, signatures to the petition—these became grist to his mill. Although

---

[18] *Newcastle Press*, 4 January 1834, p. 4.

his perspectives had now shifted from London to the regions, he still saw Chartism in terms of direct action—as a set of demands which, when firmly backed by the popular will, could not be ignored by government. This took him into the physical force camp, but rather because of his unthinking care-free optimism than from any taste for violence.

His lecture-tours for the convention and reports from his colleagues came as a profound shock, not only to him but also to O'Brien and Harney. Instead of an enlightened people wanting only leadership to claim their rights, he and they found apathy, ignorance and lack of "manly spirit", all of which confirmed his poor opinion of the ordinary man. A letter from Lowery read out to his Newcastle supporters on 16 July 1839 suggests that he was already alarmed at the situation. His autobiography does not mention it, but at the time he was keen to delay the beginning of the Sacred Month from 22 July to 12 August, to give time (as he said) for delegates to rouse their localities and strike at the moment of maximum impact, harvest time.[19] Lowery's recognition of political realities perhaps owed most to his Irish mission of August 1839 (pp. 144–148), which forced him to see how religious prejudice could divide his class. Lowery's Irish Chartist sympathisers and his trade union connexions in Dublin could not prevail over the strong-arm tactics of O'Connell's followers; public meetings were simply broken up and placards torn down. Nor could the Chartist convention supply him with the money needed for establishing a permanent bridgehead in Ireland. From late summer in 1839, he came to accept what Lovett had always believed—that men must be made fit for power before they can exercise it.

On his own account Lowery spent the winter of 1839–40 attempting to damp down extravagant proposals. On 30 September 1839 he told Newcastle Chartists that "there had been a misconception on both sides; the people expected the Convention to do what they could do themselves only, and the Convention expected the people to do that they were not as a body prepared for" (p. 243). Lowery's recollections of that winter are particularly significant —even though he does not say all he knew, and conceals names and places. For several months he had been aware of plans "to concoct a rising" (p. 155), and had been in touch with its leaders. He had some advance knowledge of the Newport rising, and when a second convention was arranged to effect Frost's rescue, Lowery was the only delegate of the first convention to attend. It met at the Arundel coffee-house in London from 19 December to 8 January, and Lowery provides our only first-hand account of it (p. 158). He makes it clear that Newport was not a spontaneous outburst, but the cul-mination of plotting since late summer 1839; that there was a skeletal national Chartist organization, strong in Wales, the West Riding and New-castle, which the convention aimed to co-ordinate; but that in January 1840, local leaders in Dewsbury, Bradford and Sheffield took matters into

---

[19] Peter Cadogan, *Early Radical Newcastle* (Consett, 1975), p. 122.

their own hands. At this point he fell seriously ill, and temporarily withdrew from Chartism.

His perspective on all these events was decidedly provincial. "Fully developed Chartism", wrote Hovell, "derives its programme from London, its organization from Birmingham, its personnel and vehemence from Lancashire and Yorkshire".[20] Lowery came from none of these areas, but from a peculiarly interesting region which has been somewhat neglected until recently: he entered national Chartism as a delegate from the North-East, and first visited London to attend the Palace Yard meeting of 17 September 1838. His response was typically provincial: he marvelled at the sophistication of the London press and husbanded his integrity amid London's temptations. Ryan, when proposing Lowery as one of Newcastle's three delegates at the 1839 convention, tried to forearm him: "should the moral force old women attempt to swamp the Convention, Mr. Lowery would tell them that the people would not wait to perish of hunger . . ." Lowery had already described London as "a sink of corruption—the wealth of the Aristocracy was spent there—and the artizan lived by their extravagance, and, therefore could hardly be expected to be so virtuous as the workmen in their own provincial towns". For a provincial radical, London was corrupt, atheistic, apathetic to reform: Cobbett's "Great Wen", Devyr's "modern Babylon . . . a Lazarretto, a prison, a hell!". [21]

Lowery's autobiography usefully complements Lovett's (London-based) and Cooper's (Midland-based), the more so because as late as 1963 the North-East had "virtually no attention" paid to it by Chartist historians, despite the fact that Chartism there "attained a stridency and vehemence which was rarely matched and never excelled elsewhere".[22] In Lowery's words, the local miners were "a century in advance of their class in any other mining district" (p. 77), the leaders of the Northern Political Union "combined philosophic astuteness, literary ability, oratorical powers, and social standing rarely equalled by the leaders of the public in any other district" (p. 64). The *Northern Liberator*, edited from Newcastle, was one of the most remarkable newspapers of a remarkable press.

Travelling for the convention, Lowery learned much about the diversity of British regional cultures, and therefore came to see just how sizeable was the task of creating radical solidarity between Cornish fishermen and Paisley weavers. He was alert to local customs and traditions: "everything was new and interesting to me in Paris in the manners and habits of the masses" (p. 168, cf. p. 148) he writes: he was equally observant when visiting Cornwall or Cumberland, Durham or Dublin. Lowery the autobiographer

---

[20] M. Hovell, *The Chartist Movement* (Ed. T. F. Tout, Manchester, 1918), p. 98.
[21] Ryan, *Northern Liberator*, 29 December 1838; for Lowery, see below, p. 220; T. A. Devyr, *The Odd Book of the Nineteenth Century* (New York, 1882), p. 155.
[22] W. H. Maehl, "Chartist Disturbances in Northeastern England, 1839", *International Review of Social History*, 1963, p. 389.

retained this nose for the rich variety of regional cultures in Britain. "There was a strong feeling of poetry, a sense of humour and witty satire displayed in their local songs", he says of the Newcastle working men among whom he learnt his radical politics (p. 82). He likes a Scots audience (p. 116), he notices the distinctive moods of Lancashire (p. 109), and Cumberland people (p. 113). His comments on the culture of Scotland (pp. 149, 153) and the North-East (p. 77) are extensive, and illustrate his taste and skill for setting his own actions in a general context.

Yet in Lowery there is none of Samuel Bamford's antiquarian fascination with dialect writing and folklore, none of J. R. Stephen's bantering familiarity with local dialect forms. William Lovett recalled on his arrival in London "my provincialisms and bad English being often corrected by the kind old schoolmaster I have referred to, I was induced by his advice to study Lindley Murray's Grammar, and by making it my pocket companion for a few months, and studying it in all my leisure hours, I was enabled to correct some of my glaring imperfections in speaking".[23] Like Lovett, Burn and Cooper, Lowery seems self-consciously to have shed his dialect as an encumbrance in the course of his political and intellectual growth. His autobiography aimed to provide "helps to young men in such circumstances as mine were" (p. 40): and dialect would be a hindrance to readers intent on self-improvement. His autobiography was itself intended to advertise the cultivation a self-educated working man could acquire. Chartist leaders' geographical as well as social mobility meant that unlike a Bamford or a Ben Brierley, they were seldom rooted into a specific locality; furthermore Lowery as a child moved five times in twelve years. Dialect appears in his autobiography only within quotation marks, often for naive and backward remarks (like those of the St. Ives town-crier, p. 132), or for the commonsensical bystander on the Chartist fringe. An autobiographer was reluctant to use what he may have regarded as purely a spoken form, and Lowery, writing in the 1850s, did not anticipate the impending interest in dialect, folklore and local customs. Lowery never sees a distinct popular culture as central to working class dignity or working class identity.

If Lowery's perspective was profoundly provincial, his outlook was also inherently artisan. Victorian artisans were of course exceptional men, and their autobiographies, it has been rightly said, "are the last places in which to look for references for anything but the most acceptable forms of behaviour".[24] But their influence, together with that of their authors, on nineteenth-century British society and politics was profound. They are of great interest as a psychological type, and in his attitude to his fellow working men, Lowery had been a "respectable" at least since the age of thirteen

---

[23] W. Lovett, *Life and Struggles*, p. 34; cf. J. D. Burn's contempt for cockney in *The Autobiography of a Beggar Boy* (1978 ed.), p. 58, and T. Cooper, *Life*, p. 57. M. Vicinus, *The Industrial Muse* (1974), Ch. 5 provides relevant discussion.
[24] Angus McLaren, *Birth Control in Nineteenth-Century England* (1978), pp. 216–7.

(p. 48). The characters of such men were moulded in a context which to modern eyes seems incredibly harsh. Frequent moves of home during childhood, off to the mine in the dark mornings at the age of ten (p. 45), orphaned and across the Atlantic on his own at thirteen, lamed soon after, and a poverty in early marriage which is described vividly but without self-pity. As for Lowery's lameness, we are brought up short by a sudden reminder of it at the Dublin meeting of 1839 (p. 146), whereas his extensive Chartist lecture-tours, uncomplainingly narrated, have almost led us to forget it. In this context, the comment of Crossthwaite the Chartist to Alton Locke becomes comprehensible: "for one who comes safe through the furnace, there are a hundred who crack in the burning."[25]

To the difficulties of life itself were added all the struggles involved in self-improvement. Lowery became a tailor in the first place because his family thought it a respectable trade (p. 59), and with him as with Alton Locke, employment in a tailor's workshop increased his intellectual opportunities. He repeatedly urges the importance of giving opportunities for reading to working men in their trades: seamen should have books (p. 51) and mechanics' institutes should be managed by working men (p. 115). "The necessity to labour", Lowery wrote, "does not debar working men from acquiring useful knowledge and intelligence, but in some degree offers facilities for their attainment which employers and shopkeepers do not possess" (p. 40, cf. p. 60)—most notably the opportunity for contact with a better-educated master, and the chance of studying and arguing while working. The wife played a crucially important role here, though Lowery says all too little about her. With him, as with Place, Vincent and Lovett, we see the dependence of the public radical on the private support of a happy home-life. As a young married man, Lowery behaved as respectable husbands should, keeping his family's difficulties to himself (p. 62) and buying books in preference to food (p. 63). After marriage Lowery, like Francis Place, "left off every thing which could in any way tend to impede my future progress in the world".[26]

But if Lowery is exceptional in a general sense, he is perhaps more typical than Cooper or Lovett of the type of respectable working man who became prominent in the Chartist movement. His autobiography resembles that of another second-rank Chartist leader R. G. Gammage—in its fascination with the movement's great men, its preoccupation with oratory, its taste for romantic scenery and its overriding emphasis on the countrywide journey for the purpose of communication. There are also strong affinities between the careers of Lowery and James Burn. Both came from the Border country, and travelled freely in Scotland and Northern England. Both joined declining trades (Burn was a hatter), and both were active in the trade union and

---

[25] Charles Kingsley, *Alton Locke, Tailor and Poet* (Everyman ed. 1970), p. 61.
[26] F. Place, *Autobiography* (Ed. Mary Thale, Cambridge, 1972), p. 11, cf. pp. 224, 254–5, 258.

radical movements of the 1830s. Lowery reveals much (though less than Cooper) about the intellectual influences which moulded his radicalism; and like Lovett and Burn his is particularly full on his childhood experience. He was an instinctive protestant, taking nothing on trust, stumbling into a full-scale study of polemical divinity only because he refused to accept the first thing on the subject that he read (p. 55). He was also innately rationalist, a man who read himself into religious belief without any early personal consciousness of sin or redemption. When as a boy he went to his first play, his immediate response was not to read another one, nor to see another one, nor even to act in one, but to write one for himself; inevitably, it was a high-land romance (p. 56). On such a man, the English puritan revolutionary tradition was far more powerful than any French influence, and he dismisses Harney (and with him O'Brien) in one sentence: he "had evidently read with avidity the History of the French Revolution, and was smitten with admiration for the social theories and sentiments of Robespiere and St. Just, and that portion of the French revolutionists" (p. 119, cf. p. 168).

The young Lowery read extensively in English history to furnish the warehouse of his mind, and in English literature to delight and nourish the imagination. Typically he considered his master "a *book* to me, in which were chronicled the impressions on his mind of the events which had taken place in his time" (p. 60). Equally typically, he found himself forming a debating society, and among other subjects talked on the Polish rising, the Irish Coercion Bill and the Tolpuddle martyrs. And like so many prominent provincial Chartists—William Rider, Joshua Hobson, Peter Bussey, Lawrence Pitkeithly—he did his stint with the Unstamped. He depicts its impact on the provinces, the crowds waiting for the London coaches to arrive on a Saturday afternoon, bringing bundles of the *Poor Man's Guardian* to Newcastle; the devices adopted to defeat magistrates; the placarding and protest when a vendor was arrested. He shows that in part the hopes of their London publishers were realized—that the "Pauper" press did help "the people" to become a recognized portion of public opinion (p. 95) and that work with the Unstamped was crucial to the radical education of many working class leaders outside London.

Lowery's relationship with the tailoring trade is particularly revealing of his attitudes to class and status. Entering into the trade late, he telescoped his apprenticeship into two years, but then found the Newcastle trade firmly controlled by its older members, who monopolized all the work when it was short. As entry to their ranks could be secured only through bribery, all Lowery's susceptibilities—moral, financial, educational and teetotal—were simultaneously offended. Inspired by the federated unionism of the GNCTU, the Newcastle trades formed a combined general union, with Lowery as secretary. By exploiting a verbal error in the constitution of the society of tailors, Lowery was able to open up the trade and prevent the senior members from keeping their machinery distinct. But the Newcastle master-

13

tailors' counter-attack against local trade unionism in 1834 soon put Lowery out of work. He was reduced to "slop-work", making cheap ready-made clothes at blackleg wages; then he left the trade altogether, and moved into radical journalism.

It is clear from these events that Lowery was no natural trade unionist. He understandably disliked an apprenticeship system which he thought incompatible with the self-help and the social and occupational mobility so integral to industrial society. But he never recognized that apprenticeship, a way of controlling entry to the trade, was one of the craftsman's few remaining weapons in what was becoming a masters' market. The relaxation of apprenticeship controls was precisely what accelerated the destruction (which Lowery himself observed) of trades like tailoring and carpentry. "Honourable" society tailors, who had served their full apprenticeship, were being swamped by "dishonourable" men who formed a pool of cheap semi-skilled labour available for seasonal and sweated work. It was this gulf that the London tailors tried to "equalize" in the GNCTU when they laid down minimum rates and maximum hours for all men—yet it was this gulf which Lowery, by his willingness to do cheap slop-work, was widening. Lowery therefore shared the position of the dishonourable men; he used the notions of the GNCTU without really understanding them. He viewed it as a doubtlessly well-intentioned but decidedly feeble attempt at federation, and not as an early attempt to grapple with the problems of sweating before they had overwhelmed the craft trades.

The tensions in the relationship between "respectables" and other working men could at times be overlain by a common sense of the dignity of labour and the injustice of privilege. But at other times they could be exposed by a continuing awareness—always present in Lowery—of the weakness and folly of the common man, his gullibility, his irrationality, his herd-like instincts. When Lowery worked to break the grip of the older society men in Newcastle, he acted in the name of individualist natural justice, not in the name of brotherhood. He was no Richard Pilling: even then he was not as instinctively loyal to the weak as he was to the able in a trade. When Lowery talked of union, it was in the language of Richard Carlile, of a moral union of intelligence. By 1856 it seems that (like Place) he doubted the need for trade unionism, and (like Mrs. Gaskell) believed that if masters could only be brought to a proper sympathy and understanding of their men's situation, and their men in turn to a proper self-respect, then trade unionism would wither away. "While we have free trade in capital and its productions" he writes (p. 59), "we still want it amongst workmen and workshops". By extension, he never criticized orthodox political economy as such, and apparently accepted that wages depend on profits and that strikes are self-defeating. By 1856 he was even expressing regret that political economists did not take the lead in social investigation, for fear that others less qualified would come forward in their place (p. 70). There is no intellectual gulf here between Lowery and the manufacturers and shopkeepers whom he later encountered in the Urquhartite, temperance and complete suffrage movements; his instinctive individualism, his distaste both for deference and demagogy, his belief that truth emerges from intellectual conflict, his reluctant but inescapable moral and educational elitism, were all artisan attitudes they would find congenial.

Provincial and artisan though his roots were, Lowery was also a highly professional lecturer, fascinated by the techniques of his trade and in his Chartist speeches always ready to condemn the press for its distortions (pp. 215, 218). Communication is, in fact, the enthusiasm of his life, the unifying feature of his career.[27] He moves forward easily from lecturing on the radical causes of the 1830s to lecturing on Chartism and from there to lecturing on other topics (p. 186) including temperance, while interspersing this with mission work. Books, speeches and newspapers fascinated him. Just as Cooper's autobiography is unified by its concern with the profession of writing, so Lowery's is unified by its concern with the profession of public speaking. Unlike their continental counterparts, Chartist leaders rarely resorted to conspiracy, but were made or broken on the public platform. Like Gammage in his history, Lowery regularly and freely digresses on the performance of his colleagues on the platform. He was interested in the subtle interaction between speaker and audience—which runs all the way from O'Connor ("he blarneyed and flattered the multitude for their hurrahs"— p. 125) through the combined restraint and incitement of his own Cornish speeches (p. 133) to the pedestrian performances he heard in the House of Commons on 12 July 1839 (p. 140).

Lowery was not helped as an orator by his build, for he was both short and lame, but Gammage says that he had "a somewhat intelligent and pleasing expression of countenance, which was much enhanced by any sudden excitement, for then his eye, usually placid, was bright and animated". According to the *Charter* in 1839, his face "albeit it is somewhat stern, is expressive of intelligence and benevolence".[28] By concentrating on technique, Lowery made the most of his natural advantages. He included an account of his preparations for his first public speech "as it may be of some use to my class who may wish to be able to address a public meeting" (p. 78). From the first, he took trouble to perform well. After speaking for some years at public meetings, he was asked to give a lecture; he immediately recognized that he must make a new beginning if he was to master this new oratorical form. "I remember well the anxiety I felt on the first night I lectured . . .", he writes: "I prepared too much material, and my chief difficulty was to

---

[27] David Jones, *Chartism and the Chartists*, pp. 102–112, is excellent on the role of lecturers and missionaries within Chartism; Chartists in the remoter parts were almost totally dependent on Chartist missionaries, who made a precarious and physically exhausting living by working their circuits.

[28] R. G. Gammage, *History of the Chartist Movement*, pp. 30–1; *The Charter*, 28 April 1839, p. 215.

compress it" (p. 105). Even a first-rate report of a speech cannot convey its flavour, let alone the mood of the audience and the all-important factors of gesture, facial expression and timing. But it is clear that Lowery's Chartist oratory was emotional and high-flown. He practised in public and polished in private until his speeches were "far above the common order . . . slow and deliberate, but . . . instinct with much force". Though he made no great effort to be logical, Gammage continues, "a vein of sound reasoning ran through nearly all that he advanced".[29]

When Lowery, like so many Chartists, refers to the voice of the people as the voice of God, he means it in an almost pantheistic way.[30] The crowd is God's handiwork, carries God's message, is his tabernacle. But the crowd is also God's theatre. Sharing a platform with Stephens, Harney and Taylor— men not noted for their moderation—he learned to play on his audience, to use provocative language which kept to just the right side of sedition. Touring the Newcastle area for the *Northern Liberator*, and speaking on universal suffrage and the new poor law, he soon learned to use the rhetorical question and the dramatic pause to some effect, to move easily from the earthy language of Cobbett to the grave periods of the Old Testament, and to speak *extempore* for as long as the weather permitted. Nor was he above the occasional eye-catching gesture: he won "immense cheering" from his Newcastle audience in October 1838 when, towards the end of his speech (p. 222), he produced an ear of wheat from "the first year's crop of the Dorchester Labourers' farms".

Fear of prosecution in the 1830s forced Lowery to wrap up his message. Gammage says that he possessed "in a pretty large degree, the useful faculty of caution, he chalked out for himself certain limits which he seldom overstepped". He would not advise the people to arm, he said at Newcastle in May 1839, but "it was no harm for one neighbour to ask another whether he had a good musket . . .".[31] In his autobiography Lowery often comments shrewdly on the delicacy of the relationship between a radical speaker and his audience, each of them inciting the other, the orator as much the servant as the master (e.g. p. 96). To judge from interruptions to his speeches, he knew how to sweep his audience along, to establish that public *rapport* which turns a crowd into a single mind, the essence of successful platform speaking. His speech at Leeds in January 1841 (p. 253) shows him handling a hostile audience. Unfortunately, no full reports of his temperance speeches have yet been found, so we do not know whether his speaking style changed in later years.

[29] R. G. Gammage, *History of the Chartist Movement*, pp. 30–1.
[30] cf. Richard Pilling's use of the phrase in his *Defence*, repr. in P. Hollis (Ed.), *Class and Conflict in Nineteenth-century England, 1815–1850* (1973), p. 297; on the crowd mentality, see R. Holton, "The Crowd in History", *Social History*, May, 1978.
[31] R. G. Gammage, *History of the Chartist Movement*, p. 31; Lowery, *Northern Liberator*, 25 May 1839.

His autobiography's best passages (the descriptions of his Cornish and Irish journeys) are understandably dominated by accounts of his own public speaking. His comments on his speech at Hayle in particular (p. 133) are both very funny and very frank. He also likes to show how orators on the same platform can complement each other in style and mood—Duncan and himself in Cornwall (p. 129), or the four stars of the Northern Political Union (p. 65); for a major radical public meeting in the 1830s was not a sequence of isolated solo performances, but a well co-ordinated symphony whose score was prepared in advance. He acquired a precise ear for the oratorical skills of his fellow Chartists and displayed a pointed surprise at the oratorical poverty of professional parliamentarians (p. 140); politics were for him a gymnasium of ideas (cf. p. 71), so how could parliament ever hope to perceive the truth of the Charter through speeches so inept?

The test of successful oratory was not only to hold an audience but to move them. Lowery is acutely aware of the relation between Chartist leaders and led, especially in the crisis years 1839–40. His narrative can be set alongside Disraeli's extravagantly-drawn Dandy Mick, George Eliot's high-minded Felix Holt and Kingsley's self-conscious Alton Locke; far from being in command of their popular following, their control was so precarious that they had to lead in order to restrain. Compare Alton Locke at the agricultural labourers' meeting ("I felt myself in a measure responsible for their conduct; I had helped to excite them, and dare not, in honour, desert them") with Lowery on the plight of the Chartist leaders in 1839 ("the whirlwind of popular passion had been unloosed, and those who raised it could not wield it"—p. 154): or Lowery's comment that "the speaker only gives vent to the hearers' emotions. His words at once find a response in their wishes" (p. 96) with Dandy Mick's "a leader, to be successful, should embody in his system the necessities of his followers, express what every one feels, but no one has had the ability or the courage to pronounce".[32] According to a government report, when the police urged the Chartist leaders to call off their London demonstration on 10 April 1848, "Jones thought this impossible, saying the leaders would gladly do so, but that the people could not be controlled".[33]

Lowery had always been keenly aware of popular pressures on the platform and had always known that the speaker was in a profound sense the puppet of his audience. By late summer 1839 his missionary tours had convinced him that his "masters" were but children—politically fickle at best, dull and lethargic at worst—and he realized he must start from the beginning. Self-control must precede self-government, moral weight must create political influence, maturity produce power. At Newcastle in September 1839 he was already claiming to have learnt an important lesson. Events of

---

[32] Quotations from C. Kingsley, *Alton Locke*, p. 260; B. Disraeli, *Sybil*, in *Works* (Bradenham ed. 1927, Vol. IX), p. 464. Compare George Eliot, *Felix Holt the Radical*, Ch. 33.

[33] Jones quo. in J. Prest, *Lord John Russell* (1972), p. 284; cf. Thomas Cooper, *Life*. pp. 180, 197.

the summer were "a necessary ordeal for us to pass through to give us experience in our future movements. We have learned much" (p. 243). The lesson he publicly claimed to have learned was that there was one law for the rich and another for the poor, but already his mind was turning towards new tactics such as exclusive dealing and electoral campaigning. The conspiratorial folly of the second convention, his illness, and his exposure to Urquhart only confirmed the lesson. By the time he came to write the autobiography, painfully-learnt lessons had become self-evident truths. Violence is now by definition folly; he talks of impatient men in their haste trying to set aside "natural laws". A younger Lowery would have ridiculed any such concept.

Lowery in the 1830s knew quite clearly what he was fighting—it was social injustice, in which those who produced society's wealth were its poorest members, those who were the most valuable part of society were its most despised and deprived. There was a holy war to be waged on privilege and parasitism. But in the 1850s this sharpness of vision had gone. Lowery suggested only two reasons for Chartism. One was a condition-of-the-people account: distress had understandably driven men to desperation and violence. The other was the example of 1832, when the middle classes had themselves toyed with violence to win their rights and reduce their taxes; Lowery argued that the Chartists were working by analogy. He nowhere recaptures the Chartist hope that universal suffrage might herald a new society, in which redistribution of wealth would redefine life-chances, in which a crippling class structure would wither away. In the 1830s he had seen poverty as immoral; but by the 1850s he saw it instead as embarrassing good will between men. Indeed, perhaps one reason why Lowery the autobiographer sympathized more with Oastler and Stephens than with any others of his old allies was that he was coming to share their organic aspirations for society, their search for harmony rather than equality, their view that class relations involved mutual obligation between master and man. Lowery was by then willing to describe society as a body, sometimes healthy, sometimes diseased; pain and suffering, he wrote in an extended metaphor, could be welcomed as signs of vitality.

Many Chartists evolved from a youthful faith in rapid institutional change towards a more gradualist pursuit of moral elevation. Radicals rather than socialists, they attacked an aristocratic system of privilege rather than a capitalist system of competition. They had often entered Chartism through short-lived political unions or journalism, itself usually an educational concern. On the other hand, those whose roots were in Yorkshire and Lancashire, who had grown into Chartism through factory, trade union and anti-poor law movements, more often retained their faith in the fitness of ordinary working men for political power. Lowery passed through Manchester once on his return from the Palace Yard meeting of September 1838, but otherwise his tours never took him to Lancashire, Yorkshire or the

Midlands. Like Vincent and Lovett, Lowery knew very little about the Chartist heartland.

And so Lowery's autobiography is important not only for its information on Chartism and its provincial, artisan and oratorical perspectives, but also for its self-consciousness about class relations, its appreciation of the growth of class harmony by the mid-1850s. This harmony had been gained through a combination of economic recovery, the reassertion of law and order, and above all the "active attempts by the bourgeoisie to win back mass allegiance" through such agencies as friendly societies, freemasonry, adult education, temperance, co-operation; hence in towns like Oldham, an outright majority of working class leaders "actually became incorporated into the new parties"[34]—with factory reformers gravitating to the Tories, and Chartists to the Liberals. Lowery's autobiography makes it clear that such a political consensus was for him not a matter of "false consciousness", of being lulled into acquiescence by concessions from above. His radicalism, his quest for political citizenship, his commitment to an active morality, meant that for him, as for so many others, his liberalism grew from the same soil as his Chartism. There was no betrayal.

III

The very title of Lowery's autobiography suggests that he was influenced by Samuel Bamford's famous *Passages in the Life of a Radical* (1839–42). It belongs to a specialized literary genre which originated long before the nineteenth century and lasted well into the twentieth. This genre ranged from Benjamin Franklin's *Autobiography*, completed before 1790, to radical autobiographies like William Lovett's *Life and Struggles* (1876), teetotal autobiographies like Thomas Whittaker's *Life's Battles in Temperance Armour* (1884) and on to the many autobiographies of Labour Party pioneers like Will Thorne's *My Life's Battles* (1925) and Jack Lawson's *A Man's Life* (1932). They were in some ways secularized versions of the spiritual autobiography so influential in dissenting circles.[35] They retained some of its classless flavour in that they showed how even the humblest working man could exercise moral self-

---

[34] John Foster, *Class Struggle and the Industrial Revolution* (1974), pp. 207, 209. Foster has restated in a sophisticated and quantitative form some of the older "wrong-turning" theories, by which working class protest was bought off by "concessions [which] were made and *kept* on employer terms" (Foster's reply to Musson, *Social History*, October 1976, p. 363). Pivotal to Foster's argument is the role of a new labour aristocracy as mediators of respectable values—a role examined by H. F. Moorhouse, "The Marxist Theory of the Labour Aristocracy", *Social History*, January 1978. Wider issues of consensus and discipline are raised in A. P. Donajgrodzki (Ed.), *Social Control in Nineteenth Century Britain*) (1977); and support for Foster's liberalization thesis comes from T. Tholfsen, *Working Class Radicalism in Mid-Victorian England* (1976).

[35] For spiritual autobiographies, see L. D. Lerner, "Puritanism and the Spiritual Autobiography", *Hibbert Journal*, Vol. 55 (1956-7); we owe this reference to Dr. J. D. Walsh, Jesus College, Oxford. See also Thomas Cooper, *Life*, pp. 70–1, 82.

discipline in the face of difficulty and so develop character as well as intellect through study.

In this respect, at least, the working man's autobiography had much in common with books like *The Pursuit of Knowledge Under Difficulties* (1830) and Samuel Smiles's *Self-Help* (1859). The myth of Samuel Smiles as the individualist exponent of bourgeois values is very different from the Smiles the Chartists knew in Leeds during the 1840s—the first person to offer Lovett a job after his release from gaol: the insecure newspaper editor who had so little in common with Baines, Marshall and the local middle class elite, so much more in common with the working men for whom his *Self-Help* was originally written.[36] Belief in a society which encouraged talent to rise to its own level was a highly radical ideal in what was then an aristocratic political system, and biography was therefore a major influence on serious-minded working men. A biographical article on Dr. Samuel Lee, who rose from apprentice carpenter to Professor of Hebrew at Cambridge University was, according to Thomas Cooper, "one of the greatest incentives I had to solid study"; and in being impressed as a boy by Benjamin Franklin's autobiography, Thomas Burt the miner's leader was far from alone among respectable nineteenth-century working men, who reinforced the tradition by writing their own autobiographies when success had been attained.[37] The genre persisted as long as the Labour Party's concern to elevate a class could be reconciled with admiration for the social mobility of an individual, and as long as such mobility could plausibly be ascribed to the individual's innate qualities rather than to his cultural and social opportunities. In the course of the twentieth century, however, the social elevation of the working class seemed best attained through more direct methods than through encouraging individual social ascent. As the structural obstacles to working class self-improvement became clearer and as class solidarity extended, so in the years after the first world war the popularity of such books declined. With the modern cult of the "anti-hero", the reaction against nineteenth-century attitudes is complete.

Unfortunately we have no direct evidence on how Lowery came to write his autobiography, or even on whether he was paid for it. No correspondence with the editor of the *Weekly Record* survives, and Lowery seems to have left no personal papers. It is impossible even to say whether he, like Lovett,

---

[36] Asa Briggs, introduction to W. Lovett & J. Collins, *Chartism. A New Organization of the People* (Leicester, 1969), p. 22; A. Tyrrell, "Class Consciousness in Early Victorian Britain: Samuel Smiles, Leeds Politics, and the Self-Help Creed", *Journal of British Studies*, May, 1970, pp. 107, 111–2, 124; K. Fielden, "Samuel Smiles and Self-Help", *Victorian Studies*, December, 1968, pp. 174–5.

[37] Thomas Cooper, *Life*, p. 55; Thomas Burt, *Autobiography* (1924), p. 19. For the influence of self-help autobiographies, see E. Baines, *The Life of Edward Baines* (1851), p. 27; G. J. Holyoake, *The Value of Biography, in the Formation of Individual Character* (1845), p. 15. Compare the nineteenth-century shift in working-class attitudes to American "rags to riches" stories, discussed in R. Bendix & S. M. Lipset (Eds.), *Class, Status and Power* (1954), p. 393 by R. R. Wohl.

began writing his autobiography long before he published it, though many of his reflections could have sprung only from long reflection on his Chartist experience. Internal evidence suggests that he compiled it largely from memory, though on one occasion he quotes briefly from the *Newcastle Journal* (p. 79). For had Lowery relied extensively on newspaper sources, he would certainly have used them to describe the 1839 convention more fully, and he would have avoided so frequently using phrases like "about this time", "within a short time" and "about this period of time" (pp. 78, 80, 90). He occasionally gets his dates wrong (pp. 122, 133), though he is also quite capable of providing precise dates (pp. 108, 119, 128, 156); his account may well owe something to a small engagement-diary like George Howell's. He never quotes from letters written at the time, and despite his fascination with oratory, never quotes from the extensive newspaper reports of his own speeches. This is not necessarily a drawback; Francis Place's autobiography is not improved by its abundant documentation, nor Lovett's by its laborious inclusion of his manifestos. Unlike Lovett and Hardy, Lowery did not envisage his autobiography as a holdall for preserving documents for posterity; his autobiography is much richer than theirs, both in its reflections on class relations and in its vivid descriptive power. A Lowery free to let the fancy roam was a Lowery thrown back on his strongest resource as an auto-biographer—on his vivid memory for scenes and incidents in the past, going right back to his childhood.

The autobiography's structure is straightforward enough: it narrates his life consecutively from childhood until he entered the teetotal movement in 1841. As with John James Bezer's autobiography, there is a trace of the pilgrim's progress here, the perilous but ultimately successful journey through hazard and temptation. It would have been understandable had Lowery paused for self-congratulation. "I may say that I have attained my present position *solely*, by my own exertions", Francis Place informs us in his introduction;[38] Samuel Bamford and Thomas Cooper were not free from this trait either. But Lowery entirely lacked egoism. His autobiography conveys no impression of ambition at the time or of complacency in retrospect; he never tries to inflate his own importance in the Chartist movement, and his autobiographical mood is rather one of self-critical relief that his youthful enthusiasm did not land him in worse straits. The self-effacement of Henry Broadhurst's autobiography comes to mind, though Lowery is not even self-absorbed enough to display Broadhurst's periodic surprise at the unlikely outcome of his unpremeditated career.

Lowery apparently considered his private family life unimportant to the reader. This may be no more than a "Victorian" reticence, but it may also reflect a certain lack of curiosity and reflectiveness about his own personality. He says nothing about his three brothers, dismisses his father's four-year

---

[38] Francis Place, *Autobiography*, p. 11; cf. *The Autobiography of John Castle* (Essex County Record Office, Chelmsford, D/DU 490), p. 150; D. Vincent, *Testaments of Radicalism*, p. 167.

illness and death in a sentence, and rarely refers to his wife after their court-ship. She arrives suddenly on the scene (p. 62) when he is eighteen but is never described in detail, though relations between them seem to have been happy and close. He travels about the country as a Chartist lecturer without once saying how she is faring, and does not even tell us whether she is still alive at the time of writing; he almost certainly outlived her, for why other-wise should he go off to Canada at the end of his life to live with a married daughter? He never carries the careers of his two daughters, whom he never names, beyond early childhood. For long sections of the autobiography, Lowery submerges his own career behind larger issues. The only exception to this lack of interest in himself is his preoccupation with his own intellectual development and his care to record gratitude to those who have been kind to him in the past, the Quebec nuns, Robert Monteith and Dr. Pearson (pp. 56, 170). If justice seemed capricious during their lifetimes, working men could at least ensure in their autobiographies that justice would be done by posterity.

Lowery makes "no pretensions to literary ability" (p. 39) and the auto-biography begins, after its brief initial declaration of intent, in the most busi-ness-like way: "I was born in North Shields, Northumberland, on Oct. 14th., 1809 . . ." Unlike Cooper, Lowery wears his learning lightly. He refers to Scott, Gray, Thomas Campbell, Emerson and Fennimore Cooper, but usually to convey a sense of place rather than to parade his own cultivation. Many Chartists wrote and published verse, including Jones, Harney, Kydd and Linton—usually under the influence of Shelley and Byron. Byron's *Childe Harold* and *Manfred* "seemed to create almost a new sense within me", Cooper recalled. But Lowery's favourite was Burns, to whom he returns again and again in his autobiography.[39] A self-educated working man would respond to a poet who spoke with the popular voice and had experienced the feelings of the poor, yet whose natural genius forced its way through diffi-culty and drew upon the romantic grandeur of his surroundings. "From boyhood his poems had been my *pocket-book*" (p. 116). These literary in-fluences give Lowery much in common with those Scottish pioneers of the Labour Party Keir Hardie and Ramsay MacDonald.[40]

In retrospect it is surprising that the romantic poets had so little influence on Lowery's style, for radical politics are often associated with radical stylistic innovation. It is "a familiar phenomenon", Marcuse writes, "that

---

[39] Quotation from Thomas Cooper, *Life*, p. 35; cf. Y. V. Kovalev, "The Literature of Chartism", *Victorian Studies*, II (1958–9), p. 126; Charles Kingsley, *Alton Locke*, p. 45. For Chartist poets, see Philip Collins, *Thomas Cooper, The Chartist: Byron and the "Poets of the Poor"* (Byron Lecture, Nottingham, 1969), p. 14. For Chartist attitudes to Burns, see Y. V. Kovalev, *An Anthology of Chartist Literature* (Moscow, 1956), pp. 298, 299, 305–6; Thomas Cooper, *Life*, p. 42; Gammage, *Newcastle Weekly Chronicle*, 27 September, 13 December 1884.
[40] K. O. Morgan, *Keir Hardie, Radical and Socialist* (1975), p. 7; D. Marquand, *Ramsay MacDonald* (1977), p. 12.

subcultural groups develop their own language, taking the harmless words of everyday communication out of their context and using them for designating objects or activities tabooed by the Establishment". The belief that "inspiration is continual and orderly" was being challenged by the Chartists at all points in religion and politics.[41] Yet their own writings did no more than palely imitate the romantic poetry of the middle class. In Chartist literature there is none of the linguistic irreverence of Marx, of Bezer's autobiography or of *Red Mole*; on the contrary, there is a pronounced concern for propriety, a pursuit of that "classless" literary language which seemed the best way of acquiring an authoritative independence and "distance". Lowery's style changed somewhat between the 1830s and the 1850s; his pamphlet on *State Churches* was full of lordlings and panders, star-bespangled skies, priestly garbs and pallets of poverty, but by the 1850s this stagey quality had vanished. Amidst the prose of seasoned and matter-of-fact maturity, there is only an occasional flicker of the earlier Lowery. "No costly viands can give the relish which the humble fare of toil imparts", he declares (p. 62); he later speaks of the "bard-child of nature" (p. 136), "the car of truth" (p. 173) and "the lark's matin song" (p. 188), and there are the occasional tired similes (pp. 73, 82, 99) and strained metaphors—the "huge Aeolian harp" on p. 52, for example, and the "merchants who seek wealth in a sickly clime" on p. 82, but by comparison with the Lowery of the 1830s, these moments are rare.

But if Lowery the autobiographer has pruned his language, he cannot restrain romantic scenery from interrupting his narrative flow, particularly when discussing his childhood (6 per cent of his autobiography is absorbed in this type of description). Its vividness must erflect the impact scenery had made upon him at the time. He has a sharp visual memory for the events of early childhoox—his father's shipwreck when Lowery was eight (p. 42), the Atlantic hurricane (p. 47) and the remarkable detail involved in his recollection of the ship "broached to" in the Atlantic (p. 52). Some of Lowery's most vivid descriptions concern storms and shipwrecks. Occasionally these descriptions of nature lead him into over-ornate prose (e.g. p. 188), but he believed that "the vast, grand, terrible, and sublime in Nature tend to expand the comprehension and views of those who are brought up beside them" (p. 41). He delights in describing the wulf of St. Lawrence, Ravensworth Vale, the Banff coastline or the scenery round Burns's birthplace. Even as autobiographer he becomes eloquent at the thought of large public meetings gathering "beneath the mighty dome of God's sublime and beautiful creation" (p. 109). Much of his indignation against industrialism, as his *Collier Boy* (p. 240) shows, came from a belief that it was destroying natural beauty. Lowery also has a memory for sounds as well as sights—

---

[41] Herbert Marcuse, *An Essay on Liberation* (Penguin ed. 1972), p. 41, cf. pp. 42, 68; Dean Winnstay, in Charles Kingsley, *Alton Locke*, p. 165.

the hymns at the Quebec nunnery and the sailors' songs. Nor did this precise descriptive memory forsake him in later life, as the disrupted Dublin meeting and the Cornish revival indicate. When to fine landscape was added the drama of historic events, Lowery's enthusiasm for a locality was boundless. The Heights of Abraham, Runnymede, Stirling Castle, the Paris of 1789 —these all intensely moved him, and made him regret that the English working man did not share the Scotsman's passionate involvement with his past. "I have gazed on Runnymede, the field of Worcester, and Shakspere's and Hampden's homes", he wrote, "but rarely found a labouring man whose spirit has communed with the past" (p. 153).

Lowery often employs direct speech. The meeting of the Newcastle tailors, the speechmaking at Hayle in 1839, the refusal to repudiate the New Move in 1841—all gain immediacy as a result. His account of the St. Ives revival in particular (p. 134) is superb in its handling of detail and dialogue. The romantic's capacity for entering into the feelings of others comes out clearly when he describes the "smitten" young woman at St. Ives, or the Carlisle factory girl ("a soul of feeling was in her eyes") who grasped his hand at the Carlisle meeting in 1839 (p. 138).[42] It also comes out in his eagerness to communicate with his readers—buttonholing them occasionally, as during the storm-scene ("Oh, the wild shriek which burst from wives there"— p. 42), and wanting them to understand what life at sea is really like (p. 52). This desire to communicate had always been only precariously restrained in Lowery by the need for rational argument and concise presentation, and in the autobiography it occasionally breaks through in the anecdote which, though irrelevant, aims to entertain. The strenuousness of the autodidact's career demanded great austerity of character. Lowery remained genial and gregarious, while retaining a vivid memory of suffering that retrospectively still made him angry and indignant. His Chartist days seemed to Lowery the autobiographer as a sequence of deeply moving episodes— the sunken cheeks and dim eyes of the Carlisle handloom weavers, the weariness and disillusion of the Paisley weavers, the Dublin beggars. It is as though his memory was essentially visual, working less in a chronological way than through imaginatively recalling a sequence of snapshot scenes.

IV

Why, finally, did Lowery write his autobiography? The question is perhaps best answered by contrasting Lowery the Chartist with Lowery the autobiographer. In this edition we have therefore reprinted some of Lowery's major radical and Chartist speeches, together with one of his pamphlets, *An Address on Exclusive Dealing*. Lowery the Chartist is jaunty, confident, funny: "trusting soon to hear the bugle sound 'the gathering', and hoping soon to

---

[42] cf. *Northern Liberator*, 6 December, 1839; Thomas Cooper, *Life*, p. 142.

meet you in the ranks" (p. 252) he can still write to the *Northern Star* after the setbacks of 1839 and the serious illness of 1840. Contrast the middle-aged Lowery who broods on how providence shields the child from "the shades and dark shadows which lie in the onward pathway" (p. 43), and on how, as a young man, he "had not . . . compared the ideal of things with the real of life" (p. 63). He is almost nostalgic about the high hopes of early married life (p. 62) and almost wistful (when speaking against the reformed poor law) about the fact that "it never entered into our minds to question the practicability of what we were seeking. We had a perfect assurance that we were right . . ." (p. 96). The older man feels he knows better, yet retains an affection for the unworldly idealism of the young radical.

This sombre quality mingles with self-criticism. It is not that Lowery is another Thomas Cooper—toning down his one-time extremism in the process of recollecting it: it is rather that he half-apologises for youthful actions which might in retrospect seem extreme. He admits that the radicals were indiscriminately hostile to the new poor law (p. 95), that the Chartists tried to go ahead too fast (p. 141). "Even my wildest outbursts always had a semblance of reason" (p. 171): and "at that time I did not properly weigh my words often" (p. 137). The speeches reproduced here reinforce the point. Lowery quotes with approval the sceptical working man or woman in the Chartist audience who proved wiser than the radical stars of the day. When a dashing young radical orator said he would fight and die for his wife, a working woman in the audience wanted to know whether he would work for her; "that woman", says Lowery, "understood the duty of man" (p. 141). Lowery the autobiographer has come to respect the down-to-earth sceptical realism of such bystanders, and anecdotes of this type feature more than once, with interjections often quoted in dialect form.[43] It is an attitude akin to the Victorian radical's penchant for eccentric "characters"—for Johnny Lawson (pp. 177, 178) and Jamie Grant (p. 181)—which Lowery also displays.

This change of tone and outlook originates partly in the fact that Lowery was in his late forties when he published his autobiography. Introducing his *Life and Struggles* in 1876, Lovett said that "the older I get the more I am finding out my great deficiencies, and perceive how lamentably ignorant I am on a great variety of very important subjects"[44]. A similar humility pervades Lowery's autobiography. A nineteenth-century autodidact pursued *self*-knowledge as well as book knowledge. His autobiography is a record not only of an apprenticeship to public affairs, but also of a private development in intellect and character. He is interested in how this occurs—in how he felt almost adult after his father's shipwreck, how his time in the nunnery launched him on study (p. 55) and how he trained himself for public speaking (p. 73).

---

[43] For examples, see below, pp. 45, 72, 137, 141.
[44] W. Lovett, *Life and Struggles*, p.v.

Supplementing the mellowing of age there was an emotional maturity which originated in suffering. There is a parallel here with George Eliot's Adam Bede and Kingsley's Alton Locke. George Eliot erodes Adam Bede's prickly intolerance through the emotional crisis of Hetty Sorrel's trial, whereas for Lowery the crisis is physical—his illness in 1840–1. At this point in the autobiography, Lowery is at his most mystical: on his sickbed he "first felt the nothingness of life here, unless conjoined to life eternal, and was led away from things of earth to commune with things heavenly. From that time forward my dear wife and I had a deep conviction that our duty was simply to live right each passing day, and not to fret for the future . . ." (p. 161). Henceforward he felt able to co-operate more fully with the middle class followers of Urquhart and Sturge: his severe illness and the help he received from relatively wealthy people brought home to him—in a way that would have delighted the heart of Mrs. Gaskell—the common humanity of men from all social classes. Private suffering can bring about public reconciliation. Lowery's encounter with Monteith and Pearson recalls the meeting between John Barton and Mr. Carson at the end of *Mary Barton*: "rich and poor, masters and men, were then brothers in the deep suffering of the heart".[45]

A third reason for the contrast between the two Lowerys is of course the fact that the autobiography was written for a temperance public. From week to week Lowery's columns were hemmed in by reviews of books like the Rev William Ritchie's *The Scripture Testimony against Intoxicating Wine*, by reports of lectures like E. Grubb's "On the Qualities and Effects of Fermented and Distilled Liquors on the Human Constitution", by correspondence on the medicinal value of alcohol ("I gave malt liquor a fair trial, and I can now say, that during the space of three months it has *utterly failed in producing the desired effect*"), and by advertisements for hydropathic establishments, temperance tracts and "tea-festival contractors".

The *Weekly Record*, founded in 1856, was the semi-official organ of the Quaker-dominated National Temperance League.[46] London-based and relatively timid in its policies at this time, the League shuddered at the radical prohibitionism of the Manchester-based United Kingdom Alliance. The editor was William Tweedie (1821–74), son of a pious Scottish land-steward. Tweedie had published James Burn's *The Autobiography of a Beggar Boy* the year before; he was a shrewd and prudent man who helped found the Temperance Land and Building Society and the London Temperance Hospital, and made himself the leading temperance publisher in London from the early 1850s to his death. His views were far from radical, and in 1859 his paper launched an attack on Ernest Jones's parliamentary candidature which would have been too strong even for Lowery (who does not

---

[45] Mrs. E. C. Gaskell, *Mary Barton* (Everyman ed. 1969), p. 345.
[46] The League is more fully discussed in B. Harrison, *Drink and the Victorians* (1971), pp. 210–18, 243, 268.

mention Jones at any point in his autobiography): "when we see our movement dragged through an election at the heels of adventurers, and made the synonyme of Chartism, and put upon the lowest platform of politics, we should be recreant to the cause if we held our tongue."[47]

A Chartist autobiography published amid the high-minded semirecreational reforming activities of early Victorian dissent needed to make certain concessions to its readers. Publication in the *Weekly Record* was constricting in a double sense—it seriously limited the readership for a memoir which deserved national attention, and it encouraged Lowery to include irrelevant and often crudely-inserted snippets about drinking customs (e.g. pp. 47–49) and the occasional long moralistic anecdote; the latter (5 per cent of the total content) are sometimes inserted on the thinnest of pretexts. Lowery clearly bore his readership in mind when describing the drinking habits of the sailors he met as a boy, the Newcastle tavern discussion groups, friendly societies and freemen, and the harm done by drink to handloomweavers and American Indians. He describes his few months as a publican as "a mistake" (p. 104) and adds that he "became more and more averse to the position every day" (p. 105). He includes the long digression about the surgeon's apprentice merely because "it presented a memorable instance of a respectable family being ruined by a popular prejudice and delusion" (pp. 57–58); the long concluding anecdote merely inculcates the trite lesson that pledge-signing can promote the happy life. It would in fact have been surprising if Lowery's autobiography had remained completely unaffected by his fifteen years' experience as a temperance lecturer.

Some of Lowery's Chartist rhetoric would have been unacceptable to the *Weekly Record*. In 1834 he described the prominent Quaker and temperance supporter Joseph Pease as "that piece of sanctified assurance and deceit":[48] at Newcastle in November 1839 he urged his audience not to listen to "the damnable priests, who would persuade them that God punishes the poor for their sins, and not the rich", and saw the working man as a Christ-like figure, crucified by Whigs and Tories.[49] To clothe political and class grievances in such vigorous phrasing would hardly have pleased the worthy Quakers of the National Temperance League. Dissenters in the 1830s may have been distant from the Whigs, but they did not see them as a hyena to be destroyed by the Tory tiger, as Lowery did in September 1839 (p. 246). Lowery the autobiographer ignores the hostility shown by Lowery the Chartist to the sabbatarian and temperance movements. In Newcastle in May 1838 he had strongly opposed Plumptre's Sabbath Bill, and condemned those who spent Sundays listening "to the voice of a man whose mind was perhaps gloating upon the emoluments of his benefice" rather than absorbing "the blue sub-

---

[47] *Weekly Record*, 14 May 1859, p. 191. For a memoir of Tweedie, see B. Harrison, *Dictionary of British Temperance Biography* (Society for the Study of Labour History, 1973), pp. 130–1.
[48] *Newcastle Press*, 24 May 1834, p. 4.
[49] *Northern Star*, 7 December 1839, p. 1.

27

limity of the mountains . . . the minstrelsy of the woods . . . the dark heaving of the mighty main". By 1855 Lowery was championing complete Sunday closing, a position endorsed in his autobiography. Lowery's Chartist speeches aim at establishing the dignity and stature of the working people, and therefore vigorously repudiate criticism of their drinking habits. It is the middle class who can afford to drink the most, he tells the Palace Yard meeting (p. 211), and it is the privacy of middle class circumstances—he tells the Carlisle meeting in September 1838 (p. 217)—which enables them to conceal their vices. In November 1839 he and Duncan saw oppression as "the principal cause of the drinking habits of the people": temperance reformers "declaimed against the vice only, without doing something to remove the cause". There is nothing of this in his autobiography.[50]

Lowery the Chartist and Lowery the autobiographer again differ in their view of Chartist-teetotal relationships in Cornwall during 1839. "The Priests are moving Heaven and Earth against us" (p. 236), Lowery and Duncan told the convention on 22 March. Duncan went further, and wrote in the *True Scotsman* on 21 March that the Methodists and teetotallers monopolized all the local talent: "were any of these young men to give the [Chartist] mission the smallest countenance, they would never again be permitted to address a religious or tee-total meeting. Toryism and Pharisaical cant is omnipotent in every tee-total committee in Cornwall. These things have been obstructions and hinderances [*sic*] in our way."[51] Not surprisingly, none of this comes through in Lowery's later account of his Cornish mission. He emphasizes that he and Duncan stayed at temperance hotels, and that at St. Ives after the Chartist meeting "a number of very intelligent working men came to us at the Temperance house, whom we found to be mostly teetotallers" (p. 132). But his emphasis in the 1850s is very much on Chartist respectability.

It is possible that editorial intervention was responsible for this contrast in mood. This may also be the reason why the autobiography breaks off so abruptly; there is no attempt at rounding it off or at summing it up with some final reflections. Furthermore, one might have expected his activities after 1841 particularly to interest a temperance readership. Yet this seems an unlikely explanation. Tweedie undoubtedly felt that Lowery's autobiography would help launch his new periodical, for it was advertised in the first number and began in the second. And editorial intervention seems to have been kept to a minimum. The autobiography's content is quite unaffected by serialization, and does not seem to have been written from week to week because it flows smoothly and without repetition. The manuscript seems to have been cut up fairly arbitrarily; extracts of varying length appeared at different intervals, and they run consecutively, instead of reaching the

---

[50] Quotations from *Northern Liberator*, 26 May 1838; *Charter*, 10 November 1839, p. 667. Contrast Lowery's view expressed in *British League*, May 1847, p. 118.

[51] His letter appears in *True Scotsman*, 30 March, 1839.

weekly dramatic climax which serialization would require. Because the original breaks appear to be artificial we have not reproduced them here. But it would be difficult to refer to, let alone digest, an unbroken 80,000 word memoir. We have therefore divided it into six "chapters" which in our view reflect its natural breaks. To each of these "chapters" we have assigned a general heading of our own which we hope will be helpful.

If Lowery's autobiography had primarily aimed at pleasing a teetotal audience, it could have been adapted much more fully for the purpose. His life could have been moulded into one of those standard teetotal sagas so often heard at temperance meetings or printed by the temperance press. Yet his teetotal conversion is by no means the climax of his autobiography: it is an episode discussed in a matter-of-fact sort of way, and the autobiography continues, somewhat inconclusively, for several pages longer. And if the conventional teetotal denouement is lacking, so also is the conventional teetotal preliminary—the sinful drinking past. Lowery makes no attempt at building up his Chartist sins as the ugly precursors of a new teetotal career. On the contrary, Lowery defends his Chartist past at several points, and explains how Chartist extremism inevitably resulted from the combination of poverty and a radical history and culture (p. 120). The *Weekly Record*'s readers received no abject apology from Lowery for his past conduct: in his autobiography he forthrightly defends the 1839 Chartist convention as "more talented than any I have known" (p. 127) and he repeatedly emphasizes Chartist integrity and intelligence. He never retreats from universal suffrage, and insists that working men pioneered the attack on protection.

All this suggests that Lowery was not asked to modify the tone of his autobiography or to curtail it. He certainly remained on good terms with Tweedie, if one can judge from the approving reports of his activities between 1858 and 1862 which appeared in the *Weekly Record*. He was employed at Hull as a temperance lecturer for the ten months ending July 1858, and he reappears in the *Weekly Record* for 16 October 1858 as finding in drink the "chief source" of the prostitution and social evils of the dock areas. "Most sincerely do we mourn his departure and revere his memory", wrote the *Weekly Record* on 5 September 1863, reporting his death: "and most earnestly do we recommend our readers to emulate his zeal in advancing the Temperance movement."

It was no mere desire to conciliate the *Weekly Record*'s readers, then, and still less editorial censorship—which caused Lowery the autobiographer to play down his Chartist critique of the teetotallers: it was his overall change of strategy since 1840 which brought him to see his Chartist past in the 1850s through temperance spectacles. Between the 1830s and the 1850s he came to recognize that working and middle class men were at last beginning to speak the same language, a language of social responsibility on the middle class side, a language of respectability and shared interests on the working class side. Lowery the autobiographer sees his class as an "order", to judge from the sub-title, a term which looks both ways—towards more stable social institutions, but also towards self-respect and recognition. Lowery had urged a dialogue between middle and working class in 1841–2 (p. 254); by the 1850s his hopes were being realized and his mood had become optimistic, though less securely so than Henry Broadhurst was at the end of the century. Transport is cheaper, Lowery points out (p. 119), writers can publish without the need for patronage, "every denomination of religion is more active in its operations to do good" (p. 100), progress is on the march (p. 173). "Time, with his steady pace, carries forward the car of truth, tests the soundness of all prophecies, and surely, though often slowly, triumphs over wrong" (p. 173). As Kingsley wrote in his 1854 preface to *Alton Locke*, "there is no doubt that the classes possessing property have been facing, since 1848, all social questions with an average of honesty, earnestness, and good feeling which has no parallel since the days of the Tudors."[52]

The function of his autobiography for Lowery is therefore to explain one class to another, to continue the task he had undertaken at Leeds in 1841 (p. 253), and in the Urquhart and Complete Suffrage movements. Indeed, it is perhaps wrong to see Lowery's articles as an autobiography at all. His title refers, after all, only to "Passages" in the life of a radical, and the emphasis is firmly on Lowery's Chartist years up to 1841, which occupy over two-thirds of the biographical passages. Lowery's purpose seems mainly to show how the lamed son of a seaman became a working class leader, rather than to portray his life as a whole up to 1841, let alone afterwards. The autobiography sets the scene, so to speak, for the class reconciliation which began in 1840. "Classes hitherto in a state of rancorous hostility are there linked together", said Monteith to Cargill of the Urquhartite movement: "operatives and merchants sit together at the same table, conning over the same papers and espousing the same convictions."[53]

Lowery the autobiographer aims to consolidate this mood by struggling to explain the situation of the middle class even when at their most hostile to working men—after 1832, for example. He tries to show how the mistakes of the new poor law, for instance, grew out of the failure of the upper class to comprehend the domestic economy of early Victorian working class families. He often admits that when conflicts between middle and working class occurred in the 1830s there had been, in retrospect, "faults on both sides" (cf. pp. 74, 138). There undoubtedly was a need for mutual explanation. A Wesleyan superintendent conversing on mineralogy with Lovett on a bus was incredulous when Lovett revealed his name. "What! William Lovett,

[52] Charles Kingsley, *Alton Locke*, p. 16; cf. pp. 2–3 (Kingsley's 1862 preface). Compare James Burn's chronicling of change, which he equates with progress, in his *Autobiography of a Beggar Boy* (1978 ed.), especially letter X; and Henry Broadhurst, *The Story of his Life* (1901), pp. 51, 53.
[53] Quotation from G. Robinson, *David Urquhart*, p. 99.

the Chartist? . . . *you don't look like one*";[54] the Chartists had been converted by their enemies into villains. In the late 1830s *Blackwood's Magazine* could describe Chartism as "composed for the most part of the lowest, the most ignorant, and the most desperate of the kingdom", and John Collins at a Manchester dinner in 1840 found authors and journalists "notoriously ignorant" of working class feelings and habits. Lowery, like Lovett and Place, notes the "painful vexation" he felt at such silly comment (p. 39).[55] But whereas at Leeds in 1841 Lowery almost passionately insisted on the need for dialogue between the classes, there is in the autobiography a quiet confidence that this dialogue is now well under way. By 1856, alternative perspectives on the working classes were being offered by the social novelists and by investigators like Henry Mayhew, whom Lowery praises in his first instalment. So Lowery hopes that his autobiography may "be useful, not only to the present thinkers amongst the working classes, but also to some of the middle and upper classes" (p. 39, cf. pp. 105, 121). Working men, he aims to show, are naturally as kindly, humane and intelligent as any other social group; or if they are not, their behaviour is understandable. "In the consideration of all moral action", he writes, "we must not only know the act but also the modifying and often complex influences which produced the result before we can clearly judge" (p. 40).

The two Lowerys therefore pursue very different strategies. Lowery the Chartist aims to develop the self-confidence and self-respect of working men by advertising their achievements and convincing them of their power (pp. 212, 215). Lowery the autobiographer aims to increase upper and middle class understanding of working men by depicting their virtues and difficulties: to show, in Kingsley's words, that it is the maligned Chartists who "have been the great preachers and practisers of temperance, thrift, charity, self-respect, and education".[56] But whereas in the 1830s his response was to attack his superiors, in the 1850s he seeks to educate them. He knew better than most how deeply rooted was Chartist extremism in desperate poverty: "there is something in the effects of hunger and of the sight of your family suffering from it", he says, "which none can judge of but those who have felt it" (p. 121). He always relates working class extremism to the context of poverty (p. 97). One of his major tasks in his autobiography therefore was that of the social novelists in the 1840s: to impress upon the

---

[54] W. Lovett, *Life and Struggles*, p. 244.
[55] *Blackwood's Edinburgh Magazine*, September 1839, p. 289; Collins, *Northern Star*, 22 August 1840, p. 8. Compare Henry Solly, "*These Eighty Years*", or, *The Story of an Unfinished Life* (1893), I, p. 345; II, p. 166; Charles Kingsley, *Alton Locke*, p. 65; J. S. Mill, "Reorganisation of the Reform Party", in G. Himmelfarb (Ed.), *J. S. Mill; Essays on Politics and Culture* (New York, 1963), p. 291. See also F. Place, *Autobiography*, p. 109; B. Harrison, "Two Roads to Social Reform. Francis Place and the 'Drunken Committee' of 1834", *Historical Journal*, 1968, pp. 283, 296–7.
[56] Compare C. Kingsley, *Alton Locke*, p. 41; [J. S. Mill], "The Claims of Labour", *Edinburgh Review*, April, 1845, p. 189; *Northern Star*, 29 January 1848, p. 4; F. Place, *Autobiography*, p. 128.

relatively prosperous *what it felt like* to be poor. Lowery on his early poverty echoes Mrs. Gaskell on Ben Davenport's fever-stricken family in *Mary Barton*; he wants the other side to understand what drives a man to revolution. Lowery's message is less insistent than Kingsley's, but it is the same: when placed in the same situation, rich and poor would behave alike.[57] Henry Broadhurst's autobiography was to preach the same message half a century later.

But Lowery shared Kingsley's view that education was also needed by the working classes. He published his autobiography partly from "a belief that its incidents may be made useful to my fellow working men" (p. 39)—or in the somewhat complacent words of Francis Place, to "prove how from very inauspicious beginnings, by a little honesty, a little practical good sense, a due portion of self respect, and continued exertion a great deal of what is most desirable may be accomplished".[58] So the autobiography is didactic in tone: "Oh! working men, guard faithfully and jealously . . . the 'day of rest' " (p. 45), he insists: and his account of his publican days is included "that it may be of use to others" (p. 105). He condemns sailors who use their leisure only for drink (p. 48), working men who get into debt or use "credit shops" (p. 62), the "unthrifty habits and mismanagement of some of the working men and of their wives around us" in his early married days (p. 63), and like Bamford and Lovett he hoped that politically active readers would learn from his personal and political mistakes:[59] from his unwise decision to take a public-house, for instance (p. 105), or his nervousness as a young radical orator (p. 78). It seemed important—within the working classes as within the elite—to pass on accumulated experience.

The transition from Lowery the Chartist to Lowery the autobiographer was not easily accomplished: in the process Lowery faced O'Connor's hostility, the loss of his livelihood, the painful need to rethink his first principles of political action. But the scale of the transition and its difficulties should not be exaggerated. He had never been an atheist: "we are the true practical christians", he insisted at Carlisle in 1838; in July 1839 he even "appealed to the sacred Scriptures to show that men were justified in righting themselves by physical force."[60] And his Christianity was always staunchly protestant: his heroes were the Reformation and puritan heroes, and his language was that of the Bible, the first book he records himself as reading (p. 41). The Biblical echoes which abound in his autobiography[61] can also

---

[57] C. Kingsley, *Alton Locke*, p. 7; cf. pp. 50, 62, 137. See also Mrs. Gaskell, *Mary Barton*, p. 56, cf. p. 21; *Alton Locke*, p. 193; and Henry Broadhurst, *op. cit.*, p. 54.

[58] F. Place, *Autobiography*, p. 12; cf. Joseph Arch, *The Story of his Life* (3rd ed. n.d.), p. 2 (foreword); J. D. Burn, *Autobiography of a Beggar Boy*, preface.

[59] cf. W. Lovett, *Life and Struggles*, p. 1; S. Bamford, *Passages in the Life of a Radical* (Ed. W. H. Chaloner, 1967), pp. 36, 277.

[60] Quotations from *Carlisle Journal*, 6 October 1838, p. 3; 13 July 1839; cf. *Northern Liberator*, 11 April, 1840, p. 6.

[61] For examples, see below, pp. 75, 100, 111, 121, 131.

be found in his Chartist speeches, where they appear somewhat fresher and less stilted (cf. pp. 227, 239). Lowery's *State Churches* is rhetorical in mood and somewhat flowery in phrasing, but its message was entirely acceptable in nonconformist circles during the 1850s and for several decades later. In an argument adorned with a panoply of Biblical quotations and showing extensive research into episcopal revenues and Anglican pluralism, Lowery argued strongly against established churches in principle as infringing freedom of opinion and conflicting with the aims of the Reformation. "If ever freedom had a foe, if ever tyranny had a tool, it was priestcraft . . ."[62] He also argued against their practice—as exemplified by the Church of England, with its corruption and its aristocratic connexions which ensured that it diverged markedly from the humble origins of Christianity and held up social and political progress. Who but the dissenters, Lowery asked, had covered the country with Sunday Schools and civilized the Northumberland and Durham miners? The wealth of the Church should be distributed in educating the people. Sentiments of this kind expressed in the 1830s made it easy for Lowery in the 1850s to co-operate later with a predominantly dissenting moral reform movement.

Nor was Lowery's zeal for thrift, temperance and respectability acquired only after 1841. He may have been distant from the temperance movement in the 1830s, but he was a real enthusiast for sobriety. "Give a man a cheap newspaper, and he will not become a pot-house politician" was his argument for repealing the taxes on knowledge in 1834. He told a Carlisle meeting in 1838 "I hate a pot-house politician, who, to satisfy his own desires, robs his wife and family of those comforts he ought to administer to them; such are not the men on whom we must depend".[63] The 1841 conversion to teetotalism merely pushes forward an earlier trait in Lowery's mentality. Illness and Urquhart's influence drove home to him the recognition that governmental power could be subverted only by a people fully equipped to assume its role. "Hitherto I had simply applied my mind to forms of government and popular rights, thinking that if these were attained improvement would be at once achieved. But he turned my mind to the fact that all law was dead unless its spirit was in the people . . ." (p. 167). It was easy for Lowery to move forward to the high-toned moral idealism of mid-Victorian Liberal reforming causes.

Chartism had always enjoyed strong links with the middle class at some times and places: Lowery himself mentions the shopkeepers who "freely contributed" to Chartist funds (p. 117), the free franks received by the Chartist convention from sympathetic M.P.s (p. 120) and the clergyman Dr. Wade marching at the head of a trade union procession (p. 139). Manu-

[62] R. Lowery, *State Churches Destructive of Christianity and Subversive of the Liberties of Man* (Newcastle, 1837), n.p.
[63] Quotations from *Newcastle Press*, 4 January 1834, p. 4; *Carlisle Journal*, 6 October 1838, p. 3.

facturers like Thomas Doubleday and Charles Attwood, surgeons like Larkin and Fife, a wine and spirit merchant like James Mather, and Lowery's Newcastle employer the Primitive Methodist master-tailor—these were the decidedly middle class men who had presided over the growth of Lowery's early radical ideas. In his later Chartist days he did of course attack shopocrats and "middle men", but never without the hope that they might one day join the masses in attacking privilege. Lowery, the autobiographer, speaks of "my class" five times, but never uses the segregating term "working class": his favourite terms are "the people" (used 27 times), "working men" (25), "working classes" (22), "masses" (8) and "multitude" (5). When "the classes" were under attack, their opponents could include very varied social groups, both in the 1830s and 1850s. It is quite untrue to say that "a breadth of aspiration, a passion of protest and an intensity of resolve . . . had no place in the politics of Liberalism"; nor did a turning away from Chartism to Liberalism involve any abandonment of the Chartists' "social programme"[64] such as it was. Once he had overcome his distrust of the mainly middle class leaders of Liberal reforming movements, Lowery was well able to appreciate the affinity between Chartism and the many crusades which built up Russell's and Gladstone's Liberal Party.

Furthermore Lowery's belief that "suffering is the divine voice that bids us to be up and find a remedy" (p. 99) was shared by the mid-Victorian Liberals and radicals who were working in the same direction as Lowery from the middle class side. Together they transformed the early-Victorian Whig-Liberal party into a vehicle of popular politics. Lowery's autobiography displays none of that pessimism about trends within the working class which can be seen in some later Chartist autobiographies—in Lovett and Cooper, for example. Like his Chartist speeches, it moves in a world where progress is occurring, but with the difference that in the 1850s the authorities constitute less of an obstruction. A tactical change after 1840 there may have been, but there was no capitulation. In 1841 Lowery retained his earlier ideals and had the courage to face out hostility from those who mistook a blind tactical consistency for superior personal integrity: to repudiate pressure from those who had forsaken the movement's initially broad objectives for a clannish personality-cult and a political blind-alley.

He therefore moved out of the Chartist mainstream and applied himself in the short term to winning middle class friends for the working people; and in the long term, to preparing working people for entering politics on their own account. He never fully acknowledged the difficulties Whig governments inevitably encountered in the 1830s when trying to administer a pluralist society which faced unprecedented problems without efficient administrative machinery; nor did he lose his somewhat unreal views on English history and on the processes of government. Nonetheless, Lowery the Chartist emerges as

[64] Quotations from Dorothy Thompson (Ed.), *The Early Chartists* (1971), pp. 4, 15.

a courageous, romantic and even mischievous radical, less earnest than some of the London Chartists, less flamboyant than most of the northern men whose platform he shared. And Lowery the autobiographer is sane and serious-minded, quick to acknowledge kindnesses done to him, seldom unfair in his judgements and never conceited. In the 1850s he created for us the quiet but moving record of his intellectual and spiritual journey .

Passages in the Life of a Temperance Lecturer,

Connected with the Public Movements of the Working Classes for the last Twenty Years.

BY ONE OF THEIR ORDER

I
Childhood and Apprenticeship:
1809–1826

Making no pretensions to literary ability, it is not a desire to attract attention or acquire distinction in that sense which induces me to present the leading passages of my life to the public, but a belief that its incidents may be made useful to my fellow working men. I have also often been urged to do so by many of my friends who are labouring to elevate the working classes, who think that my life would be interesting and instructive in incidents and events connected with those movements which have engaged the attention of these classes for these last twenty years. During that time I have attentively observed these movements, and have been one of the prominent actors of my class in some of the principal ones: thus I have mixed with the working people privately and publicly, at their firesides, in their workshops, and in committee; and I have publicly addressed them in cities, towns, and villages, from the Lands-end to the Orkney Islands, and can therefore state the general thought and feelings which I found amongst them. I was placed in a position to observe their changes—what I considered to be their errors and wrongs—their intelligence and virtue and means of improving their own condition. Thus, these passages of my private and public history may present useful materials for thought. First, from my public life many facts and events will be better understood by those persons who came later than I into these movements, or who at the time were not acquainted with the springs of action which moved the movers of the masses. These facts may be useful, not only to the present thinkers amongst the working classes, but also to some of the middle and upper classes; for I have often observed, with feelings of painful vexation, the erroneous assertions and reasonings of some of these, and even of the public press, on many of the errors of the working men in their public movements, present and past. The masses know these assertions to be wrong, while still they instinctively feel, because of failure, that there has been error in some other way, while the more intelligent of them are still more offended and ascribe to the animosity of these classes what proceeds but from an error of judgment, given without having all the facts of the case and a proper arrangement of them. Thus, the best of the working men are often placed in antagonism to the upper classes, and much of the truth uttered by the press is neutralised in their minds. Until lately, and to a great extent even yet, there was but little communion or sympathy on either side between the working people and the wealthy orders; labouring men only met with their employers in the workshop, or counting-houses, receiving orders, or disputing wages or time; neither knew much of the home life, inner thoughts, or virtues of the other. The wealthy and independent classes only saw the people in the public streets, meetings, or processions; while, with but few exceptions, the writers in the press wrote rather from theories of the inner thought and life of the labouring class, than from an acquaintance with the facts of their condition. But, in the consideration of all moral action, we must not only know the act but also all the modifying and often complex influences which produced the result before we can clearly judge; yet these writers never having mixed with the working classes only saw what was thrown out from them in times of suffering and excitement—knowing nothing of what worked underneath. Then the labouring classes deemed the press, in most instances, the mere special advocate of the interest of the richer classes. Then there were no sanitary commissions or societies for improving the dwellings of the people or inspectors of factories and workshops. No Lord Shaftesburys, or Mr. Mayhew's letters in the *Morning Chronicle*, and the press was then almost totally engaged in questions more immediately affecting the welfare of the upper ranks of society.[1] Now, thank God! this is not the case.

The second point of view in which I think these passages of my history may be useful, is to the rising youth of the working classes, who will learn the means I used to obtain knowledge under the difficulties of toil and poverty from an early age upwards. My aspirations to be "a man among men," and the effects of these aspirations on my after circumstances, welfare and happiness, my modes of study and means of attaining what little information I acquired—these may serve as suggestions—helps to young men in such circumstances as mine were, and tend to prove that the necessity to labour does not debar working men from acquiring useful knowledge and intelligence, but in some degree offers facilities for their attainment which employers and shopkeepers do not possess.

---

[1] Lowery refers to documents like Chadwick's *Sanitary Report* (1842) and *Health of Towns Report* (1845); to legislation like the Factory Act (1833) and Mines Acts (1842, 1850), enforced through a specially appointed inspectorate; to philanthropic activity like Shaftesbury's work for ragged schools, improved housing and missions: and to the remarkable journalist Henry Mayhew, whose letters on the life of the London poor were first published in the *Morning Chronicle*, 1849–50. See E. P. Thompson & E. Yeo (Eds.) *The Unknown Mayhew* (1971), which reprints material from these letters. On social reform legislation, see S. E. Finer, *Edwin Chadwick* (1952); D. Roberts, *Victorian Origins of the British Welfare State* (Yale, 1960); W. Lubenow, *The Politics of Government Growth* (1971); O. MacDonagh, *Early Victorian Government 1830–1870* (1977). For philanthropy, see E. Hodder, *Lord Shaftesbury* (3 Vols. 1886) and, more generally, D. Owen, *English Philanthropy, 1660–1960* (1965). For a remarkable though highly controversial account of the structural determinants of class relations in Oldham, Northampton and South Shields in the early nineteenth century, see John Foster, *Class Struggle and the Industrial Revolution* (1974): the review of it by John Saville in *Socialist Register*, 1974: and the discussion between A. E. Musson and John Foster in *Social History*, October 1976, pp. 335–66.

I was born in North Shields, Northumberland, on Oct. 14th, 1809. My father was a younger son of a large family of an agriculturist, who resided somewhere up the Tyne above Newcastle on the Durham side, who died when his children were young, leaving them unprovided for; in consequence my father received no education. At an early age he came to North Shields and bound himself an apprentice to sea. My mother was the daughter of a master boot and shoemaker of that town; they had four children, all boys, of whom I was the eldest.

I have no definite recollections until about five years old, except some boyish freaks and mishaps; my more distinct remembrances begin at Banff, a small sea-port in the north of Scotland, where my father went as mate of a Greenland ship, called the Earl of Fife, the only whaler out of that port. I remember the strangeness of the language and the fare of the Scotch people, but being like all children, both impressible and active, I soon became a Scotch "bairn," and was as fond of porridge and milk-cakes and kail as if I had been born kilted. I had been at a Dame's school at North Shields and could read the Bible; here I was sent to a master, and commenced writing, arithmetic, and grammar.

The coast and inland scenery around Banff were beautiful and sublime. Before this I had become acquainted with the stirring sights and sounds of a sea storm on the rocks at the foot of Tynemouth Castle, "Shields bar," or the "herd sand," and here, in these more northern parts, I became more and more familiar with and fond of the ocean. From after reflection on the effects of mountainous and ocean scenery on my own mind when young, I feel convinced that the vast, grand, terrible, and sublime in Nature tend to expand the comprehension and views of those who are brought up beside them, and from which they receive feelings of a strange intermixture of pleasure and pain, which the inhabitants of the inlands cannot feel or fully understand. In the level inland country plains, a storm at its height calls up thoughts of personal inconvenience—damaged roofs and trees, rain, sleet, or cold, and forests moaning from the gale. But to me, in addition to these, they also call up the roaring of the mountain torrent in the glen, which the cotter seeks in vain to cross, while he is troubled with anxious thoughts about the safety of his family on the other side; tempest-driven ships with shattered sails; boats and bulwarks washed away; dismantled vessels and their signals of distress, or scenes at firesides, where anxious wives, children, and friends, as the storm blast raves without, exclaim, "Oh! Heaven pity the poor sailors! Where will your father be? What will they do with a wind like this? it is dead on the coast!" I never hear the song of the "Minute Gun at Sea",[2] but it calls up to my mind various reminiscences of sea storms, and more especially of one which is as vividly remembered by me as if it happened only yesterday; yet it

[2] Presumably "The Minute-Gun" by Richard Scrafton Sharpe, a popular early nineteenth-century versifier.

was about forty years ago, in which the ship Earl of Fife, in which my father sailed, was wrecked in Banff Bay. The harbour of Banff being a shallow one, the ship had to go out into the bay and take in her heavy stores when about to sail for Greenland, and to unload before entering on her return. She was anchored in the Bay lading when a severe gale of wind came on which blew right into it, so strong, that even at its commencement the captain and a boat's crew who happened to be on shore with him could not get off. The storm continued to increase, and I can recollect standing on the banks of the shore watching the ship as she was tossed at her anchors by the violent sea, which rolled and roared onwards towards the shore. The ship was about a mile from the beech, one side of the bay was rocky and a portion of the other sand. Hopes were expressed that the storm might lull; but it did not in the least, while the waves continued to rise higher and higher. My mother with some of the other men's wives sat in a fisherman's cottage during the night, and I remember as the sound of the gun came from the ship, on the storm blast to the shore, the looks and tears or passionate exclamations of grief and distress uttered by these women, and their going often to the window or door and straining their anxious vision to endeavour to see the ship on that stormy night. Daylight returned and the gallant vessel was still there, and that day, as the news had spread into the country, many people came to see her, and large numbers of them and the townspeople were continually on the banks of the bay, watching with that intense anxiety which a crowd ever feels when they see their fellow creatures in imminent peril of their lives.

Some thought "she might ride it out if the anchors and cables held," others "hoped the wind might lull or shift, for no ship could long stand that strain." Another night came, the storm did not abate—again the tears and prayers silent, and expressed, of the inmates of that cottage—the fears that the ship would not endure the storm for that night. As the booming of the occasional gun fired from her, came down on the blast,—"thank God, she is still afloat" bursting spontaneously from all! so impressed my young mind and heart, that I seemed at once in those moments to have attained the thoughts and feelings of years, and for the time ceased to be a child and to have become invested with the cares and gravity of manhood. The morning dawned, and already many of the townspeople and those of the cottages were there, watching the ship with wistful looks. The boom of a gun came down on the blast and it seemed to sweep the lingering darkness away, and discover the vessel clearly as she rose on the crest of the waves in relief against the windward sky—"she's parted from her anchors," exclaimed some of the bystanders, and all could see her wheeling from her position. Oh, the wild shriek which then burst from wives there, whom a few moments might make widows! On she came towards the rocks, on which she would have soon been beaten into fragments—strong men's cheeks were blanched and women wrung their hands in agony,—looked in despair, or cast their eyes imploringly to heaven, when providence caused a wave to strike the vessel so that it forced her from the line in which she was coming and she drifted on to the sandy beech. "Thank God," burst from the surrounding tongue, and men and women rushed to the beech, the fishermen and sailors expressing confident hopes that all the crew would be saved. The ship had come on shore at high water, and when the tide receded all her men were rescued uninjured, except my father, whose head had been severely cut, by being thrown against a gun-carriage on the quarter-deck, by the violence of the concussion when the vessel first struck the shore, but as there was no fracture he soon afterwards recovered.

The next year we went to live at Peterhead, a seaport town north of Aberdeen, with some 14,000 inhabitants. My father being engaged as mate or nurse of a large Greenland whaler, the master was chief owner, but being uneducated, was unable to navigate her to and from the country. At that time, although a small harbour, Peterhead had eighteen sail of Greenland ships, which caused it to present a busy scene in spring in their fitting out and sailing, and in autumn on their return and unlading, which was much earlier than the whalers at present from "Davis Straits," for I recollect that my father went regularly a voyage to Petersburgh with the vessel after her return from the fishing.

Peterhead lies on a low point of land which projected eastward into the North Sea; on the south side lay the harbour and a fine bay, about three miles across and two deep, with a sandy beech. On the southern point stood the fishing village of Buchan; beyond this, a little off the shore, stood the rugged Skerry Rocks, on which, until a light-house was erected, ships were often wrecked.

Here begin the distinct remembrances of the consecutive events of my after life, and to this day the scenery and society of Peterhead stand out in that vivid sunshine with which memory gilds the romance of childhood. When the bounding blood and quick flow of animal spirits give a zest to material life, when we only see the beautiful and joyous, and a kind providence veils from us the shades and dark shadows which lie in the onward pathway, that age and experience alone can enable us to perceive. Here I was sent to one of the principal schools, and, from my remembrance of that school, I think it presented a practical solution of the present difficulty felt regarding a union on the education question, in the religious instruction of children in the same school, whose parents are dissenters and churchmen. There were in it children whose parents were members of the Church of Scotland, and of those who were dissenters from that church, also of those who were members of the Church of England and dissenters from it. There were no strictly religious books read during the week except on Saturday, which was especially devoted to religious instruction, when the Scriptures were read, and either the Scotch or English cateschism taught the children according to the request of their parents. I trace my desire for reading to the class-book we used, which was called the "Scotch Beauties," being composed of extracts from the chief historians, poets, and didactic writers of Great Britain, and I remember the strong desire I felt to be able to get the books from which these extracts were quoted. Often, while playing on the seashore, have I cast my eyes on Morven Mount, which lay inland, and thought on Ossian's[3] heroes, or on the ships sailing, and imagined the voyage of Columbus and his first landing in America. There were two extracts from "Robinson Crusoe" and "Gil Blas",[4] and these were the first books I got the loan of to read, when about seven years old.

Our boyish sports were daring and exciting; one was chasing or hunting the diving sea-birds, who rarely take the wing and then cannot fly any height off the water; they are thus almost continually swimming—and dive under the water, following the fish, their prey, using their wings to swim with. Four of us in a boat would watch one, row up towards it, and the water being clear, we could trace its flight under it, and as soon as ever it rose to the surface to breathe we were close above it with stones ready to throw at it; thus at last we ran it out of breath, disabled or killed it. We often went in parties to the cliffs south of the bay where the sea-fowl laid their eggs and hatched their young. These cliffs are a portion of Buchaness, an iron-bound coast extending southward for many miles; they are often perpendicular and hundreds of feet high, assuming wild fantastic outlines, with caverns extending far into them, in which the sea-swell rushes with sullen sound while the outward ocean lies in comparative calmness; but when the storm rages, then the waves, foaming onwards, dash high up these cliffs, presenting scenes of wild grandeur and sublimity such as can only be seen on such a coast. Here the various sea-fowl flocked in thousands, resting on the rocks, circling the air between their summits and the sea, or swimming about their base. Parties used to shoot the birds and gather their eggs and young ones, going across the bay by boats and climbing up the cliffs, or by land aiding one another to descend. This was extremely dangerous and produced a daring rivalry among us boys, and on one occasion one of our companions fell and was killed, which produced such a warning that we never went again while I was there. My characteristics then were those of a "wild laddie" foremost in "devilry," often playing the truant, and seldom out of scrapes, so that if the author of any boyish mischief could not be at once discovered, I was pretty sure to get blamed. But I was a favourite amongst my schoolfellows, being always one of their leaders in our rival school fights, and in our individual encounters possessing that quality of endurance that, if I could not beat the bigger lads they could never beat me. I had a hearty laugh in 1842 when I revisited Peterhead from Aberdeen for two days. Some of the temperance friends there invited me to deliver a

---

[3] James Macpherson, a Scottish schoolmaster, published *Ossian* in 1760. He claimed that these extremely popular (but faked) epic poems had been written by a Gaelic bard of that name.

[4] An early eighteenth-century French picaresque romance about an unsophisticated young man's rise to power, self-knowledge and a benign worldly wisdom, by A. R. Lesage.

lecture, and an old man, who had been neighbour to us when we lived there, attended the lecture, and warmly invited me to tea with him and his wife. During tea the old lady had very little to say and her mind was evidently bewildered with some idea; at last, looking at me, she earnestly exclaimed, "A' man, but ye wer' a deil (Anglice, devil) when ye war' young." The old lady could not comprehend how the wild callent[5] had become a lecturer. In the autumn, when my father's ship returned from Greenland, she had to un-load in the bay; this was the high festival of the year for me, for I then had leave from school to stop on board of the ship, and was a favourite among the men, going with them in the boats when towing the rafts of blubber casks to the shore, or fishing with my lines from the ship's stern, or climbing about the rigging as I liked.

When my father had been three years at Peterhead he became ill with a pulmonary disorder, no doubt brought on by having been upwards of twenty consecutive years at Greenland, and we removed up to Sheriff-hill for change of air, which lies on the heights south of Newcastle-on-Tyne, where, after an illness of four years, the last two of which he was bedridden, he died of dropsy.[6]

At the commencement of my father's illness I was taken from school, at the age of nine, and never had the privilege of returning afterwards. I had passed through the common rules, into Practice, been drilled twice through Lenny—but by rote, and had rather received a desire for, than learned much of Geography and History.[7] The little savings of my mother were soon exhausted and she opened a girls' school, and I went to work after I was ten years old, to pick the brasses out from the coals at the mouth of the mine, by which I earned five shillings per week. I had to rise at 4 p.m. every morning and walk nearly two miles to work, which continued from 5 a.m. until 6 p.m. and I well remember how I longed for the "day of rest", when the voice of the "caller" no longer broke in on the sound slumbers of the morning, and during the day the noise of the engine, the rattle of the waggons and the dust of the coals were exchanged for the soothing and holy influences and restoration of the Sunday-school and public worship.[8] Oh! working men, guard faithfully and jealously, as ye love your families and your country—guard faithfully the sacred privileges of the "day of rest" from temporal labour and reserve it

[5] Callent, or callant, Scottish dialect for boy.
[6] Lowery was not the only orphaned Chartist leader. Compare the early histories of William Lovett, Thomas Cooper, and Thomas Dunning.
[7] William Lennie (1779–1852), a Scottish teacher, published a very successful *Principles of English Grammar*, to which he added a key in 1816.
[8] Most nineteenth-century radicals wanted Sunday to be preserved as a day of rest. Some (like Lowery the autobiographer) wanted Sundays to be spent only on religious activity; but others (like Lowery the Chartist—see *Northern Liberator*, 26 May 1838) wanted working men to enjoy all types of "rational recreation" on Sundays. See B. Harrison, "Religion and Recreation in Nineteenth-Century England" *Past and Present*, December, 1967, pp. 103–6. Lowery presumably rose at 4 a.m., not p.m.

for instruction in things divine; it is the "Magna Charta" of all your rights and liberties.[9]

Here again the scenery was picturesque where we lived; on the left lay the beautiful vale of Ravensworth and the Tyne—Newcastle in front, with Elswick and the Town Moor stretching beyond, while to the right, Tynemouth Priory and the ocean could be seen. I remember often standing in twilight on the brow of the hill, overlooking Ravensworth Vale and perceiving, long before I read of it, the distinctive superiority which word painting has over oil painting in being able to add sound to sight as instanced by critics in Grey's elegy; as the bay of the watchdog and the low of the cattle or the tinkle of the sheep bells fell on my ear I would repeat to myself the lines—

"Now fades the *glimmering* landscape on the sight,
And all the air a solemn stillness holds,
Save where the beetle wheels his droning flight,
Or drowsy tinklings lull the distant folds.[10]

When I was thirteen years of age my mother decided to remove to our native place, North Shields, that I might be apprenticed to sea, for which I had a strong desire. Had she been merely anxious to live on our earnings without reference to the future, in two or three years the joint earnings of myself and brothers would have brought in a very good income; but she urged the change saying, "you and your brothers can have no opportunity of being anything here, we must make a struggle to get you to sea; it will be a hard one for us, but I trust in God."

I was bound apprentice to the London, a brig of 300 tons or 20 keels burden, belonging to North Shields, which was generally in the North American timber trade, and I sailed on my first voyage to Quebec in May.

Having before made some short passages, I never was sick. The weather was fine through the Pentland Firth and until we were about half-way across the Western Ocean, when we encountered severe westerly gales, and we had to "lie-to" with the helm lashed down for nearly two weeks; except the "look-out," all the crew kept below, going occasionally to try the pumps, but fortunately the vessel remained tight. I remember two light ships running past us dismasted, under "jury" masts.[11]

---

[9] The early nineteenth-century radical view of English history combined a "Norman Yoke" theory that the Normans at the Conquest had destroyed the freeborn Saxons' constitutional democracy—with the republican populist view that constitutionalism had been restored through Magna Carta and the revolutions of 1640-42 and 1688. See C. Hill, "The Norman Yoke", in J. Saville (Ed.), *Democracy and the Labour Movement* (1954); Lowery particularly favoured "Magna Carta, that bulwark of English freedom", *Northern Liberator*, 15 September 1838.

[10] Verse 2 of Gray's *Elegy*. Line 4 is slightly misquoted—"Or drowsy" should read "And drowsy". Gray is spelt "Grey" two lines above. It is not clear why Lowery puts "glimmering" in italics.

[11] A temporary mast which replaced a broken one.

It is well for the sea-boy that a tincture of romance, recklessness and ignorance veils from him the hardships of his profession, or few would follow it. Those who go verging on manhood never like it and rarely make good mariners. I had no sense of danger, and when rough weather came used to wish that it would "blow great guns," for while the wind was merely heavy there was a frequent taking in of "reefs" and sails, causing loss of rest by having to "call the watch" frequently; but when the great guns blew, and the sails had to be furled and the vessel "laid-to" rolling and pitching so that you had to sit or hold fast when standing, then all the men were below, and one was generally telling a yarn most interesting to me. One day we lost a man; the wind had somewhat altered, and the captain deemed it necessary to "ware the ship," and had ordered a new forestay sail to be bent, the one in use having been shattered by the storm. I had been out on the bowsprit keeping the sail down in the "net" while it was being bent, but about twelve a.m. being called in to do some cabin work, a Scotch baker, about twenty-five years of age, who had come as a three years' apprentice, took my place; through inattention, he let the wind get into the folds of the sail, and it flung him over to leeward. "A man overboard" was echoed through the ship, and in an instant the whole crew was on deck looking all around; but he never rose to view. I recollect being struck forcibly with the impropriety of one of the drinking customs on this occasion. The captain was a religious man, and with some others felt deeply shocked at this sudden death; he asked the crew below, and read the prayers for the occasion; but when we returned to the deck, some of the mess requested me to go and tell the captain that it was usual to give the crew a "DRAM" ON SUCH AN OCCASION. Such is habit formed by evil custom, so associated is men.

When we arrived in the Gulf of St. Lawrence, we fell in with a number of ships which had encountered as stormy a passage as ourselves, and we took a portion of the crew of a wrecked vessel which one of them had picked up. We now had a fair wind, and expected to be up to Quebec in a few days; but it was not to be before we tasted a gulf squall. One night, about eleven p.m., when we were running with a fine wind and studding sails[12] set, and except the men on the "look-out," we of the watch on deck had settled under the lee of the long-boat, some smoking and all listening intently to the pro-gress of a yarn which had already proceeded for "two watches," hearing the sails shake, we looked aloft. "The wind's changing," was the remark; but scarcely had the remark been made before it was pitch dark, and the vessel was struck by a hurricane right a-head, while the forked lightning flashed in various directions. The studding-sail booms broke, and the sails got entangled with the ropes, while the ship was blown as it were on her beam ends. This was my first initiation into such a sudden squall and its effects. When up the rigging, clearing the broken booms, adjusting and stowing the sails, so

---

[12] A studding sail was set beyond the leeches of any of the principal sails during a fair wind.

blinded were we by the lightning that we could only see how to clear the entangled ropes by the light of the flashes, which often lasted for a minute or so at a time. Shortly a torrent of rain came down, all was put right; a steady breeze blew down the Gulf, and the ship was put on a "tack" to "beat up,' and we were a fortnight from then in getting to Quebec. A ship within a short distance of us lost her masts by a stroke of the lightning. These lightning and thunder hurricanes are common in North America. Sometimes they are confined to a spot, and I remember afterwards to have been one day in the Gulf when some ships were blown on their broadsides and their sails shattered, while others in another part were sailing with a steady breeze, while others, again, were lying becalmed, and some had a gentle wind in another direction.

We arrived at Quebec after an eight weeks' passage; fifty ships were lost bound out there alone, yet some few vessels, which kept two degrees farther north than the others, had favourable winds and fine weather all their passage out to Quebec, which they made in a month.

The scenery of the Gulf in its vastness and grandeur delighted me. The sombre forests covering its shores, with the highlands of Labrador and New-foundland in the distance. Here, at Quebec, there was a junction of the majestic with the softer scenes of cultivation. The island of Orleans below the town presenting a beautiful appearance, with its fields studded with houses and churches, whose tin-covered spires glittered in the sunshine. The town, so romantically situated, the noble river, with the numerous ships at the wharfs or anchored in the stream, and the loud songs of the sailors, rafts-men, and boatmen, were a gratifying change for eye and ear after being cooped up in a vessel for eight weeks. During the four weeks that we lay here to take in our cargo of timber, we were anchored in "Wolf's Cove," about three miles above the city, and I went to see the heights of Abraham, on which the young hero fell covered with glory, and the rock on which he died going up from the shore, which is steep and high, by the path which Wolf's army cut during the night before the battle.[13]

Even as a boy I was then struck with the want of interest in, and desire for information, and almost total want of observation, which the seamen evinced. Some of them had been frequently at Quebec, but had very little knowledge of its history or general characteristics. They knew that there were French inhabitants, because some worked on board, and they had met others on shore with whom they could not converse or make themselves understood, except in buying rum or swearing; but this seemed all they knew. When on shore they seldom got farther than the grog shops of the low parts of the town.[14] Some of the older ones deemed it strange that I knew more about

[13] General Wolfe (1727–1759) captured Quebec by scaling the Heights of Abraham in 1759, in the course of which he was killed. The attack was part of Pitt's attempt to destroy French-Canadian trade, on which the French war effort appeared to depend.

[14] Compare Thomas Cooper's nine-day career as a sailor: "the coarse language, the cursing and swearing, and brutality . . . rendered me so wretched that I told the master of the vessel I wished to go home"; see T. Cooper, *Life* (1872), p. 40.

Quebec than they did, before I was there, I having read a description of it in some Geography or Gazetteer, while in some of the older men there was evidently a disrelish of "boys" knowing so much, as if from a suspicion that it lessened the superiority of the men. We had a fine passage back to England, and came to Colchester and delivered, thence to Shields; and I had so improved in person that when I went into my mother's house with an older fellow-apprentice whom she knew, she asked us when "her Robert would get on shore?" but my merry laugh soon brought her arms round my neck and the paternal embrace.

The vessel then went into the London coal trade for the winter; and on a passage up to London, when off Flamborough head, deeply laden, a severe gale from the westward came on, and some ships foundered and ours lost all her sails, boats, cook-house, bulwarks and their staunchions,[15] and she was blown above a hundred miles off the land. The gale lasted three days, during which the sea was frequently washing over the vessel. Some of the crew gave up and took to their hammocks, and the hatches were battened down. Those who kept to their duty were in the cabin and with ropes round their persons. Whenever a "lull" came they used to rush out on deck to the pumps, and pump until they sucked; but fortunately there never was much water in the hold. Here I can remember the self-evident superiority of warm tea and coffee to enable men to endure cold, wet, and fatigue better than ale or spirits. The master had both on board, and gave them to the men, both warm and cold, but they very soon preferred the hot tea and coffee; and my office during the storm was to look after the fire in the cabin stove and have a constant supply there in readiness. On the fourth day the wind changed, and the weather turned fine, and the men were busy getting ready a fresh suit of sails, when a large ship hove in sight, our North country sailors made remarks on the superiority of the master, who was a navigator and coaster also, over a mere "long shore" captain, as they term those who constantly sail to tropical climes. The vessel lowered a boat, and her captain came with a chart in his hand, he having no knowledge of his exact position; ours was walking smoking his pipe on the quarter-deck when the boat came up on our quarter, and the other asked him if he could tell him "where they were?" "I am steering for Yarmouth-roads," was the answer, "and think we are on the outer dousings, but if you will step on board we will take a cast of the lead, and I will tell you directly." He came on board and the chart was spread out on the top of the companion, and when the men cast the lead and shouted out the soundings, our captain put his finger on the chart on the outer dousings, saying, "just as I expected, we are there." Although a much faster sailer, the large vessel kept by us during the day, and we hung out a light that he might keep our company at night, which he did until we made

---

[15] Upright posts around which ropes were coiled.

Yarmouth-roads in the morning.[16] One sea voyage is like another, and the incidents of sea life are monotonous; so to pass our next spring we went to Quebec and had a new captain, combining the daring seaman with the intelligent commander, who wielded a dignified authority without austereness or its mere display, and while he stood above his men was not isolated from them. In the autumn, after unloading at Liverpool, we sailed for Picton,[17] where we loaded some of our cargo, and took the rest in a lone bay where there was but one settler's dwelling in sight, and a wooden building left by some family who had attempted a clearing near the beach, but who had gone to seek a better place. In it we used to make up a fire for those engaged with the timber on the beach, and we had a number of Indians who helped to load the vessel, and who stopped in the hut. I remember that they were very fond of the rum, and care had to be taken to keep it from them in any quantity; for if they could procure sufficient, they at once drank to intoxication, and became worse than useless. We often went on shore on an evening when work was done, and they would dance us the war dance, and although ordinarily they looked dull and stupid and had none of the elastic step or eagle glance of the eye which Cooper[18] describes in their forefathers, yet as the whirl of the dance increased in rapidity and they sang their song of defiance, yelling and brandishing their tomahawks, their whole nature appeared to be altered and their forms to be more dignified, their countenances became lit up with animation and their eyes glistened with courage and daring.

The snow was lying on Cape Breton island as we came through the Gut of Canso homewards; and to those who wish a romantic fever for sea life cooled, I recommend a "fall" passage from North America in a timber-laden vessel, their stores of comforts exhausted, and nothing left but salt junk and pork, which perhaps has sailed three times round the world since it was first salted. The timber is stowed to the cabin door, and almost to the roof of the steerage where the men sleep, they scarcely having room to sit upright, to get their victuals, or change their garments. Their hammocks are almost lying on the wet timber; thus their bed-clothes and those in their chests are always damp, and if the weather is severe they cannot get them dried on deck or below. My bed was close to the deck or floor entering the cabin, and frequently when a sea struck the vessel the water would rush right down into it. I know not

---

[16] The run from Flamborough Head (Yorks.) around the Wash and East Anglian coast to Yarmouth was notorious for the lack of shelter it afforded ships in bad weather. Nearer Yarmouth, the narrowness of the channels (the "Yarmouth-roads") and the shifting sand-banks (the "dousings") which were difficult to chart, made it a hazardous port. Information kindly supplied by Professor J. R. Jones, University of East Anglia. Compare Bamford's account of this run, when he was apprenticed to a coaster, in S. Bamford, *Early Days* (ed. W. H. Chaloner, 1967), pp. 236 ff.

[17] A port on Lake Ontario, in Canada.

[18] J. Fennimore Cooper (1789–1851), American novelist famous for his Leatherstocking Tales, including *The Last of the Mohicans* (1826), in which Indians and woodsmen were splendid heroic figures.

what changes have been effected since then in the lodgings of the men in the merchant service, but at that time they were not fit for horses or dogs, and no wonder the sailors thought only of animal tastes and enjoyments when on shore, and were gross and brutal. Lodge men worse than brutes, and they will in time become brutish. How could intellectual tastes, studies, and improvement progress in such conditions? Yet on long voyages no class of workmen have the time for improving their minds and studying the science of their profession that sailors have. To illustrate this I will relate some instances afterwards. Why should not each cabin have a library and intellectual provision, as well as grog, beef, and pudding for the crew? Not only would such provisions nourish and develope characteristics which would give the country a better class of sailors, but it would produce a superior class of masters. I am aware a great change for the better has taken place in the latter class, but know that many of them still have no resource by means of which to pass their time during a passage but the "pipe and the glass", and they sink into sots—exercising a cunning care not to expose themselves when in the port, but sinking again as soon as they are at sea. I remember our captain, who was one of those who had no constitutional tendency towards alcoholic drinks, presenting a proof of such a want as I have described, as also of the danger of the moderate drinking customs of social life. After clearing the land and getting fairly into the "blue water" in the passage out, he felt that vacancy of mind which is sure to steal over those in such circumstances who have no intellectual pursuits. He never used to drink grog after dinner, or at any time except when he had company and courtesy required it; but he then proposed that he and the mate should have a glass and their pipes every day after dinner. It went on apparently to the satisfaction of his reason, but by-and-by the glass grew larger, and they sat longer, and at last he frequently proposed another glass. This startled his reflective powers, and one day as I set the decanters down he exclaimed "No, no, boy! take them away, I must drop this practice, or I soon will get too fond of it. I begin to be so already, for I want to take twice as much as I did at first." He from thence returned to his usual practice of water drinking, and although abstinence as a principle was not known to him, except when the drinking fashions compelled him, he was a water drinker; and I saw him the other day, hale, hearty, and elastic as many grog-drinking captains are at forty, while he is sixty years old, having been upwards of twenty years in the East India trade, and is now the oldest captain in that service out of London.

With all the generosity and natural kindness of the sailor, there is no class who have less feeling for the weak or sick of their fellows than they have at sea—at least, such was my observation; this may be that every man and boy has a round of duty to perform, and if he cannot do it it must be done by the rest. This is particularly the case as to the apprentices. Small ships are generally short-handed, the owners endeavouring by apprentices to give the quantity but save the cost of the quality of hands. Although but cabin boy, I

51

now took my regular "truk" or turn at the helm, and could steer well enough, except on extraordinary occasions; yet when these came, unless I had complained of being too weak to "manage her," there would not have been any remission of the duty, and pride forbad me to confess such weakness, although men of consideration would have seen it. Now an occurrence took place, which although not strictly my fault, produced a change. The ship "broached to"[19] while running in a storm before the wind, but fortunately without damage, and as a description of such a scene may be interesting to those who have not been at sea, I shall briefly describe it. We were about half way across the Western Ocean; the wind, although fair, had been blowing very heavy for some days, and the sea was running very high. Now, when in a storm with a heavy sea, it is much more dangerous for a ship to continue running before the wind than to be "lying to," for then she lays with bows slanting to the wind and waves, and pitches to them as they come, but when a ship is running before the wind, in the Western or other wide oceans, a wave coming fast on the vessel may strike her on the stern; sweeping all before it, or she may founder at once under it; but as we all are loath to lose time in a fair wind, although a gale, they run as long as they dare, and when they feel endangered it is dangerous to "lay to," because before they can do so the ship's head has to be turned or wore round to the wind and sea, and were a wave to strike her when she lay broadside to it in the hollow, almost certain destruction would follow. We were under close-reefed topsails, and had passed some ships lying to during the afternoon, and towards dark the storm was unabated. Some wished the master had "laid to,"—"hoped the wind would lull, for it was dangerous to run in such a sea." Twelve at night came, and the captain went to bed, leaving the second mate in command, and all the watch were below except the look-out. It was my turn at the helm from two to four a.m., and I went to the wheel; as a matter of course the man resigned it to me. Such a night it was! the Atlantic in all its sublimity—the wind sung in the cordage as in a huge Æolian harp,[20] while the phosphoric light emitted by the agitated sea seemed here and there as a rolling mass of light in the darkness. Although it was hard work for me, I managed to steer the ship very well, being quick to watch her slightest wavering by watching the position of her fore yardarm and some star, which enables you to detect a vessel swerving sooner than the compass. It was within a few minutes of four when they were about to heave the log, and I should soon be relieved. So far well; but just then the main-boom, which had been lowered on to the "taffrail," or stern, and lashed down, the ship rolling so heavily, had chafed through the lashing, and the boom broke loose and struck the wheel. Fortunately I stood lower than it, and to have the more ready command of the vessel had, as it were, constantly kept it on the move,

[19] A ship "broached to" by turning its side windwards.
[20] A stringed instrument operated by a current of air. Aeolus was God of the winds.

and had not my shoulder under one of the "spokes;" so when it struck I let go and called for help—a man came and seized the wheel, attempting to stop the vessel from veering from her course, which she was then doing. She again rolled, the boom again struck the wheel, and knocked him down. By this time the ship "broached to," that is, wheeled broadside to the wind, and the sails were shaking. The captain feeling her altered position and motion in his bed, rushed up in his drawers and shirt, as he had lain down, storming and shouting, "Why have you let the ship broach to?" With a glance he saw the ship's position, and at once decided to bring her to the wind; but to do this was dangerous—a sea might sweep the decks forward in doing so; he ordered the second mate and another man to the wheel, and the mate to go forward with himself to the braces, forbidding any other to follow, and the ship was safely got round, "laid to," and the fore-topsail stowed. On inquiry into the matter he soundly rated the second mate and men for being so lazy as to allow a weak boy to steer at such a time, and from thence there was more consideration. The next afternoon the gale abated, while the wind still remained fair, and we again set sail and turned her head for England. It was on Christmas night, we saw the "Lizard Light,"[21] about 10 p.m., the wind being strong and fair—and such a Christmas! All our corn, beef, tea, and sugar consumed, and we had only salt junk and pork, which, perhaps, had sailed three times round the world. Frequently the conversation turned on conjectures "what they were doing at home", and sincere wishes for some of their fare in the half-deck. Morning came, and the wind blew strong up Channel, and the captain carried all the sail he dared; frequently, as the wind blew a little stronger, and his judgment told him there should be a reduction of the sail, and the men were about to "let go the halyards," he would set his teeth, and bend as the mast bent to the squall, and then cry out as they righted, "No, no! hold on; try her yet!" "We'll carry on her and share their Christmas loaf yet." However, at last, in one of the gusts, the jibboom broke, and sail was reduced. When we got to Yarmouth Roads we found a fleet of "light colliers," and borrowed some tea and sugar of one. With a fair wind we passed on, and on the eve of New Year's Day, a little before dark, saw Tynemouth Castle. Nothing was spoken of but the pleasure of home, wives, sweethearts, and friends. About six p.m. we were abreast the bar, knowing it would not be high water for us to enter until near eight. The harbour lights were bright and clear, as if beckoning us in, and we had hoisted our signal for a pilot, and expected one quickly, and all was expectation and delight. Suddenly the sky darkened, and a violent blast blew from the westward, and it came so suddenly and with such force, that our chief sails shattered to pieces, and we were blown far off the land, almost over to Norway, and we did not get into Shields harbour until a fortnight after, and by that time our loan of tea and sugar had been done for some days. Our

[21] The Lizard is the southerly tip of Cornwall.

candles and oil were consumed, and we had to burn strips of pine in the binnacle[22] to enable us to see the compass; or steer by the stars during dark.

Next spring we sailed for Quebec. I had frequently been troubled by pains in my left knee when a boy, and on one occasion a "bonesetter" had declared it to be dislocated, and put me through his process of "setting" it. During this winter I had felt a return of these, and when about half across the ocean it was seized with violent pains, and swelled severely, from a little below the hip to the foot included, and I could not bear my weight on it; the pain often assumed a spasmodic action, as if an electric shock was passing from the hip to the knee, when I would have to hold it with my hand to keep it still, and shout with agony.[23] Some remedies were tried, as bathing it with steaming hot flannels; but there was scarcely any abatement of the symptoms. In three weeks' time we reached Quebec, and the captain procured me admission into the Hotel Dieu Nunnery, which took in twelve boarders of each sex. The nuns attended on the sick, and a surgeon and physician visited daily. They did not take in those afflicted with fevers or contagious disorders; chiefly accidents. It was a very large building, forming a square, in one corner of which there was a church belonging to it. It stood on the brow of the heights on the east part of the town, with the Isle of Orleans in front, overlooking the space where the St. Lawrence bends or widens here to the Falls of Montmorency on the left, or north; thus the scene from the window next which my bed was placed was most picturesque. There was a large garden on the declivity in front, belonging to the nunnery, in which some of the nuns were always working. At this time commenced the more complete exercise of my thinking and reflective faculties.[24] Up to this time I had read but few books, merely feeling interest in the poetry, imagination, or incidents; and had therefore no ideas, so to speak, of my own. Those I had, had been given me by others, and had not been analyzed by me, or made my

---

[22] The compass box, kept near the helm.

[23] Lowery's illness apparently resulted from tuberculous involvement of the left knee joint. Dr. Alastair G. Mowat, consultant rheumatologist at the Nuffield Orthopaedic Centre, Headington, has been kind enough to read the relevant passages of Lowery's autobiography, and in a letter to the editors he says that this would "explain the long history with final settling of the disease, in particular the absence of fever which allowed his admission to the nunnery in Quebec. The failure of help from an osteopath could also be explained, as would the final settling of the condition in his mid 20s". He thinks that the disease caused the knee to "become permanently flexed" and the muscles to become wasted. "This would give the appearance that the left leg was thin and short . . . It seems unlikely however that the flexion deformity of the knee could be completely corrected by simply walking again, but it would certainly be the case that most of the muscle would return to the limb and hence his appearance would look largely normal". Dr. J. M. Potter, Director of postgraduate medical education and training at Oxford, kindly put us in contact with Dr. Mowat; he informs us that Lowery "is the first patient to be treated under a medical consultation service for historians which he and his colleagues are hoping to operate from Wadham College".

[24] For Lowery, as for another Chartist leader G. J. Harney, early illness gave opportunity for sustained reading which might not otherwise have occurred. See A. R. Schoyen, *The Chartist Challenge* (1958), p. 3.

own. As I sat in bed day and night, the shocks still frequently coming, reflections seemed to come, and the mind as it were rose and came forth, to ask of, and examine, this and that of life and its future, which I had scarcely thought of before. During the night, when I could not sleep, I was constantly reflecting on what I had been reading during the day; and this being on the questions of religion, the surrounding associations were peculiarly calculated to dispose me to religious feelings; my sick-bed—thoughts of my mother and brothers far away—the silence of the night—the nuns noiselessly moving through the room in their occasional visits, in their white robes and black veils, seen by the dim night lamp; and then some time between four and five in the morning, I could hear the distant swell of the organ, and music of their voices, when engaged in their matin devotions.

The nuns were exceedingly kind to me, and whenever I had any nauseous medicine to take, were sure to bring me a little jam or something pleasant tasted along with it. There was a student of medicine, a French Canadian youth of upwards of 20 years of age, who frequently sat and conversed with me, he being then studying the English language, and from his superior information I received advantage. One of the nuns, between 40 and 50 years of age, also a French Canadian, who was the one who was most constantly in attendance on the patients, and superintended the preparing and administration of the medicine, often held conversations with me, and gave me Catholic books to read, some devotional and some were controversial, expressing her wish that I might see the errors of Protestantism; but there was nothing officiously urgent or bigoted in her perseverance. There were daily calls from two Catholic and Protestant clergymen. The Catholic was an *emigree* from France during the troubles of the First Revolution. He had seen much of the world, and was fond of relating his reminiscences of the revolution and the war between France and England; he seldom or rarely entered into religious topics. The Protestant was a sincere and attentive clergyman, cautious of the Catholic influences, yet not bigoted. On finding that I was reading some of the Catholic controversial works, he lent me others on the same questions by Protestant writers. This was decidedly an important starting-point, from which my mind progressed most rapidly. From morning until night I read these books, and on certain passages I was continually comparing their inferences with the Bible, which scarcely ever was out of my hand; in fact, for two years afterwards I was constantly reading polemical divinity, until amongst the conflicting opinions of the various sects my mind felt so convinced of the clearness of some doctrines, and their harmony with the revealed Word, that they have remained ever since firmly impressed on my belief and understanding.

There was something romantically interesting in that nunnery; all the associations were so new: the country, the scenery, the people, the religion— that to this day imagination pictures it, and I dwell on it with pleasure. I used when sitting on an evening to hear the songs of the "Canadian Boatmen," as the chorus of "Row brothers, row," rose from the waters and swelled in the still air, the clear moonbeams falling on the isle of Orleans, or hear the "vesper bell," or pealing organ, and solemn music sounding through the vaulted roof, the narrow aisles, and the corridors of the nunnery. The nuns were so kind to me, while from my situation my heart was warm to receive impressions, that had it not been for the love of my mother I should have remained with them. They expressed a desire for me to stop and be brought up there, and they would provide for me. There was introduced to me a priest about 25 years old, who had been left in the convent sick when a sailor boy, whom they had educated for the priesthood, he having turned Catholic. When the ship was ready to return home, the captain brought some of the men to carry me on board, and I shed tears profusely at parting from my friends in the Convent; and to this day those nuns and that Convent are remembered with affection and gratitude.

On my return home I was put under the best medical care, and every means used to restore the use of my limb; but all proved unavailing. The swelling disappeared and the pains ceased, but I could not bear my weight upon it and had to use crutches, which I continued to do for upwards of two years. For twelve months hopes were entertained that I might recover. During that time I was continually reading and writing. I read without any order or method, yet my mind appeared to have a ready power of arranging the information this desultory reading presented on any subject when I wished to do so. But I had no definite aim before me to which my studies were directed, still I kept gathering a store of various materials which might afterwards be useful, although in what precise manner I did not then foresee. I rapidly acquired a general knowledge of history, and poetry and imaginative literature were my delight. I remember I read the whole of a cheap lending library kept by an old bookseller. I had a strong desire to be able to write poetry and imaginative tales, and tried to compose so much rhyme every day. I would take a passage or an idea suggested from some author and endeavour to enlarge upon it. I found this enabled me to trace ideas in their connections, gave me a wider view of subjects, and a facility of expression in writing. At that time I was evidently a compound of warm feelings and fleeting imaginings, confused perceptions of life, its capabilities and destinies. I was ever ready to receive strong impressions from the passing moment, and strong in faith that I could learn to do anything. I remember the first time I was at a theatre was at a bespeak[25] by the member for the county. The play was *As You Like It*. I sat the whole time as if in fairy-land, and, as the audience were retiring, I stood enrapt in the idea of writing a play, which I began next day, and continued until I had written a very long one about some romantic adventure of some Highlanders in Spain during

---

[25] A benefit night performance. Compare Alton Locke's first attempt at poetry: "my hero was . . . a pious sea-rover, who . . . set forth . . . to colonise and convert . . . a South Sea Island." C. Kingsley, *Alton Locke* (Everyman ed. 1970), p. 93.

the middle ages. Yet such was my ignorance of the architecture of a play, that I was bothered for a long time to know the difference between a scene and an act.

These compositions of youth were gradually thrown away as my mind and tastes developed. I had no ambition for seeing my name in print, nor money to pay the cost of doing so. I must except, however, a few stanzas written on the mysterious disappearance of a young man, an apprentice to a surgeon in the town, who was supposed for many years to have been murdered by the resurrectionists. As it presented a memorable instance of a respectable family being ruined by a popular prejudice and delusion, I shall record it. Shortly after the arrest of Burke and Hare[26] at Edinburgh for their numerous murders to sell their victims to the dissecting-rooms, there was a morbid dread of such characters being everywhere. People were afraid to pass lone places in the dark at late hours. A woman belonging to a very respectable family, who kept a large earthern and chinaware establishment, was taken ill about 4 p.m. of spasmodic pains in the stomach or bowels. The surgeon was sent for, and this young man came and prescribed for the woman. She revived quickly after he left, but he never returned to his masters with whom he lodged.

The next day every search and inquiry was made for him, but no information could be obtained. He had left his watch and clothes in his room, and nothing betokened an intention to leave altogether. The person whom he had been called up to attend having recovered quickly was in the shop in the usual hour in the morning. When two or three days had elapsed without any traces having been discovered of the missing man, the blame was laid on her, although the family of this woman up to that time bore the most respectable character in the estimation of the public. All classes of the inhabitants at once entertained the improbable and horrible suspicion that her illness had been feigned, and was part of a conspiracy to entrap and murder the man by the "resurrection men." Their shop and society were shunned by all, and thus their business was ruined. The grief of the young man's mother unsettled her reason, and his parents being in poor circumstances subscriptions were raised for them.

Some years passed away, and one day the father of the accused family, having a dispute with a tradesman in Newcastle, the latter violently accused him of being of the conspiracy. He then brought an action for libel against this man at the assizes, who was found guilty, and the report of the proceedings having been published in a Carlisle newspaper was seen by a surgeon in that neighbourhood, who instantly wrote to the family who had been so long labouring under the imputation, stating that he knew the young man

---

[26] William Burke, a Scottish navvy, lodged with William Hare in Edinburgh. Both were accused of smothering people whose corpses could be sold for medical research in 1827–28. Burke was hanged in 1829, Hare was released. Their murders were all the more notorious because of the popular hatred of dissection.

in India. He had enlisted as a soldier at Chatham, and was draughted into the regiment there, in which he served as surgeon. Becoming acquainted with him, and finding what he had been, he got him appointed to assist him; that after being some time in the country he died, and that if application was made to the India House they would ascertain the correctness of his information. Inquiry was accordingly made, a committee of the inhabitants being formed for that purpose, and it was discovered that the parents had received a letter from him in India nearly two years after his departure, detailing his reasons for leaving home, and the manner in which he left, yet his father had never divulged the facts, not even after he received the official notice of his death and effects, although he knew the unjustly-accused family were suffering so much. The only reason supposed for this unworthy conduct was that the father, having received so much aid and sympathy from the public, a false shame had hindered him from confessing his son's unworthy conduct. The reasons assigned by the son were—a dissatisfaction with his position, that as his father was too poor to put him to college he could not perceive the possibility of his becoming a surgeon, so he determined to enlist for the Indian service; and as they might have traced him if he had taken his clothes, he formed the determination to depart in the manner he did, and thus throw a mystery over his disappearance. A public meeting was held to congratulate the accused family on the providential exoneration of them from the unjust charges under which they had laboured so long, and to express their pleasure at the complete establishment of their innocence. A public subscription, too, was raised to compensate them for their losses in business. To this Earl Fitzwilliam[27] sent a handsome subscription, the father of the accused having been a tenant-farmer on his estate for many years.

But to return from this digression. After being under several medical men and divers quacks for twelve months, it became obvious I could not return to sea. Although I now had no pain in my knee, I had to walk with a crutch, and it became important that I should lose no more time, but go at once to some employment which I could learn. Some of my mother's friends urged her to get me into an office, as I could write well, but I disagreed with that, saying, "No, no—let me learn a trade first, and then I can be a clerk afterwards."

From my own experience, after much reflection, I am convinced that there is much obstruction to the free exercise of the industry of the working classes in the common mode of apprenticeship. In many instances they are far too long, and hinder the adults from changing from one trade into another. Out of six and seven years' apprenticeships, the boys generally pass two or three years in mere drudgery of odd work, which, although useful to them and to their masters, are not essential to enable adults to learn such trades. This might have done very well in the times of our ancestors, when society

[27] Earl Fitzwilliam (1748–1833), Whig Lord Lieutenant of Yorks, until dismissed for censuring the actions of the magistrates at Peterloo in 1819.

and its industries moved in fixed forms, and a youth could fix on an employment by which to maintain himself all his life; now it is no longer so; society
moves at a railway pace, and the transitions of industry are quick. There are
few trades now that a youth can be put to with a certainty that they will
furnish employment to him for life. In ten years' time they may be revolu-
tionised, or almost cease. The operatives in them should be able, therefore,
at once to turn to some kindred trade, and learn it in two or three years.
Meanwhile, it would be easy by some scale that might soon be adjusted to
pay the learner his worth, while the master or men who taught him should
both have an advantage in doing so. While we have free trade in capital and
its productions, we still want it amongst workmen and workshops. Why
should a man be shut up for life to make furniture only, if he can better his
condition by turning pattern maker, house or ship carpenter? So of many
trades in which similar processes are employed. The present apprenticeship
is a continued source of irritation and strife between masters and journeymen. In many trades, the master can introduce a disproportionate number
of apprentices, and by the low wages thus paid, undersell those masters who
are not so situated. Even in shops where the journeymen are at piece-work,
and have the apprentices under their charge, being paid so much per day for
teaching them, and the profit is thus shared between the men and the
masters—in such shops the masters are never desirous of an extra number of
apprentices. The apprenticeship system does not obtain to near the same
extent in America, and the idea of never looking for employment in any trade
but that which they may have served their time to, would be deemed
absurd. I knew a person who was some years there, and he learned three
different trades, in addition to the one he knew before he went there. The
old adage, "Jack of all trades, and master of none," does not hold good in
practice, for it will be found that many of the cleverest masters and men in
some trades and professions—even those who have most improved them—
have previously been engaged in other employments before they turned to
them.

On consideration, the trade of a tailor was deemed the best for me. It
was then very good—wages were high, and it was considered a very respectable employment. An agreement was made with a master in Newcastle (who
had no apprentice), who sat and worked himself, and employed a journeyman
or two occasionally. I was to receive my board and lodging for my services.
I set myself to work earnestly to learn, and having, when at sea, learned to
mend my own clothes, I was able to cut and make a pair of trousers in six
weeks. I used often to rise in the morning at four o'clock, and read until six;
and at night I frequently sat up until twelve or one over my books.[28] During

[28] Compare Thomas Cooper, who rose at 3 a.m. to study theology, languages and history;
then worked at his bench till 8 or 9 at night; then tried to memorise Shakespeare or
Milton "until compelled to go to bed from sheer exhaustion", *Life*, p. 59. Not surprisingly,
Cooper had a nervous breakdown when aged 22. Lowery seems initially to have had more

the day, as it is a business in which you may still converse and study while you are working, I used to reflect on what I had read the night before or in the morning; or I would converse with the master about the religious bodies, or the politics of the day. He had not been an extensive reader, but he had seen and remembered much of society. He was a *book* to me, in which were chronicled the impressions on his mind of the events which had taken place in his time. He and his wife were Primitive Methodists, pure and guileless, full of godly simplicity, ever ready to do what good they could for others. Had I been of their own family, they could not have been more kind to me. Indeed, I became as one of them, being made acquainted with, and consulted in, their difficulties. This sometimes led me to take more freedom than I should have done if I had been under formal stipulations, by reciprocating kindnesses and attentions. After I had been awhile there, and was found useful, I used to go down to Shields every Saturday night or Sunday morning, and come up on the Monday morning. Sometimes, when busy, we would work very late on Friday night and Saturday, and I would not get away until Sunday, and then, occasionally, I would not come back until Tuesday. If still very busy, I could, on entering, at once see he was displeased, although he never spoke of it. I never used to make any apology, or enter on any explanations, but at once silently sat down to my work, and gradually the atmosphere seemed to harmonise us; and when I saw, from the expression of his countenance, that this was the case, I would ask some question about the most interesting subject of the day, and he would at once enter into conversation on the matter, and all unpleasantness would soon be forgotten.

Shortly after this time I became able to walk without crutches. While standing looking at a procession of "barges" on the "Mayor's day" in Newcastle, a gentleman kindly inquired how I became lame, and how long I had used crutches. When I informed him, he stated that he had a son who had become lame in the same manner, but that as long as he had used crutches his leg had continued weak. Being persuaded, however, to try to use a stick instead, although he felt it difficult to do so at first, he by that time could walk without either, and the gentleman told me he felt confident that if I adopted the same plan I would receive the same benefit. I did so, and although for the first few days I could scarcely go above a hundred yards at a time—in six months I was able to walk from Newcastle to Shields, a distance of eight miles. But the knee-joint has still remained stiff, and the leg did not

---

stamina, and his health did not break down till his early thirties. Dr. David Vincent has also drawn our attention to the late night studying in C. Thomson's *The Autobiography of an Artisan* (1847), p. 67, and Ben Brierley's *Home Memories* (1886), pp. 31–2. See also W. E. Adams, *Memoirs of a Social Atom* (1903), I, pp. 111–13. J. Leatherland, a Chartist poet from Kettering who worked as a velvet weaver, wrote "My plan therefore was to read at leisure intervals, and to ruminate on such reading whilst engaged in manual occupation. If in the course of my thoughts, anything struck me particularly, I made a note of it in a memorandum book, which I kept by the side of my loom for the purpose". (J. A. Leatherland, *Essays and Poems, with a Brief Autobiographical Memoir*, 1862, p. 12.)

grow as the other, becoming fixed and shorter. When I had been with my master fifteen months, seeing that I would not be able to learn the business in its most fashionable forms, I endeavoured to make arrangements with a superior shop in my native town, desiring to have a perfect knowledge of the best modes, especially in cutting. I effected an agreement by which, in three years, my education as a tailor should be completed in all the branches. But the men in Society stated their objections to this transfer, it being against their rules, declaring to the master that they would not work in the shop if I was taken on these conditions. In consequence I had to leave, and I went and got work with a country master near Walls-end, receiving six shillings per week, bed and board. We frequently went out to work in the houses of the people at the charge of two shillings per day and victuals. And, as I passed for a journeyman, he cleared one half of that sum by me. I continued here for nine months and then went back to North Shields and commenced as a journeyman. I then could sit down as a journeyman with the very men who had refused my admission to the shop as an apprentice, which I frequently did. I liked the business of a tailor very well, but as there had been a rush into it, from its being considered an easy and genteel business with good wages, there was soon a surplus of journeymen, and, except for a few, there was but little chance of regular work for more than six months in the year. I procured a share of customers among my acquaintances, who found their own cloth; yet, not having any capital to purchase a stock and give credit, I had but little work during the slack time of the year. Afterwards my circumstances grew better, by getting work from a family, the head of which, during a depression of the wool and hosiery trade in Yorkshire, had come to the north to settle. From a small shop he rapidly rose till he had one of the chief hosiery and seaman's clothes trades in the town. He now has two large hosiery and woollendrapers' shops in the three towns of Shields, Newcastle, and Sunderland, besides ships. Besides the work for his family, I could, at any time when I had nothing better to do, go and get some "slop-jackets" to make for the shop sale, and although I could not earn more than an average of two shillings a day, yet it was a surety, and I used to term this shop "my parish."[29]

---

[29] "My parish"—Lowery's alternative to poor law relief. At a time when apprenticeship controls were the main way of preserving craft status, Lowery did not serve the full 5 or 7 year apprenticeship, but belonged to what Mayhew later called the "dishonourable" trade. An "honourable" tailor would have been obliged to refuse half-price slop work (cheap ready-to-wear clothing). Lowery's comments on the apprenticeship system were perhaps valid, but they were not disinterested. Professor Norman McCord of the University of Newcastle, in kindly responding to our enquiry, suggests that the head of the family which employed Lowery was Robert Spence, Sen., who moved to North Shields in 1804 and created the drapery firm in collaboration with his cousin Joseph Procter. R. Welford, *Men of Mark III* (1895), p. 426, says that Spence "was for years one of the most respected residents in his adopted town, ably filling many of its public offices". A Quaker with literary interests, Spence joined Edward and William Chapman in a banking firm which also operated in Newcastle and (after 1836) in Sunderland.

II
Marriage and Politics:
1827–1834

At the age of eighteen I was married to my cousin, who was a year older than myself, and in three years we had two daughters. My wife's mother had died when she was ten years old, and she was then stopping with my mother; her father, captain of a ship, being still a widower.

In passing, I would remark that however in a prudential sense we both afterwards perceived that it would have been more prudent for us to have waited until we had been older, and I had time to fix myself in something, whereby a better provision could have been made for our wants, yet as Emmerson[30] has said, in our struggles we had "compensation." We were knit into one; and however we improved in circumstances afterwards, we looked back to these days of poverty and love as the happiest in our lives.

With love in a garret at twenty years of age hope was high, and we were the world to each other. I am aware that too often, when the difficulties of such early unions come, if there is not sufficient stamina, the parties lose hope and become careless. The husband often turns reckless, and selfishly seeks in the pot-house or elsewhere to escape these difficulties. But if there is manhood in us, a struggle for the sake of those we love will develope it; and of all the stimulants to exertion, affection for wife and offspring must prove the strongest to a well-constituted mind. We murmured not, but looked forward with hope, and kept our difficulties to ourselves. At that time my mother was better off, my brother aiding her, and I have often refused to sit down to roast goose with them to go home, to do without dinner, and take an early tea. Virtuous poverty may have its bitter struggles, but its bread is sweet; no costly viands can give the relish which the humble fare of toil imparts. I have been at "great dinners," and dined "among rich folk," but never in my life did I enjoy such delight at these as I enjoyed a meal under the following circumstances in the days of my poverty. Work had been slack, and we had had to make up our rent, and we had nothing in the house but a little bread on a Monday night. We did not use a credit shop, but any one that we thought best and cheapest, and we shrunk from the idea of borrowing.

---

[30] Ralph Waldo Emerson (1803–82), American transcendentalist, whose writings advocated "self-culture". John James Bezer also depicted his early marriage as a bitter offence against Malthusian principles, in his *The Autobiography of One of the Chartist Rebels of 1848* reprinted in D. Vincent (Ed.), *Testaments of Radicalism* (1977).

We then had two children, girls. The first thing our eldest child did when awake in the morning was always to ask for a "piece of bread." Now I had a slop-jacket to begin to next day, and it was a day's work; and until it was done we knew we could not get any more victuals. So at night we put what bread we had aside for the children's breakfast in the morning, and I rose at five, and my wife gave me what assistance she could during the day. Neither of us broke our fasts, nor had the children anything from breakfast time until the jacket was finished at 5 p.m., when I took it to the shop, and returned with some bread, chop, tea, and sugar. I never ate a chop or bread which tasted so delicious as that chop and bread, nor ever drank tea which had such a flavour as that tea had.

My wife had the same desire for reading which I had. Our clothes were now "too shabby" to go out with on Sunday. The question would be on a Saturday night sometimes, "Well, we cannot afford to have anything for dinner to-morrow, and to pay for a week in the library also (the library cost eight-pence per week), what do you think, shall we get something for dinner, or get a book and have an early tea? We always thought alike—that the dinner would soon be over and gone—but if we did without it, we would not miss it much, and we would have the advantage of the library all the week.[31]

I remember well being struck with the unthrifty habits and mismanagement of some of the working men and of their wives around us, so much so that I feel certain that at a time when my income did not average more than 14s. per week, we had as good a house, more comfort, and were better clothed and as well fed as others who had only the same family as we had, and yet earned four-and-twenty shillings per week or upwards. Until I was twenty-three years old I had mixed very little in society, even of my own class, and I continued to read at every opportunity, and knew more of what the world had been in former times than what it was in my own day. My heart warmed with sympathy and admiration when I read of the struggles of Greece against the Persian despot, or of the citizens of Rome for their liberties, or of Rienzi, or of Zell, or of Wallace, or of Bruce. Our own Sidney, Hampden, and Russell were my heroes, while Godwin's History of the Commonwealth and the History of the Scottish Covenanters charmed me.[32] I had not then compared the ideal of things with the real of life, and on first view the mind of

---

[31] The shelves of Lovett's early library "were often supplied by cheating the stomach with bread and cheese dinners"—*Life and Struggles* (1876), p. 36. Lowery's early days of marriage closely resemble those of Francis Place—see his *Autobiography* (Ed. Mary Thale, Cambridge, 1972), pp. 106–9, 115. Compare T. Cooper, *Life*, p. 59; and James Burn, *Autobiography* (1978 ed.), p. 129 f.

[32] Lowery's heroes were cast in the romantic mould. Rienzi was a notary who seized power in 1347 and became self-styled tribune of Rome. He reformed some of its laws and tried to assert Rome's dominance, but within 6 months he was broken by Pope Clement VI and Emperor Charles IV. Zell was presumably Matthew Zell (1477–1548) pastor in Strassbourg from 1517 and German Lutheran reformer. Sir William Wallace was the Scottish hero who, after the Union of 1290, drove the English out of Scotland until defeated

youth instantly admires and sympathises with all who act heroically, and struggle and suffer for freedom, whether civil or religious. Now I began to mix with the living world, and to hear its conflicting utterances, and often at first thought it passing strange that others did not think and see things as I did. I soon perceived that we rarely can give a clear answer to the whys and wherefores of our opinions, until we come into the courts of the active world.

The excitement on the Reform Bill now agitated all classes of the community, although at first the multitude were more attracted by the contests of the upper classes and by party feeling than an understanding of the principles involved in the Bill; yet it developed thought among the more reflecting, and begat discussion on the principles of government and of national prosperity. It produced thinkers indeed in every class, and more especially the working classes. Out of this thinking the after movements of the working classes originated, and from this arose some of their errors also. No part of the country exceeded in fervour the district around Newcastle-on-Tyne for the Reform Bill. Nor did any association surpass that of the "Northern Political Union" in talent and influence.[33] Its principal leaders combined philosophic astuteness, literary ability, oratorical powers, and social standing rarely equalled by the leaders of the public in any other district. And with their varied powers they bound the people to them with confidence and admiration. The chief of these was Charles Attwood, brother to Thos. Attwood, of Birmingham, and who possessed a mind of more deep research and wider expansion than his brother. He was engaged as a capitalist in extensive works in the neighbourhood, and had, as a man of science, discovered improvements in the manufacture of glass and soap, which he had patented. Thomas Doubleday, a partner in an extensive manufactory, a gentleman of acknowledged literary ability, the author of the "Philosophy of Populations," also of some essays and tragedies of acknowledged eminence; John Fife, who was afterwards knighted, was one of the most eminent surgeons of the north of England; and Charles Larkin, a surgeon who had been educated for the Catholic priesthood, was an eminent classical scholar, and one of the most commanding orators I have ever heard. Their varied styles of

---

by Edward I in 1298. Robert Bruce (1274–1329) was claimant and then king of Scotland after he had defeated both Edward I and Edward II. Sir Philip Sidney (1554–86) was a romantic Elizabethan figure—soldier, statesman and poet. John Hampden (1639–83) helped lead the country party's resistance to the accession of the Catholic Duke of York (James II). Executed for high treason, his attainder was reversed by William and Mary. For Godwin, see below, p. 68. His *History of the Commonwealth* (1824–8) argued that "England is indebted for its liberties" to the opponents of Charles I: by executing the King, they brought all men under the law.

[33] From late 1829 radicals formed political unions, modelled on Thomas Attwood's Birmingham Political Union, to organize public opinion behind parliamentary reform. The Northern Political Union, centred on Newcastle, was one of the most prominent. Like the B.P.U., the N.P.U. was revived in September, 1838, by local Chartist leaders, with the *Northern Liberator* as its main journal.

address produced an effective oneness.[34] Attwood would open a meeting with a wide historical survey of the operation of any evil complained of, tracing it in its various forms at different times to our own day, and showing the necessity of its removal. Doubleday would trace the principles sought to be established back to Anglo-Saxon law and usage, and enforce them by the authority of the best writers on political philosophy, and Fife would dissect and lay bare the fallacies of those opposed to the Bill; while Larkin, with his commanding form and voice, would utter forth, in swelling tones and powerful sentences, a torrent of indignation against those who opposed the measure, which would rouse the passions of the multitude vehemently. Frequently, on particular occasions, a hundred thousand people would come to these meetings, which were held on Newcastle Town Moor, the surrounding villagers marching in rank, with military step, to bands of music. It is well known that the language was often violent, and the opposition was threatened with physical resistance if they should proceed to enforce any laws to stop the unions in agitating for their demands.

---

[34] All four feature in R. Welford, *Men of Mark* (1895)—see I, pp. 149–55; II, pp. 109–19, 226–35; III, pp. 6–12—and are praised in William Cobbett, *Rural Rides* (Ed. G. D. H. & M. Cole, 1930), III, p. 713. Charles Attwood (1791–1875) came to Gateshead at age 20 as a glass manufacturer, and in three years bought out his partners. Difficulties with patents led him into lawsuits and he later became a successful ironmaster. He came bottom of the poll as radical candidate at the 1832 general election, and in later life was much less prominent in Newcastle politics. In the 1850s he was an Urquhartite, and made his last public appearance in Newcastle defending the Poles in 1863. Thomas Doubleday (1790–1870) was pushed into his father's soap-boiling business when his real interests were literary. He went bankrupt, and was appointed registrar of births, marriages and deaths for Newcastle, and secretary to the coal trade. He wrote poems, plays and angling songs, but also *The True Law of Population* (1842), *A Financial, Monetary and Statistical History of England* (1847), and *The Political Life of Sir Robert Peel* (1856). He strongly opposed Malthusianism and the new poor law. In the 1830s he was secretary to the Northern Political Union, but "far from being a fluent speaker . . . his diffidence, which never left him to the last, caused him to hesitate where a less able man would have gone freely on" (Welford, II, p. 118). He chaired several Chartist meetings on the Town Moor in 1838–9, but he later left the movement. He remained an active reformer, and supported Urquhart and the Complete Suffrage Union. Sir John Fife (1795–1871), a surgeon's son and an Anglican, was popular with the local poor for launching a medical charity in 1822 which developed into the Newcastle Eye Infirmary. For thirty years he was surgeon to Newcastle Infirmary. "To his skill in tactics the [Northern Political] Union owed no small part of its success" (Welford, II, p. 229), but he soon left the Union and in 1838 was elected mayor of Newcastle. He became very unpopular with local Chartists for breaking up their demonstration by force in summer 1839, an incident which Lowery perhaps surprisingly ignores. He was knighted in 1840, and re-elected mayor in 1843, and active in the Anti-Corn Law League. In later life his views became Whiggish, and he was active in the volunteer movement. Welford says that he "formed county connections, and began to consider himself as much a country gentleman as an alderman of Newcastle" (II, p. 235). Charles Larkin (1800–79) was a local orator who wrote several pamphlets on political and religious questions, attacked sabbatarians and stoutly defended Catholics against Protestant attack. In the 1840s he antagonized many local Chartists with his zeal for free trade. He made his last appearance on a local political platform in October, 1872, advocating the release of Fenian prisoners. We are most grateful to Dr. David Rowe, Department of Economics, University of Newcastle, for help with this footnote.

The Bill was carried, but popular expectations had been formed not easily realised. The working men thought that the enfranchised middle classes did not do what they might to attempt to realise them, but that they looked more to their own class interests than to those of the unenfranchised who had helped them to attain the Bill. This might have been expected. On the first rush into the constituencies possessing power from which they had been previously excluded, and forming a major portion of that constituency, it was to be expected that they would first apply themselves to things which most affected themselves, and as a general rule look to the interests of those without only in connection with their own. Perhaps too, even when the claims of the unenfranchised conflicted with their own, would many conscientiously conclude that, in serving themselves, they were serving the excluded and absent also. This produced feelings of disappointment and vexation among the working classes towards the middle classes, and a current of popular distrust and ill-feeling set in strongly against them and the Whigs, whose strength they were thought to compose.

Until of late years I always found the personal character of the titled and landed gentry more esteemed than that of the manufacturing and trading classes by the people, and the apparent anomaly that while the working men professed Liberal politics they thought more highly of the Conservative gentry, with whom they disagreed politically, than they did of the trading classes, whose professed principles were similar to their own.[35] This arose from the social condition and close connection between the parties. The trades classes and the working classes, through the competition of profit and wages, were more frequently brought into conflict, and thus the capitalists were the medium through which some of their chief hardships reached them, and even when difficulties come inevitably from the state of our position, we are apt to think that the more fortunate should transfer these difficulties from us and take them on themselves. At that time there was more of isolation and selfish inattention in the trading community to their duties towards the labouring classes than is now common. The declaration of "Finality"[36] soon convinced the masses that, as far as the franchise was concerned, they had got "nothing but the Bill," and finding themselves deceived, the people turned to other modes of improving their condition.

---

[35] Compare Lowery's Newcastle speech, reprinted below, p. 246. Lowery points up a central dilemma of nineteenth-century working men. They were often attracted by the Liberal party's policies, but were sometimes repelled by its local leaders (frequently their own employers). This problem was exacerbated in the 1890s, when technological and other changes strained employer-employee relations. See Henry Pelling, *The Origins of the Labour Party, 1880-1900* (1954), p. 174. The predominantly rural Conservative gentry could afford to show more concern for the urban working man, and were active in the factory, public health, and anti-poor law movements.

[36] On 20 November, 1837, Lord John Russell declared the Reform Act to be a final measure and not the first of many reform instalments. Hence his nickname, "Finality Jack". See John Prest, *Lord John Russell* (1972), p. 123.

The repeal of the combination laws[37] had given the operatives more facilities for uniting to support one another to attain a common object: to maintain wages, to increase them, or to limit the supply of labour. These things they thought they could do, and there is no doubt but that the fact of the combination laws having hindered them from uniting had induced them to entertain erroneous notions respecting the great benefits to be acquired by their repeal, and by the formation of trade unions. This idea, however, was at first confined to the leading minds of the class. They thought and began to promulgate the idea that, shut out from the franchise, the masses would have much power to effect beneficial changes in their position through the medium of laws or regulations of their trades. This they could manage without waiting for Acts of Parliament. These ideas soon spread through the workshops and trades societies, and as the reform agitation had accustomed the operatives to the excitement of disputation and zeal in favour of a common idea, they began to combine. Prior to this their societies had been passive, or only engaged occasionally to repel any attacks on their established rules of working, but now they desired to be aggressive, and to change the order of things. Speculations were entered on, questioning the usual relations of labour and capital, charging the social system and trading classes with injustice towards the people. They had no idea how essential is capital to the employment of labour, and that they were but a portion of the power to create national wealth and prosperity, and that while they prided themselves on their numbers, too often their numbers constituted their weakness. In consequence of these notions social or political unions sprung up all over the country.[38]

About this time Robert Owen[39] and his disciples began to address the people through lectures and public meetings, endeavouring to show that the basis of society was unsound, and the principle of individualism radically wrong, that it obstructed production and misapplied its powers to sustain folly, vice and idleness. They therefore urged the producing classes to co-operate to form communities, which they asserted were the true mediums to

[37] Pitt's Combination Acts (1799, 1800) prohibited all trade combinations and substituted summary jurisdiction for the cumbersome legal procedure of conspiracy charges under common law. But by 1824 they were seldom invoked; the magistrates disliked interfering in trade disputes, and employers preferred either to persist in using common law or to rely on the market. So in 1824 a select committee advised repeal. Henceforward the law allowed the right to strike and to hold funds, though not intimidation associated with picketing.

[38] Lowery was no socialist. He attributed antagonism between master and men to misunderstanding, ignorance and insensitivity—not to irreconcileable class-interest, still less to any notion that profits were theft. At no point, even in the 1830s, did he attack the principles of orthodox political economy.

[39] Robert Owen (1771–1858), cotton manufacturer, educationalist and social reformer. His analysis of competition, unemployment and underconsumption provided the common vocabulary of 1830s co-operation and trade unionism; it invoked Spencean notions of land nationalization and O'Brien's arguments for currency reform. Owenism seemed to offer a communitarian restructuring of society without invoking either political reform or moral self-help. Compare Lowery's remarks on shopkeeping in his pamphlet on *Exclusive Dealing* (1839), printed below, pp. 195–204.

remove the fear of want, by enabling men to live in harmony, and to realize the highest amount possible of physical and intellectual enjoyment. Trade was at that time in a depressed state, and such ideas were naturally attractive; the possibility of the producers of wealth at once associating to produce for each other was plausible and appeared practical. It was forgotten by the multitude that capital was needed in production, and that they had not enough to erect dwellings, schools, workshops, and machinery on the estate, or money or credit to purchase it, or reserves of food to enable them to live while they were producing their first crops and stores for their future consumption. At this time certain London publishers brought out cheap and popular editions of "Wade's History of the Working Classes," "Turner's History of the Anglo-Saxons," Moore's "Utopia," Harrington's "Oceana," Godwin's "Political Justice," and Porson's "Pig's Meat for the Swinish Multitude," and other works, endeavouring to show an ideal superior to the real, and that our aristocratic and class legislation caused the poverty and degradation of the working people; and that by our old Saxon laws the lands were the common property of the whole people vested in the crown, which acted in trust for the people, and were granted to the holders on condition of their rendering certain aids and bearing certain charges for the benefit of the common wealth.[40] Projects were propounded for grafting the co-operative principle on these old laws, by returning, after a proper indemnification to the present holders of land, to the principle of these old laws. No longer were individuals to be allowed property in the soil, which should be the common property of the nation, held in trust by the crown and managed by it and

---

[40] John Wade's *History of the Middle and Working Classes* (1833) popularized orthodox political economy. Starting with a labour theory of value, he argued that capital was stored-up labour, that the rate of wages depended on the rate of profits, and hence that the interests of masters and men were identical. His *Black Book* (1820–23) gave details of pensions, sinecures and nepotism, and became the quarry for all enemies of a corrupt aristocratic political system. Sharon Turner (1768–1847) produced the first instalment of his *History of England from the Earliest Period to the Norman Conquest* in 1799. He described the battles, dress, customs and kingship of the Anglo-Saxons and traced the emergence from the barbarian mind of "moral, reflective and improving men". Sir Thomas More's *Utopia* (1516), one of the earliest classics to portray the New Society, described an ideal communitarian state, in which the economics of business enterprise and the morality of entrepreneurship were satirized, and the moral economy of a co-operative commonwealth reaffirmed. James Harrington's *Oceana* (1656), dedicated to Cromwell, described an imaginary republican commonwealth, with an elaborate structure of indirect representation, ultimately dominated by the ruling landed gentry. Harrington saw more clearly than most of his contemporaries that the structure of government was dictated by the structure of property relations. William Godwin's *Political Justice* (1793) was one of the key radical texts, and together with Paine's writing, shaped radical thought for the generations before Cobbett. He argued, like Owen later, that men were products of their environment, essentially reasonable and potentially benevolent beings who would flourish in a just society. But government, he insisted, was by its very nature unjust, coercive and repressive: it robbed men of independence and rationality and depended for its survival on keeping the masses ignorant. Porson was an eminent Greek scholar (died 1808) whose *Pig Meat for Swinish Multitude* was a savage Hone-type parody. It was originally published in the *Examiner*, but Carlile reprinted it as a pamphlet in 1818.

the parliament. These should appoint collectors to draw the rents, and thus support the expenses of the government, which could then remit all other taxation, provide means for a national education and for the maintenance of the poor. It was reasoned that the land needed not to be divided, nor ought to be so, each generation only having a right to the usufruct. It could therefore be let as at present, the tenants simply contracting for terms and paying their rents to the government factors, under the direction of a local authority, instead of paying it as now to stewards or to individual proprietors. It was contended also that the privilege of making money by the banking class injured trade and the working classes by tending to confine the use and power of capital to a certain class instead of benefiting the whole nation. That the right of coining money being vested in the crown, so the right of creating paper money should be also confined to the crown; the state, public lands and taxes being the best security for the convertibility of the paper so issued, while the profits derived therefrom would revert to the nation. The dreams of a new world propounded by Owen by and by began to fade from view, and as it were to elude the grasp of the people. This arose from various causes; at first Robert Owen and his followers had the sense to see that while the New Testament left men free to choose the forms of society best suited at the time to sustain the spirit of its teachings, Christianity enforced broad principles of a brotherly bond of common interests, sympathies, and pursuits, by which the more men loved the Lord the better they would love each other, not minding their own things alone but the things of each other, succouring the widow and the fatherless, and relieving the distressed, and by all feeling purely, dealing justly, and living righteously, they would profit in the highest degree in the present life and be best prepared to inherit life everlasting. Thus at first the views of Robert Owen presented nothing contrary to the spirit of Christianity, but on the contrary seemed to be required by it to ameliorate the condition of the multitude, and many sincere Christian men adopted or favoured them. Frequent were the appeals to the day of Pentecost and to the effects of Christian love in causing them to unite as one body, holding all things in common. That the same might now be done was a natural aspiration for all good men; here was a beautiful ideal which at once attracted all those pressed by want and care, and many who sympathised with them in their distress. But they overlooked the fact that the times are as men make them, that the blessings of truth can only be realized in virtuous action. Mankind must first have godlike spirits before they can enact godlike lives, and therefore ignorance and vice are impotent to work out heavenly visions; men must first receive new hearts and understandings before they can work the works of love and righteousness.[41] In other words it was forgotten that none but Christians could put Christianity into practice and

---

[41] Here, as so often elsewhere, Lowery's views echo Lovett's. According to Lovett, "the great obstacle" to the realization of Owen's scheme "is, that the perfect and wise arrangements are to depend *on imperfect men and women*"—*Life and Struggles*, p. 45. Likewise Bamford came

realize this vision of a good time to come. Gradually Robert Owen propounded his theories of fatalism[42] and unaccountability, and the lecturing of his followers became the means of propagating opinions opposed to the Christian faith and practice. This at once produced a reaction, and Christian people separated from this body of socialists and opposed its teachings on these questions, while on the other side a large amount of the speculative infidelity of the country, which had paid little attention to the practical portion of the social theory, joined their ranks to enable them to enforce their speculations on the people's attention. From this time each party became pitted against the other, and the less educated but sincere of the Christian people confounded the ideas of social science or improvement with infidelity, so that the question was under their bann. Hence it became injurious to his influence for any public writer or speaker to enter into investigations of our social system, unless in the most guarded manner, for he was at once suspected of being an infidel. Thus, until lately, not a few of our public writers, who were well fitted to investigate our system of society—to point out advantages or detect defects and propound remedies—have held back from doing so, while the writers of France, not being so fettered, previous to the excesses of Fouriereism[43] and of the national workshops, have investigated more completely the principles on which society moves. The English economists have confined themselves to explain how things are as they are. This they have done ably, but few reflecting people are contented with things as they are, and desire changes for the better, if they can be attained in consonance with justice to all, which alone could guarantee national advantages. Hence the English economists have seldom entered on more than the first stage of social and political economics, how things are as they are, and have not entered on the enquiry as to how they might be made better than they are. It is wrong and in vain to seek to ignore these subjects, and if those fitted to lead the people do not guide them in their desire to investigate this branch so essentially interesting to them, others unfit for the office of guides will assume it, or the people in their ignorance will attempt to find the way.

---

to see "self-examination, self-control, and self-amendment, as the basis for all public reform. Canst thou not control thyself, and wouldest thou govern a household? Canst thou not govern a household, and yet wouldest thou direct a nation?"—*Passages in the Life of a Radical* (Ed. W. H. Chaloner, 1967), I, p. 279. Perhaps the act of autobiography presumes in part a "self-made self" incompatible with the environmentalism of Owen.

[42] Owen's theories of fatalism were educational in origin: that men's characters were shaped by their environment, and that by reforming the environment you could reform mankind. To Christians, this seemed a denial of free-will, an abnegation of moral responsibility. From the late 1830s, as the co-operative stores and exchanges died, Owenism became increasingly identified with secularism.

[43] Charles Fourier (1772–1857) was one of the French pre-Marxist socialists. In his "phalansteries" (primarily agricultural communities, like Owen's) rich and poor would benefit each other and the community. Middlemen, uncertainty and competition would be eliminated, and all would be prosperous and liberated.

Owenism spread through all the large towns rapidly, and had its lecturers, halls, and institutions, but after its first novelty was over, it seemed to collapse and perish of inanition, and as there is a wide difference between profession and practice, the observant work-people soon saw that those who projected the formation of a new and superior social state were deeply tinctured with the vices of the old one, and as full of selfish scheming, as fraudulent and as money-mongering as those whom they condemned. This produced a corresponding reaction on the multitude, who although not accustomed to enquire into abstruse questions, are quick to perceive differences between profession and practice. Thus in time the socialist or Owenite co-operative party died away; while individuals here and there retained their opinions, they ceased to be influential on the working men as a body. Their halls passed into other hands, and were used for other purposes.

From reflecting on what I then saw, and have since observed too in similar movements, they appear to me objectionable as tending to destroy Christian faith and virtue. The blame rests more on the Christian instructors and professors than their opponents. Whether infidelity proceeds solely from sincerity in error, or whether it is also aided by knavery and hypocrisy, with a view to worldly advantages, we must expect it to be active in such an imperfect state of society as we are in. Christians, then, are bound to arm all rising youths with an education which will introduce them to a knowledge of the attacks which they will have to meet, training them as it were in a gymnasium of thought which will fit them to wrestle with the doubts and denials of their faith which they will meet with. Too often are they warned as of a sin against allowing themselves to listen to or think of them, so that when they do meet with them, as most surely they will if they mix in the general world, they are not prepared or skilled to baffle the blows of their adversaries. Thus while the native strength and endurance of truth enable many to stand, as unmoved rocks, under these attacks, the superior agility and trained art of their opponents cause them to appear the most clever, and too often are those weak in the faith overpowered and fall. Even in the best and strongest of minds there have been periods of doubt, and I have observed that while a large number of people, rightly instructed and trained in youth, pass on to manhood and death in the right way, yet to a certain extent it is rather owing to the impulses given from without—opinions impressed on them from without—than due to those which arise from personal examination and conviction. Men of strong minds rest not till they have a reason to give for the faith that is in them, and in passing from boyhood into the full manhood of their existence—some sooner, others later—they begin to question the opinions which they have received. It is not a state of denial, but the unfastening of the ropes of these outward influences. They desire to be masters of the opinions which hitherto they have only submitted to. Then in these momentous questions and enquiries doubts, fears and sometimes darkness will obscure their vision; but if there has been a discipline of the understanding and the will, with a consciousness of the little they know, and of their duty to search and to know more, and with the polar star of faith in God still shining overhead in their darkness, they push on, and soon streaks of light appear in the horizon. Day dawns again and dispels their doubts, fears and distrusts; then a flood of light shines on their path—they see all is stamped with the hand of Divine love and wisdom, and behold the glory of God in his Word, his work, and his providence. I remember being much amused with an instance of this reaction from Owenism in a working-man from Yorkshire, in London. We had been sitting on a committee connected with political matters, and one evening, seeing an announcement of a social lecture in a place we were passing, we went in. The lecture was, as usual, an exposure of some grievances felt and acknowledged by society, with a large infusion of Robert Owen's unscriptural views, and assertions of what his system would do for mankind. Afterwards the lecturer invited questions: our Yorkshire friend then put some, pointing out practical difficulties and errors; the lecturer admitted some of these, but painted in glowing colours the inhabitants of their new world, and the harmony and superior influences which would reign among them. "Na! na!" cried out the Yorkshireman, "That winna de for me; I've been amang ye, yer not sa; I am not to be gammon'd that way, I ken a' about ye, I've been amang ye, I tell ye."

About this time I was invited with others to form a debating society.[44] It consisted of about twenty members of the mechanic and shopkeeping trades, among whom were a foreman of a printing establishment, two chemists, a medical student, and a reporter for a newspaper. We hired a private room, and met once a week. We admitted the discussion of any subject but pole-mical divinity.[45] A week's notice had to be given of the introduction of any subject, and the proposer had to introduce it either orally or by a written discourse. Fifteen minutes were allowed him to do so, and ten minutes to those who followed. The discussions began at eight o'clock and closed at ten, when, if the majority agreed, the subject could be adjourned. I derived much advantage from these discussions; they set us a-thinking and reading on the topics, and accustomed me to try to arrange in consecutive order all the arguments I could think of. This developed constructiveness, and helped to give me a readiness of thought and a greater facility of expression. I remember I was so diffident and deficient in language before that I could not speak a few consecutive sentences extempore; but I gradually got quicker in arranging my ideas, so that, when listening to an adverse argument, I could dot

---

[44] Debating societies and discussion-groups were as much a passport into political activity for J. S. Mill as they were for Bamford, Cooper and Lovett. See Mill's *Autobiography*, Ch. 4. For other working-class debating societies, see W. E. Adams, *op. cit.*, I, p. 116 (reference supplied by Dr. D. Vincent). Lowery's emphasis on the need to examine received doctrine critically in order to assess its truth shows how close he was to some of the intellectual strands of Victorian Liberalism.

[45] Compare the London Corresponding Society, in Francis Place, *Autobiography*, p. 198.

down the answers as the argument went on. I could rise thus to repeat them with more clearness and force. My chief care was to note down these answering responses, for if I did not do so, but trusted to memory in listening, the latter part being most fresh would render less distinct the impressions of the first, and I could not answer *seriatim* the positions my opponent had laid down. I found this society very improving to us all; for the different textures of our minds, pursuits, and experiences, enabled us all to present something advantageous to each. Of the twenty who composed the society one half became public speakers or writers. From my observation since then I have seen much good done by mutual improvement classes, especially if attached to a library and reading room; they enable the thinkers to compare notes, and the younger reader is saved much time when he gets acquainted with one who is far in advance of him, who, being directed to the best and clearest writers on any branch of knowledge, the younger derives at once the benefit of the elder one's experience. As when about to journey on a road you have not previously travelled, and you question another who has travelled it, he puts you at once at your ease by communicating to you his knowledge of that which you could only have acquired step by step, so an hour's conversation with a mind further advanced than your own will often make plain to you at once that which unassisted it would have taken a long time to comprehend. At this time the Polish insurrection[46] broke out, and the people in the north were strongly moved in sympathy and admiration for them, and being one of those who had agreed to hold a supper on the question, I was invited to take a toast. I remember well this maiden effort; it was a new position to occupy, and produced a new class of fears. Instead of twenty people, as in our debating society, above one hundred had taken tickets, and instead of being able to sit down if one liked after a sentence or two, or five minutes time, it would have to be twenty minutes, speaking, or a failure, and hit on the following mode of preparation, which although not quite as sublime as that of Demosthenes[47] speaking to the roaring waves on the sea shore, was perhaps equally applicable to my purpose. I took a walk into the neighbouring fields in the afternoon until I got to an elevated part of one, where I could see all round, and thus know if any person was approaching within the sound of my voice. I tried to conceive the full tone and manner of speech which I thought it necessary I should deliver, and see how

---

[46] The partition of Poland in 1815 as part of the peace settlement left Russia with most of Poland, which at first enjoyed some degree of self-government. This was suppressed by Czar Nicholas, and in November 1830, a rising spread out from Warsaw. The Russian troops withdrew, but by September 1831, they had returned, and Poland was annexed. English radicals naturally sympathized with Poles against Russians, as later with Hungarians against Austrians, and (rather more ambiguously) with Turks against Russians in the Crimean War. See Henry Weisser, "Polonophilism and the British Working Class, 1830–1845", *Polish Review*, XII (Spring, 1967).

[47] Demosthenes was the great Athenian statesman and orator. His original attempts at oratory were supposedly unsuccessful, but he led much of the resistance to Philip of Macedon from 350–330 B.C. Eighteenth-century parliamentary orators often imitated his speeches.

long I could sustain myself without faltering for matter or expression. This I did, and I remember well there was a flock of sheep grazing close by, and they were on the whole perhaps a superior audience to many, for if they did not reflect on what I said, they were quiet and orderly; they did not run away, but remained to the end, and there were some old ewes and rams, which occasionally turned up their countenances and observed me with serious gravity.[48] I satisfied myself that I could "talk awhile." Evening came, and I got through without a falter, and was deemed by the company to have a wonderful memory to be able to give the history of Polish prowess, patriotism, and suffering which I did.[49]

About this time the strike of the pitmen of Northumberland and Durham took place, and as it much affected the trade of the district, it interested all classes.[50] The points in dispute were not only about wages, but the manner by which the men's work was reckoned. They wished to be paid for working the coals rather by weight than by measure, as was the practice; besides which there were sundry other matters of dispute. As usual, there were faults on both sides—the employers stood by selfish and one-sided rules, and the men, instead of confining themselves to the removal of obvious injustice, wished for extensive changes in their condition. After above six weeks' strike the masters granted their demands, and they thought they had nothing to do but to carry out their own wishes in future. The owners, however, took the alarm at these unions, and shortly after, when better prepared for the market, entered into a combination to destroy the combination of the men; about half of the works agreed with the men, and they were bound; the other half objected, and men were sought for from a distance to supply their places. Thus, all along, the collieries were enabled to supply the London market. It being the custom of the employers to provide houses and firing for the workmen, whole families were turned out of their houses, and had to encamp in the lanes and road-sides during the turn out. If ever strike could be conducted with firmness and self-denial on the part of the men that one was. The colliers out of employ, along with others, would be about 10,000; while the masters had agreed with the other half, yet those in work regularly every pay week contributed, for six months, one' half of their wages for the support of those who were not allowed to work. But gradually the men, procured from a distance, increased in number, and the turn-outs began to see that by

[48] Compare Archie Lush on Aneurin Bevan's speech practice in the Duffryn Valley: "Aneurin made some wonderful speeches up here, and the only people who listened to him were the sheep. I used always to judge the next meeting, as to how effective it would be, by the number of sheep who ran away when he started speaking"—BBC Radio 4 broadcast on 22 June 1978.

[49] Lowery's fears were not unusual among working men. Compare J. C. Farn, in *Reasoner*, 21 October 1857, p. 235: "in after years I more than once have addressed the stormiest public meetings . . . but then the slightest show of opposition would have thoroughly affrighted me."

[50] The strike began on 5 April 1831, and is discussed in Richard Fynes, *The Miners of Northumberland and Durham* (Sunderland, 1873), Ch. 5.

remaining out any longer they ran a risk of being shut out altogether, and they had, therefore, to submit to the terms of their employers. The employers did not use their victory mildly, but inflicted all the punishment they could upon the leaders and influential men. In this they made a great mistake—a mistake that I have since observed often occurs in the minds of the upper classes regarding the leaders of these strikes. It is assumed that these leaders are the lazy and immoral of the working classes,[51] who sow the seeds of discontent until they ripen into a union and a strike, whereby they install themselves into good pay, and acquire a positive interest in fomenting divisions between the men and their employers. This may be the case with some who gain after the discontent commences, but it is not general. In this strike, and in many others which I have known, while it was but natural for the more talented to feel what they deemed wrong as acutely as their fellows, and to express their sentiments freely, they were in most instances compelled into the leadership by their fellow operatives. They were rather averse to the risk and labours, and were mostly men of good religious and moral character, a large number of them being local preachers in the Wesleyan denomination.[52] Where a mixed multitude of twenty thousand men or so are engaged in a dispute calculated to rouse bad passions in the bad, pressed with hunger and want, and filled with a burning sense of real or of supposed wrongs, few of the other classes know of the care and toil which the conscientious leaders of these men undergo. Abused by the employers, and also by the improvident and unjust of their own class, and in continual dread of the ignorant and violent of them compromising the safety of the whole by committing some unlawful act, they cannot sleep on beds of roses. And although at first sight the reason may not appear, yet I have observed that, as a general rule, the bad men of the class do not like bad men to be leaders—in confirmation of the Scripture that there are no bonds binding the wicked together. They instinctively think the men of good character will manage their affairs best, and thus all of them unite to force the leadership upon these men. They are urged to it as a duty they owe their class, and accused of cowardice or of a leaning to treachery and to the side of the masters if they do not. If success attends their efforts even then unthankfulness or hostility from those whom they have tightly held or watched is often their reward; and if defeat ensues they are often marked and persecuted by the employers, who, as in this instance, combine to hinder some of these men from ever getting back to

---

[51] Several hostile early-Victorian novelists depicted trade union leaders. See Harriet Martineau's treatment of Slack, the union orator, in *A Manchester Strike* (1832); Mrs. Gaskell's attitudes in *Mary Barton* and Charles Dickens's account of Slackbridge in *Hard Times* (Everyman ed. 1969), pp. 123 ff. Compare George Lloyd's defence, quoted in P. Hollis (Ed.), *Class and Conflict in Nineteenth Century England* (1973), pp. 240–2.

[52] Compare T. Burt, "Methodism and the Northern Miners", *Primitive Methodist Quarterly Review*, July 1882. See also R. F. Wearmouth, *Methodism and the Trade Unions* (1959); J. Obelkevich, *Religion and Rural Society: South Lindsey 1825–1875* (Oxford, 1976), also explores the relationship between Wesleyanism and trade unionism.

work again. Such conduct is highly impolitic, for if the men were not vindictive or desirous to foment discord between the classes that they might live on it, this course is calculated to make them so. A dignified use of their power and a generous reconciliation and trust of these men would have been much better and more beneficial to all concerned; for it does not act on the mass of the workmen as a punishment to warn them. They may stand by and see their leaders thus suffer and perhaps not aid them, but they do not believe the charges of the employers against them, as they know better; meanwhile the seeds of discontent remain, and these leaders are again called forth to counsel them in some fresh dispute. But were these leaders admitted into the amnesty, being mostly men of superior intelligence the very failure of their scheme would open their eyes to its fallacies, and they might become the pacificators and exponents of improved views to their class.

During this strike one of the oldest magistrates[53] of South Shields was murdered; he was passing between Jarrow and that town, on an afternoon and from his office. He had been concerned in the ejectment of some of the men from their houses, and in suppressing some of their attempts to hinder the "black-legs," or non union men, from working. Two colliers, seeing him come out from a public-house, attacked him; one was considered a decent quiet man, but the other was known to be a blackguard, and he struck him a severe blow which caused his death. They fled; he who had murdered him was never traced, the other was taken the same evening in the tents then on the South Shields sands for the races. He was tried and executed, and hung in chains on the river opposite the shore where the murder had been perpetrated. The body hung some weeks, but during a dark night it was removed and buried somewhere by his friends. The man who struck the blow never was discovered by the authorities.

Years after, when conversing with one of the most superior of the leaders of that strike about the difficulty we had found in the political movement springing from the evil passions and recklessness of the ignorant, who were ever liable to be misled, he related an occurrence showing the dangerous position which the leaders occupy, and the care and anxiety the conscientious among them undergo while endeavouring to act faithfully by their fellow-workmen and guarding against any acts of illegality being committed by the ignorant or designing. It was during the time when the feeling was most bitter against the men whom the owners had brought from a distance, as the "standing-out men" began to perceive that through these they would be defeated. One of the out-standing men came to him one day, and called him aside, and not in the excited virulence of angry passion, but in that silent calmness of purpose which a fixed criminal idea—approaching to insanity— so often assumes, told him that one of these black-legs passed early every morning when going to the pit past his garden, and that with his gun he

---

[53] Nicholas Fairless, assaulted on 11 June 1832, died 21 June. See Richard Fynes, *op. cit.*, pp. 31–2.

could shoot him without being seen as easy as possible, and stated that he had been going to do it, but "thowt he woul' aks him first an' see what he thowt about it." My informant started as by an electric shock, vividly painted to him the cowardice and atrocious nature of the act, and the destruction he would bring upon himself, and the disgrace on his family and fellow working men. He exacted a solemn promise from him that he would not allow such wicked thoughts to rest in his mind, but pray God to keep him from temptation. The man promised, replying, "I thowt I'd better aks th' first." From that time while the strike lasted this leader passed many a wakeful night, from the care and responsibility of his position, and he never enjoyed a sense of security until the strike was over. He was a man of superior intelligence, strict integrity, and religious principle, yet while he had unquestionably exercised a beneficial influence on the men he never could succeed in getting employment afterwards, and had to hawk tea to maintain his family.

The colliers of Northumberland and Durham are a century in advance of their class in any other mining district in England, Scotland, or Wales. This I would ascribe to the works being large and belonging to rich proprietors or companies, and to there not being any intermediate contractors between the colliers and the proprietors. Thus the truck system never was attempted, nor the temptations of public houses employed to derive profit from the expenditure of the men.[54] A colliery lasting for a long period, houses with gardens attached were built for the men, who were bound from year to year. As a general rule there was but one public-house allowed in the neighbourhood of each mine, unless to accommodate the surrounding population. Other houses of the kind were opened; the "coal-hewers" were but six hours in at the "face" of the mine at a time, so that there was not more than eight hours from their leaving home to returning from work. They had thus much leisure to read or to follow any light or intellectual pursuits when they desired. The owners had early seen the capability of the organisation and labours of the Methodists being especially adapted to improve the population; for the colliery people were collected in places mostly lying apart from the established parish churches, which then had no curates or scripture readers going forth to reach such people. The owners wisely facilitated the operations of the Wesleyans in opening Sunday-schools and chapels. Many of the colliers

---

[54] The truck system, or payment in kind, was illegal; but middlemen butties still forced their employees to buy at their shops or public-houses. According to an appendix of the 1842 royal commission on mines, the miners believed that these abuses would be ended if only the owners knew about them, and took responsibility for managing the mines themselves. See also W. H. Maehl, "Chartism in North Eastern England", *International Review of Social History*, 1963, p. 393, for the outlook of miners in the North-East at this time. Lowery's respect for the political complexion of the North-East at this time echoes Cobbett. See *Rural Rides* (ed. G. D. H. & M. Cole, 1930), III, p. 733: "a *better* race than that at NEWCASTLE and its vicinity, I am quite satisfied that there is not upon this earth." (October 1832).

became able local preachers, and promoted the mental culture of their own class. While there was much occasional intemperance and ignorance amongst them, yet there was a large number of reading, thinking, and ingenious men; you would often meet with a good library in their cottages. There were many superior mathematicians, and the booksellers of Newcastle were known to sell, chiefly among the workmen of the north, a larger number of works on that science than were sold in any other similar district of the country. Some of these men were excellent horticulturists and florists. They cultivated their little garden plots with much taste, and I was acquainted with one of these men, who frequently carried away prizes at the floral exhibitions held by the societies at Newcastle-on-Tyne. His pronunciation was of the broad vernacular, with its deep burr, and as he walked among his flower beds he would sound their scientific names in his provincial tones, intermingling his conversation with remarks on the philosophy of Locke, or quoting passages from Milton, Byron, Shelly, or Burns. Having been thrown out by the strike, he was for proceeding at once to America; but a clergyman and some gentry of the neighbourhood, who admired him as a florist, enabled him to get a lease of a five-acre pasture field for twenty-one years, at a rent of £50, on which the owner built a cottage and outhouses, charging interest of capital thereon. He thus commenced as a florist and market gardener, and brought up a large family in comfort and respectability from the produce of that garden.

About this time I made my first speech to a large audience. The Government of Earl Grey were then passing the Coercion Bill for Ireland,[55] which was strongly objected to by the Radicals, and a meeting of the inhabitants was called by hand-bill to petition against it; it was to be held in a large room in one of the principal inns, and the leading speakers of the Union were to attend from Newcastle. I was asked to second a resolution, which I consented to do, thinking I could accomplish this satisfactorily in a room, and as it may be of some use to my class who may wish to be able to address a public meeting I will relate the preparations I made for this, my first attempt to address a large audience: I felt that the difficulty would be to encounter that trepidation which is sure to be felt in such circumstances at first, a nervous flutter that deprives the speaker of that collectedness of thought which is essential to arrange his thoughts or select his words; so that I might have nothing to do but to acquire the requisite coolness of utterance, I wrote out what I deemed would occupy me twenty minutes, trusting that by that time I would have surmounted all trepidation, and could then proceed with

---

[55] Lowery's speech was given on 15 July 1833. The Coercion Bill (1833) was the Whig response to the collapse of law and order in Ireland and the growing agrarian troubles. The Bill empowered the Lord Lieutenant for one year to forbid meetings in disturbed areas, to suspend *habeas corpus*, and to substitute courts martial for ordinary courts. O'Connell bitterly opposed it, and England radicals joined Irish nationalists in attacking the Whigs. In working class circles, opposition to this Bill kept political unionism alive long after the Reform Act had passed.

the subject extemporaneously. This plan I always carried out for some time at important meetings until practice and want of time enabled me to speak more extemporaneously. The hour at which the meeting was announced arrived, and the Newcastle friends came down in a steamer, with music playing, and colours flying, and guns firing. The inn in which we were to meet stood on the "New Quay", facing the river, and the room might hold four or five hundred. But before our friends got landed the guns and music had gathered at least 10,000 people in front of the inn, so that it had to be at once decided that the speakers would have to address the people from the top of the door entrance. Here was a new situation. It was one thing to try to speak in the room, another to attempt doing so to such a crowd in the open air; and to increase this perplexity it was found that only one of the speakers from Newcastle had come—Mr. John Fife. It had been expected that they had to supply speakers, and except appointing another and myself to nominally move and second a resolution against the measure of Government, the Shields friends had made no arrangements. The person called to the chair was no speaker, and merely introduced the business and called on the speakers to address the meeting. It was decided that I should follow him and move the first resolution. It was well I had committed to memory what I had, for although I felt no desire to be excused, yet the earnest look of that multitude of expectant faces bewildered my mind, and so excited me that I could not have sought for matter or words to express myself. As it was, in my excitement I made no calculation of the volume of voice requisite to extend over such a crowd, and had no knowledge then of the pitch of voice from which its rising or falling may be regulated, but I began at the highest pitch and soon was obliged to stop from exhaustion and take a mouthful of water. This enabled me to get into a lower key, but still too high; my voice became hoarse, still I gradually acquired confidence as I observed the effects of my remarks, which were well received. I managed to continue to speak for upwards of twenty minutes. I was then but little known to the general public of my native town. The speakers were only known as gentlemen of the Union, their names not having been announced, and as the *Conservative Journal* condescended afterwards to admit "the speaker possessed a considerable talent for declamation."[56] Strange and amusing conceptions ran through the crowd. I had the honour to be set down for different persons of importance whom they had learned through the news-papers to be active in other districts. When it became known that "he was a tailor lad," a native of the town, I became a marvel of admiration among

---

[56] If by *Conservative Journal* Lowery means the Conservative *Newcastle Journal*, his quotation is puzzling, for in its immediate report of the meeting, the *Newcastle Journal*, 20 July 1833, p. 2 merely listed the major speakers and added that "several of the Shields Unionists per-formed inferior parts". The *Journal* reported all radical meetings in a sarcastic spirit, but the radical *Newcastle Press*, 20 July 1833, p. 2, was equally brief: it described Lowery's speech as "energetic", but did not report it.

the working classes, who always feel proud of the speaking talent of their own order. The trading classes, however, who could not think the Whig Government could do wrong, condemned the objects of the meeting, but admitted that the "lad was a clever lad," and some of the more prudential who did not trouble themselves about politics were of opinion that such talent would do me no good, for it was dangerous to the interests of a poor man to meddle with politics.

Within a short time I was called on to address some large meetings, and my second public speech was at a dinner given by the radical electors and non-electors to Charles Atwood[57] on his defeat as a candidate for the representation of Newcastle-on-Tyne, when upwards of one thousand electors voted for him. No public hall in the town being large enough for the dinner, a rope-walk was procured, in which upwards of one thousand people dined. My third public speech was at a public meeting of the "trades" held in the town Moor, to condemn the sentence of transportation passed on the "Dorchester labourers".[58] Full 100,000 working men came in procession from the surrounding neighbourhood, and the feeling against the sentence and the quick carrying of it out by the Government was intensely bitter. It was an act which was felt afterwards to be unjustifiable when properly inquired into. The condemned men were men of intelligence and moral character. But ignorance and crime had broke out in that county in almost nightly stack burnings, and while the farmers had evidently been careless of the social deterioration of the people, they and the proprietors had become alarmed at an attempt amongst the labourers to form an association to endeavour to raise their wages, which were much lower than the average of their class in other counties, as it were from the spirit of the repealed combination laws, they indicted these men for some seditious act. A jury evidently full of fears and prejudices declared them guilty; they were sentenced to transportation, a sentence which the Government instantly put in execution. But when the country was roused by the operatives and those agreeing with them on the matter, the subject was brought before Parliament, and re-investigated, when it was found that the law had been overstrained, and the "Dorchester labourers" were set at liberty. The condemnation of these men, compared with the conduct of the Whig Government regarding the

[57] This dinner, on 2 December 1833, is fully reported in *Newcastle Press*, 7 December 1833, p. 4. Lowery's speech strongly attacked the Whigs, whom power had "transformed . . . into contemptible trucklers". Lowery wanted a return to a police-free, less heavily taxed regime, and believed that against the "moral opinions" of the radicals, "the thunders of the cannon and the bristling of the bayonets are in vain".

[58] For Lowery's speech, see below, pp. 207. The Dorchester labourers of Tolpuddle resisted wage-cutting by forming an agricultural union, deliberately copied from urban working class methods of self-defence. Despite considerable public protest, they were transported for taking unlawful oaths. George Loveless's autobiographical *Victims of Whiggery* (1838) shows that capitalist farming and dissent were both dissolving the traditional bonds of the rural economy.

illegal acts of the Duke of Cumberland in the "Orange" lodges,[59] which they hushed up while screening him from the consequences, produced a strong conviction among the people of partiality in the governing powers towards their own order.

[59] Ernest, Duke of Cumberland and King of Hanover (1771-1851), fifth son of George III and a tough-minded Tory Ultra, was the leading opponent of Catholic emancipation. The Orange lodges, which emerged during the 1790s, were strongly anti-Catholic and influential with Ulstermen and Tory Ultras. With their oaths, para-military organization and ritual, they bordered on illegality. The Duke (as grand master of the lodges) encouraged their military activity, and they were temporarily disbanded in 1836. Compare Lowery's speech in *Scotsman*, 3 July 1841: "if the Dorchester labourers had been sent abroad by the Whigs, why was the Duke of Cumberland and his friends [*sic*] allowed to escape when they broke the same act?"

III

Tailoring and the Unstamped Press:
1834–1838

I now removed to Newcastle to live, having, as I thought, secured more regular work in one of the best shops in that town. I now mixed more in society, and my study of men and character became more extensive. At that time the masses of Newcastle presented a state of mind peculiar to themselves. There was a strong feeling of poetry, a sense of humour and witty satire displayed in their local songs. A fondness for company, and a passion for speculative inquiry and discussion, prevailed along with much intemperance. Thus, while the intelligence of the people was strong and they had their literary and philosophical institutions and a number of public libraries, and every week public lectures on various subjects, the old tavern system still prevailed. All classes met there to compare notes and to hear individual remarks and criticisms on what occupied public attention, and there was in consequence much intemperance. Every branch of knowledge had its public-house where its disciples met. Each party in politics had their house of meeting—there was a house where the singers and musicians met—a house where the speculative and free thinking met—a house where the literate met—a house where the artists and painters met—also one where those who were men of science met. Thus the drinking customs put on its most seductive form, and enlisted the mental energies of the people in its service. It was not the sluggish sensual sipping of the drink to pass away the time, but the quickly swallowed draught amid the warmth of disputation or the excitement of interesting ideas that was most dangerous. The aspiring young men were thus led to seek the company whose talents and knowledge they esteemed, and although at first the appetites which God gave them were averse to these drinking customs, yet like merchants who seek wealth in a sickly clime, and submit to it unwillingly for the sake of gaining gold, but at last catch the fever or plague and die, so those seeking intellectual wealth, submitting at first to the drinking atmosphere in which it had to be sought till their moral sensitiveness ceased, and they caught the fever and plague of intemperance, their manhood became diseased, and death to all the realities of life ensued. At that time the journeymen tailors, as a class, in that town were a low, immoral set, especially those of the house of call.[60] Yet the best of the old men admitted that there had been much improvement in the body since they "were young." To have apprenticed a boy in many of the shops was as it were sending him to pandemonium to be trained. The journeyman of truly moral and religious habits being the exception, such mostly kept silent, whilst the conversation was chiefly engrossed by the intemperate and immoral. Their day's theme was generally the last night's excesses or the relation of some "sprees" of debauchery and vice in which they had been engaged. They would pride themselves in recounting acts of meanness, unmanliness, and dishonesty, unconscious of their degradation. Very often when an innocent youth came into a shop from the country, and while working, hung his watch up, a wink would go round, and his watch would be sent off and pawned for the value of a gallon or two of ale, which being brought in, amid joking and laughter the ticket would be presented to him, with an invitation to serve out the drink; to this robbery, not wishing to quarrel with the shop, and, perhaps, looking to improve his workmanship by the men, he would submit. Stories would be told amid bursts of laughter, how certain parties had imposed on landlords and landladies, and got credit for drink; how they had cheated the "garth" or slop shops where they had gone to sell their "crib" of pieces of cloth or trimmings. For a certain amount of cloth having been cut off for a garment, along with a certain amount of stuff to make and trim it, and given to the workman, the trade morality was that the maker who spent time in planning and saving had a right to what he saved. But the gathering up of "crib" was not always restricted within this limit. An amusing instance of this used to be related of an old journeyman in one of the principal shops:— The custom of the foreman or cutter was to cut from the web the requisite length of cloth for a coat, and having cut the outsides sent the remainder of the cloth up to the work-shop for the maker to plan the facings and collar cuffs. But on this occasion, being in a hurry, and having taken cloth enough for a suit he merely cut the coat and sent the rest up, intending afterwards to get the remainder down again to cut out the trousers and vest. The message boy said nothing about this, but with saying "there is a coat for

---

[60] The "house of call" was the public-house which served as the headquarters for a local trade. Meetings were held there, funds were kept, and men on the tramp called for work and relief. For pubs as meeting-places, see B. Harrison "Pubs", in H. J. Dyos & M. Wolff (Eds.), *The Victorian City* (1973). The standard work on drinking customs is John Dunlop, *The Philosophy of Artificial and Compulsory Drinking Usage* (1839). Lowery makes it clear that the artisan workshop of this period scarcely represented a homogeneous "respectable" culture. Dr. David Vincent has drawn our attention to Thomson's comments on his experience as an apprentice shipwright: "I could not share in their mad roysterings, and hence was their butt, at which they shot plentifully their coarse jokes and taunts, which they generally wound up with a satirical addenda of 'parson', 'lawyer', 'painter', 'player', anything; they considered refinement and reading as a degeneracy fit only for 'lubbers and gentlemen.' Our average number of apprentices was about fifteen; and wallowing daily in such an immoral miasm, they were fearfully ignorant of every thing necessary to build up the moral man, or fit themselves for a world of progression" (C. Thomson, *The Autobiography of an Artisan*, 1847, pp. 72–3).

you"—closed the door. Mr. ——— who had spread the cloth out, and was surveying intently, exclaimed, with an oath, "I can save as much as will make a coat! Who'll buy a coat cloth!" It was put up to auction, and knocked down for seventeen shillings to one of the men, and a boy sent instantly to the beer-house for a gallon to "wet it". During the afternoon the foreman being through his work was going to cut out the trousers and vest. Up comes the message boy—"the foreman wants that cloth left off the coat," "What cloth boy? I've got none. I was sore pinched." "Why, he says he cut off as much as would make a suit, and he wants to cut out the trousers and waist-coat?" Amid roars of laughter ——— had to get his customer to refund the cloth, and it was admitted it would be coming it too strong to attempt to stand it out.

At that time the old corporations exercised a most pernicious influence on the morals of the journeymen in the different trades of Newcastle. A very large number of them were freemen and they had some excellent privileges as such off their guilds. The different employers sought to get all the freemen they could into their employment that they might ensure the support of the influential gentry of the party they sided with. These feasted the freemen at every election, and money and drink were profusely squandered. During a contest, the poll being then open for fourteen days, it was one saturnalia of dissipation and vice. Thus as a body the freemen became dissipated and degraded, and whatever knowledge they might have of right principles was drowned by their vicious habits; these rendered them the willing instruments of every corruption.[61] The public vices of influential bodies are sure in the long run to permeate general society, and the instruments in humble life begin to imitate the actions and laws of their betters in that circle where their rule and influence extends.

This was peculiarly seen in the rules or laws of the tailors' society, which presented a scheme of selfishness, monopoly—injustice—corruption and waste that appeared to have been conceived from the model of those of the Corporation. The Recorder of the Borough had sanctioned them and they were considered the Magna Charta of the trade, and the rock on which its prosperity alone could stand. There were three divisions of the men in the society, the first called the members—the second composed of those who had been upwards of one year journeymen in the town—the third the strangers who had not been twelve months in the town. Each division had a book in which its men set down their names when out of a job, to ensure a

---

[61] Freemen possessed the vote in certain of the old corporations. The freedom could be obtained by purchase, gift or apprenticeship. In towns like Norwich and Newcastle, therefore, it was notorious that there was a sizeable working class vote up for sale; where the corporation was Tory, so was the freeman vote. The 1832 Reform Act left the freeman vote untouched, and a radical motive for advocating municipal reform in 1834–5 was to purify local elections. In 1837 Norwich, for example, had a population of 60,000; 1,400 of its 3,700 electors were willing to sell their vote—at an estimated cost of £44,000. See N. Gash, *Politics in the Age of Peel* (1953), Ch. 7.

"call" to a shop when a man was sent for. So far just—but the rule was that so long as the first or members' book could supply the "calls" none had to go to the second book, and so long as the first and second books would supply them none went to the third book; so that, except during the three months in summer, the third book never brought a day's work. The men on the second were a little better, while those on the members' had almost constant work. Every man on all the books was obliged to pay so much a month to the society and so much per week to a sick and burial fund, from which any falling sick got a weekly allowance, and so much was paid at their death.[62] Apparently this was proper, but there was a rule that when a person left the town to work elsewhere he ceased to have any claims on the fund, and as the third bookmen and most of the second were constantly leaving after a season it was a most unjust tax upon them. When any of the members died or left the town an election took place to fill up the vacancies from the other books, which was just an imitation of the elections of members of Parliament with all their follies and corruptions. The poll was kept open fourteen days, during which time the candidates were visiting the shops canvassing and inducing them to come forward and poll for them by treating them with intoxicating drinks. Suppers, too, were given to the influential few, sometimes by running into debt, by selling and pawning part of their furniture, while after all many of them must lose their election.

As a matter of course none thought the members' privileges just or reasonable but the members themselves. Complaints were continually made known by a general grumbling, or were openly expressed when opportunity offered at a trades meeting. More liberal ideas had sprung up even among some of the privileged ones, but the excuse was, it was the "law," the constitution which the recorder had sanctioned. The house of call was held in a public-house, and those out of work had to attend at 8 a.m., at 12, and 6 in the evening, when masters might send for men. Thus those who had any money were induced to tipple and to spend it, and the more knowing ones who had none schemed by skittles, quoits, or dominoes, to win beer. Habits of idleness, tippling, and drunkenness, were thus formed. Some of them were scarcely ever out of that public-house. Drunkenness was not esteemed a degradation, nor were the mean and dirty schemes to attain drink looked on in the same light as a similar dishonesty would have been if exercised in connection with other things. Bad as the state of things were then, they described them as having been worse "when they were young," especially in the managing committee, who were more narrowly watched now in their expenditure of the funds. They said that at one time the committee never complained if the secretary did not charge more than five or six quarters' salary in one

[62] See P. H. J. H. Gosden, *The Friendly Societies in England, 1815–1875* (Manchester, 1961). Trade unions forced underground between the 1790s and 1824 transformed themselves into friendly societies and thus obtained both legal standing and some protection for their funds.

year. That was deemed fair, and they said nothing, he in return saying nothing about certain pranks of the committee, who deemed it a sin to allow the money in the box to exceed £10, and at once got up a spree to reduce it to the necessary limits when it exceeded that sum.

The combined trades-unions[63] were now formed, and it was thought by this combination a strike of any single trade might be supported by all the rest, and its success made certain. They forgot that human selfishness is ever on the watch, and that every trade would conclude it should be first supported by others, instead of supporting any of them. They had scarcely got formed when the central committee found they had two or three "strikes" already on their hands. One of these was that of the London tailors, whose wages were very good indeed at the time.[64] The press generally condemned them, and the middle classes felt alarmed at these combinations. Sir Henry Hardinge[65] in the House of Commons said that he would walk down to the House in his shirt-sleeves if his tailor could not get his coat made without submitting to the unjust exactions of the journeymen. The funds were soon exhausted, the common sense of the men began to see the impracticability of the scheme, and it gradually came to nought.

---

[63] This was the Grand National Consolidated Trades Union, formed around the London co-operative labour-exchanges by followers of Owen during winter 1833–4 as a result of the Derby silk-weavers' strike in November. Lowery's speech on 19 May 1834, reported in *Newcastle Press*, 24 May 1834, p. 4, makes it clear that he had become a trade union member since giving a speech at the trade union meeting on 14 April 1834. The GNCTU was originally an attempt by London trades like the tailors to close the gulf between honourable society and dishonourable men such as Lowery himself. It capitalized on public outrage at the Dorchester labourers' sentence and at its height attracted some 11,000 London and 16,000 provincial members. It aimed to build up strike funds; to promote co-operative schemes for self-employment and economic independence; and to offer the full range of friendly society benefits. Each trade was vertically linked up from branch level to Grand Lodge, and linked horizontally with other federated trades. But some leading unions never joined, and unlike the amalgamated unionism of the 1850s it was unable to centralize its finance. Owen's conciliatory attitude towards the masters became suspect, and after several unsuccessful strikes had drained its resources, the GNCTU collapsed in summer 1834. See W. H. Oliver, "The Grand National Consolidated Trades Union", *Economic History Review*, 1964. Compare Lowery's involvement with that of James Burn, who similarly reorganized the journeyman hatters in Glasgow (*The Autobiography of a Beggar Boy*, 1978 ed. p. 144).

[64] In November 1833, the London tailors were reorganized to form a single union covering all classes of journeymen, thus "equalizing" the conditions between the honourable men (who had served their full apprenticeship) and the semi-skilled dishonourable men (who undercut them by making cheap ready-to-wear clothes for the slop shops). The London tailors were the main support of the GNCTU, but in Spring, 1834, they went on strike to prevent (according to *Poor Man's Guardian*, 3 May 1834) "work done 90 per cent under its fair value"; they demanded 6s. for a 10-hour day in summer, 5s. for an 8-hour day in winter. The masters retaliated with the document and broke the strike. Lowery's comment that their wages were "very good" applied only to the minority who comprised the honourable trade; the rest earned less than half their wage.

[65] Sir Henry Hardinge (1785–1856) was prominent in Wellington's Peninsular campaigns, and became Tory M.P. in turn for Durham, Newport and Launceston (1820–44), Secretary at War 1828–30 and 1841–4, Irish Secretary 1830 and 1834–5, and Governor-General of India 1844–7.

The entrance into the union was by a secret initiation, when a promise of secrecy was given, and a pass-word communicated, which enabled a member to enter any of the union meetings; these were held with closed doors watched by "Tilers" or officers both outside and in, to guard against the entrance of any who were not members. The titles of the officers and modes of conducting business were contemptibly pompous and puerile, yet in much they might be traced to the weaknesses of the upper classes, whose forms in some institutions they imitated. [It was what "Carlyle"[66] would have considered a chapter in the philosophy of clothes, for in addition to the dress, forms and ceremonies, through which the courts of law and divinity work, there had also arisen an order called the Odd Fellows, which as well as the Freemasons had its secret signs, closed meetings, and peculiar styles of dress and address.[67] This order, too, was patronised by wealthy men, magistrates, and the nobility.][68] However in the midst of this shaking and shifting and trying of additional plans, by the people, streaks of light got into the dark spots of their societies, and some began to see things there not in keeping with the improvements they wished to make. The old wished often to retain the effete and useless, but the younger members wished for a new modelling of the society. The committee of the society could not resist the desire to become amalgamated with the other trades in this union,[69] but kept its machinery separate. This could not last long, for mixed with its impracticable schemes the union recognised certain principles of equity among workmen which the selfishness of the older and more close society did not act on. The new ideas, therefore, soon began to work their way. The right and justice of retaining the three books was denied and a "reform" was demanded. The privileged prophesied that if their privileges were taken away the prosperity of the "trade" would be ruined. The young rejoiced they had no prosperity to lose, and could not expect any while such an unjust system continued. I had been chosen secretary of the union

---

[66] Thomas Carlyle (1795–1881) essayist, historian and author of *Sartor Resartus*, argued that the "spirit of the times" was deplorably mechanistic, acquisitive, shallow and insensitive; he diagnosed the "condition of England" question as neglect of the spiritual as well as the material well-being of the poor. His remedy was to return to the close-knit paternalist society of the medieval Abbot Sampson. His comment, "the first purpose of Clothes . . . was not warmth or decency, but ornament . . . The first spiritual want of a barbarous man is Decoration . . ." presaged a savage attack on utilitarian values. (*Sartor Resartus*, Book 1, Ch. 5, "The World in Clothes".)

[67] Rose's Act (1793) allowed friendly societies to possess a legal corporate personality, which enabled them to defend their funds. The Oddfellows were a friendly society founded in Manchester in 1810. Together with the Foresters they became the leading Victorian friendly society, and offered insurance, sick benefits, burial expenses and occasionally pensions. By 1872 the Oddfellows had nearly half a million members, substantially more than the trade unions in total.

[68] It is not clear who is responsible for the passages enclosed by square brackets. Although the passage on p. 99 could be an editorial insertion, other such passages, including this one, were probably written by Lowery himself, cf. pp. 139, 161.

[69] i.e. the GNCTU.

of trades, and one night, when we had a full society meeting, with about two hundred in the room, the proposal of remodelling it came up. The privileged ones stood by the articles of the constitution—"Let me see the articles," I exclaimed, for I had never seen them, they being kept locked in the box with as much care for their safety as ever the Jews took for the "Law." The box was opened and the articles brought forth—I sought the "rules of membership," when, in a moment, I detected the omission of a word which completely altered the sense of the rule from that which had been intended—a remarkable instance of the importance of a single word in fixing the signification of a sentence. The document was drawn up after the legal form, with marginal statements of the purport of each paragraph. In the one described as rule for making members, the intention had been not to fill up any vacancies which might occur during the winter half year, that being the slack season of the year. The intention had been to express it thus, "There shall not be any members *made* from Martimas to Lammas, on account of the usual scarcity of work during that season of the year," but the word *made* had been left out. At a glance I saw the omission and the advantage (though an unfair one) that might be taken of it. "What!" I exclaimed—"why, by your own rules the right of membership ceases during the winter half-year!"—cheers and cries of "No! no!" greeted this assertion. I read the sentence—the cheers were louder and the noes more vociferous than before. "Come, read for yourselves," I retorted; "you cannot deny the fact." One of their committee looked at the sentence, which I held before him. "By Jingo! it's true," he exclaimed—"he's right," and the uproar grew louder still, as I at once proceeded to propose that as their membership was then in abeyance by the rules, and as this privilege was unjust at any time, there should be a committee elected at once to remodel the whole constitution of the society. I continued to urge the condemnation of the monopoly, and described the harmony and security which their repeal would produce, amidst a storm of opposition and applause, for upwards of an hour. The result of this was the passing of the resolution, and three-fourths of the assembly going to another house, carrying the box along with them. The rules were remodelled in fairness, and continued to give satisfaction afterwards.

For awhile the old body tried to keep up, but in a short period it died out; yet, for a long time, those who had enjoyed these unfair advantages over their fellow workmen used to exclaim that I had ruined the society and the trade. Changes from that time went on in the trade which have produced a complete revolution. Wages fell very low, and small masters, as a class, were almost swept away by what may be termed the ready-made clothes manufactories. While the wages of the makers are reduced to a starvation point, these houses enjoy very large profits, and while the public get a more showy article at a low price, they get an inferior article. The error of the former system, which this one superseded, was, that it allowed nothing between the best clothes with elaborate workmanship, and uncouthly cut and made slops. This arose from the journeymen attempting to maintain a uniform price for making all garments, and employing, therefore, too much labour on those for the poor classes, who could not afford to pay for it. While the cloth they wear is inferior, the poorer classes naturally wish to have the cut and general appearance of their clothes to present what is deemed a fashionable appearance. This the ready-made or slop system accomplished; but it flung the trade into the hands of large capitalists, and reduced wages to a minimum, while the profits to these masters are higher than they were before.[70]

I had taken every precaution before I went to Newcastle regarding the prospect of constant work; having been employed there in one of the principal shops, a branch of a London house, which had the chief work for the officers of the regiment; this was deemed the most fashionable business. Being desirous of hearing a course of lectures which were being delivered, and the "calls being open," in a busy week, I thought I would take a week's work to be on the spot, and went in as a partner with a person I knew who was a regular "coat hand" in the shop. The master had spoken to him after I was a few days there, stating that as I suited and was a sober person if I wished I might continue. I went on as usual for some weeks that I might feel the more certain I did suit them, and then removed with my family to Newcastle. But when the tailors' strike occurred in London the press and the upper classes became alarmed at the combined unions. The principal masters caught the panic and took what steps they could to weaken and destroy the combination. Being already known to be influential among the men, I got the "silent sack," as it is called, that is, I was not told I was not to have any more work; but as the slack season had come on, I was told "I had better put my name on the books of the house of call, as there might be a chance of something more than they had that week to offer." I did this, but never had another day from that shop; I knew I had no chance of getting employment in any of the other shops, as the same cause operated there to hinder me; so I determined at once to return to my native town, where in general, our work was better in the winter than in the summer, because the inhabitants, chiefly seamen, were more at home during the winter. There I had my first lesson of the neglect by working men of their front ranks amidst the troubles into which they may be brought when engaged in any dispute for the advantage of all. It was with difficulty I was enabled to remove my

---

[70] Lowery describes the growth of the dishonourable and increasingly sweated trades. Compare Henry Mayhew's *London Labour and the London Poor* (1861–2 ed.) II, pp. 300 ff: piecework produces a glut of goods, prices fall, wages are cut, men therefore increase their output by working longer to maintain their income, the glut is accentuated, and prices and then wages fall still further. This downward spiral Mayhew formulates as "over-work makes underpay and underpay makes over-work". The artisan trades being invaded by sweating (tailoring, cabinetmaking and shoemaking) were the strongest in London Chartism.

furniture to Shields; some few of my acquaintance lamented the hardship of my case, but although the general body knew the cause of my having to leave, no trouble was taken to inquire whether I was ill off or otherwise.

The strikes and the changes in trade which were springing up in consequence had exposed the fallacies of the trades union system. The sensible were losing their faith in the principle, and the selfish in their success. The spirit of political reform was again rising. As Government have power to make and alter laws, and to raise money to carry out its purposes, it is natural at first sight for people to suppose that improvement can be most easily obtained through possessing political power, and this idea is strongest in the classes excluded from political power, who conceive that their exclusion is the result of selfish injustice on the part of the ruling class. Thus, until experience opens their eyes from time to time, the crowd ever turn to Parliament as the means to improve their condition. The popular mind began now to take up the idea of improving their condition by Acts of Parliament. They sought not for the mere supremacy of any party in the state, but for the removal of class taxation, for greater facilities to trade, and for the better employment of the people. The *Westminster Review*[71] had done much to show how unequally the taxation pressed on the wages of the labouring classes as compared with that on property. Col. Thompson's[72] catechism of the corn laws and expositions of the doctrines of free trade had been published in a cheap form. These were being widely circulated, and at that time were well understood and advocated by the working classes, while the middle classes and shopkeepers as a body never petitioned for the repeal of the corn laws, and but few of them were conversant with the subject. It was not until the working men had held meetings and petitioned till they were tired, and had turned to seek an entrance into political power in order to carry these and other changes, that the trading community began to study these subjects and to seek for free trade.

It was about this period of time William Lovett and Henry Hetherington and John Cleave and their friends formed the Working Men's Association in London,[73] which combined a library, meetings, lectures, and discussions on

---

[71] Founded by Bentham in 1824 as a radical and utilitarian journal, rivalling the Whig *Edinburgh Review* and the Tory *Quarterly Review*. It was first edited by Dr. Bowring, and later (when it joined the *London Review*) by J. S. Mill. It advocated franchise extension, reform of the legal and political systems, and political economy. For its relations with the philosophic radicals, see J. S. Mill, *Autobiography*, ch. 4.

[72] Thomas Perronet Thompson (1783–1869) campaigned in the Peninsular War, wrote on political economy and free trade, published his *Catechism on the Corn Laws* (1827), and was owner-editor of the *Westminster* (1829–36). He was a philosophic radical M.P. for Hull 1835–7, and M.P. for Bradford 1847–52, 1857–9. See L. G. Johnson, *General T. Perronet Thompson* (1957).

[73] What Lowery describes as the Working Men's Association, was not the London Working Men's Association, founded in 1836, but the National Union of the Working Classes, founded spring 1831. This was originally a general trades union but it was captured for political unionism by the adherence of co-operators (like Lovett), parish radicals and Irish. At its height in 1832 the NUWC had some 2,000 London members organized in classes,

political and social economy, the object being to attain the political enfranchisement of the working classes. Amongst the first objects which they perceived obstructed the diffusion of knowledge on the subjects they had in view, was the 4d. stamp then on newspapers, which had evidently been imposed at first to restrict the purchase of newspapers to the richer or enfranchised portion of the community.[74] This they determined to get repealed, and for that purpose got up petitions in different parts of the community, and waited on various members of Parliament. Lytton Bulwer[75] took up the question actively, bringing it frequently before the House of Commons. But the Reform Parliament did not entertain the question, and always had some plea of not being able to spare the tax, until it became evident that they did not want to do so. Whatever of Earl Grey's pledges of "Peace Retrenchment and Reform" they might wish to carry out, reform of the laws affecting newspapers was out of the number.

A determination was come to publish newspapers for the people without the stamp, which was held to be an unjust and impolitic tax. Henry Hetherington, publisher in the Strand, put out the "Poor Man's Guardian", at

and was in contact with dozens of provincial political unions. It was a product of the reform agitation, and when the storm over Irish coercion died away, it was displaced in autumn 1833 by the growth of trade unionism. William Lovett (1800–77), cabinet-maker, was a leading figure in the London co-operative movement, NUWC and LWMA, where he drew up the Charter. He was secretary to the 1839 Chartist convention and was imprisoned for denouncing the police after the 1839 Bull Ring riots in Birmingham. While in prison, he and John Collins published *Chartism. A New Organization of the People* (1840), in which they outlined "knowledge Chartism", with its emphasis on education and moral self-improvement. Henceforward he was outside the mainstream of Chartist activity, but he retained his radicalism and remained active as an educational and moral reformer, and published his classic *Life and Struggles* in 1876. Henry Hetherington (1792–1849) was a printer, publisher and bookseller, and hero of the Unstamped Press. He was a leading figure in London trade unionism, in the NUWC, LWMA, and early London Chartism. John Cleave (*c.* 1790–*c.* 1847) was probably Irish, and like Hetherington prominent in the Unstamped and the NUWC. He was London delegate to the Convention in 1839 but unlike Hetherington and Lovett he remained in the O'Connorite strand of Chartism after 1840, and became treasurer of the National Chartist Association's Convention Fund.

[74] Legal restrictions on the cheap newspaper included a comprehensive definition of what counted as a newspaper, together with stringent control through the libel law of what could be said in it. Richard Carlile fought this battle in the 1820s—see W. Wickwar, *The Struggle for the Freedom of the Press* (1928). Financial controls included stamp duties on almanacs, pamphlets, advertisements, raw paper and above all the 4d. stamp on newspapers. Middle class radicals, anxious to circulate proper notions of political economy, opposed these "taxes on knowledge": working class radicals, keen to teach working men their rights and wrongs, defied the law by selling the Unstamped. See P. Hollis, *The Pauper Press* (Oxford, 1970), for background to this and to footnotes 76–86. The stamp duty was reduced to 1d. in 1836. Lowery's speech on the taxes on knowledge is printed in *Newcastle Press*, 4 January 1834, p. 4.

[75] Edward Lytton Bulwer (1803–73), a literary figure who kept a watching brief on literary and theatrical matters as M.P. for Lincoln (1832–41), and retained a loose connexion with the philosophic radicals (Hume, Grote and Warburton). In June 1832 and May 1834, and finally in August 1835, he introduced parliamentary debates on the taxes on knowledge, but did not always press them to a vote. He returned to politics in the 1850s as a Conservative.

1d., "Published in defiance of the law," was inscribed on it as a motto. John Cleave published his "Gazette," and Mr. Cousins the "Penny Satirist," while the others gave the general news and comments.[76] The *Guardian* was the most vigorous in its articles on the people's rights to political power—in its condemnation of class legislation, and in its investigations into the banking and monetary system. The Working Men's Association sent out John Cleave and Henry Vincent[77] into the country districts, and similar societies sprung up in the chief manufacturing towns. The societies established shops for the sale of the unstamped papers. Some went into it enthusiastically from a desire to free the press from all imposts, while it presented an opening for a large class who are ready to engage in any trade that promises remuneration.

Subscriptions[78] were raised to support those who were prosecuted, and a common risk seemed to unite them in a common interest. They mutually aided each other in getting their papers out and in extending their sale, for an active demand instantly sprung up which no single office could supply. The more liberal of the stamped papers also facilitated the publishing by furnishing part of their set-up type, and frequently the unstamped were machined in the same office, especially in that of the *True Sun*.[79] A person resident in London, of some property, gave his time, money, and labour freely in aiding these publishers in their struggle against the law.[80] He gave, I think, £300 or upwards to each of the above-mentioned papers, besides two others. The law was soon put in force, and men and women were

---

[76] Benjamin Cousins was a young printer and publisher of the Unstamped. He also had ties with the parish radicals, and as part of their campaign in 1833 he refused to pay assessed taxes.

[77] Henry Vincent (1813–78), Chartist and lecturer, came to London from Hull in 1835 and joined the LWMA. He was a missionary to Wales and the South-West and delegate to the 1839 Convention from London and Bath. His language became more extravagant and he was imprisoned for sedition and illegal meetings in autumn 1839. It was supposedly to release him from Monmouth gaol that Frost led the abortive Newport rising. After his release, Vincent came to favour middle and working class co-operation, supported the Complete Suffrage Union, and repudiated his former extravagance. His career follows Lowery's quite closely, and it is curious that Lowery says so little about him. There is a fuller memoir by B. Harrison in J. M. Bellamy & J. Saville (Eds.), *Dictionary of Labour Biography*, I (1972), pp. 326–34.

[78] From July 1831 Lovett organized the subscriptions into a Victim Fund, to help men and their families imprisoned for selling the Unstamped; some £360 was collected and distributed in London.

[79] *The True Sun* was established in 1832 by Patrick Grant as a radical newspaper. Among its editors were William Carpenter and John Bell (of the Unstamped) and Laman Blanchard. It campaigned for radical parliamentary reform, social reform, and for repeal of the stamp duties and of the libel law. It was prosecuted twice for libel in 1834, and its finances were always precarious; it collapsed in December 1837. Uniquely among the stamped press "it identified itself with the working classes" (Lovett). See C. H. Vivian, "Radical Journalism in the 1830s", *Modern Language Quarterly*, 1954.

[80] This was "Palafox" Julian Hibbert (c. 1800–34), a radical philanthropist and Greek scholar, whose money was made in the West Indies; he allegedly spent £5,000 on helping Richard Carlile.

imprisoned for selling them.[81] The publishers were frequently fined and imprisoned, but they stood their ground. The law then was not so stringent regarding the sale of illegal papers as it was made after the 4d. stamp was repealed: afterwards, either the printer, seller, or purchaser of the paper could be prosecuted, while at that time the printing and the sale had to be sworn to, and clearly brought home to individuals. In the metropolis it was easy to get a large number of vendors to sell them in the streets. These were furnished with a dozen to begin with, paying for them as they sold them. When they were put in prison for selling them the committee looked after their case and allowed them a trifle per week. In the provinces the London publishers liberally credited a stock, and either sent a man down or the local association got one to sell them, and co-operated with him to extend the sale. Whenever a seizure was made and the parties imprisoned, the circumstance was turned to account, and the town placarded, and public meetings held to petition Parliament to repeal the obnoxious law. All at once the people became readers of these newspapers, and of kindred publications that were sold in the same shops. Lord Brougham, Charles Knight, and their friends, about this time brought out the "Penny Magazine," and other standard works.[82] The "Cornucopia," a very superior penny weekly literary sheet, was published at Edinburgh—the first of that class of which so many have sprung up since—but for want of capital it went down, and *Chambers's Journal*[83] instantly appeared, whose circulation increased weekly. The publication of these more standard serials did not lessen the sale of the newspapers, but rather increased it, as the class of readers was extended. There was thus an outburst of popular thought and inquiry among the working-men, and the number of readers and thinkers in their class was increased tenfold. There

---

[81] The usual way of obstructing the sales of the Unstamped was to arrest vendors for selling papers in the street without a hawker's licence (16 Geo. II c. 26); this was punishable with a maximum of 3 months in prison. Around 750 people were imprisoned in London alone for selling the Unstamped between 1831 and 1836.

[82] The Society for the Diffusion of Useful Knowledge was founded in 1826 by Lord Brougham, one of the more radical of the Whigs, and by Charles Knight, the printer and publisher of much useful knowledge. It was widely supported by those generally interested in popular education, and especially by those anxious to popularize political economy. It published inexpensive editions of the classics, and above all the *Penny Magazine*, a weekly miscellany of short pieces on kangaroos, Rouen cathedral and popular science—designed to divert the popular taste away from the Unstamped. Sales reputedly reached over 200,000 a week. The Society collapsed in 1846, bankrupted by its Biographical Dictionary.

[83] The *Cornucopia* was a folio-sized 4-page paper, selling at 1½d., and was owned and edited by George Mudie. According to William Chambers "as the *Cornucopia* contained a quantity of amusing matter, and in point of size resembled a newspaper, it was deemed a marvel of cheapness"; it was the model for Chambers's own *Edinburgh Journal* (W. Chambers, *Memoir of Robert Chambers*, 1872, p. 225). We owe this information to Dr. D. Vincent. See also James Burn, *Autobiography* (1978 ed.) pp. 164–5. *Chambers's Journal* was launched in February 1832 by Robert and William Chambers "to elevate and instruct, independently of mere passing amusement" along the lines of the *Penny Magazine*, (W. Chambers, *The Story of a Long and Busy Life*, 1882, p. 30). Within a year, sales were steady at 50,000, of which Scotland took the greater part. See R. K. Webb, *The British Working Class Reader* (1955), Ch. 3.

had long been a class of Radical politicians among the working-men who were readers of Hone's works, "The Black Dwarf," Cobbett's "Register," and such like,[84] but they were few compared to the body of the people, and worthy men of mental powers and peculiar intellect superior to the masses and standing apart from them rather than acting upon them; but the whole multitude seemed to be roused to interest themselves in the matter of the unstamped papers and their collateral subjects. Even those who could not read themselves often became subscribers with others who would read to them. The parcels generally arrived by the London coaches on the Saturday afternoon, and I have frequently seen a crowd waiting their arrival, and if by any mishap the newspaper parcel did not arrive they would be evidently much disappointed. The women, too, would be often waiting with their children in their arms, and when any apology was offered and a hope that it would come, perhaps next mail, would say, "Yes, yes, but I like to get it on the Saturday, and then he doesn't go to the public-house after he's done work, but stops at home and reads it." Meantime a taste for reading was created, and while afterwards it sought a change in some of its fare, the appetite still continued. The shop at Newcastle was extended to two large establishments, which continue still, while there are many smaller ones. The exertions of the authorities became more active against these shops as they saw their influence increase, and prosecutions were instituted in all parts of the country. First they managed to convict the man who kept the Newcastle shop,[85] and his wife was assisted by the friends to keep it open. Then they convicted her, and both were put in gaol. In my enthusiasm I went in until other arrangements were made, and another person was got from London.[86] An excellent plan was hit upon for evading prosecution. A person having one of the cellars under the arch of the Bridge on the "Quay side," notice

[84] These papers all emerged in the radical years before Peterloo, and most were killed by the Six Acts. William Hone (1780–1842) was a radical bookseller famous for his political satires and parodies, which included the *Political Litany* and *The House that Jack Built;* for the first of these he was prosecuted and acquitted in 1817. *The Black Dwarf* was started in 1817 by Thomas Wooler to urge political reform and the reduction of taxes; at its height in 1819, its sales may have reached a weekly 10,000, but it could not survive the Six Acts. Cobbett's *Political Register* acquired mass circulation in November 1816 when he reduced its price to 2d. and denounced Old Corruption—that system whereby the aristocracy levied taxes and lived off the poor. More than any other paper, the *Register* was the voice of popular radicalism, and it linked the press of 1819 with the Unstamped. It died with Cobbett in 1835. Other significant papers of the period included John Wade's *Gorgon*, Carlile's *Republican*, and Davidson's *Medusa* and *Cap of Liberty*. For this journalism, see W. Wickwar, *op. cit.* and E. P. Thompson, *The Making of the English Working Class* (1964), pp. 718–40.

[85] This was Edward Wastneys, a Sheffield man who had been persuaded by Carlile to move to Newcastle in October 1833 to start an agency of the Unstamped. He was soon imprisoned, and his wife took over. She too was imprisoned, and their children were sent to the workhouse. They were released in July 1834, when Lord Denman decided that the *Guardian* was not a newspaper, and that therefore they had committed no offence in selling it.

[86] This was David France, one of Carlile's London shopmen, and brother-in-law of his Bolton agent.

was given that the newspapers might be had there. Two holes were cut in the door, and on the outside it was printed, "Put in your money and say what you want," and the paper asked for was put out through the hole when thus requested. Three or four volunteers were always inside, and so had the authorities broken open the door they could not have sworn which was the person who had sold the paper. The magistrates became convinced that it was impracticable to convict, and ceased to attempt it. I have known £20 taken through these holes on a Saturday evening. Thus the law was at last completely evaded. Public feeling was as one on its injustice and impolicy. Government could not enforce the Act, and would not have been able to get Parliament to give them more power to do so; so in the end they determined to repeal it and to bring in the late Act, which was repealed to pass the present one. That was not done, however, before they had imprisoned men and women in all parts of the country, having had nigh 300 persons incarcerated in London at one time.

The unstamped had freely reported the meetings and discussions of the working men's associations, and thus it might be said they were the means by which the people were admitted to the press, for from that time their influence grew stronger, and their wants and wishes were more and more inquired into by the standard press and by Parliament. They thus became a recognised portion of public opinion. Speakers and writers rose from their ranks, and a gradual change took place in legislation regarding them. Free scope for their industry and facilities for their mental and moral elevation were given; whilst many of the taxes which pressed more hardly upon them were remitted. But this position of things was not attained all at once, and in their struggles, as might have been expected, ignorance and folly often obstructed their progress. The manner in which the old Poor Law was amended gave great and, in many instances, deserved dissatisfaction, and furnished another element of discontent.[87] In its endeavour to remedy the obvious evil of the old law, others as obviously unjust were introduced. Some of its enactments were those of men who knew little of the inner life of the class on which the law was to operate, and they sought to reduce the moral feelings and action of parties widely differing to one uniform state, doing violence to Christian feeling and to common sense. These errors in the Act roused the feelings and the prejudices of the multitude, who overlooked the real improvements in the Act and bitterly opposed it. This was peculiarly the case in withholding out-door relief, and forcing the people into the unions, as

---

[87] Amended in 1834 to ensure that relief was less "eligible" than local wage-rates, and thus that the able-bodied had an incentive to work. However unemployment was endemic both in the trade-cycle North and in the arable South and East. On the new poor law, see D. Fraser (Ed.), *The New Poor Law in the Nineteenth Century* (1976), and in particular N. McCord, "The Poor Law and Philanthropy" therein. See also D. J. Rowe, "Some Aspects of Chartism on Tyneside", *International Review of Social History*, 1971, for Newcastle attitudes to the Act. As Lowery shows, outdoor relief was never abandoned, even in the rural areas, on grounds of cost as well as of humanity.

has been proved by the working of the Act, which is no longer stringently enforced in this matter. It is found more beneficial to ratepayers and people to keep the clause in abeyance, or only enforce it in special cases. In the northern counties this clause was much opposed by the people and the rate-payers. The people were not like those in some mere agricultural places where wages had sunk so low and the selfish masters conceived they had an interest in paying them from the parish funds. Education being higher here, and their wages and social condition better, an honest pride was taken in personal appearance, and they had mostly well furnished dwellings. When a number of sudden deaths among the seamen occurred from a storm, or among the miners from an explosion in the mine, it had been the practice to relieve the widows with families liberally at first, so as to enable them, with some of the club money and the aid of friends, to get into some mode of employment, such as keeping a mangle, a child's school, or a little shop, and then the allowance was reduced or withdrawn. This policy kept the house together, as it was called, gave security to the family tie, and encouraged them to hope for better days, while to withhold relief, except they went into the house,[88] would have broken their spirits, destroyed their family bond, and rendered them incapable of struggling to maintain themselves. So obvious was this that the guardians never carried out the law. I have been, too, in agricultural districts where it appeared that those parishes which relaxed the law and gave out-door relief in deserving cases had lighter rates to pay than others where the law was inflexibly applied. At this time those of us who could address meetings were frequently doing so, for two or three nights every week, and I have frequently, nay in such cases generally, sat and wrought a day's work and then walked four or five miles to a village, and, after having spoken for an hour, walked home again. It never entered into our minds to question the practicability of what we were seeking. We had a perfect assurance that we were right, and that we would soon have everybody of our opinion. Thus the speaking consisted of that kind which is ever the most eloquent and impressive to the feelings of the multitude, where speaker and audience are one in feeling and desire. The speaker only gives vent to the hearers' emotions. His words at once find a response in their wishes. The speech may not be elegant in phraseology nor select in its words, nor com-posed of nicely-balanced sentences, but the souls of all being in accord, the ideas and words flow in one earnest, rapid torrent from the heart of the speaker to the hearts of all. None need convincing, but all pant for action to carry their conviction out.[89] This style of speaking depends thus more on the circumstances of the time than on the speaker, and all great movements have these juvenile periods. I have observed them in the case of the Reform Bill,

---

[88] i.e. workhouse.

[89] Compare Transport House, *Henry Vincent MSS.* 1/1/9: Vincent to Miniken, 18 August 1838, from Manchester: "I cannot describe the way the people flock round me. I can[']t understand how it is, but I play the Devil with them on all sides."

Catholic Emancipation, Chartism and the Temperance movement. Afterwards the speaking may be more critically correct, more elegant in its phraseology, and enlarged in its philosophy—but the first fervour of faith has gone. The movement has not succeeded so rapidly as they expected. The world's ignorance or selfishness retards it. It now commences as a work of education and conversion. Facts and reasons must be given to inform, instruct, and convince mankind. The eloquence of enthusiastic faith which felt that all men would believe it as Gospel when uttered is gone.

The reflecting working-men in London, on reviewing the desultory agitations which had been held on various special subjects, to get Parliament to attend to their wrongs, concluded that it was a waste of time and energy to have to agitate and excite the masses to bear on Parliament, in order to procure a remedy for the political grievances of the unrepresented; they thought it would be wiser to organise to procure the enfranchisement of the working classes, who could then express their opinions and enforce their wants, through their representatives in the House of Commons. It was advised that all other political grievances should be placed in abeyance until they had removed this fundamental one. Their right to vote for the members of Parliament which voted the taxes that they had to pay, and which enacted the laws that they must obey, should be first enforced. On reviewing the condition of the working-classes, of commerce, and of society in general at this time, it is easy to perceive the causes of the Chartist agitation, and to understand the errors that were made in it. They arose very much from the condition of the people, and from the ideas which the middle classes had given them of political rights and of political power. The common doctrine of the middle and upper-class speakers in the meetings for the Reform Bill was, that the people had a legal right to vote in the election of representatives to Parliament; that taxation without representation was tyranny, and ought to be resisted; that the small boroughs, which in the early periods of our history were the seats of our then scanty population, and the proper places to send members to Parliament, had fallen into decay or remained stationary, while the chief population and commerce had sprung up in other towns of the country, which were unjustly deprived of political privileges and taxed without their consent; that this unjust monopoly of the franchise had engendered corruption in the electors of these small boroughs, in the members of Parliament who purchased these boroughs, and in political parties in the state who trafficked in them, and whose power rested on them. And therefore a reform of the electoral system was to be enforced, to procure a retrenchment of taxes, improvement of the laws, and a government which at all times would govern for the interests of the whole people rather than for a class or party.[90] When, as might have been expected, those who had

[90] Lowery analysed the parliamentary reform movement in the language of traditional radicalism: a selfish corrupt Aristocracy—with its placemen, pensioners and rotten boroughs—is being opposed by a disinterested and enlightened People. When parliament

the power in these old boroughs and in the monopoly of the representation resisted this change, associations and unions had been formed, meetings held, and the populace congregated in large masses to demonstrate the numbers who were for the Bill compared to those against it. The right of resistance, even armed resistance, had been more than hinted at.

There was a time when physical force was believed in in England. The Hampdens, the Fairfaxes, and the Cromwells of the army of the Parliament, who fought for the right of the people to vote their own taxes, were praised, and during the Reform Agitation open threats had been made that the payment of taxation would be refused unless the Bill was passed; moreover, if the borough-mongers who governed dared to enforce the levying of these taxes they, the reformers, would resist force by force! They might in many instances never expect that it would ever come to physical resistance, but hoped that the threat of physical force would accomplish their ends without its use. The ignorant, however, do not enter into these subtleties; they take words in their plain meaning, and apply to their own case and circumstances the principles which the other classes of society apply to theirs. Nottingham Castle was burnt down, the Bristol riots occurred;[91] and while the intelligent and virtuous of all classes in the Reform movement deplored these excesses, there were few who doubted that eventually the Reform Bill was extorted from the fears of physical resistance, rather than granted as a political concession to right or justice. It was impossible but that this state of ideas would affect the popular mind. Political power seemed a remedy for all social evils; Acts of Parliament were to do everything; and this idea permeated the people, however they might differ about forms or details. The new press circulated these ideas. The desire for equal political privileges appears to reign in every class. Should they have any fears or doubts regarding the eligibility of others, they rarely have of their own. All seem democrats to those above them, but aristocrats to those below them. Once in a mixed company of tradesmen in Edinburgh the conversation turned on the extent to which the suffrage should go in the Bill, the details of the proposed franchise under it not having then been made public; some were for one rental, some for another; and on inquiry it was found that each one had advocated the enfranchisement of householders whose rental was similar to his own. This aspiration after equal political privileges in the masses is an

---

represents all interests and reduces taxation, harmony and prosperity will result. There is no class language here, and nothing to offend Francis Place or Richard Cobden.

[91] Nottingham Castle belonged to the Lord Lieutenant of the county, the Duke of Newcastle: he was one of the most hated peers in England, and owned several rotten boroughs. It was destroyed in October 1831, when the House of Lords had rejected the second Reform Bill. Sir Charles Wetherell, who had been Wellington's Attorney-General and a diehard opponent of reform, was Recorder of Bristol. He visited the city on 29 October 1831 for the usual gaol delivery. For the next couple of days the mob sacked Mansion House, broke into the city's prisons and burnt the bishop's palace; the officer in charge of the troops refused to fire on the mob, and when about to be courtmartialled, committed suicide.

honest and elevating ambition, and developes and preserves what is good in a people. Though they are liable to err in their modes of attaining it and in its use, it should ever be the duty of a government to encourage this desire, and to point out a way of attaining it, and not to say to the people, "the doors are finally shut, and ye cannot enter." It is in the very nature of the intelligent and virtuous to feel self-respect, and the claims of manhood as man. They can bear poverty and exclusion from the circles of the wealthy. They know they are not equals in wealth, but they cannot bear insult, and to be told that because they are not their equals in wealth they are not capable of being equal in intelligence, integrity, and manhood. Such exclusions ever breed discontent in the excluded, and place the ruling powers in a false position. It is the duty of a government to facilitate all progress in education, self-respect, individual justice, and morality; but as these increase in any population excluded from the franchise, their discontent with that franchise and with the class who maintain it must increase also, so that the only chance of having the people content with this exclusion is to keep them ignorant, and to occupy their attention with other things. Such rule being thus in antagonism with a nation's progress has ever incipient elements of disunion in the growing virtues of its intelligent people. There are materials and tools in its contented ignorance for the promotion of knaves and fools. In the very best states of society which the world has yet seen law is still imperfect, wrongs creep in, organs become diseased if they cannot be sustained by the deportation of effete matter and the assimilation of new. Thus a certain amount of discontent appears to be a necessity in the normal condition of society. There is always some wrong, some sin,—thence some suffering; this suffering is a blessing. Pain could not be felt if life were not still left in the suffering parts. Suffering is the divine voice that bids us to be up and find a remedy. When pain ceases mortification has ensued; so when contentment with wrong ensues the life of a nation has passed away. If we look carefully remedies are to be found for mental, moral, and social evils. It is the boast of our constitutional writers that there is no wrong but the law has provided a remedy. If it is so of man's law, how much more is it of God's, which cannot err. No evil can beset us but He hath provided a way whereby we may escape. Agitation in a right spirit seems to be our normal state. The process of our refining is disturbance—struggles—writhings—heavings, by which the alloy or dross of ignorance and vice is separated from the pure metal. [As the fires of love to God and man wax warmer and hotter, and burn more steadily and intensely in the hearts of the good and wise, the ore of society, in which are commingled the pure metal and impurity, is put in commotion as in the furnace; disturbance, separation, and refining are the result; but when separation is completed all is placid, the refiner's face is reflected back from the metal—the image of Godlike men from the regenerated soul, of Godlike men from purified society; then all is peace—the peace of active harmonies.] How much changed for the better all classes of society are since that period none can feel so well as those who mixed in the active world at that time. However much of evil we have still to deplore, those who have marked well what has passed have hope in the progress of good, and feel the truth that, if they weary not in well-doing, in due season they shall reap, if they faint not.[92]

It is pretty generally admitted that at present there is a much higher sense of class and individual responsibility. There may be less talk perhaps about rights, but there is much more of duties. There is less class antagonism; people of wealth and station are more alive to their responsibilities, and take more interest in aiding improvement, especially in the higher or more wealthy commercial class; then they thought little of those whom they employed, except as mere workers in their establishments. Now they take interest in all their concerns; they look to their dwellings, their pursuits and recreations, to their means of mental, moral, and religious culture; they mix more frequently with them, they feel gratified in having good men in their establishment as well as good workmen. Formerly there was rather a race after gold than after happiness within. They got them houses and lands, gold, and silver, but felt that these could not be preserved except by a good employment of them. While ignorance, vice, and crime, with their attendants, want and suffering, surrounded them, they could have no high enjoyment. Fears of insecurity would trouble them. Experience convinced them, that in widening the sphere of their activities, in using their wealth and position to promote mental and moral improvement, they would find their highest profit and pleasure; better workshops, dwellings, schools, public parks, libraries, peoples' colleges, social jaunts and festivals for the work-people, were promoted by them. By these means the characters and enjoyments of both classes are improved, while mutual confidence and respect are increased. Here and there in the management of companies or large firms there may be some inattention to the social and moral condition of their workmen, but the rule is as I have stated. The evils of the truck system, and the encouragement to drunkenness among the men, generally spring from petty contractors and employers, men who care nothing about anything but the percentage they can gain from those whom they employ. They open shops, contract for a percentage with public-houses, and contrive to send the men there, they give the best part of the work to those who spend the most, and during the slack periods contrive to give the work to the greatest drinkers. They thus surround the workman with temptations that it requires a strong resolution for a steady man to resist; while those who have fallen into habits of intemperance have to exercise much self-denial. Every denomination of religion is more active in its operations to do good since then, and especially the Church of England clergy. The mere fox-hunting, sporting, and jolly living parson who entered the church for the *living* has almost died out, and a new race of earnest men devoted to the duties of their office have sprung up. Twenty years ago when

---

[92] *Galatians*, chapter 6, v. 9.

moving about I found a general disrespect for the parsons, as they were called. The word was used to express contempt and condemnation, as of one who drew the salary and did not fulfil the duties of an office. For though conscious of their own misconduct, bad people will not bear to be reproved for wrong and exhorted to do right by those whom they know to be as bad or worse than themselves. The old parish church, once well situated for the attendance of the people, became inconvenient when public works and their population sprung up further off. The inhabitants increased four-fold, but there was only one church still; hence the dissenting chapel became a necessity, if not a choice. This is altered now. Now the churches are extended, the clergy and the curates generally respected, and active in instructing the poor. In some there may be a contractedness in their views, confining their sympathies to the church as an institution; but even such are earnest and devoted workers. In the parish of Westbromwich, once comparatively rural, now thickly peopled with iron workmen, colliers, and public works, the one church has become three. There is, besides, regular service by two clergymen in two large public works. Each incumbent has a curate, besides scripture readers, and there are night schools where they attend to teach the adults to read and write. Frequent lectures and addresses are given to the working classes by these ministers on subjects interesting to their welfare.[93]

The prominent topics of the new press which had sprung up was class legislation, the unequal pressure of taxation on the working classes, as shown in the taxes on leather, soap, tea, coffee, sugar, and corn.[94] These, with the obstructions they caused to the development of foreign trade, were the constant themes of condemnation. In all the manufacturing districts, with decreasing work and decreasing wages, and the progressing transition from hand labour to production by machines, there was much want bordering on

---

[93] Lowery was a domestic missionary at West Bromwich in 1852: see *British Temperance Advocate*, 1 March 1852, p. 33. In the 1830s the Church of England set itself in order. The ecclesiastical commission, established in 1836, reformed the structure of the Church, reduced pluralism, abolished cathedral sinecures, levelled salaries and created new parishes in heavily-populated manufacturing areas. The Whigs in turn met some of the dissenters' grievances: they commuted tithes into a rent-charge in 1836, and introduced the secular registration of births, deaths and marriages (though church rates were not abolished till 1868). Thirdly, Church laymen and clergy undertook "church extension", the building of new churches with an attached network of welfare agencies—from lying-in clubs to libraries and schools. Bishop Blomfield of London was particularly active here. See O. Chadwick, *The Victorian Church, Part One* (1966), chs. 2 and 5; J. Welch, "Bishop Blomfield and Church Extension", *Journal of Ecclesiastical History*, 1953.

[94] The evidence of R. M. Martin (an authority on the incidence of taxation) to the select committee on handloomweavers in 1834 showed the regressive nature of indirect taxation. Levied especially on food and beer, it fell hardest on working men. His own estimate was that "half of his [i.e. the labourer's] income is abstracted from him by taxation" (*Parliamentary Papers* 1834 (556) X, QQ.3875–7). As half of these taxes (some £27 million out of £50 million) went to service the national debt, the taxation system was not only regressive but redistributed wealth upwards. When Cobbett attacked taxation, he had a stronger case than O'Brien and other socialists allowed him. The Anti-Corn Law League made much of the obstacles which such taxes presented to the development of foreign trade.

positive destitution. The average earnings of the hand-loom weavers of the coarser fabrics proved, on inquiry, to be less than five shillings a-week in many places.[95] Yet, hand-loom weavers in many parts of Lancashire, in the chief parts of Cumberland, and in the west and centre of Scotland, formed a principal part of the population. No wonder that discontent generally prevailed in these districts, and that they were ready to entertain projects which promised them relief. Seeing the unequal pressure of the fiscal system on their class, they sought earnestly for political power for the same purpose as their employers had sought it under the Reform Bill, which they had enabled them to carry. All the indignation expressed by the trading classes at a later period against the injustice and impolicy of the taxes which were repealed under free trade were a confirmation of the justice of the previous discontent of the working classes with this system. The difference of their relative political position was this:—The trading class had first secured the franchise, and had thus some chance of enforcing their demands in the legislature. It was their evident duty to enlighten the ignorant, and to arouse the apathetic of the electors to change the law. The working men, however, had yet to acquire the privileges of electors to enable them to change these laws; and had then little hope that the constituencies would aid them to effect the change; for from ignorance and apathy the trading classes were quite inattentive to these subjects. It is true, when the Working Men's Associations had organised themselves to obtain the suffrage that they might make these changes. The trading classes who had organised to repeal them wished the working classes to unite with them. But the feeling and general answer was "No; we sought you to do this duty to us and yourselves when you did not feel these laws so much an evil on yourselves as we felt they were on us. You then turned a deaf ear to our calls for aid—we lost faith in your sagacity or justice, and have determined first to seek an entrance into the representation, that we may be able to speak and act more efficiently in these matters. We cannot turn back, but will press on for the franchise. Then we shall be more able to aid you in repealing these and all unjust laws!"

As I have stated, William Lovett and his friends had established the Working Men's Association,[96] which spread rapidly over the country. The end was the political enfranchisement of the working classes. The means proposed were Libraries, Reading-rooms, Lectures, Public-meetings, and petitions to Parliament. The policy of the working men and their friends was to

[95] The select committees on handloomweavers (1834–5) showed how handloomweaving had become the first of the sweated trades. Even before the power-loom was introduced after 1820, wages were falling—from 30s. in 1790 to 14s. in 1811 to 8s. in 1820. The trade was destroyed by the influx of cheap labour, often Irish; the introduction of machinery only accelerated the process. Physically scattered, the handloomweavers lacked both the artisans' craft controls over entry into the trade, and the spinners' and clothiers' group solidarity and consequent control over hours and wages. See Duncan Bythell, *The Handloom Weavers* (Cambridge, 1969).

[96] The LWMA was formed in 1836, when old NUWC members came together to press for universal suffrage and newspaper duty repeal; but unlike the NUWC it restricted its

cease to agitate for the removal of any of the minor grievances, and to concentrate their whole energies in organising, agitating, and petitioning for their political franchise; they insisted on their right to vote in the election of members of Parliament, who passed the laws which they had to obey, and who voted the taxes which they had to pay. If the franchise was once attained, they could then enforce the removal of the general grievances, by electing members of Parliament pledged to carry out in the legislature those reforms which they now petitioned for in vain. These convictions led to the organisation for the People's Charter, the history of which need not now be given. It was published by the Working Men's Association on the 8th of May, 1838.

It was printed in a cheap form and circulated by the associations in the country and by the unstamped news-sellers, whose shops then were in their vigour, and who sold four times as many of these newspapers in almost every large town as were sold of the stamped. Discussions and lectures on the Charter were held in the towns and villages, and it was the common theme of conversation in the workshops.

Thus with few exceptions the general intelligence of the non-electors was in favour of the principles, and it would have been as rare to have found any of these against them as it was to find a non-elector amongst the £10 renters opposed to the Reform Bill during the discussions before it became the law of the land. There is something so natural to men to desire to be invested with equal civil rights and privileges with their fellow countrymen, that question who you will, you will scarcely ever find a person who will admit he is unfit to exercise the franchise. It is always others, or some one else, that he thinks unfit.

I had resided in South Shields from 1835 to 1838, when I left the tailor business and was engaged by James Mather, Esq.,[97] wholesale wine and spirit merchant, who added a tea and coffee and West Indian preserves business to the establishment. He engaged me to mind it. I had become acquainted with this gentleman through politics, in which he took a warm interest, being of the Hume radical school. He treated me in every way as a gentleman, and as an equal rather than a servant. He was a man of superior mind and literary and scientific tastes, and had edited an edition of the "English Magna Charta and Bill of Rights," the constitutions of the United States of America

---

membership to "the *intelligent* and *influential* portion of the working classes". Its members quickly became missionaries and built up provincial associations; in this way, the basis for Chartism was created.

[97] James Mather (1799–1873) studied medicine and philosophy at Edinburgh University, and invented the first lifeboat used in the merchant service. He published *The Constitutions of Great Britain, France, and the United States of America* (1834) and visited the U.S.A. in 1838. He chaired the first corn law repeal meeting at South Shields, championed the miners in the North-East, and published a pamphlet on preventing mining accidents. Richard Fynes, *op. cit.*, p. 299 says "few men amongst us have rendered so many public services, or done more to advance the interests of the neighbourhood". See also John Foster, *Class Struggle and the Industrial Revolution* (1974), pp. 122–3.

—and the "Charter" of France established at the Revolution of 1830, to which he had appended the blasphemous Russian Catechism published by the Emperor Nicholas, and ordered to be taught in schools after the Polish insurrection. We opened at nine in the morning and closed at seven in the evening. I assisted in the wine and spirit department when not busy with that of the tea, which was more especially under my charge. Mr. Mather lived at Newcastle, and often invited me to pass the Sunday with him. He had a well selected library, and kindly lent me any of his books I wished. He had studied for the medical profession, and was well acquainted with general chemistry and geology. He was a member of different literary and scientific societies, and a good public speaker. I received much benefit from my intercourse with this gentleman, who had moved in a superior circle, and received a strictly scientific education. My salary was small, but I was happily situated, and whenever I wished to speak at any public meeting in Newcastle or the neighbourhood I had only to state my wishes to get away. During this time I closely read and studied the economical works of Adam Smith, Ricardo, Colonel Torrens, Colonel Thompson, Poulett Thompson, and others of that class.[98] I read a good deal of "Jeremy Bentham,"[99] and was interested in the Malthusian controversy.[100] As I made a mistake during my

[98] Lowery's crash-course in political economy seems to have included Adam Smith's *Wealth of Nations* (1776) and Ricardo's *Principles of Political Economy* (1817), the two classic statements of *laisser faire*. Robert Torrens's *Essay on the Reduction of Wealth* (1821) criticized Malthusian population theories, extended Ricardian notions on the labour theory of value, and with Perronet Thompson [see above, p. 90] developed the under-consumptionist aspect of anti-corn law writings: to abolish the corn tax would release working class purchasing-power for other goods, and thus help curtail depression. Poulett Thomson (brother of Poulett Scrope and in 1834 President of the Board of Trade) argued that government should withdraw from the workings of a free market. Other authors whom Lowery does not mention, but who were widely studied by working men, were J. R. McCulloch, and James and J. S. Mill.

[99] Jeremy Bentham (1748–1832), philosopher and legal reformer, whose *Introduction to Principles of Morals and Legislation* (1780) and *Fragment on Government* (1776) underpinned the group of philosophic radicals (including Joseph Hume, Grote and Warburton, Francis Place and J. S. Mill) prominent in the 1830s and 1840s; the advocates of political economy: and those who, like Edwin Chadwick, promoted governmental and social reform.

[100] Rev. Thomas Malthus (1766–1834) argued in his *Essay on Population* (1798) that without checks such as war, population would outpace food-supply. Catastrophe could be avoided only if the working classes (especially the paupers) limited their numbers. The implications were clear: "the concession of a right of full support to all that might be born . . . and a right of property, are absolutely incompatible and cannot exist together"—*A Summary View* (1830, Mentor edn. 1960), p. 57. Malthus's views were challenged. J. S. Mill, Place and Carlile simply advocated (without themselves practising) birth-control; Cobbett denied that population was rising; Owen argued that full industrialization would release the enormous wealth required to support a growing population; McCulloch and Nassau Senior, speaking for orthodox political economy, argued that the significant relation was that between population and the amount of capital for its employment—not that between population and food supply; and that in any case Malthus's prophecies were relevant only to an island economy, and not to a major trading nation. Nonetheless, Malthus hardened public attitudes to paupers and to casual philanthropy; the new poor law's tone owed much to his pessimism. See K. Smith, *The Malthusian Controversy* (1951); D. V. Glass & D. Eversley (Eds.), *Population in History* (1965), part 2.

stay in South Shields which many in similar circumstances are liable to make, I shall briefly give that passage in my life, that it may be of use to others. I took a small public-house.[101] Some friends thought as I had a general acquaintance and was often invited to a public-house by them they would come to see me in my own, that my wife could manage the business during the day, the profits on which would increase our small income and comforts. Once in, my aversion to it increased every day. This did not arise from my holding Temperance views as to the inherent evils of intoxicating drinks and the drinking customs; for I had not then heard, read, or conversed on the abstinence question. But from my own experience I am convinced that, except in a large inn where he merely superintends the general arrangements, an intelligent high-minded man, sensitive to self-respect, cannot keep a public-house any length of time without losing these qualities day by day— unless becoming more and more dissatisfied and disgusted with his position he soon quits it. Before this I could visit other houses and accept a glass with others, and enjoy the conversation, taking an active part in it, and while they continued to drink, refuse to take any more, yet continue as keenly as they in the conversation or discussions, and that to a late hour. But in my own house I felt my position to be anomalous—my self-respect lowered. I was galled by the idea that they were drinking that I might profit. I became more and more averse to the position every day, and after a very short time could not bear to be in the house, preferring to meet or seek company anywhere else than at home, and I generally kept out in the evenings until it was time for shutting up. The consequence was that the public-house was a losing affair, and I was glad to get rid of it, which I effected at the end of half a year. At this time I delivered my first lecture. The voluntary controversy[102] ran high at that period, and Mr. Mather, as well as myself, were warmly interested in it. I remember well the anxiety I felt on the first night I lectured. The position was a new one to me. Hitherto when speaking it had always been at public meetings along with other speakers, and when I felt short of ideas I could at once wind up and cease. But in delivering a lecture I would be expected to occupy the meeting for a certain length of time; if I ran out of matter or of ideas before that time ended how silly I would look! The consequence was, I prepared too much material, and my chief difficulty was to compress it. This was soon remedied. Afterwards Mr. Mather offered to undertake the risk of the expense of publishing the lecture if I would prepare

[101] Compare the experience with that of James Burn, *The Autobiography of a Beggar Boy* (1978 ed.), p. 145: "I . . . entered upon a new line of life, perhaps the most dangerous of any I had ever been engaged in. I opened a tavern." See also his comments on pp. 50–1 on intemperance. As with Lowery, Burn's innate dislike of the culture of drinking rendered his business unprofitable. We owe this reference to Dr. D. Vincent.

[102] The voluntary controversy concerned the propriety of an established church, with its financial claims on the whole community; its effective monopoly of education; its Tory politics and seats in the House of Lords; and, by implication, its discrimination against dissent. Lowery's pamphlet was *State Churches Destructive of Christianity and Subversive to the Liberties of Man* (1837).

it for the press. If there were any profits derived from the sale, I was to have them. He warned me, however, not to be sanguine, for, as a rule, pamphlets were losing concerns. He generally lost by any he published, and he laughingly told me of a Scottish friend of his who occasionally went to press, who deemed himself fortunate if he had not lost so much as he had done by a former pamphlet. So the sequel proved. The edition was sent to a London publisher at the Royal Exchange, and the expense of advertising was incurred by Mr. Mather, but shortly afterwards the Royal Exchange was burned down and the whole expense of printing also had to be borne by Mr. Mather.

IV
Chartist Delegate:
1838–1839

A change took place in my position in 1838, which, although unforeseen at first, eventually led to my being wholly engaged in public speaking and lecturing. A relative of Mr. Mather's, who had been brought up in the West Indies, had occasion to come and settle in England, and was in want of a situation. Mr. Mather received him, and as the business did not require another, I had to leave. Mr. Mather kindly offered to use his endeavours to procure me one similar to what I had had, and, I dare say, would eventually have done so. I removed to Newcastle, and in the meantime, until something should turn up, was engaged by the proprietor of a newspaper called the *Northern Liberator*[103] to visit the principal places round the district, to establish agencies and promote the circulation. I did this chiefly by addressing meetings on the most interesting topics of the day, and as the Anti-Poor-Law and political agitations were then rising to importance, and the paper had been established to support these views, its circulation rapidly extended. Its editors were Mr. Blackey, Mayor of Morpeth, author of the "History of Moral Science," and afterwards a Professor in one of the Queen's Colleges in Ireland, and Mr. Thos. Doubleday, author of the "Theory of Population," and other works.[104]

At this time the Working Men's Association of London decided to hold a public meeting in London, to petition Parliament for the points of the People's Charter; and they invited the towns in the country to send delegates to this meeting. I was accordingly elected as a delegate from Newcastle. I had no idea whatever of becoming a public labourer, but went up to London, thinking I would be looking about me in the meantime for some private

---

[103] *The Northern Liberator* (1837–40) was begun in Newcastle by Augustus Beaumont (1798–1838), a Byronic and extravagant figure born in New York and orphaned young; he led the physical force wing in Newcastle, and sold the paper to Robert Blakey. Thomas Ainge Devyr became one of the paper's subeditors; see his *Odd Book of the Nineteenth Century* (New York, 1882). Lowery's job was to lecture on radical topics and so help to sell the paper. See W. H. Maehl, "Augustus Harding Beaumont: Anglo-American Radical", *International Review of Social History*, XIV (1969), pp. 237 ff.

[104] Robert Blakey (1795–1878), self-educated mechanic's son and radical hatter, published a *History of Moral Science* (1833) and many other works. He became mayor of Morpeth in 1836 and on 1 January 1838 became proprietor of the *Northern Liberator*; he sold the paper in May 1840. In 1849 he was appointed Professor of Logic and Metaphysics at Queen's College, Belfast. See R. Welford, *Men of Mark*, I (1895), pp. 329–33.

employment. But one circumstance arising after another led to my being completely engaged in public life, and dependent totally on its casualties for my income. Up to this time my labours had been gratuitous. I had often worked until six o'clock, and then walked miles to speak and back again to be ready for my morning's work without receiving any money recompense even for expenses. I now proceeded to London to attend the meeting which was held in Palace-yard, Westminster, on the 17th of September, 1838, called at the request of a numerously signed requisition to the High Bailiff of Westminster, who took the chair. Rooms had been engaged in Brown's Hotel, and hustings were erected in front. The five points of the Charter were passed as resolutions, with one to embody them in a petition to Parliament. Colonel T. P. Thompson, J. T. Leader, M.P. for Westminster, Ebenezer Elliott, the corn law rhymer, William Lovett, Feargus O'Connor, and Abraham Duncan, a working man from Scotland, and others addressed the meeting.[105] Having been appointed as one of the speakers I had then the first opportunity of addressing a metropolitan audience. I remember being forcibly struck with the perfection which the London press had attained in the rapidity with which it published the proceedings. The leading daily press had a number of reporters there, and every arrangement had been made for their convenience. Each took notes for a quarter of an hour or so, and then was relieved by another. The speaking commenced at one o'clock p.m., and continued until near six, and at half-past four o'clock we had copies of the *Sun* on the platform,[106] with a full report of the speeches up to within an hour of that time, with remarks of the editor on the meeting, so that some of the latter speeches made at the meeting consisted of observations on the report of it, and on the remarks made by the editor of the *Sun*. I only stayed a couple of days in London, but in that time I got personally acquainted with William Lovett, in whose house I stayed, whom the more I knew the more I esteemed.

[105] For T. P. Thompson, see above, p. 90. J. T. Leader (1810–1903), radical M.P. for Bridgwater and then Westminster, stood bail for Lovett during the Bull Ring riots prosecution of 1839, and presented Lovett's petition against his prison conditions. Leader was a close friend of J. A. Roebuck, the radical M.P. for Bath. Ebenezer Elliott (1781–1849) was a Sheffield ironworker famous for his verses: a radical who supported the Anti-Corn Law League against Chartism. Feargus O'Connor (1794–1855) was the outstanding Chartist orator. He was radical M.P. for Cork, 1832–5, associated with London working class radicals from 1835, founded the *Northern Star* at Leeds in 1837, and thenceforth dominated northern Chartism. Abram Duncan was a Glasgow wood-turner and spokesman of the Glasgow trade unions in the 1830s. A member of the 1839 and 1842 Conventions, he became a close friend of Lowery, and travelled with him in their lecture-tours through Scotland and Cornwall. Like Lowery, he came to advocate moral force, and rejected O'Connor's leadership. He became a Chartist pastor in Arbroath and an itinerant lecturer on temperance, Chartism and political economy. He later emigrated to the U.S.A.

[106] For the *Sun's* report of Lowery's speech at the Palace Yard meeting, see below, pp. 210–212. It is perhaps a little surprising that, apart from his comments on the reporting of the London press, Lowery does not offer any recollections of his first impression of London. He seems to have been remarkably poised and self-possessed at what must have been an awesome experience.

I returned again by steamboat to Hull, intending to proceed onward by packet to Newcastle. But I there received a notice from our committee that I had been appointed as their delegate to attend a meeting to be held at Hull, when the people of Manchester and neighbourhood were to adopt the charter. I proceeded by packet to Selby—thence by rail to Leeds, and left by mail for Manchester at midnight, arriving there at six in the morning. I found the whole population on the move. After breakfast I went to the committee-room, where I found F. O'Connor and a number of delegates from the different towns in the district, as well as representatives from the local committees. The programme of speakers and resolutions was arranged with a view to adopt the charter and to petition Parliament for it. The meeting was to take place on Kersal Moor, outside the town. Local and district processions soon began to fill the streets and we joined them. Although I had often seen 100,000 at a meeting in Newcastle I never had a clear conception of a multitude until that day. The day was exceedingly fine, and there were processions from Rochdale and Oldham and the chief places for fourteen miles or upwards round about Manchester; I should think there were hundreds of bands of music. I could not conceive where the people came from, for at every open space or corner there would be thousands standing, besides the crowd passing. When we got out of the streets it was an exciting sight to see the processions arriving on the Moor from different places, with their flags flying and the music of the bands swelling in the air, ever and anon over-topped by a loud cheer which ran along the different lines. On ascending the hustings a still more exciting sight awaited us. The *Times* estimated the meeting at about 300,000. One dense mass of faces beaming with earnestness—as far as you could distinguish faces—then beyond still an immense crowd, but with indistinct countenances. There is something in the appearance of such multitudes,—permeated with one thought or feeling, —whom no building made with human hands could hold, met beneath the mighty dome of God's sublime and beautiful creation, and appealing to Him for a cause which they believe to be right and just,—something which, for the moment, seems to realise the truths of the ancient saying—"The voice of the people is as the voice of God." Their deep response to the utterances of great truths coming swelling up from their very heart's depths all indicated an honest, virtuous intention. Your northern, and especially your Lancashire, man, with all his want of polish, has a sterling outspoken candour,—his differences or agreements with you—his "A' will" or "A' wunnd" come direct from the heart. Here I first met the Rev. J. R. Stephens[107] and Richard Oastler,[108] who then were exercising a powerful

[107] Joseph Rayner Stephens (1805–79) son of a methodist minister, ordained methodist minister 1829, suspended for attending disestablishment meetings in Ashton-under-Lyne circuit, and resigned 1834. Powerful orator who agitated for the factory movement and against the new poor law in "physical force" language. Arrested December 1838 for attending an unlawful meeting at Hyde, and sentenced to 18 months' imprisonment. Settled at Ashton 1840, and passed out of national political activity. Place considered that

influence on the working-men in Yorkshire and Lancashire, by opposing the New Poor-law,[109] and seeking an Act of Parliament to regulate the factories. To address the whole assemblage from the hustings was obviously impossible, so Mr. Oastler and others went to the outside and addressed part of it from waggons, so that there were half-a-dozen addresses going on at the same time in different places. Among others whom I heard from the hustings were the Rev. J. Stephens, F. O'Connor, and Dr. Fletcher.[110] Being appointed to express the sentiments of our Newcastle association I had also been placed in the list of speakers. In the committee after the meeting we had an amusing instance of O'Connor's tendency to exaggerate facts. Our different estimates of the number at the meeting were from 300,000 to 500,000, but O'Connor maintained stoutly that there could not be less than 600,000, and he proceeded to demonstrate this by calculations of the acres on which the meeting took place, and the density in which the people stood.[111]

Next day I passed down by rail to Liverpool to attend a demonstration there. Here the population did not appear so imbued with the ideas, and the meeting was not so large as we had expected; but there was a dinner held in the Queen's Theatre, which was densely crowded in every part. Here I first marked the effect of the Rev. J. R. Stephens' speaking on the English people, which was most powerful. His voice was clear and impressive, and his words came home to the thought or feeling he wished to arouse. He did

---

Stephens "professed himself a tory, but acted the part of a democrat". See J. T. Ward, "Revolutionary Tory: The Life of Joseph Rayner Stephens of Ashton-under-Lyne", *Transactions of the Lancashire and Cheshire Antiquarian Society*, LXVIII (1958); T. M. Kemnitz & F. Jacques, "J. R. Stephens and the Chartist Movement", *International Review of Social History*, 1974.

[108] Richard Oastler (1789–1861), Anglican, Tory protectionist, who bitterly opposed the Whig manufacturers and launched the factory movement in 1830. Like Stephens, a "tory democrat" who asserted the rights of "cottage, altar and throne". Steward to Thomas Thornhill at Fixby Hall 1821–38, but was discharged for opposing the poor law commissioners. Imprisoned for debt for 3 years in December 1840. Released February 1844, and agitated for ten-hour day 1844–7. See Cecil Driver, *Tory Radical. The Life of Richard Oastler* (1946).

[109] See Michael E. Rose, "The Anti-Poor Law Agitation", in J. T. Ward (Ed.), *Popular Movements c. 1830–1850* (1970).

[110] Dr. Matthew Fletcher. A Bury medical man who led local opposition to the poor law and thence drifted into the Chartist movement. O'Connor described him in 1839 as "the cleverest man in the Convention". As early as 1839 he was feeling uncomfortable in his new position, and advocated a middle class alliance. There is a memoir in *The Charter*, 31 March 1939. See also Dorothy Thompson (Ed.), *The Early Chartists* (1971), pp. 73–81.

[111] Several Chartists commented on the impressiveness of the larger Chartist public meetings. See, for example, Benjamin Wilson, in D. Vincent (Ed.), *Testaments of Radicalism*, pp. 197–8. Major public meetings—Kersal Moor, Newhall Hill, Palace Yard, Calton Hill—stand out like landmarks in Chartist history. Chartists claimed that 500,000 people attended the Hartshead Moor meeting near Bradford on 18 October 1838, but the unreliability of such estimates has been stressed by R. Currie and R. M. Hartwell, in their "The Making of the English Working Class?", *Economic History Review*, December 1965, p. 635. See also E. P. Thompson's rejoinder in his *The Making of the English Working Class* (2nd edn. 1968), p. 935.

---

not reason on abstract rights or ideal improvements, but dwelt on facts and feelings, on pains and privations. By appealing to men's feeling he endeavoured to seek some redress from the pains and privation which they suffered. He did not talk about political rights or unjust taxes, but about social evils, the wrongs of the factory system, and what he deemed the evils of the New Poor-law. All these subjects came home at once to the wants and to the bosoms of the masses. When virtuous their enjoyments and affections are concentrated in the home circle, and the family relation is strong among them. The routine of their daily enjoyments is circumscribed, and they immediately feel the absence of any portion of them. This Stephens knew, and he at once struck these chords. "This is a knife and fork question," he would exclaim, and he would arraign the unequal taxation pressing on the consumption of the poor, the decrease of their earnings and their over toil, and the destitution too common in their dwellings; contrasting with this the increase of the factories and the fortunes of their proprietors. In his speech at the Queen's Theatre he described how his attention was first drawn to the evils of the factory system when he first settled as a minister of the Gospel in Lancashire. He found that certain members could not attend their class meetings on the week day evenings—that any religious service he might have was attended by few of the factory people of his congregation; the children were more ready to sleep than attend to instruction in the Sabbath-school. He described the mere children carried in their father's arms at five in the morning to the mills—the mothers having to leave their younger children at home to work in these places, and their sucking infants being taken to them at the dinner and breakfast hours. He pointed out the ignorance of the masses, the want of provision for the education of that population, and the impossibility of their benefitting by any such provision if opportunity for so doing was not secured to them by law. Then after painting vividly the unchristian apathy of the proprietors to this state of their workpeople, and the cold selfishness in which they appeared only to look on them, as producing machines—not as men with immortal souls and destined for another world—he exclaimed with a burst of overpowering fervour, "I am no Chartist, that for your five points,"—snapping his fingers—"I am no O'Connor's man,—but while I live and where I live there shall be the law of God and righteousness." Then he painted the struggle as still going on; and spoke of the hopelessness of law seeking to stifle inquiry and to stem the rising intelligence of the inquiring people,—as did the Philistines of old to Sampson—by binding him—and just as Sampson did when they taunted him in triumph and fancied security[112]—so would the people do now, if so fettered and blinded, they would at last, when their oppressors thought themselves safe in their wrong-doing, grasp the pillars of the State and wrench them from their foundations, so that the whole structure

[112] *Judges*, Ch. 16, vv. 5 ff.

would fall and all be buried beneath its ruins." He held the whole audience spell-bound and thrilling, as it were, in actual view of such a scene. Yet his power over the multitude was greater when he preached in the open air, as was his wont. I have read of no such power exercised in this country by open-air preachers since the time of Whitfield,[113] and he had not such vast concourses of people to address. Stephens was a riddle to many a man of a shrewd judgment and talent, yet again and again uttering the most indefensible sayings. This could not be the result of ignorance, yet he might have been assured the authorities would indict him for them. He had far too much penetration not to know that the law could not be overthrown by the mere force of numbers. Few have understood Stephens; I never could until I came into personal contact with him. He cared nothing about the Charter or the Political Right questions. He and Richard Oastler simply went to the Chartist meetings to advocate a Factory Act and a repeal of the New Poor-law. It was mostly in opposition to the latter that he uttered his wildest language, and I believe he so spoke with the hope and expectation that the Government would indict him for seditious opposition to that law. It will be remembered that the ex-Lord Chancellor, the celebrated Lord Eldon,[114] who was deemed the greatest constitutional lawyer by the Tories of his day, resigned his office rather than be one of a ministry to pass the Catholic Emancipation Act.[115] When the New Poor-law Bill was before the Lords he strongly opposed it, declaring it was unconstitutional, and that Parliament would be acting illegally if they passed it. Oastler and Stephens and a large class of Tories wished to be indicted for opposing it, that its legality might be tried before the judges; but the Attorney-General was too wary. Stephens was indicted under a sweeping arrest after some political meeting where he had spoken. The working men laughed at the idea of Stephens being arraigned and condemned with them. Large sums were gathered for his defence fund. He defended himself, trying to bring his real seditions against the Poor-law before the jury, but he was condemned only as taking part in a seditious assembly, and sentenced to two years' imprisonment. When he came out he did not mingle in public with any party again. Richard Oastler was highly esteemed by the factory operatives in Yorkshire and Lancashire.

[113] George Whitfield (1714–70) in 1738 began the course of preaching which, with Wesley, established methodism as a popular movement. Whitfield started open-air preaching near Bristol in 1739, to great effect, but his stern Calvinism provoked a breach with the Wesleys. He founded the Calvinistic Methodist denomination in Britain, and was one of its leaders in Wales.

[114] John Scott, first Earl of Eldon (1751–1838), was called to the bar in 1776. M.P. 1783, solicitor-general 1788, attorney-general 1793, lord chief justice of the common pleas 1799, lord chancellor 1801–6, 1807–27. Towards the end of his career he led the ultra Tories. He was a forceful character of reactionary views, and strongly opposed Catholic emancipation. When Canning became prime minister in 1827, Eldon resigned from the cabinet.

[115] This Act (1829) was a response to the pressure O'Connell applied from Ireland through the Catholic Association. The Wellington administration was forced to enfranchise Catholics who took an oath of loyalty; this enabled them to sit in parliament and hold almost all government posts.

He was then up in years and had laboured incessantly all his life to improve the condition of the factory population, in seeking to restrict the hours of labour, the employment of children below a certain age, and for a limited time each day. He tried to establish arrangements in the mills for the safety of the operatives from the machinery, for their health, and for the preservation of their morals; all of which were sadly neglected at one time by the proprietors of the mills. He had succeeded his father in the stewardship of a large estate in Yorkshire belonging to a wealthy commoner. Thus he was surrounded with all the influence and respect which attaches to a judicious kind landlord interested in the social improvement of the district in which he resides. He was sincerely attached to old Tory ideas of the Constitution, and of the benefits to be derived from the influences of nobility, landed gentry, and the Established Church, when they should fulfil their duties. He considered that the new order of things introduced by the Whigs had set aside these influences in favour of the mere mercantile capitalists who had no fixed and permanent connections with the masses. His desire was to rouse the landed gentry to take an interest in removing the evils of the factory system and the obnoxious clauses of the Poor-law, and to strengthen those bonds which ought to exist between the working men and their employers. The institutions of the country could thus only be safe from the faulty legislation of the Whigs. His countenance beamed with philanthropy, his manners were mild and gentle, his language had none of the violence of Stephens, and altogether he was more like the present Lord Shaftesbury, who very much resembles him in his general tone of mind.

From Liverpool I passed on to Carlisle, being deputed to attend a demonstration there. There was my first acquaintance with the Cumberland people, and I was charmed with their frankness and open-heartedness. O'Connor, Rev. R. Stephens, and A. Duncan,[116] from Scotland, and myself addressed the meeting, which was a very large one, considering the population of the neighbourhood. The chief portion of the working men in Carlisle, and in many of the villages round about, were hand-loom weavers, weaving comparatively common fabrics, in which it was impossible for them to compete with machinery and earn a livelihood. It took husband, wife, and children to work constantly to earn twelve or fourteen shillings a-week when work was plentiful. But too often this was not the case, and, from investigations previously made, it had been found that the average incomes of a very large number of families during twelve months was but from five to eight shillings per week. Hence their fare was deficient, their clothing scanty, and the numbers of wan faces told too plainly of their wants. When conversing on these subjects, many a tale was told of the weakly, ailing husband, wife, and daughter, or son, sinking slowly into a premature grave for want of that nourishment which the sad survivors around were unable to give them.

[116] For Duncan, see above, fn. 105; and below, pp. 213, 223 for reports of Lowery's Carlisle speeches.

Unused to such scenes of general privation, it was peculiarly painful to observe so many of the females who, for want of a sufficiency of blood-forming food, had sunken cheeks and dim eyes, instead of the beaming brightness and ruddy glow which belonged to their ancestors. Is it to be wondered at that a population in such circumstances were ready to hope for the success of any cause which sought to change the state of things under which they suffered so much?[117] I found some very superior men among the weavers. As a whole they were intelligent, fond of reading, and well acquainted with the debated topics of the day, which I afterwards found to be the case generally with hand-loom weavers to a greater extent than with any other class of workmen. This arises from the facilities which their employment gives them for conversation. Yet there was one anomaly in these men which, although it did not strike me then in all its evil aspects, gradually, as I became more and more acquainted with the condition of the working-classes, appeared to me to be *the wrong which perpetuated all other wrongs*—the stumbling-block in the way of all improvement—I mean *their drinking customs*. Low as their wages were, the public-houses were supported by them. The men who rarely saw beef too often got beer. Here, as well as at Newcastle, the public-houses were filled with politicians. Now at this time I had no idea of Temperance as a principle, nor had I considered the drinking customs in reference to work, wages, moral, social, or political improvement. So, while in the well-paid districts of the Tyne and Wear I had merely felt annoyed at the excess, here, where I knew the people were starving, I felt that the drinking of the men was a selfish and unprincipled robbery of their wives and children. Although I have not been in Carlisle for fifteen years, I have often since then been gladdened to hear from time to time of the advance which Temperance has made in the population, as well as of the success of their working-class reading-rooms or true mechanics' institutes. They present a practical model on which all real mechanics' institutes should be fashioned. A beneficial harmony has arisen between the workmen and the gentry from their generous aid to these institutions, and from their desire to improve the condition of the people. The committees and members of mechanics' institutes through the country should read the account given by the Mayor of Carlisle of the success of the working-men's institutions in that city, also the account of Lord Brougham. In almost every place where I have been, in every district the mechanics' institutes are failures. Nay, in most cases what appear as exceptions are still failures. For the members and committee are almost all of the middle classes—shopkeepers, clerks, and such like. Institutions for the working-classes should have weekly as well as quarterly

---

[117] Compare *The Life of Thomas Cooper Written by Himself* (1872), p. 142: "I saw lounging groups of ragged men in my time. I hope what I saw will never be seen again. And I heard words of misery and discontent from the poor that, I hope, are not heard now. I should not like to hear them again, for I know not what they might again impel me to say or do." Compare the comments on poverty in Lowery's Leeds (1841) speech, reprinted below, pp. 253–6.

payments, and always include a reading-room with newspapers and periodicals. They should be left to the management of the working men as far as possible by the upper classes, who should kindly aid with contributions of books and money.[118] The mutual improvement societies begun by the friends of Temperance in many places, combining the library, newspapers, conversations on various interesting subjects, classes, and lectures, are the models of what such institutions should be for working men. But unfortunately too many of the friends of education, from their prejudices against the Temperance movement, keep aloof from these mutual improvement societies. The working classes do not feel at home in institutions where the middle classes are the chief members, contributors, and managers. They feel a restraint, as they would if meeting in the parlours or drawing-rooms of the richer classes. They feel their education has been inferior, that they have less general knowledge, and express themselves imperfectly. While this continues they will even, while seeking to remove these deficiencies, prefer the company of their own class. To enjoy the fellowship of any society, we require to feel on a par with the average of the members. In England the working classes are undoubtedly behind the middle classes in education, reading, and general information. Hence they cannot amalgamate in such societies. In Scotland it is different, for there, as a general rule, I have found the working men fully equal to the middle classes in general reading and information.[119]

Mr. Duncan having to address some meetings in and around Dumfries, I determined to acccmpany him, along with Mr. Arthur, the bookseller of Carlisle. We arranged to take a gig, that Mr. Arthur and I might return next day. We started on a lovely morning, and breakfasted at the far-famed inn of Gretna Green, the high priest of which was, at that time, a friend of Mr. Arthur's; we were favoured with a view of the select apartments for the happy pairs. In the register of the marriages we saw the signatures of many known to fortune and to fame. I enjoyed the ride, and when we arrived found the working-men on the *qui vive*. The grant of the market-place was

[118] Mabel Tylecote, *The Mechanics' Institutes of Lancashire and Yorkshire before 1851* (Manchester 1957), p. 259 says that of 204 institutes in England and Wales in 1849, only 43 were mainly supported by operatives and mechanics. Compare Thomas Kelly, *George Birkbeck. Pioneer of Adult Education* (Liverpool, 1957), pp. 244–5; J. F. C. Harrison, *Learning and Living 1790–1960* (1961), pp. 59–62, 67–9, 129–30. Lowery's speech in *Newcastle Journal*, 15 November 1834, p. 3, takes a different view from the autobiography: "Let our oppressors attend the Mechanics' Institutes and they will find thousands of working men who would put to shame the boasted intelligence of many of our senators."

[119] Compare *The Life of Thomas Cooper by Himself*, p. 326: "I know no people so keenly appreciative of the value of thought as the people of Edinburgh; and I would sooner lecture to an Edinburgh audience than any other audience in the world." For other comments by Lowery on the Scottish intellectual climate, see below, p. 137, 153. See also Alexander Wilson, *The Chartist Movement in Scotland* (Manchester, 1970), and Leslie C. Wright, *Scottish Chartism* (Edinburgh, 1953). A very high proportion of the extant working class autobiographies are Scottish. H. H. Asquith was still praising the intellectual calibre of Scottish audiences in 1920—see his *Letters . . . to a Friend. First Series. 1915–1922* (1933) p. 126.

procured and a meeting at once announced for eight o'clock that night by "tap o' drum". I went to see the tomb of Burns as soon as possible, and in passing to the churchyard was shown the house in which he died; I stood for a few moments reflecting on the scenes of the convulsive struggles and aberrations of that noble nature, whose land was not worthy of him; he was its glory and its shame. From boyhood his poems had been my *pocket-book*,[120] and now that my mind was more expanded by contact with the hard realities of life, and I had felt some of the cares, struggles, and indignities of a poor man's lot, I had read and studied his letters, in which the heights and depths of his noble mind are more fully seen than in his poetry. I could conceive the agonising tortures which his soul must have undergone ere the spirit of hope had fled and he became reckless and insane, as he did before the dark scenes of his latter days closed his struggles. On entering the churchyard, and standing by his tomb, we see him at the plough in his peasant's garb, having lifted his bonnet to the message of Genius who is hovering over him. As I stood by, the sunshine burst through the cloud, its rays falling on the person of the Poet and Genius. This combination of nature and art gave a peculiar beauty to the statuary, which does honour to the heart and genius of those who erected it. Oh! had Burns but lived in this day, when genius and literature are more independent and can appeal to the public for patronage and reward instead of to the rich or titled few, how different might have been his history! In these days of comparative Temperance, when intellectual sociality can meet apart from the fumes of the tavern, how different might have been his career! Who can read his heart in his works and catch the warm glow of his brotherhood with man "the world o'er" and doubt but he would have been of the noble band of Temperance reformers? Reformers who seek to destroy drinking customs that have blighted the lives of men of genius, talent, and industry. How he would have sung the beauties, virtues, and social delights of Temperance, ridiculing with his wit the insane follies and false estimates of life and happiness propagated by the drinking customs; stinging with his sarcasms or crushing with his withering scorn the ignorance or knavery which defend them! It being then dark at eight P.M., the meeting was held by torch-light. This practice became common, as the committees could not always get halls, and a larger crowd too could hear when the meeting was in the open air, besides saving expense. The meeting was large, and I at once saw the superiority of a Scotch audience of working men over those of the south of England; for they are proud of their national poetry, can

[120] Burns was a strong influence on many early nineteenth-century radicals and Chartists. Compare Samuel Bamford, *Early Days* (Ed. W. H. Chaloner, 1967), p. 289 on his first reading Burns's life and writings: "did I not sit down, beside my quiet desk, under the sky-light, and read, or rather compress to my very soul, every word of that precious book." See also *The Life of Thomas Cooper by Himself*, p. 42; Y. V. Kovalev, *An Anthology of Chartist Literature* (Moscow, 1956), pp. 298–9, 305–6; and Lowery's comments below, pp. 136, 229. Alexander Somerville's *The Autobiography of A Working Man* (1951 ed.) describes the impact of Burns's personality and poetry on him at pp. 42–3.

read their national history, and you could quote or appeal to any of these and they understood—not so the English working-men. Stopping but a night in Dumfries, we returned to Carlisle; I then proceeded to Newcastle, where I was engaged addressing meetings almost every night round the district. The injustice of the bread tax, as well as the duties on tea and sugar, and coffee, and soap, and other articles necessary for the people, and the extravagance of the pension list, furnished the general themes as inducements to seek the Charter.[121] The past unavailing labours of the Radicals in the district and elsewhere were held as proof that until the suffering masses attained the right to vote, which the Charter would confer, these taxes could not be repealed. Wherever you went, however remote the place from general intercourse, these opinions had spread amongst the more reading and reflecting, who formed a nucleus ready to arrange for public meetings which at once responded to and adopted the sentiments expressed. I was sent on a tour up through Hexham, thence across the moors into the dales bordering on Durham, Westmoreland, and Cumberland amongst the lead miners. It was a wild hilly moorland district, yet I was astonished at the number of people who gathered at the meetings. The distance which many of them came, and their earnest attention, showed a great interest in the cause. I was also much delighted at the intelligence of those with whom I conversed in that district.

It was now determined that instead of local petitions for the Charter there should be one general or national petition—each district to gather and send in signatures to it, and that as many districts as could should, after due notice, elect a representative, or representatives, to a national convention to meet in London on the day on which the Government might announce the assembling of Parliament for 1839. That the duty of this convention should be to present this petition to the House of Commons and urge its support on the members of that House. Every district was expected to contribute to a fund for the general expenses of the convention, and those places that elected delegates were left to make what personal arrangements both parties might agree to. Collectors and treasurers were at once appointed for the national rent fund, as well as for the delegate fund, to which the working classes and many of the shopkeepers freely contributed.

During the autumn of 1838 a public meeting was held in the open air to elect the delegates for the Newcastle district.[122] The different associations of the district had been consulted as to the number of members to be elected, and the persons whom they would put in nomination. The choice fell on Dr. John Taylor, of Ayrshire, in Scotland, and Julian Harney, of London, along with myself. When the meeting assembled, which was numerously attended,

---

[121] For an excellent account of taxation policy at this time, see Lucy Brown, *The Board of Trade and the Free-Trade Movement 1830–42* (Oxford, 1958). Here, as on p. 198, Lowery's theme is that the Charter will remedy unfair taxation and high pensions. There is no hint of a more socialist critique.

[122] Lowery is incorrect here. He was in fact elected as delegate for Newcastle on Christmas Day 1838; *Northern Liberator*, 29 December 1838.

we were elected unanimously. I had only seen Dr. Taylor once, when he spoke at a meeting in Newcastle, some time before, in aid of the committee of the Glasgow cotton-spinners, whose trial was then about to be held in Glasgow. I was then struck with the extreme eccentricity of dress of Dr. Taylor, yet charmed with his style of speaking, which was exceedingly attractive. But when I afterwards heard him oftener, and knew more of his personal history, I had no confidence in him, and deemed him one of the most dangerous characters in the movement. He was then dressed in a green hunting-coat, white breeches, top-boots, broad-brim, and had on a red flannel shirt with open neck—man-of-war's-man fashion. He stood middle size, had a dark complexion, piercing black eyes and large whiskers, with hair of the same colour flowing down to his shoulders. The Tory newspaper styled him an Indian chief. His father had been a Scotch gentleman of property, and his mother was an East Indian; they had left him a handsome fortune, but he had squandered it in gambling and dissipation. For some years before he had been living on friends; he had outlived all sense of shame and honesty, and would without hesitation make use of any money he could get into his possession, and laugh the parties in the face, telling them he had been obliged to use it, but he was to receive such and such sums by-and-bye, when he would be able to accommodate them. These characteristics were only known then to the leading Radicals in Glasgow and the west of Scotland, and as he was a prominent writer in the *Glasgow Liberator* they had hesitated to expose him, although often suffering from him. He had received a classical education, and I have rarely heard his equal at a speech after a soiree or dinner in a hall, there was such a happy blending of historical and classical allusions, polite literature and poetical sentiment. Vanity was his ruling passion. He had no principles, and having nothing to lose was prepared to pander to the passion of the hour without heeding the future; yet, as in all such characters, there were some good traits. He would share his last sixpence with anyone, and freely offer the loan of any he had at the time to those whom he knew to have none; so that often of that which he defrauded others he would give the greater part away.[123] Julian Harney was a native of London, and then

[123] See Alexander Wilson, "John Taylor, Esq. M.D. of Blackhouse, Ayrshire (1805–42)", *Ayrshire Archaeological and Natural History Society Collections*, 1947–9 (2nd. Ser. Vol. 1). As a young man, Taylor spent several years in France, and also helped the Greeks against the Turks. In the 1830s, he became a newspaper owner and editor of the *New Liberator*, championing the Glasgow cotton spinners. Bankrupted by a libel action, and imprisoned for challenging his creditor to a duel, he became a prominent physical force Chartist and attacked the national convention in 1839 for being timid in launching the sacred month. He was arrested for sedition on 23 November 1839, but the case was abandoned. By this time, he was suffering from bad health, and took to studying theology before he died in 1842. Gammage's overall judgement of Taylor is more favourable than Lowery's: Taylor was, he says, "without a doubt, one of the most frank, honest, fearless, single-minded, and disinterested Democrats of that day"—see his *History of the Chartist Movement 1837–1854* (1969 Cass ed.), p. 29. See also below, pp. 142, 155. However, Burn, who knew Taylor in 1837, confirms Lowery's estimate of him (*Autobiography*, 1978 ed., p. 146), and see Burn's comment in *Newcastle Weekly Chronicle*, 20 October 1883.

about twenty-two years of age. He had been born in poor circumstances, and received no education in childhood. While a pot-boy he had discovered a taste for reading—and had written some articles for the unstamped press. He was a fluent speaker. He had evidently read with avidity the History of the French Revolution, and was smitten with admiration for the social theories and sentiments of Robespiere and St. Just, and that portion of the French revolutionists.[124]

Parliament had been summoned to assemble on Monday, the 4th of February, 1839, and the Convention had to meet in London on the same day. I left Newcastle-on-Tyne by coach on the Saturday at noon, and it did not arrive at Fetter-lane, Fleet-street, in London, until after twelve on the Sunday night. To solace the grumblers at the slowness and dearness of railways, I may mention that I paid £2. 10s. for my outside seat. The snow covered the ground, and at night when we got to York it came on to rain. I then paid fifteen shillings more to get inside to Grantham, where we were to breakfast next morning. We changed coachmen every forty mile or so, and changed guards at York. I gave him five shillings when we reached London, and he said I was no gentleman to offer him so little. Thus I paid £3. 5s. fare, and thirteen shillings fees, and was thirty-six hours on the road. Now you may leave Newcastle by parliamentary train at five a.m. and be in London by seven p.m. for twenty-five shillings, and no fees.

The General Convention of the Industrious Classes met at the British Coffee House, Cockspur-street, Charing-cross on Monday morning, at 10 a.m., 4th February, 1839.

Mr. William Lovett was unanimously chosen to be secretary.[125] The members then handed in their credentials of election, and it was found that there were 53 present. Several others arrived during the week. Several changes occurred during the period of the continuance of the convention, some leaving, and others being sent by new districts, but from fifty to sixty would be the average attendance. About an hour after we met her Majesty was proceeding through the Park to open Parliament. The British Coffee House being close by, those of us who had never seen her Majesty made a general rush to see her and the procession. Some of the gentlemen in waiting would have been astounded at the free criticisms and remarks made upon the beef-eaters and paraphenalia of the procession.

---

[124] For Harney, see A. R. Schoyen, *The Chartist Challenge* (1958). Lowery might have stressed the similarity between the childhood of Harney and of himself, for both acquired the taste for reading while suffering from a long illness. When discussing Harney's revolutionary views, Lowery might have mentioned James Bronterre O'Brien, whom Schoyen (p. 12) describes as "the strongest single intellectual influence of his [Harney's] formative years", and for whom he worked on the *Poor Man's Guardian*.

[125] Lowery is wrong here. O'Brien objected to Lovett's appointment because he was "not in agreement with the men of the North as to the methods by which the Charter was to be obtained"—see Mark Hovell, *The Chartist Movement* (Ed. T. F. Tout, Manchester, 1918), p. 123.

General rules for the order of debate on any question or subject which might come before us were agreed to; a committee for the management of finance, and another for the arrangement of preliminary business, were chosen. It was announced that the sum subscribed for the National Rent was upwards of £1,900.

As the rent of our place of meeting in the British Coffee House was £10 a day, it was soon agreed that we would remove to the large room at the Dr. Johnson's Tavern, Bolt-court, Fleet-street, which was equally eligible and very much cheaper. So we continued to meet there from 10 a.m. until 1, and from 2 until 4 p.m. every week day except Saturday. Each of us waited on the members for his own districts, and a number were appointed to wait on the members of the House generally. We also engaged a person as a messenger for 30s. a week, who had often been in London in connection with the Factory question, and was well known to all the Liberal and to many Tory members. He was sent every day to the clubs to solicit postage franks, and I dare say on an average got as many as saved us, in those days of the old postage, 20s. a day.

I shall give here, as briefly as I can, a sketch of the materials which composed the convention and the sentiments of the leading men in the provinces. From this will be perceived the causes of our eventual disunion, follies, and failures. The factory districts of Yorkshire and Lancashire were the centres of an exciting organisation, animated by bitter hostility to the factory masters, who were mostly Whigs, and advocated the new Poor Law.[126] Trade being very bad their wages were at starvation point. The language was often unguarded and violent when maddened by a sense of their own sufferings, for too many of their local speakers spoke their own feelings and did not merely describe the experience of others. One delegate,[127] a hand-loom weaver, described to me his privations for want of food, and how his starving wife, unable to supply nature's nutriment to her sucking babe, the infant had frequently drawn blood from her breasts instead. Was it to be wondered at that these men with the history of the Magna Charter, of the Commonwealth, of the revolution of 1688, and the threats of the Whigs during the Reform Bill agitation, all within their knowledge, should not hesitate to declare they would meet force with force if they were stopped in seeking a redress for their grievances? They knew that their want of work was to be chiefly attributed to the corn monopoly, and to other unjust taxes and fiscal arrangements. If afterwards the middle and upper commercial classes, surrounded by comforts, however, smarting under monetary losses from these Corn Laws, often lost their temper and command of language, when urging

---

[126] Yet see Lowery's earlier comments on the new poor law, implying that the masters were hostile to it—mainly on grounds of cost, p. 96.

[127] This was Richard Marsden. See his vivid description of poverty in Dorothy Thompson, *Early Chartists*, pp. 182–3. Marsden was a poor handloomweaver, elected as delegate for Preston to the 1839 Chartist convention, and an enthusiast for the general strike.

their repeal, what allowance should not be made for the operatives who knew they lacked food because of these laws? From the first, as a body, they had seen their injustice and asked even their employers in vain for many long years to help them in seeking for these reforms. No wonder that these people were ready to listen to any advice which promised redress, whatever personal risks they might chance to encounter. Imagine such people listening to Stephens, or to one of their own fellow-workmen, preaching from a, then, often used text, "They that be slain with the sword are better than they that be slain with hunger," (Sam. iv. 9) and you may have a conception of the state of that population. There is something in the effects of hunger and of the sight of your family suffering from it which none can judge of but those who have felt it. The equilibrium of temper and judgment is deranged as your child looks up with piteous face and tearful eye, asking with suppressed voice for the bread it knows you have not. I have heard my own child so ask for the bread I had not to give, and my prayer is, God help the man so tried.[128] Were it pestilence or famine, plainly sent by our Heavenly Parent, faith in His wisdom and goodness might be summoned up to bear the chastisement, under the conviction that, however hard, it must be for good in the end, and that behind the dark cloud of the hour his sun still shines, and will at length burst through and gild with light and joy what, for the present, is all darkness and distress. But when you know it is man-made scarcity, and therefore to remove it is manhood's duty, then to rest idle contented under it becomes a sin. You turn with disgust from a system of which the Word of God says, "He that withholdeth corn, the people shall curse him," Prov. xi. 26. At Newcastle-on-Tyne wages were better though work was often scarce, and the feeling was general that the Whigs and middle-classes had cheated them in not using their votes under the reform constituency to enfranchise them.[129] The upper classes were wofully wrong, and are yet so, in thinking that it was only the ignorant, idle, and vile among the masses who embarked in that movement. As a rule, it was the more intelligent and thinking portion of them; admitting that here and there might be a clever unprincipled demagogue, the majority could have no interest in cheating themselves, in giving time, labour, and money for what they did not care about—for all

[128] Compare Lowery's earlier remarks on poverty, p. 63, and Charles Kingsley, *Alton Locke* (Everyman edn. 1970), p. 193: "and here let me ask you, gentle reader, who are just now considering me ungentle, virulent, and noisy, did you ever, for one day in your whole life, literally, involuntarily, and in spite of all your endeavours, longings, and hungerings, *not get enough to eat?* If you ever have, it must have taught you several things." Chartists on trial very often attributed their desperation to acute distress: see the speeches of George Lloyd in April 1840 and Richard Pilling at the Lancaster trials of 1843, quo. in P. Hollis (Ed.), *Class and Conflict* (1973), pp. 240-2, 293-8. Bezer's *Autobiography of a Chartist Rebel* after a savage portrayal of bread-and-cheese-philanthropy, concludes that "politics, my Lord, was with me just then, a bread-and-cheese-question" (D. Vincent, Ed., *Testaments of Radicalism*, p. 187).

[129] Contrast D. J. Rowe, "Some Aspects of Chartism on Tyneside", *loc. cit.*, p. 22, where he comments on "one of the lasting features of Chartism in the region, the links between people we would place in the middle and working classes"; see also *ibid.*, p. 38.

the local labour and agitation was done gratuitously, unless a person was sent on any special service, and this very seldom happened, until the convention met. Each delegate was only one among myriads, and in many instances was chosen from the class of tradesmen and others in better circumstances. The working-men, therefore, who organised and sustained the movement might have been in error on some points, and incapable of guiding the whirlwind which was eventually raised, but they honestly deemed their object true and just. The whole mass being once enlisted, they had the ignorance and vice of that multitude on their hands. When their ignorance and passions broke out, what had been intended as mere words to frighten the more prudent became the realities of violence. The intelligence and virtue which had created the movement, and could alone eventually sustain it, gradually withdrew from it until it died, as it were, through exhaustion for want of healthy blood.

The people in Newcastle generally considered it justifiable to meet force with force if stopped in seeking what they deemed their constitutional rights. At this time that spirit became particularly strong from the great popularity of Augustus Beaumont, of whom it is necessary to give some account here. He had been in the district only a few months, but in that time he had imbued the masses and many of the shopkeepers with his spirit. He was one of those men who, from education, talent, temperament, and social status, possess uncommon powers for good or evil, calculated to inspire a multitude with admiration for him as a man, and with confidence in his courage and ability to head any dangerous enterprise. He was full of enthusiasm, which justified to itself the use of armed resistance. The danger of this doctrine lies in its almost inevitable tendency in the multitude to justify attack as well as resistance. He had spent some years in Jamaica, conducting a newspaper. He had some property and had been a member of the legislature in that island; through his attacks on the Pro-Slavery and Monopoly parties he had been engaged in frequent duels, in one of which he had shot his opponent. He had left Jamaica, come to England, and with his brother, a Dr. Beaumont, had entered warmly into the struggles of the Parisian Press with the edicts of Charles X. He fought along with the people in Paris during the celebrated three days of the Revolution of July, 1830. Afterwards he was engaged in the revolution of Belgium, for which he had been presented by the inhabitants of Brussels with a sword.[130] There being a general election he had been

---

[130] Charles X's three ordinances dissolved the Chamber, virtually abolished freedom of the press, and reduced the size of the electorate. Three days' fighting, on 27–29 July 1830, forced Charles X to abdicate and Louis Philippe replaced him. The revolution in France sparked off a revolution in Belgium against the rule of King William I of the Netherlands. The leading part in the Belgian revolt was taken by Brussels, aided by volunteers from elsewhere. The revolutionary government on 4 October proclaimed Belgian national independence, and on 20 December a conference of ambassadors in London announced the dissolution of the unitary kingdom of the Netherlands. On 20 January 1831 the conference decided that Belgium should be an independent and perpetually neutral state, under the guarantee of the powers.

invited at the eleventh hour to come and stand as candidate for Newcastle, on the Radical and Chartist principles. He polled some 1,000 votes, and was immensely popular: he established the *Liberator* newspaper there. Thus it will be seen that he had all the qualities which fit a man for armed resistance. I often reflected afterwards what a blessing it was that death removed him before the convention met, and the excesses of ignorance and violence developed themselves; for had he been alive undoubtedly there would have been an insurrection in the Newcastle district, and it would not have been a Newport affair if he had led it. No, the constituted authorities would have prevailed; many lives would have been sacrificed before it was accomplished. A short time before this, during the heat of the excitement on the Canadian revolt,[131] he had expressed himself warmly on the subject, and justified their revolt, and declared his intention, as soon as he could arrange his affairs, if their wrongs were not redressed, to go out and tender them his sword. Such, too, was the enthusiasm that a large number of working men sent in their names to him expressing their desire to volunteer and go out to Canada with him. He passed down to Glasgow with Feargus O'Connor and Stephens to attend a meeting about the trial of the Cotton Spinners,[132] and the last time I saw him was on his returning south to attend a large meeting at Leeds. We walked the flags during the short time the mail stopped, and I then found his keen perception of men had at once read the character of O'Connor in their short intercourse. "O'Connor is not to be trusted," said he; "he's a coward, and if ever we should have to fight he is not to be depended on. I am convinced he is a coward, and ought not to be trusted." I knew little of O'Connor then, but often thought of these words when after events showed their truth. Beaumont passed on to the Leeds meeting, spoke at it, and was seized with a brain fever and died in two or three days.[133] Such was the Newcastle district.

Politically, Feargus O'Connor was the popular man in Yorkshire and Lancashire, and in every district he was beginning to attract the admiration

[131] The Canadian revolt in 1837 originated in French-Canadian colonists' distaste for British rule in Lower Canada, and in the distaste felt by all Canadian colonists at their lack of direct control over taxation. The revolt was easily suppressed, but it caused the Whig government to send out the radical Lord Durham as high commissioner. His report (published in 1839) laid down the new pattern of British government in Canada: it proposed to solve the French problem by amalgamating Upper and Lower Canada, which would put the French colonists in a minority: and to solve the taxation problem by ensuring that the executive in Canada was responsible to the representatives of the Canadian people. See also Michael Brook, "Lawrence Pitkeithly, Dr. Smyles and Canadian revolutionaries in the United States, 1842" *Ontario History*, LVII (1965).

[132] Lowery refers to the trial in 1838 of the five Glasgow cotton-spinners for conspiracy, violent intimidation, and murder of their fellow workers. The result was a select committee on trade unionism in 1838. Radical working-class opinion supported the trade unionists, and their sentence of 7 years' transportation became as notorious as the sentence passed on the Dorchester labourers 4 years before.

[133] For Beaumont, see above, p. 107. Lowery fails to emphasise that Beaumont had at first *defended* the planters' interests and turned against them only later. Beaumont won only 290 votes in 1837, but Professor N. McCord suggests that Lowery may have confused the 1837 result with the 1,092 votes Charles Attwood won in 1832.

of the unthinking crowd, while the far-seeing few already perceived the deficiencies of his character, and the evil results that his language would eventually lead to. He had never mixed with the English working men until after Lovett and the associations had established an agitation based on intellectual and moral means. Having lost his seat for Cork and quarrelled with Daniel O'Connell,[134] he left the Irish agitation and appeared at the meetings of the English Radicals. He went down into the factory districts, and speaking to please he soon became popular. J. Hobson,[135] Mr. Hill,[136] and others in Yorkshire, seeing the want of a newspaper as an organ for the rising movement, had succeeded in raising some few hundreds of pounds by shares to establish one. O'Connor persuaded them that they would not be able to get the necessary amount, and that the mixed authority of a committee would hamper the editor, and render the paper inefficient. He proposed that the shareholders should lend him the money already raised, for which he would guarantee interest, and that he would find the rest of the capital and commence the paper at once, that Hobson should be publisher and Hill editor. This was done. It was entitled the *Northern Star*. But there is every reason to believe that at that time he had no capital, and that the money of the shareholders was the only money ever invested in the paper. Fortunately for him it soon rose to a very large circulation, reaching at last to some 60,000 a-week, and when, during Frost's trial,[137] he gave one week's profits to the defence fund he handed over £200 as that week's profit. Thus the *Star* at once gave him and his party a general influence, while the sayings and doings of his special favourites were regularly reported and eulogised. Feargus O'Connor was a strange compound, and at first sight was very attractive. He was tall, well made, of sanguine complexion, had a fluency of language and a good voice, a ready Irish wit and oratorical flourish. Being a

[134] Daniel O'Connell (1775–1847), Irish lawyer and organizer of the successful Catholic Association founded in 1823 to secure Catholic emancipation. His policy after 1835 of collaborating with the Whigs was extremely unpopular with the Chartists, and Feargus O'Connor (who entered parliament as one of his followers) favoured a more aggressive campaign for repealing the Union, and soon broke with him. It was O'Connell who persuaded the Whigs to set up the inquiry into trade unions (1838), and this worsened his relations with working class radicals.

[135] Joshua Hobson, self-educated handloomweaver, was born in 1810. He was prominent in the factory hours movement, produced much of its literature, and later became editor of the *Huddersfield Chronicle* and then *Huddersfield Weekly News*. He was publisher and printer of Owen's *New Moral World* (1839–41), and published the *Northern Star* 1837–44. He was twice imprisoned for circulating unstamped periodicals. See Asa Briggs (Ed.), *Chartist Studies* (1959), p. 90.

[136] William Hill was the son of a Barnsley handloomweaver. He became a lecturer on phrenology, and in the mid-1830s settled at Hull as Swedenborgian minister of a New Jerusalem Church. He edited the *Northern Star* 1837–43, but was dismissed by O'Connor in 1843 and died in 1867. Lowery's account of the origins of the *Northern Star* is broadly correct: see E. Glasgow, "The Establishment of the *Northern Star* Newspaper", *History*, 1954. This is the passage quoted (somewhat inaccurately) in William Lovett, *Life and Struggles*, p. 173; see above, p. 1.

[137] For John Frost, see below, p. 137.

barrister, he was an adept at special pleading, and had much tact to please those whom he wanted. He was no reasoner, saw no deeper than the surface of things, and looked no farther than the next moment for the effects of a present action. Thus he was totally unfit to lead a great movement. Had he possessed a better balanced character, and wrought in conjunction with others of superior judgment, he would have been in his right position—for his physical strength and extraordinary activity and style of address would have left him with few superiors to work out plans first arranged by more philosophical heads. But his vanity and self-esteem were diseased, and upset all the rest of his powers. His heaven was in the applause of a crowded meeting. He would endure any fatigue and sacrifice everything else to attain this. No adulation could be too gross for him, and strange as it may appear, he must have intellectually thought little of many whose flattery he courted. So much was this the case that I have often wondered whether he was a fool or a knave. I have often been asked, "did I think he was honest"; my answer is, in one sense yes—in another, no. He was honest in his desire to attain the Charter, but his self-esteem would at once induce him to oppose and render nugatory any means which he had not originated or did not manage. In his bombast and exaggeration he led himself at last to believe his own imaginings. He blarneyed and flattered the multitude for their hurrahs. Of two reports of a meeting sent from the same place, that which was most thickly interlarded with (cheers for O'Connor) was sure to be inserted, however false or gross in other respects. He did not want earnest superior men in the movement. He did not labour for the future, but for present excitement. If he could not get these superior men to be his flatterers, he at once set to work to denounce them and drive them from the movement. This he would not boldly do at first himself, but by his ignorant rabid tools; and when these men, conscious that he was the moving-spring of these attacks, accused him, he would hypocritically complain of these accusations, and accuse them of being the tools of the Whigs and middle classes. He called on the working men for their sympathy and support. Secure in the admiration and confidence of his worshippers, he did not care for being seen through by the intelligent. While they were around him, he would boldly proceed with his exaggeration and flattery up to the point that only the fanatically ignorant could not see through. He never placed confidence in his dupes, and evidently had no faith in virtue and integrity. I could never find that he had spoken in confidence with any of his friends about any plans; all was indefinite. He cared not so long as there were crowds, demonstrations, and plaudits for him, whether they were met to petition for the Charter, or for the lives of Frost, Williams, and Jones to be spared.[138]

[138] The trial of Frost, Williams and Jones for their part in the Newport rising of 1839 is discussed in Mark Hovell, *Chartist Movement*, p. 186; see also below, pp. 155–9. Lowery resembles Gammage on O'Connor: "noise was O'Connor's proper element; even in disapprobation it was sweeter to him than the calmness of indifference". This view

The leading men of the Birmingham district had been active in the political union with T. Attwood during the passing of the Reform Bill.[139] They retained all the boldness of that union, but cautiously confined their language to constitutional expressions, and perceived that O'Connor and Stephens would lead the body into the meshes of the law if not checked. Mr. Salt, a leading manufacturer, Mr. Douglas, then editor of the *Birmingham Journal*, Mr. G. Edmonds,[140] who afterwards became town clerk, and John Collins,[141] were the leading men and delegates from there. Scotland, with its native shrewdness and sagacity, saw the necessity of struggling under the protection of constitutional forms, and remembered the spy system and Richmond's victims in the Tory reign of terror;[142] yet at first there was division, not so much on their fundamental ideas regarding the necessity of being cautious,

---

(Gammage, *History*, p. 64) was accepted by Mark Hovell, and has now become the orthodoxy. But compare John Saville in *Bulletin of the Society for the Study of Labour History*, No. 20 (Spring, 1970), p. 16; in the secondary literature on Chartism "nowhere is there a serious assessment of Feargus O'Connor as a political leader". See also below, p. 157.

[139] Thomas Attwood (1783–1856), Birmingham banker, organizer of the Birmingham Political Union founded in 1830, and active in promoting parliamentary reform. He revived the Union in 1837 in the belief that currency reform (stimulating mild inflation) was the cure for poverty, and on 19 December declared for universal suffrage. Collaboration between radicals in Birmingham and Scotland helped launch the Chartist movement. But the BPU's moderate tactics, its mood of class collaboration, and its currency theories eventually prevented it from retaining control over the Chartist movement.

[140] Salt, Edmonds and Douglas shared a common admiration for Thomas Attwood, and (by October 1838) a common suspicion that O'Connor was fomenting violence. All three attended the 1839 Chartist convention as delegates for Birmingham, and all three left, with other middle class moderates, when more militant Chartists took control. Salt was a lamp manufacturer who employed a hundred men, and was influential with local working men. R. K. Douglas was a Scotsman who edited the *Birmingham Journal* and at first chaired the Chartist convention. George Edmonds (1788–1868) was prominent in the history of early nineteenth-century Birmingham radicalism. He had been imprisoned in 1820–1 for conspiring to elect an M.P. for Birmingham. He campaigned for the town's incorporation, and became town clerk in May 1839.

[141] John Collins was a Birmingham shoemaker and member of the BPU. His covenanting style of oratory made him a key figure in linking up the revived Union with Scottish radicalism in 1838. He continued to attend the convention after the leading Union members had withdrawn in February 1839. He always opposed violent tactics, and favoured co-operation with the middle class, He was arrested with Lovett in 1839 for publishing a seditious libel; they then jointly published *Chartism* (1840) while in prison. According to Burn (*Autobiography*, p. 152) he was "a decided loser, both in a pecuniary point of view, and in his domestic comforts. After John had retired into private life, and was succeeding to make a comfortable living for his family, some of his foolish friends carried him into the Birmingham town council, where he had not been long until he became divested of his reason". Collins came under the influence of the Christian Chartist Arthur O'Neill, and died *c*. 1850.

[142] Alexander B. Richmond, supposed *agent provocateur*, was a weaver who championed the Scottish weavers' campaign for fair wages in 1812. He was outlawed, gave himself up, and was imprisoned for a month. He became involved with Kirkman Finlay, M.P. for the Glasgow district of burghs, and provided him with information which led to the arrest of several weavers in 1816. Richmond failed to secure a conviction for libel against a writer who had accused him of instigating the plots which he revealed. See William Ferguson, *Scotland, 1689—the Present* (Edinburgh, 1968), pp. 273–4, 278–9. See also below, p. 174.

but as to the expression of this necessity in a formal manner to the O'Connor party, lest it might sow division and bring the authorities upon them. But the Rev. Patrick Brewster, a minister of the Established Church in Paisley,[143] and John Frazer,[144] proprietor and editor of the *True Scotsman* newspaper, of Edinburgh, called a meeting of delegates to attend on the celebrated Calton Hill, where numbers assembled in the open air, when a series of resolutions were passed condemning all violent language, and protesting against it as calculated to lead to the destruction and failure of the movement; calling on the people to pledge themselves to discountenance all illegal or unconstitutional proceedings. The leading men of London held the same views. Of course everywhere there were some with more zeal than knowledge, who sought O'Connor's favour by opposing these men when they dared to question his judgment as a pilot.

Now that we were fairly installed in Bolt-court, the individuality of the members became more marked, as well as the divisions of party. Some could think for themselves, and at once gave utterance to their own opinions. Others were pledged to O'Connor, and deemed him their leader; yet it often happened that on some open questions their own unfettered judgments took different views from his, and then it was amusing how he would wheel round and chime in with the majority. As a discussion was about to close, and he saw the views he had expressed were in a decided minority, he would rise, assuring them that they had misapprehended him, and he would make it obvious to them that they had. He then entered with ardour into some proposition, as far from the question on hand as the east from the west; and after a while, without having given any explanation, boldly conclude, saying they would now clearly perceive that his opinion was their opinion, and withdraw his resolution, assuring them that the amendment best expressed his views.

With all its faults, as a body, that convention was more talented than any I have known. I believe they were honest, and did not foresee the results at first. I myself was as wild in hopes and expectations as any one, when I

---

[143] Rev. Patrick Brewster (1788–1859), younger brother of Sir David Brewster, was a strong opponent of O'Connor and a member of the Anti-Corn Law League. Minister at Paisley 1818–59, he preached vehement Chartist sermons. Suspended in 1842 from his ministerial functions for his *Seven Chartist and Military Sermons* (published 1843). Campaigned also for temperance and poor law reforms, and against slavery. A solitary Chartist, contemptuous of other men's ideas, uncompromising in repudiating criticism, adept at making enemies.

[144] John Fraser (1794–1879) a Johnstone schoolmaster of advanced educational views, whose radicalism led him into prison in 1820. He moved to Edinburgh *c.* 1836 and founded *The True Scotsman*. A pioneer temperance reformer, and advocate of Hygeism; also an agent for Morrison's Pills. He denounced O'Connor's violent tactics, but later moved out of the Chartist world and began giving regular performances of Scottish songs with his daughters in London. Visited America, but in old age returned to Johnstone as a wealthy and respected citizen. The *Paisley Daily Express* on 7 March 1879 spoke of him as "a stern moralist" who "placed high above mere political privileges the necessity of the working classes, by education and strict sobriety, elevating their character and position in the world". See also J. R. Fraser, *Memoir of John Fraser* (Paisley, 1879).

first came up to the convention, deeming the whole country, as we had been led to expect it, and as the *Star* had expressed it, "up to the mark". I thought we had nothing to do but demand and receive. But after the first few weeks I found we had deceived ourselves. Still, I thought we had only to go to the unawakened districts, proclaim our principles and objects, and they would at once become as ardent as ourselves. But when I had once seen the state of the people, as a whole, my dream was broken by the stern realities. I saw that it was a work yet to be done; to create a thinking, virtuous, self-denying, noble, and free people. We had begun to build a structure for which, however noble and beautiful the design, we had neither the stones, the timber, or other materials. We must go back to the quarry, the forest, the mine, and the forge, to procure, fashion, and mould these materials, and then recommence the building.

On the 11th of March, 1839, a crowded meeting was held at the Crown and Anchor, Strand, Mr. Frost, in the chair, when O'Connor, Harney, and others, spoke in the strongest language, and urged the people to be prepared for the approaching struggle. When the speeches appeared in print they were alluded to in terms of reproach by those hostile to such language, and speedily after, Messrs. Salt, Hadly,[145] and Douglas of Birmingham, tendered their resignation as members of the convention. Meanwhile, at the beginning of May, on counting the signatures we had received to the National Petition, we found the numbers did not exceed 600,000 instead of 1,000,000, which was the lowest number we had expected. It was then decided, with some opposition,[146] that sixteen of the delegates should be sent out for a month, in pairs, to those districts which had not sent up signatures or been agitated.

Abram Duncan, delegate for Dumfries,[147] and I were appointed to proceed to Cornwall, and labour for a month there. Neither of us knew a single person in the county, nor had we been in it before, nor had there been any correspondence from any one in the county with the convention. On looking at the *Gazetteer* and the Map we determined to take packet and proceed direct to Falmouth, and take a circuit, which we could go twice round in the time we were to remain. We chose the mining district, where, although the towns and villages were not large, the population on the whole was pretty

---

[145] Benjamin Hadley was alderman and churchwarden at Birmingham and a disciple of Attwood.

[146] See K. Judge, "Early Chartist Organization and the Convention of 1839", *International Review of Social History*, 1975, for an account of the disputes and divisions within the convention. For a recent narrative account of Chartism, critical of O'Connor, see J. T. Ward, *Chartism* (1973).

[147] For Duncan, see above, fn. 105; according to British Library, *Add. MS*. 34245A f. 61, Lowery attended the "Committee for Extending Political Information", which had been appointed by the convention on 8 February and met on 23 February. The Committee originally assigned Lowery and Duncan Devon and Cornwall, but Devon was in fact covered by Cardo and Moir. The missionaries were given local maps, sheets for signatures, copies of the National Petition and Chartist credentials from the convention, and £10 pay and expenses.

thick. The circuit we took was from Falmouth to Truro, Redruth, Camborne, Hayle, St. Ives, St. Just, Penzance, St. Austin, and back by Falmouth. When we landed at Falmouth we took a survey of the place. Like all such seaports it presented an abundance of drunken sailors and prostitutes, with a large class of shops which profited by their expenditure. Hence our impression that, however good some individuals may be, yet, as a class, they could not feel an interest in the moral, social, or political improvement of the people, so we at once decided to pass on to the county town, Truro, and begin there. We found that we could not get a room, so determined to address the people in the open air. We chose a very broad and central street, and sent the town-crier round the town announcing that Mr. D., &c., members of the National Convention, would address the working-classes on the People's Charter and the National Petition, at such an hour in the evening. When the time came, a neighbouring joiner lent us a small bench. Across the street, and at the adjacent corners, little groups of people had gathered, but there was not above a score in front of the bench.

"Well," said I, "I don't feel courage to begin with so few, will you, or shall we wait?" "We must begin at once," said D, and mounted the bench. He stood above the middle height, was some thirty-five years of age, his countenance bore the stamp of vigorous thought, and his voice was clear and commanding. His first sentence was distinctly heard all around, and in a very short time we had above a thousand people, who listened most attentively, and frequently responded warmly to our sentiments. We continued the meeting for two hours and a-half, our general rule being to speak one hour and a-quarter each. We were both in the prime of health and vigour for the labour of public speaking. Long experience had enabled us to do even without preparation or notes for a general address, except to remind us of some special facts which we designed to mention, and were afraid we might forget. We thus possessed coolness and readiness to seize on any local or temporary circumstances. Personally we were well fitted to speak after each other. The tone of our minds and modes of address being different. My friend although possessing strong reasoning powers did not use them to lead his audience to a belief of his views, but by his earnest and impressive declaration of their truth at once produced a conviction that he was right; while his withering denunciation of the selfish injustice of the past and present *party legislation* at once humbled and silenced its supporters. On the other hand, I generally took some acknowledged principle in religion or morals, and endeavoured to show that the evils we complained of, and sought to remove, were opposed to it, and that resistance to such wrongs was obedience to God. Hence the old prophets were my armoury, and the brotherhood of man: his equality of claims on law and justice as taught in the New Testament:—That God had made of one blood all the children of men. That we were to do unto others as we would others should do unto us. That none were to lord it over the brethren—that we stood equal before God

—before his law—and in his church. That the privileged classes dare not gainsay these truths, but admitted us as equals in the church. Yet they unjustly denied us equal privileges before *their* laws and in *their* high courts of legislature, because we were poor. While the Cornwall people knew nothing about "Magna Charta," Commonwealths, Bills of Rights, and such like, yet, being devout readers of their bibles they had a quick eye to perceive the inconsistencies of British legislation with the principles taught in the Scriptures. My favourite expression was, the Bible is the "Peoples Charter." A people that read and understand the Scriptures can never sit contented under wrong, or become willing abettors of it. As we brought forward the evils of the Corn Laws, and other fetters on trade, the misapplication of educational endowments and charities, extravagant pensions, and such like, to compare them with these Scripture teachings, their attention was at once roused to the obvious anomalies, and it was called the "new light."[148]

After this meeting the news of the "Chartists" being in the district spread rapidly, and, from various motives, we were sure to have audiences. The people at once sympathised with our sentiments. The middle classes were more cautious, while the gentry and magistracy were evidently on the watch lest we should exceed the bounds of the law.[149] The working-classes in general were a simple primitive people, with strong religious feelings, of an excitable temperament—quick in their perceptions of subjects which came within the range of their experience. But they knew little of general society, its state or conflicting opinions. Living in a remote corner of the land, with the ocean almost around them, they had not mixed with the rest of the population. The Methodist style of preaching, however good to work upon their feelings, wanted some of the Presbyterian reasoning to cultivate their understandings. They were very superstitious, and we were assured of ghosts and apparitions in many places.[150] Here, as well as elsewhere in England, we found the

---

[148] Compare *The Life of Thomas Cooper by Himself*, p. 162 on the Sunday evening speeches to Chartists given by Thomas Cooper at Leicester in the early 1840s: "we always commenced with worship, and I always took a text from the Scriptures, and mingled religious teaching with politics."

[149] See below, pp. 232–237, and Dorothy Thompson (Ed.), *The Early Chartists*, pp. 187–90 for three interesting reports from magistrates on the Chartist lecture-tour. It is curious that Lowery nowhere mentions the work of his Chartist predecessors in Truro—notably the activities of Richard Spurr, who presided over a Chartist meeting there on 29 January 1839. See J. G. Rule, "The Labouring Miner in Cornwall *c.* 1740–1870" (Unpublished Warwick Univ. Ph.D. thesis, 1971), p. 363. *The Falmouth Express and Colonial Journal*, 23 March 1839 in an editorial spoke of Lowery and Duncan as "these poisonous and prowling animals". In *The Charter*, 14 April 1839, p. 187, Duncan referred to the opposition they encountered when arranging a meeting in Gwennap Pit: "every obstacle had been thrown in the way,—the magistrates had condemned, the parsons had preached, and the tyrant masters had threatened. They had published every falsehood malignity could invent to blacken the character of the missionaries, and raise the fears of the people."

[150] See William Lovett, *Life and Struggles* (1876), pp. 11, 13 on Cornish superstition. And compare Lowery's account with the letter reprinted below, p. 235 and with the report sent by Abram Duncan to the *True Scotsman*, 30 March 1839: "you can have no conception of the ignorance of the people upon general politics . . . they might have just as well sent mis-

average mind and manners of the women much superior to the men among the more uneducated poor. Their powers of thinking and observing had evidently been more exercised. One night this was particularly evident. It was on a Sunday evening in the Methodist Chapel, in Camborne, and we were sitting in the front gallery before the services began, and had the whole congregation, which was a large one, before us. They sat after the old fashion, the women by themselves on one side and the men on the other. We were at once struck with the evident superiority of expression in the countenances of the females, and my Scotch friend, being a phrenologist,[151] observed, emphatically, "The development of the women is splendid, but did ye ever see such a set of bad heads as the men have?" We found strange stories afloat regarding who we were. We were evidently a mystery to the people, they could not believe that we were working-men and had not received a "learned education." We refused to receive any monies which were frequently offered to us, allowed no collections, paid for the expenses of all our meetings, and always put up at Temperance houses or private lodgings, so that we were set down as independent gentlemen, and many had it that we were two noblemen in disguise. Many came like Nicodemus[152] and expressed their sympathy with our doctrines. Among these was one person, a proprietor of a mine, who came to the meetings at different places. At last, one night, evidently thinking that by that time we would certainly have confidence in his being a friend, he earnestly said, "Now, gentlemen, you will not persist in saying you are working-men and have received no better education." When we assured him we were, and had each been at work from eleven years of age,[153] he was evidently still in doubt.

We passed on to St. Ives, which lies on the Bristol Channel, beautifully situated, the coast rising steeply above it. We got out of the conveyance to walk down the hill into the town, and so fell in with an old man, whom we found to be quite a character. As we knew no one in the town we thought it a good opportunity to make inquiries—"Was there a Temperance house?" "Oh, yes, he could show us the Temperance house." "Did he know the town crier?" "Yes; he was crier, and he was parish clerk and the sexton."

When I told him we intended to hold a meeting in the open air that evening and would engage him to give notice of it, he assured us he would get the people to come. Thinking to gather some information of the political state

---

sionaries to the South Sea islands, to instruct the natives there in the principles of a free government, as to Cornwall . . . The people have no dreams of the past—no historical epochs to fall back upon, calculated to light the torch and inflame the soul anew for the battle of liberty. They never fought, bled, or died for liberty. They have never been taught to know that knowledge will improve their social and political condition."

[151] Follower of George Combe, whose *Constitution of Man* (1828) argued that one could discern character by studying the shape and size of the cranium.
[152] *John*, Ch. 3, v. 2.
[153] cf. p. 45, where he says he began work at the age of ten.

of the place, I then asked him if they had any Radicals in St. Ives. "A' what, Master?" said he with a vacant stare. "Any Radicals or Chartists?" said I. I shall never forget the vacuity and bewilderment of his countenance. "No," answered he, with a grave shake of his head, "they catch no fish here but pilchards and mackerel." I burst into a convulsion of laughter, and for long afterwards the remembrance of our interview with the parish clerk, sexton and crier of St. Ives furnished us with mirth.[154]

After we had procured refreshment my friend went out to reconnoitre, while I remained to write letters. On his return, "Well," said I, "what do they look like?" He answered, "I don't think there can be much love of liberty here; it's too full of Methodist chapels, and they are too priest-ridden to like freedom. As I was walking ever so many of the working men lifted their hats to me in passing; it could only be because I had a good coat on. I cannot bear such servility to the appearance of wealth." But he was wrong, for when the time came we had a large enthusiastic meeting. Although it began to rain shortly after we commenced, nearly all stood to the close of our addresses, which lasted for upwards of two hours. After the meeting a number of very intelligent working men came to us at the Temperance house, whom we found to be mostly teetotallers.[155]

My friend having been one for some years, and a frequent speaker on the subject in Scotland, was at once at home with them, and we were strongly urged to stop another day or two; but having made arrangements to pass on, we promised them to come back in a fortnight, when they assured us we should have a very large meeting, for the people were very much pleased with what they had heard. We procured a hall at Penzance, and had some crowded meetings there. At St. Just, St. Michael's, St. Austle, and onwards, we were well received, and invited to return to every place we visited. We were amused with a town crier at a village above Falmouth when we sent for him to announce the meeting. He informed us that the clergyman had told him that he was not to cry it, or he would be deprived of his situation; therefore he durst not go round and cry it, but if we were willing he would go round the houses and tell the people "that the parson would not let him cry the meeting." As may be supposed, this made the people more eager to come. By the time we reached Hayle on our second round our visit and our subject was the common topic, and many of the people were enthusiastic in favour of our views. Wherever we had left copies of the "Charter" and

---

154 Compare Lowery's letter to Lovett, in B.L. *Add. MSS.* 34,245A (22 March 1839) reprinted below, p. 235.

155 Teetotalism was making good progress in Cornwall in the late 1830s. The energetic missionary work of James Teare, the Preston teetotal lecturer, helped to ensure that there were 2,571 enrolments into the St. Ives temperance society by June 1839; 1,200 at St. Just; 800 at Gwennap; 4,060 at Penzance. For a good discussion of Cornish teetotalism at this time, see *British and Foreign Temperance Intelligencer*, 22 June 1839, p. 242; on 21 September 1839 (p. 379) the same periodical estimated that there were "about 40,000" teetotallers in Cornwall.

National Petition to be sold, they were disposed of. The convention supplied us with these to sell at a penny each. It was a beautiful May evening when we held the meeting on our second visit to Hayle.[156] We addressed it from almost opposite the chief inn of the place, in the windows of which some of the leading gentlemen, magistrates and clergy of the neighbourhood had assembled, to hear us and judge for themselves, no doubt with the conviction that our language would be seditious. My friend preceded me and warmly denounced certain selfish evils of class legislation. Having stood awhile watching the expression of the countenances in the windows of the inn as his speech operated on their minds, a desire at once possessed me to startle what I conceived to be their fears, by appearing to confirm them. Sometimes such fits will come over you as you stand conscious of your power, and of the sympathy of an audience. I calmly surveyed the crowd, and then looked direct to the gentry in the inn windows, and in a strong and emphatic tone of voice said,—"Fellow countrymen, I stand here to preach Revolution," then paused, and enjoyed their startled looks, the stretching of necks, and the straining of ears to catch the confirmation of their opinions, which they expected was to follow. After due pause I continued. "But mark well my words and do not misconstrue them, Revolution simply means change, and the revolution I advocate is a change from bad to good, from corrupt and extravagant government to a real representation, retrenchment, and reform."[157] I then proceeded to draw a comparison between the exhortations of the prophets and apostles as to Church and State and the condition of things in our own country. The next morning my friend went into a neighbouring boot and shoe-maker's shop to make a purchase, and he observed the master reading a Bible at his desk very intently. On asking the shopman for what he wanted, the sound of his voice caused the master at once to raise his head, when, recognising my friend, he exclaimed—"It was all true that gentleman said last night, sir, for I have been reading the Prophets Isaiah and Jeremiah this morning, and find just what he said." We passed on to St. Ives, expecting to have a good farewell meeting, but on arriving we found that a Revival had broken out the week before, and that for the last three days a large portion of the shops had been closed, and most of the people had ceased to work, the chapel being full night and day. On going to a tradesman with whom we were more intimate, we were informed that their servant girl had gone to the chapel the night before and had never come back. To arrange for our meeting was impossible, so we determined to go to the chapel and see how things went on there. I shall never forget that

---

[156] Lowery is incorrect. It was in fact 26 March—see British Library *Add. MSS.* 34,245A f. 169: Lowery to Lovett.

[157] Compare Lowery's speech in *Newcastle Press*, 7 December 1833, p. 4 "Revolution is a vague ambiguous term; tories would term the destruction of tyranny a revolution, even if it made Europe the seat of liberty. Ours is a revolution that turns bad to good, turns wrong to right". Compare Gammage's tantalising of the authorities at Ormskirk, *Newcastle Weekly Chronicle*, 10 January 1885.

scene; it was altogether indescribable. A large chapel was full of people; there was an open space within the door in front of the pews, where a number of people—neighbours who had slipped out without hats or bonnets, as they would to see a passing sight—were looking coolly on and passing their remarks. They evidently had not caught the enthusiasm. But all within the pews were in a state of delirium. Amidst the confusion of tongues it was impossible to connect coherently the utterances. There were three persons in the pulpit, one of whom was preaching, or rather uttering, unconnected exclamations. In the gallery some were singing rapturously, others were praying aloud. Similar proceedings were taking place under the gallery and in the body of the chapel. I shall never forget the sight we observed in one of the large pews close by us. A young woman was "smitten," as they called it. She was uttering loud, passionate, and convulsive exclamations of grief, and tearing her hair, which hung dishevelled round her neck. Afterwards she sunk on the floor, physically exhausted, panting for breath, and foaming at the mouth. There were two men beside her not at all excited themselves, who coolly watched her emotions, and excited her as if they were merely applying galvanism. One of them particularly disgusted us. There were no traces of honest fanaticism in his looks; on the contrary, he was cold and calculating, and of a "Fagin-like" Jew appearance, and seemed fitted for any dark deed. When her spent nature could no longer utter ravings, and seemed to be recovering its reason, he would kneel down by her and exclaim close to her ear, "Shout! shout! shout! there is no quietness until the devil is cast out, and then you will find mercy;" and then the ravings of the poor creature would again commence. We felt so disgusted at the fellow that we were obliged to quit the place. On conversing with intelligent persons we found that such scenes frequently occurred, sometimes to the total stoppage of all industry for a week together. While undoubtedly some good is done, yet when the *furore* has passed away too many of the conversions were found to be evanescent, and much evil and immorality had arisen from them. The population possesses all the materials for such explosions, being full of warm religious feeling which overrules knowledge. Their daily language and the religious services they attend are replete with rapturous exclamations. Perhaps the mother is out on some errand; she has left the children to play with those of a neighbour until she returns. By-and-bye, in imitation of their elders, they begin singing a hymn and uttering the expressions which they have heard at chapel. In the midst of this the mother returns. Her paternal feelings are delighted, and she exclaims, "Bless the Lord!" She joins the hymn, calls on her neighbours, who become similarly affected, and the enthusiasm spreads from house to house; then the chapel is sought, and the whole neighbourhood are infected.[158]

[158] Compare Lowery's excellent description of the revival with that by William Bunton, the Banbury secularist, discussed by Barrie Trinder in *Cake and Cockhorse* (Banbury), Autumn 1966, p. 75. See also *The Life of Joseph Barker. Written by Himself* (Ed. J. T. Barker, 1880),

We had previously arranged with the surrounding places to hold a final meeting at "Gwenapp Pit," a place where John Wesley was once stoned and maltreated when preaching to the people, but which afterwards, when God had blessed his labours with their marvellous fruits, became the place of the central gatherings or camp meetings of his followers. Although the day was very unfavourable, upwards of 14,000 people were assembled, and stood to hear us for upwards of two hours in the rain.

On returning to London we found that Dr. Wade, Mr. Matthews, of Perth, and Mr. Cobbit[159] and Mr. Rogers, had seceded from the Convention. The rest of the missionaries reported that they had been well received wherever they had been. It was determined to adjourn to Birmingham, where the Convention would be in the heart of the country, and surrounded by a population amongst the most enthusiastic of its supporters, and it adjourned to Birmingham on May 13th. Plans and projects for ulterior measures in the event of the prayer of the Petition being rejected now became frequent. To abstain from excisable articles, urge a run on the banks, and recommend exclusive dealing by the people, were among these, but the national holiday seemed to be the most fixed idea in the districts. Our part in the late mission effort having been in a district where the principles were previously unknown to the people, I had not as yet had an opportunity of judging on the average state of the country except by what I could gather from others, and having been requested to vote for the sacred month, my opinions still tended that way, although doubts of the fitness of the general country were beginning to be forced on me. On May 16th the Convention determined on a series of large simultaneous meetings through the various districts, to test the spirit of the people, and their preparedness to stand by them as a body in their future movements, if the prayer of the Petition was rejected. A series of resolutions were passed, recommending the people to follow peace, law, and order and sobriety, and avoid attending the approach-

---

pp. 185 ff. The best study of revivalism is W. G. McLoughlin, *Modern Revivalism* (New York, 1959). Revivalist methodism was as likely to disrupt work-patterns as to reinforce them. For an excellent account of participation, in a Cornish methodist revival at this time, see John Harris, *My Autobiography* (1882). Harris was a tin-miner, lay preacher and poet. We owe this reference to Dr. David Vincent.

[159] These were all middle class moderates. For Wade, see below, p. 139. Patrick Matthew was a prosperous grain dealer and landowner, and represented East Fifeshire at the convention. For his attitudes see Alex. Wilson, *Chartist Movement in Scotland*, pp. 71–2; he was later denounced by O'Connor as a "middle-class traitor". J. P. Cobbett, son of William Cobbett, was a lawyer active in the anti-poor law movement, and ran a periodical, *The Champion*. He left the convention when it refused to confine itself to petitioning and agitating; he was the first of many such defectors. Hovell, p. 127, describes George Rogers as "a mild-mannered tobacconist" from Bloomsbury. Together with Thomas Murphy and the Savage brothers, he was a parish radical of 1830, active in the National Political Union, and supported Wakley and the campaigns against assessed taxes and newspaper stamps. He became a signed adherent of Lovett's "new move", but later retracted.

ing simultaneous meetings with pikes, pistols, or any offensive weapons; but should their enemies substitute war for peace, and suppress lawful agitation, it would be their sacred duty to meet force with force. After arranging which district meetings each of its members should attend, the Convention adjourned until July 1.

I was appointed with others to visit Scotland. After addressing meetings at Newcastle and the neighbourhood, I proceeded to Glasgow, and attended a large meeting on the public green. There were upwards of 100,000 people assembled, and a crowded tea-party was held in the Lyceum-rooms in the evening, and I at once felt myself at home with a Scotch audience. Her Ossian, Burns and Scott being my favourites, I had even as a school-boy felt my spirit stirred by the struggles of Wallace and Bruce, and had sympathised with the resistance of the Covenanters and wept over the death of her martyrs. John Frost, B. O'Brian and myself next visited Kilmarnock, Ayr, Kilwining Maybole, and Girvan, where we held public meetings. During our short stay there, Baillie Craig,[160] with whom we stopped, took Mr. Frost and myself to see the land of Burns. We passed through Ayr, having previously visited the New Brigg and the Auld Brigg;[161] and, it being a clear day, we had a fine view as we proceeded of Ailsa Craig and the Isle of Bute in the distance, with the cliffs of Carrick shore on the south. We stopped at the lowly cottage where the poet was born and died,—humble, 'tis true, but a fitting spot to cradle a bard-child of nature. There were no splendid mirrors, costly sculpture or paintings, or rich carpets from Turkey or Persian looms; but the "Banks and braes o' bonny Doun"[162] were close by, and its clear stream would mirror the fair forms that look on it, and the elegant drapery of trees and flowers which adorned its banks—which ever way his eye turned, it would rest on a picture-gallery,—the hills, the plain, the sea, and the mountain ailes, would show the soft, the beautiful, and sublime, in all their endless varieties of sunshine and shade, which ancient and modern artists have tried in vain to equal, while ever and anon fair and manly forms would pass by, defying the sculptor's art to equal. We "Stood by Allowa's auld haunted kirk"—by the trees where bewildered Tam-o'-Shanter saw it in a bleeze, and the witches dancing. We crossed the Bridge of Doun, where noble Maggie lost her tail, but saved her master and herself.[163] We passed on, and viewed the monument, which is beautiful in design and execution. But his true monument is his poems—household words engraven on the hearts and memories of his fellow-countrymen, where they will remain while a spark of nature's fire burns in their bosoms.

---

[160] Baillie Craig was a respected Chartist, first chairman of the 1839 convention but resigned from it in July. He became a successful Kilmarnock draper, principal proprietor of the *Ayrshire Examiner*, and in later life a Tory.

[161] See Burns's poem "The Brigs of Ayr", in James Kinsley (Ed.), *The Poems and Sayings of Robert Burns* (Oxford, 1968), I, pp. 280 ff.

[162] See *ibid.*, II, p. 575, for Burns's poem "The Banks o' Doun".

[163] The references are to Burns's "Tam o'Shanter", in *ibid.*, II, pp. 558, 563–4.

I had been appointed to attend some meetings at Paisley and Edinburgh, and John Frost was suddenly called away to Wales on matters of private business. We proceeded on the same coach together, and his connection with the Newport affair has ever been unaccountable to me. He was the last man in the Convention that I should have ever expected to be connected with such a proceeding. His language was ever mild, though firm, and in no way did he appear to favour the spirit of violence. As we rode along he inculcated prudence on me, for at that time I did not properly weigh my words often. He endeavoured to show me that it would be a work of time and progressive instruction and labour which would attain the franchise for the people, and that violent language would only retard it. The only solution of his conduct to me was that his letters to Lord John Russell, and his continued support of Liberal principles, had made him exceedingly popular in his neighbourhood, —that the *teaching of others* of a physical force character had acted powerfully on the excitable temperament of the population, and that when others had proposed the rising, in conjunction with certain places in England, he lacked the moral courage to say "the act would be madness and wickedness."[164]

The meeting at Paisley and *soirée* were large and enthusiastic. Yet, on observing many of more advanced in years of the weavers, I marked a settled thoughtfulness on their pale care-worn countenances, which seemed to say, "Your utterances are true; we have long suffered what you describe; push on, ye younger ones, in the spirit of faith and hope; but for us, our hopes so oft and so long-deferred have made our hearts sick, and we well nigh despair of redress." The people of Paisley are a highly-intelligent class, and deeply imbued with the spirit of literature and poetry. The town has produced many talented and remarkable men, perhaps more so than any other in Scotland. A shrewd old weaver, standing in front of the hustings at one of the meetings, totally upset Dr. John Taylor's assurance. The doctor had ended one of his rhapsodies about writing his liberty with a pen of steel in letters of blood, when the weaver drily exclaimed—"Aye, aye! Doctor, ye kill them an' I'll eat them: I'll eat a' ye kill." Our meeting at Edinburgh was on the Calton Hill, whence the view of the City, the Castle—with the Pentland Hills behind, where the Covenanters took refuge—filled the mind with the memory of the past, and stirred the heart with patriotic feelings.

I returned to Newcastle, and, after a few days, passed on to Carlisle, to address meetings in that neighbourhood. The people were looking to the Convention as their hope of relief from their starvation wages; and, the weather being fine, a hearty meeting was held in the market-place. The

---

[164] Lowery's attitude to Frost resembles Henry Vincent's. *The British Statesman*, 9 July 1842, p. 10 reports that Vincent at Edinburgh "bore testimony to the excellency of Frost's character, and expressed his conviction that the Newport outbreak was the result of a foul conspiracy, carried through by tools of the government". See also David Williams, *John Frost. A Study in Chartism* (Cardiff, 1939). G. D. H. Cole shared Lowery's puzzlement about Frost's action: see his *Chartist Portraits* (1941), p. 145 and below, p. 156.

audience presented that heart-stirring and deep attention which people never show qn mere abstract or remote questions. The responses from the women, many with their children in their arms, related to the facts which they deeply felt. As I exposed the evils of the bread tax, the limitation of our trade, the reduction of their wages, which forced man and wife and child into the workshops where all could not earn the livelihood which the husband alone ought to be able to procure, I endeavoured to point out the wrongs to the rising generation, debarred of that training essential to enable them to fill the office of wives and mothers. I shall ever remember a circumstance which occurred when I stepped down from where I spoke. I had observed a female just in front of me in the working-dress of a factory girl, and perceived, by the workings of her expressive countenance, her strong interest in the subject; she was some twenty years of age, had a Saxon face, with a fair complexion, light hair, expressive blue eyes, and an intellectual forehead, while her coarse vestments could not conceal her graceful form. Numbers shook hands with me, thanking me and wishing success—but she grasped me by the hand, not in a forward manner, a soul of feeling was in her eyes. She uttered no words; the utterance was in the grasp and look. We stood as if both were mesmerized for a minute, when the pressure of others seemed to recall her recollections; she unclasped her hand, but still spoke not, and passed away. I never saw her afterwards; and, on describing her, could not learn her name.[165]

When I got to Cockermouth, news had arrived of the attack of the police on the people of Birmingham in the "Bull-ring," and the arrest of Lovett and Collins; and all sorts of fears and imaginings were rife amongst the inhabitants. A party of them insisted on watching the house where I slept, believing that warrants to arrest the members of the Convention had been issued; they declared I should not be taken there.

I passed through the Lake district on to Birmingham, when I found that the Convention had passed up to London, and that Lovett and Collins had been committed to prison, charged with uttering a seditious libel. The facts of the case were that, during the Reform agitation and onwards, the "Bull-ring," an open market space in the centre of the town, had been used for holding large popular meetings. As long as the authorities and the populace marched together there was no fault found with this; but when, in the then excited state of the populace on the Charter question, meetings were held there night after night, the authorities forbid them to do so. The people held they had a prescriptive right to hold meetings there. No doubt there were faults on both sides. It may be very right to hold a numerous meeting occasionally in such places; but to do so night after night would evidently damage

---

[165] Lowery does not record the vigorous language he used in Cumberland. His speech in *Carlisle Journal*, 13 July 1839, adduces religious justifications for the resort to physical force, recommends a run on the savings banks, and announces that "the hour of action was come . . . He came there to preach revolution, and would do it as long as his tongue could give utterance to the sentiments of his heart".

the trade of the neighbouring shopkeepers. But the magistrates might have proceeded in a more judicious manner than they did. When they found that the populace still met after their warning them not to do so, they ought to have taken possession of the ground the next evening, before the meeting assembled, and not allowed the people to gather. Instead of doing so, they had sent to London for a large number of the police, and had them ready somewhere near. When the meeting had gathered, they appeared, and the people were commanded to disperse. On their not doing so, the Riot Act was read, and the metropolitan police called into action. The police acted most savagely, and struck all indiscriminately, even the most defenceless. On the other hand, a few of the more desperate of the people wrenched many of the iron rails and even the gates of the Bull-ring churchyard down, and procured stones to defend themselves; for a time the scene was desperate, and many of the people and police were severely wounded. The Convention passed a resolution condemnatory of the conduct of the authorities and the police, and ordered it to be printed. William Lovett signed it as secretary, and John Collins took it to the printer. On its being placarded, they were arrested on a charge of seditious libel, and imprisoned to await their trial. [Forty members had re-assembled at Birmingham, so that the Convention was thus lessening instead of increasing.] When I arrived in London, I found the committee for that purpose very busy attaching the sheets of signatures to the petition, in order to have it presented to the House of Commons as soon as possible. It had been determined from the first that Thomas Attwood should present it and bring forward the motion founded on it. The petition was borne to the House on a car by the members of the Convention from Bolt-court, Fleet-street. Dr. Wade, of the Established Church, being a member, was in the front rank. For years he had taken an active part in Radical proceedings; and when the processions of the Trades' Unions went to the House of Commons with the petition for the release of the Dorchester labourers, he marched at their head dressed in his canonicals. He was frequently joked by us for sticking to the "loaves and fishes." His defence was, that he always paid his curate liberally, and laboured to improve the condition of the people. He was full of kindness, benevolence, and good humour, inclined to corpulency, and evidently one who loved good fare and inclined to sleep at nights rather than, Cassius-like,[166] lean and restless, ready for plots and dark conspiracies.

The Petition had received 1,250,000 signatures.[167]

---

[166] Cassius (d. 42 B.C.) was the prime mover in the conspiracy against Julius Caesar. Dr. Wade was the jovial Owenite Anglican vicar of Warwick, who weighed 20 stones and won popularity with working men by defending the Dorchester labourers. He was active in Owen's Grand National Consolidated Trade Union, in the National Union of the Working Classes and the Birmingham Political Union. He was Nottingham's delegate to the 1839 Chartist convention, but resigned on 28 March because of the continual talk about resorting to arms.

[167] The accepted figure is 1,280,000 signatures.

On the evening of July 12th, Mr. Thomas Attwood moved that the prayer of the petition be taken into consideration in the usual form necessary to embody it in an Act of Parliament.

The delegates were all in the gallery. Many of the country delegates had not been in the House of Commons before, and all viewed the proceedings with intense interest. The petition and its subject were treated with every respect compatible with a settled determination not to grant its prayer. Statesmen are not guided so much by the first principles of justice, and liberty, and reason, as by traditional policy. With them, practicability means that which they have been used to practise rather than that which might be practised. The present order of things working well for them, they reason it must be just and beneficial for all classes. Lord John Russell, Sir Robert Peel, Disraeli, Roebuck, Wakley, Whittle Harvey, Molesworth, Leader, and others were among the chief speakers for and against.[168]

The speaking in the House of Commons did not equal our expectations; there was a want of fluency and facility of expression in Lord John Russell that astonished us, and even Sir R. Peel and many of the Whig and Tory speakers would not have commanded the attention of a working man's meeting. Macaulay, Sheel, O'Connell, Wakley, Whittle Harvey, Roebuck, and others, came fully up to our expectations. The speech which pleased me most as indicative of thought was that of Disraeli, yet it was the most miserable deliverance I had ever heard; he could not get through two sentences without hesitating, and he stopped every three minutes to consult his notes and papers, and suck his oranges—yet there was something of his future looming through his matter, showing that there was no common mind in the speaker. Our political feelings apart our visit to the House lowered its dignity in our estimation. This appears to be the case with most men and things. The poet truly says,

"'Tis distance lends enchantment to the view,"[169]

and Hume has well observed that mostly great and extraordinary men have much in common with the commonest. Close contact with dignities seldom increases our admiration of them. It does not do to sit too close to the foot lights or behind the scenes of a theatre. You there perceive the unrealities.

[168] *Hansard*, 3rd series, XLIX, cc. 220 ff. does not list speeches by all the M.P.s whom Lowery mentions here. Of the names he records, all except Harvey, Roebuck and Sheil can be found in the division list, but speeches are recorded only for Russell, O'Connor, Disraeli and Wakley.

[169] The quotation is from Thomas Campbell's *The Pleasures of Hope*. Lowery gives his immediate reaction to the debate in *The Charter*, 21 July 1839, p. 412; he despised Lord John Russell's speech: "more infamous lies had never been stated than Lord John Russell had last night uttered." See also his Newcastle speech of 30 September 1839, printed below, p. 242. Lowery's reaction to seeing M.P.s in the flesh is paralleled among several early Victorian radicals. "And are these, thought I, the beings whose laws we must obey", said Samuel Bamford, *Passages in the Life of a Radical* (Ed. W. H. Chaloner, 1967), I, p. 27. See also J. Pearce (Ed.), *Life and Teachings of Joseph Livesey* (2nd ed. 1887), p. lviii; J. Taylor, in *The Freeholder*, 1 May 1850, p. 68; Henry Vincent, in *Plymouth & Devonport Weekly Journal*, 9 July 1846.

It is a frequent observation in Scotland, that if you want to lower the exaggerated reverence of a devotee for ministers as men, take him to the General Assembly during its sittings, and he will soon see that they are "just like ither folk."

The petition had now been presented—the House of Commons was adverse to its prayer, and from this time began the difficulties of the Convention. The movement had been conducted on a false basis; the exhortation had been, join the Chartists—sign the petition—send and support the Convention and you will get the Charter. They had looked to the Convention to originate a power which could only spring up in themselves—men in earnest do not need urging, they only need guiding by their leaders. They rather need restraint than external excitement, the stern indomitable purpose appears in a steady onward step with compressed lip, not in noise, rant and threats. It is the force of the silent unbroken wave or lightning's stroke which we dread, and not the roar of the thunder or the foam of the broken wave. Instead of having settled down to besiege a fortress, as it were, and patiently prepared to work at trench and mine, however long it might take, we had thought to march up to the legislature, demand leave to enter and at once to get the Charter. F. O'Connor had boasted to the people that they should have their "Michaelmas Goose." Men of sense had scarcely expected that the petition would at once be answered favourably, but were willing to try. Now they were prepared for patience and progressive work to create the intellectual and moral power, but there stood in the way the false idea of getting it at once, and how to change that state of feeling was the question. Impatient parties always think they can set the natural laws aside in their case and attain their objects without the needful patience, time, toil, and perseverance. The leaders and people had been in too great haste and had commenced without counting the cost. The physical force rant tended to weaken the moral stamina of the party. Many men can easily talk of fighting and dying for a cause which they would at once turn their backs on if they were required to work patiently to attain it. I and my wife were much amused at a meeting at Newcastle, while we were sitting among the audience listening to the address of a southern orator who was tinged with the physical force folly. Alluding to want and distress amongst the working people and the New Poor Law he exclaimed, "If I had a wife I would fight for her, I would die for her!" A group of females of the working-class were sitting in the seat before us, and one of them observed to the others, "He disen't say he would work for her." That woman understood the duty of man. By this time we had seen the real state of the whole people and felt we must "learn to labour and to wait." We must educate, agitate, organise societies and extend our movement. I and others who had thought all the country to be up and demanding their privileges now said it must be only a gradual process, however sure eventually. In London I found the Convention; although as a body it still spoke the same language it felt itself in a difficult position. It had assumed a false position. The mistake had been that they had promised to get the Charter for the people. The people looked to them to do what they themselves alone could have done. The wish had been father to the thought that the people were up to the mark, and in this belief excitement had been the order of the day. But one-half of the people scarcely considered the question at all, especially in the agricultural districts. Not that these were against us, or likely to be so, but to change political institutions you need those who will aid you. The boasting and exaggeration of the general strength had been believed by many individuals. The multitude took language for facts, and expected them to be realised; while the leaders, becoming more perfectly acquainted with the facts of the whole country, were forced to change their ideas, they still used the same language. They had not the moral courage to say "We have been wrong—you have been wrong; we are not as strong or as numerous as we supposed. Examine your organisation, compare it with the population—do you think that men who will not give a portion of their time, their names, and their pence, will risk high perils?" Strange inconsistency and perversion of judgment appeared in some of the members who had come first as prudent moral force men. They now became mostly reckless and violent in language. Those like Dr. Taylor, in proportion as it became evident that we would not at once succeed, became more braggart and violent in expression, evidently wishing it to be inferred that the failure in attaining immediate redress was because the rest of the Convention did not possess the courage which they did. The "National Holiday," or "sacred month" of cessation from all labour, was an idea which had originated with the Birmingham men.[170] Whatever might have been meant by it at first, it meant in the people's minds the chances of a physical contest; not an insurrection or assault on the authorities, but that by retiring from labour, like the Roman plebeians of old to the Aventine-hill, they would so derange the whole country that the authorities would endeavour to coerce them back, and that they would resist the authorities unless their rights were conceded, and thus bring the struggle to an issue. Hence the *Northern Star* and the speakers had advised the people to arm. Birmingham had manufactured cheap muskets, which were sold in various places at 20s. each. Winlaton, a village some five miles from Newcastle, the population of which were nail makers, manufactured and sold large numbers of pikes, and I remember they presented one to me, and a formidable weapon it would have been to strike

---

[170] Lowery should really have given the credit to the shoemaker William Benbow, who wrote the pamphlet entitled *Grand National Holiday, and Congress of the Productive Classes* (1832) which recommended the general strike as a political weapon. Benbow had been denounced by a government spy in 1816 for manufacturing pikes for a projected rising, and was prominent in the anti-poor law agitation. He was arrested in 1839. Attwood took over Benbow's concept of a national holiday and deprived it of its connection with class war; Attwood saw it as a peaceable protest by employers and employees together against the misdeeds of government—a demonstration of moral force. See A. J. C. Rüter, "William Benbow's Grand National Holiday and Congress of the Productive Classes", *International Review for Social History*, I (1936).

and thrust with. My wife at once put it to a proper use, and took it to break the large coals in the cellar.[171] Had the idea been practicable, it could only have been so by the proper preparation for it. But the masses had no provisions laid by or money saved; and even where they had the latter, to have ceased work, and lived on their saved moneys, would not immediately have affected the shop-keepers. The largest portion of the working-classes live on credit—when they can get it. In fact, so do the major portion of the trading classes. Nothing, however, had been done but talk about the national holiday. I had inquired of the thinking men in many places how they were prepared for this sacred month and its possible results, and the invariable answer was, "Oh, not at all! we are not ready here!" It was always "other places" that were prepared to do the work; but you in vain sought for these "other places." Seeing that if the Convention recommended the sacred month it would assuredly lead the people wrong and most likely cause breaches of the peace, I succeeded in getting the question discussed with closed doors, and carried a proposition that every delegate should give in answers in writing as to the state of his district, its organisation, and means to keep the sacred month, and the supposed number of arms which he thought the people possessed. There was evidently a conviction that the national holiday could not be kept, but a total lack of courage amongst the leading men to say so. Dr. McDowell[172] and others wanted still to recommend it. He was wont to boast of the thousands of armed men in Lancashire, and P. Bussy,[173] the Bradford delegate, would often boast of 10,000 armed men there; yet, on close questioning, Dr. M. admitted that if he named 400 armed men for his neighbourhood he would probably overstate the number. With one or two exceptions, none of the delegates could say their districts were prepared, and the vast force was found only to exist in imaginative rant. The Convention passed a resolution stating what they had done to attain the Charter, and left it to the people to decide whether they would keep the sacred month or not.[174]

---

[171] This general picture of opinion round Newcastle is confirmed by R. G. Gammage, *History of the Chartist Movement*, p. 80, and by W. H. Maehl, "Chartist Disturbances in Northeastern England, 1839", *International Review of Social History*, 1963, pp. 394 ff, though D. J. Rowe's article, "Some Aspects of Chartism on Tyneside", *International Review of Social History*, 1971, finds it exaggerated. There is a rejoinder by W. H. Machl, "The Dynamics of Violence in Chartism: A Case Study in Northeastern England" in *Albion*, Vol. 7, No. 2 (Summer 1975).

[172] Dr. P. M. McDouall entered Chartism as a young, handsome and impulsive Bury doctor. In 1840, he advocated a middle class alliance, but he strongly opposed Urquhartism and did not completely rule out violent tactics. He broke with O'Connor in 1845. See Dorothy Thompson, *Early Chartists*, pp. 139–54, 160–7.

[173] Peter Bussey (1805–1869), a blunt Bradford beerhousekeeper and advocate of physical force, was the son of a draper. He led the Bradford Political Union during the reform crisis, and supported the factory movement and the Grand National Consolidated Trade Union. At the crucial moment of the Frost rising, he was supposed to be hiding, and he never lived down the disgrace. He emigrated to America, but returned to the West Riding in 1854 and became a publican.

[174] Lowery does not clarify his own standpoint in the convention. As late as July 1839, he advocated a stoppage of work from 12 August, but he encountered some criticism for his

This was the finishing stroke. From that time the Convention, as a body, had only to wind up its affairs; its prestige was gone. The political feeling for the Charter did not abate, however, but became more zealous than ever; the ideas permeated fresh places. The *Northern Star*, as the organ of the committees, was looked up to as the guide, and O'Connor, passing from district to district, became the idol of the masses. And when the more thoughtful would point out his inconsistencies to them, they invariably answered, "He is the only one of his class that is willing to help us; the Whigs and Tories want to destroy him, but we will stick by him."

O'Connell frequently attacked the Chartists in his addresses, and as he was one of those who drew up the Charter, we felt his attacks to be most galling.[175] It was evident he feared that our agitation might extend to Ireland. It was therefore determined to send a deputation of two of our members to Dublin, to give a true statement of our principles and to correct his misrepresentations. F. O'Connor and O'Brien[176] were chosen, but O'Connor declined on account of his other engagements. I was then chosen to go with O'Brien, but afterwards he declined. I did not know Ireland then, and wondered why they declined, but they knew they would not be heard in Dublin. I knew that the Irish were worshippers of O'Connell, and full of party spirit; but I still expected to get fair play, and be allowed to address a meeting, and did not care who opposed me. In our wildest Chartist meeting we always allowed either Whig or Tory to speak if they wished; but I had no idea of Irish "liberty of speech" at that time in Dublin.[177] F. O'Connor

refusal to bring forward this date. The *Northern Star* on 3 August announced that although Lowery had voted for the strike, he was "now decidedly opposed to it, from a belief that it would be a failure"; cf. *The Charter*, 19 May 1839, p. 268, and 21 July 1839, p. 412. For the most part, Chartists followed O'Connor's position—that a month's strike was totally impracticable, but that a three-day "general holiday" had some chance of success. (*Northern Star*, 3 August 1839, reprinted in P. Hollis, *op. cit.*, pp. 235–6).

175 Marx also realized the importance of removing Anglo-Irish antagonisms from within the labour movement. In a letter dated 9 April 1870, he described this antagonism as "the *secret of the impotence of the English working-class*, despite their organisation. It is the secret by which the capitalist class maintains its power. And that class is fully aware of it". *Marx and Engels on Britain* (Moscow, 1953), p. 506.

176 James Bronterre O'Brien (1805–64) was the outstanding journalist and theorist of the unstamped, editing the *Poor Man's Guardian* 1832–5, writing for the *Northern Star* from 1838, as well as publishing his own *Operative*, *Southern Star* and *National Reformer* in the 1840s and 1850s. He integrated the new labour economics of Hodgskin, Gray and Owen with the classical political radicalism of Paine, Cobbett and Hunt to produce the most coherent account of socialism before Marx. He was fascinated by the French Revolution, and published a life of Robespierre in 1837. He was imprisoned 1840–1 for seditious speaking, and then quarrelled with O'Connor, opposing the land plan with schemes for land nationalization of his own. See G. D. H. Cole's memoir in his *Chartist Portraits* (1941), P. Hollis, *The Pauper Press* (1970), Ch. 7, and A. Plummer, *Bronterre. A Political Biography of Bronterre O'Brien 1804–1864* (1971).

177 In the convention during February, Lowery expressed the belief that "the prejudices existing between the labouring classes of the two countries were fast dying away", *The Charter*, 24 February 1839, p. 77; he was soon to be sharply disillusioned.

introduced an Irish gentleman who had been mixed up in the Anti-Tithe Agitation in that country with O'Connell, and had lost the lease of three farms by it. He represented him as the very person who should go with me, for he knew all the leading Liberals in Ireland, and could give me every advice and direction. I found afterwards that this person had come to London, and having then no fixed engagement, had applied to O'Connor to help him to something, who accordingly thus adroitly recommended him as "just the man wanted to go with me." Some letters had been sent to the Convention from Dublin by a person named Clancy, urging it to send a deputation over, and stating that there were a large number favourable to the Charter in that city. I had a letter of introduction to a gentleman there engaged in the wool trade, who I was informed was a Radical of the Cobbett school, a man of superior intelligence and firmness, who, although a Catholic, had resisted Daniel O'Connell's expediency movements and left his party. On arriving in Dublin, I proceeded with my letter of introduction along with the person sent with me, who had given me a list of names which he recommended we should call on. On presenting my letter a conversation ensued, and I showed the list of names. He looked them over, and put some questions to my colleague, inviting me to call again. When I called again he inquired who my colleague was, and told me there was not one of the names but would hand me over to the "Castle." I soon found that the person with me knew little of parties in Dublin, and had evidently selected names from what he deemed the Liberal party. I waited on Mr. Clancy, whom I found to keep a hairdresser's shop. On questioning him about his friends I said I wished at once to get up a public meeting that I might explain our principles and objects, that the public might judge for themselves—that I did not expect there would be a majority at first, but would like to be certain that a few of his friends would attend, so that I might get a fair hearing. He felt confident we would have a majority, and assured me that he knew a number of Chartists who would be there.

A public meeting was announced to be held in a hall adjacent to Sackville-street. I was aware there would be opposition, but had no conception of what an Irish opposition meant in Dublin at that time. O'Connell had soon heard of the Convention appointing the mission, and had written a letter to his friend Reay,[178] maligning our purpose, and hinting that we deserved to be tossed into the Liffy. I was told this Reay was his right hand man and regent

---

[178] The three individuals in this passage are: Mr. Hanesy, the incompetent "Irish gentleman" sent by O'Connor (Add. MSS. 34,245B f. 154); Patrick O'Higgins, the "gentleman . . . engaged in the wool trade"; and (presumably) Thomas Matthew Ray, the efficient secretary of the Repeal Association in Dublin. O'Higgins was president of the Irish Universal Suffrage Association, and leader of the Irish Chartists. He believed that O'Connell, in his bargains with the Whigs, was merely promoting his own self-interest, but the Tory victory in 1841 brought Irish Chartists and repealers closer together. Chartism always remained weak in Ireland, however. O'Higgins was arrested for hoarding arms in 1848, and was imprisoned without trial for 7 months.

in Dublin when he was absent, ready to follow his instructions, and to oppose everything he did not agree with, and that however keen O'Connell was of rent, he devoted a large portion of it to keep up a staff in Dublin to maintain his influence. Reay was the commander-in-chief of these, who always had funds at command, and, being paid, could devote his whole time to carry out his master's policy. Connected with him was a person named Arkins, a tailor, who was familiar with the *ruffs* of the coal porters, and such like. When any meeting was to be *packed* and *upset*, having money at command, with the aid of whisky, and urging them to come and defend Ireland's Liberator, he was soon able to collect a force sufficient to do his work. I went to the place of meeting by myself at the time to commence, and found the room full. I walked up to the platform, and took my seat. The platform was large, and a number of persons were on it; Mr. Clancy rose, and commenced to state for what the meeting was called; but before he had spoken a few sentences Mr. Reay rose, amid loud cheers for O'Connell. "Gentlemen," said he, "there are delegates here from Feargus O'Connor and the Chartists in England. I say we will have nothing to do with them. They want to abuse O'Connell, the friend of Ireland. I advise you not to hear them speak, they have no business here. We won't let the meeting go on. There shall be no meeting, so let us clear the room at once".[179]

To try to describe the noise and shouts were in vain. Whether there were any friends of the Charter or of fair play in the meeting I do not know, but I saw no signs of them. I observed Clancy most vociferous in his condemnation of the proceedings, but the noise and threats of those round him drowned his voice. The *gentlemen* on the platform were evidently ready for any ruffianism. One of them, whom I was afterwards told was the son of Arkins, brandished a stick in my face when I cried, "Is this free discussion." He was quite mad with passion, and I believe he only wanted an excuse to use it. They began to pull the tables and seats off the platform, and some of them were broken. I do not think they knew exactly that I was the person who was to speak, yet they could perceive that I was a stranger. It was obviously dangerous to remain, as they were fast putting the lights out, and I was afraid that in getting through the mob in the hall I might receive blows; but I was safely taken out by one who furnished a rich specimen of the extremes of the Irish character, in its prejudice, partisanship, violence, gentleness, and kindness. He was a porter, full six feet high, and had been among the most clamorous and violent to clear the room and cheer for Dan.; yet there was something in his looks which gave me confidence that there was good nature in him; so he being in front I put my hand on his head and said, "friend, I am lamed and afraid I'll get hurt in getting out of the room, will you be so good

[179] Lowery's letters to the Convention on this Irish mission record this meeting as "one of the most disgracefull proceedings I ever was at". Reay, Lowery wrote, "went over the old sling slang of abuse about violence Tory Gold, love of plunder etc." (B.L. *Add. MSS.* 34,245B f. 153).

as to help me down stairs." "That I will, come down," exclaimed he, and helping me off the platform he put his arms round me, exclaiming, "come along now, and — — into one of them shall hurt you," and he helped me as carefully down stairs as if I had been a child. He took me into a room at the foot of the stairs, and, unclasping his hold of me, said, "there, now your safe, and none of them shall harm you, but O' sure you shouldn't come here to disturb a *peaceful* country." I told him that he was under a great mistake, that I was a working man like himself, and had been sent by the workmen of England to explain the principles by which they were seeking to secure their political rights and those of their Irish brethren. The gentleman to whom I had brought the letter of introduction just then entered the room, and addressing him, he said, "Och, an is that true, Mr. O'Higgins?"—"True! every word of its true." "Then sure whatfore a gentleman like you didn't get up and introduce the gentleman; sure Clancy's no man at all, at all, a gentleman like you should have given us the rights of it."

The next day I found that the respectable parties felt the disgracefulness of the proceedings, and endeavoured to fix the blame on others than the O'Connellites. One gentleman called on Mr. O'Higgins, and offered the use of his carriage to visit parties to procure their signatures to a requisition for a public meeting on the subject of my mission. In a few days it was arranged that the Council of Conciliation-hall should call a meeting, and that I should address it, and the charge of admittance being sixpence, it was expected to insure an orderly audience. So far things appeared to signify a fair intention on the part of the O'Connellites. On the night of the meeting, a little before the hour to commence, Mr. O'Higgins and I went down to the place.

The hall was up a flight of stairs, and the money-taker was at the bottom in a small office or stand. I was for paying and walking up at once, but my friend knew the tactics of the party better than I did. "Stop, stop," said he, "stand to one side until I go up and reconnoitre." I did so, and he went up. I had not stood four minutes, when a mob of coal porters and others headed by Arkins came up, and with yells and cheers forced themselves past the money-taker, rushed upstairs, and filled the room, giving three cheers for Daniel O'Connell. After a while Mr. O'Higgins came down stairs. "Come away home," said he, "it would be dangerous to go up there." He told me that after the cheers of the mob subsided, "Tom Reynolds," a well-known orator of the O'Connellites, came forward and said, "Gentlemen, we understand that there is a delegate here from Feargus O'Connor and the English Chartists; we will not allow any one to speak until he proves that he is a delegate. If he does so, it is contrary to the law to have delegates in Ireland, and he'll be handed over to the 'Castle' "; and then the cheers and yells for Dan broke out again, when Mr. H. at once came away.

I succeeded in getting two or three letters into the *Freeman's Journal*, but that was all I could do. Had I had funds at command I have no doubt but that I might, with proper caution, by holding a few select meetings at first, have succeeded in getting a fair hearing before a large audience, when I have no doubt I should have found a considerable number of the people favourable to our opinions. I was very kindly treated by Mr. O'Higgins, who after the first week that I had been there invited me to take up my abode at his house, as well as one of the Manchester delegates, who had come over to escape a warrant which had been granted for his apprehension.[180]

It was the first time I had been in Ireland, and although I had mixed with the Irish often in England, yet there were many points in their character and politics which appeared to me strange. I saw how much the mind of a population is influenced by local prejudices and party passions, and how much its opinions and actions are moved by these rather than by universal principles, and how little we can understand the state of the people of a country before we have resided in it. I found that things which we thought of little or no importance in England were by them deemed essential, while what we deemed of greatest moment scarcely attracted their attention. They appeared to view everything through the medium of religious prejudices. Whatever the Catholics undertook the Protestants opposed, and whatever the Protestants commenced was resisted by the Catholics. I had marked our English sectarianism, but from it no Englishman could have any conception of the bitterness of religious intolerance in Ireland. At that time Dublin appeared to me full of beggars; they were sitting on almost every door-step in the principal streets and squares, and the major portion appeared to be able-bodied men. Such a sight was new and painful. At first I impulsively sought to relieve it with my mite, but as day by day the evil appeared to increase, it became at last fixed on the mind as inevitable. Yet there were many points of attraction in the wit and humour of the beggars. While they were most importunate, they never suppressed their native impulses that they might succeed in their object. They always gave a retort or joke in reply. Among the poor I remarked an over estimate of the rich. They appeared to think that a rich man must know all about everything better than the poor. This did not appear to be mere deference, but a settled conviction.

After being a month at Dublin I returned to London. The Convention was busy in winding up its affairs as fast as possible. After settling all claims

[180] The second meeting is not discussed in Lowery's other letters to the convention, in B.L. *Add. MSS.* 34,245B ff. 121, 129, 165, 167, 175. His account, together with the letters, should be compared with the briefer version in R. G. Gammage, *History of the Chartist Movement*, p. 159; and R. O'Higgins, "The Irish Influence in the Chartist Movement", *Past and Present*, No. 20 (November 1961), p. 87. Lowery's memoirs tally well with the letters he wrote at the time, though it is surprising that in retrospect he did not make more of the Convention's mismanagement of the whole mission. His letters to the Convention show him misguided by Hanesy, starved of the money necessary to make the mission a success, misinformed of the local situation by the Chartist sympathisers who had encouraged the mission and embarrassed by O'Connor's premature claims for the mission's success. The Manchester delegate is not mentioned by name in Lowery's letters, but is probably the individual described in B.L. *Add.* MSS. 34,245B f. 175, as "the Attorney General".

it was found there was about £200 of the rent fund left, and it was handed over to Mr. George Rogers, of Bloomsbury, to be resumed for any future Convention; and the Convention was dissolved on Sept. 14, 1839. I then returned to Newcastle, and opened a book-shop, but as, during agitation, others had been established, and supplied the people with the papers and periodicals, I had not the same opportunity to establish a business as I should have had at the commencement of the movement for the Convention. After I had got my shop put in train, and seeing that it would not maintain my family, I determined to take a lecturing tour into Scotland with my friend, A. Duncan, who had been my colleague in the Cornwall mission.[181] I joined him at Hawick, and we gave lectures in the chief border towns onwards to Edinburgh, where we were very kindly received. We went up to Falkirk-Stirling, and the towns along the base of the Ochills, and then down through Fifeshire and on to Dundee. In every place we had good audiences, and the people were warmly interested. The Scotch Chartists had never been so heated and impatient as the English. They looked on their franchise as a work to be perseveringly wrought out. Hence they were not disheartened or disorganised because the prayer of the National Petition had not been granted, but were organising more perseveringly than ever. Almost every Sunday we were requested to preach sermons, and I found that it had become very general over the country. This practice had arisen from the attacks of the opposing press, who had stigmatised the movement as "Infidel." Now while, unfortunately, in England a large portion of the working people, although they are not disbelievers, have no faith, and attend neither churches nor chapels, almost every family of Scotland is connected with some place of worship, and has a desire to be esteemed religious. Added to this, as might have been expected, the keeping aloof of the middle classes in some instances had produced bitter feelings between the poor and upper class members of places of worship.[182] These things had determined the Scotch Chartists in many places to carry on public worship of their own, and in others to engage a hall occasionally, when they had a lecturer or any friend of the cause who could properly undertake to conduct the religious services. The party in Glasgow engaged a larger church that was then unoccupied, formed a committee, and arranged a plan of preachers who conducted the services, and supplied neighbouring towns and villages. This church from the first has had a good congregation and useful preachers, and done much good with its local missionary efforts. It still exists in vital activity. The Scotch present a great contrast in some points to the English in the forms of religious services. In England we are apt to suppose the Scotch unnecessarily strict in every

---

[181] Like G. J. Harney, Lowery evaded arrest at this time, partly by going to lecture in Scotland. Compare G. D. H. Cole, *Chartist Portraits*, p. 278. See also below, p. 171. The Scottish travels of Lowery and Duncan late in 1839 are quite extensively reported in the *Northern Star*.

[182] For Chartist attitudes to religion, see H. U. Faulkner, *Chartism and the Churches* (1916, Cass reprint 1970), and Mark Hovell, *Chartist Movement*, pp. 200–3.

particular respecting their religion. This is the case regarding the principles of its services, but not as to the places where they are held. They attach no idea of sacredness, or reverence, or consecration, to anything material. Everything is done "decently and in order" from beginning to end of the ordinance of religious worship, whether in a church, a barn, a hayloft, or in the open air; but the services concluded, the blessing asked, and dismissal over, they look on the church or cathedral as no more sacred than the field or barn. Hence you have no difficulty in getting places of worship to hold meetings on any moral political, literary, or scientific subject. The pulpit is deemed the vehicle of delivery for doctrine, and can only be granted by the minister, but the managers can grant the church for any of the above purposes whether he will or not. Even the Dissenters in England, although they ignore the consecration of material things, entertain a superstitious reverence for their places of worship, and seldom or never use them for any other purpose than religious services, often being obliged to meet to hear addresses and lectures on secular matters in very inconvenient places while their commodious chapels are standing empty and useless. In the Chartist churches the fundamental principles of Christianity were understood as the bond of union. All sectarian doctrine was avoided, and the sermons were on practical duties, among which the social and political held a prominent place. In Hawick and the Borders the people partook of the characteristics of their forefathers. With disdain of authority where they considered it unjust, and a readiness to run any risk in order to attain their rights, they had a decided leaning to physical force; they were kind and hospitable, candid and outspoken as to their differences. They had erected a large tent on some vacant ground where they held their meetings and had religious services on the Sunday. I found many of them sincere Christians as well as ardent and intelligent politicians. The population were engaged in the woollen hosiery trade, and at that time there was a strong feeling amongst the operatives against their employers, whom they charged with being ever on the watch to take selfish and dishonest advantages of them. A system had sprung up during the dullness in trade called the "stent." The masters not being able to give full work, had agreed to add to the limited (or "stented") amount of work for which they could pay cash wages more work, which was to be laid up in stock until full trade came, and for which they were to be paid in goods. On the face of this it appeared reasonable, but the masters in general then took the opportunity to put on the "stent" when trade was good. Thus goods were forced on the workmen for which they were charged high, and on which they had to make a sacrifice before they could turn them into cash. There are many petty annoyances and exactions introduced by employers in such matters which fully account for the bitterness with which the operatives regard them, but which the public are unacquainted with. I remember well one intelligent working man, with a large family, relating to me how he had been imposed on by his employer, who was a member of the same church with him. "I wish we could establish a chapel for ourselves," said he; "I strive all I can to banish ill-feeling from my mind towards him, but often when I have seen him in the church, and have sat down at the 'Lord's Table' with him whom I knew to be defrauding me and other labourers of our hire, I could not help feeling bitterly. I would be better away at such a time." Too much of the inattention to the ministrations of religion are the result of our social anomalies. However mildly disposed we may be to hope the best, still we cannot persuade ourselves that a man is good whose conduct we know to be hard and unjust. How much less can we expect working-men to do so who are suffering daily from their injustice. Dundee being a factory and hand-loom weaving population, I found there much distress from want of employment and low wages. The hand-loom weavers, being engaged chiefly on sail cloth, did not average above six shillings per week.

I resume the account of my visit to Dundee. During my lectures, having invited questions at the end of one of them as usual, I was blamed for not joining the Corn Law Association. This led to an engagement to discuss the relative merits of the Chartist and the Corn Law Associations for two nights in the hall of the Watts' Mechanics' Institute, and as I had similar discussions afterwards, and many of the Chartists were misunderstood on that matter, I shall briefly relate the grounds of our policy regarding the Corn Law Association at that time. Much animadversion was cast on the Chartists for their refusal to join the Anti-Corn Law League and for interrupting their meetings; but the origin and nature of these differences were not understood by those who had not mixed with the working classes.[183] However ignorant and unfit the labouring class may be considered to exercise the franchise by the upper classes, past history shows that they have mostly been the first to complain of unjust laws. This appears but natural, for as a body they are the first to feel them. They may err, but they have no interest in error on these matters. They had ever opposed the Corn Laws, and for many years had petitioned in vain for their removal. As a body they had been the life of all the great reforms, and when they had organised to some extent for the Charter and were preparing the national petition, the Anti-Corn Law party took the field. At first they were chiefly composed of Whigs, mostly of the shopkeepers, whom the working men had aided to get the franchise, but who would not now with their votes aid them to get theirs. They felt they could not succeed without the people, and urged them to join them. This the people felt they could not do and retain their own organisation. Seeing this the answer to the Anti-Corn Law men was, "No, you should join us. Ours includes yours, and without an extended franchise you have little chance of success. We expose the evils of the Corn Laws and sign petitions against them, but have no vote to help you to repeal them. We are organising to procure the vote that we

---

[183] There is a good discussion of this by Lucy Brown, "The Chartists and the Anti-Corn League", in Asa Briggs (Ed.), *Chartist Studies* (1959). See also below, p. 230 and Norman McCord, *The Anti-Corn Law League 1838–1846* (1958).

may repeal them and all other unjust taxes." Hence a discussion of policy was general. This widened into attacks on the position of many of the capitalist employers, who were charged with being ever ready to beat down labour to the lowest point, even when profits would enable them to give better wages.[184] At that time there was little or no intercourse between the employers and employed; no tea parties, at which the one met the other; no care to improve the comforts and condition of the workman. They knew little of the inner spirit or life of each other. The workman only saw in his employer an authority to command him; the masters in the men those who disliked it and evaded it when they could. Looking on the employers as seizing on every opportunity of reducing wages, many of the operatives laboured under the false impression that unless they had the franchise masters would reduce wages correspondingly with the reduction in the price of food. These opinions varied, but the general reply was, "We want our political rights; help us to get them first, and then we shall be better able to go hand in hand with you to repeal the Corn Laws." The gentleman with whom it was arranged I should discuss the question was Mr. G. Troup, then editor of the *Montrose Review* newspaper, and afterwards editor of the *Daily Mail*. We were confined to half an hour each in our speeches, and a quarter of an hour each at closing. As the hall was seated for 700, 350 tickets were given to each committee. I contended that we had an organisation, while they were only beginning, and should join us instead of our joining them. His argument was that there were more people for the Corn Laws being repealed than there were for the Charter. Yet on the vote being taken on the second night we had a large majority, a proof either that we had gained converts, or that their friends were very lax in their support. I had never seen my opponent until I went on to the platform. I found him a practised debater, having long been used to public discussion. Being a professed Liberal, he truly said, when I pointed out certain reforms along with the franchise as essential to the improvement of the people, that he was for all these also, but urged a concentration of power to repeal the bread tax. I replied that we needed a concentration of power to get into the House of Commons in order to remove the bread tax and other evils also, and that to admit the truth and justice of our claims was one thing, but to work for their attainment was another. I remember he fairly lost his temper when hearing him so often admit the right of all that we were contending for, and yet maintain that it was better policy to keep to the simple Corn Law repeal, I exclaimed, "I find Mr. T. is a mere political pedlar; he has samples of all wares but stocks of none." Public discussions rarely cause men who have previously chosen their side to change

[184] Lowery's confrontation with Mr. Forbes, an Anti-Corn Law Leaguer, at Arbroath on 19 November 1839 is reported in *Northern Star*, 23 November 1839, p. 8; Lowery rejected Forbes's reproach of the Chartists for not supporting the League by saying that "cheapened corn would bring lower wages to the weaver", and that "it was of no use to have increased work if we had not increased benefits. Cheap provisions and increasing exports did not give higher wages and increased employment to the people".

it, but they frequently extend information on the subjects under dispute to that part of the audience which have not previously studied them. The Chartist Association of Dundee received a weekly accession of numbers at its sittings. I here entered into an engagement to lecture for three months to the Forfar Associations. They had an organisation which extended from Dundee to Arbroath and Montrose, and up inland to Forfar and Kerrymuir, at the base of the Grampian hills. Everywhere in this district the spirit was warm and active. Dundee had a number of large halls. Its population, composed chiefly of the handloom weavers and workmen in the mills, was, to a man, chartist. It had lectures on all the interesting topics of the day, a good mechanics' institution, and the leading minds were well-informed, and the masses intelligent.

I had now had an opportunity to observe the Scotch, and to estimate the difference between them and their fellow workmen in England. The English are quicker in perception and more impelled by their feelings than the Scotch, but very often it is but a surface perception. Activity and success warm and stimulate their feelings, and they fearlessly and at all risks speak out their mind. The Scotch are not so quick in perception, they like their understandings to be convinced, "to see th' reasons o' 't," as they express it; but once convinced they keep their "grep o't," they hold fast by what they deem true, not that they do not feel as well as the English. On the contrary, mind and feeling thus united in them are shown in the force of deeds rather than in sounds of the voice. In England, the quick common sense of the crowd and instinctive love of fair play, added to their manly contempt for the mean and time-serving, make them alive to any defects in the routine of the "services" of "Church or State." But except where the audience was intermixed with the middle classes, you could not safely venture to support your arguments with history or general literature for fear you would not be understood. I have gazed on Runnymede, the field of Worcester, and Shakspere's and Hampden's homes, but rarely found a labouring man whose spirit had communed with the past, or who could do more than act as guide-post to point you to the spot.

Everything spoke fair for a steady progress in Scotland. There never had been violent language generally in Scotland, yet they would not allow their English brethren to be attacked for theirs. The consciousness that their fellow countrymen were as a rule educated and intelligent took away from the upper classes the objection which they could use in England, "That the people were uneducated," and they would at once admit to the chartists, "Oh, it is not you we's feared to trust wi' the vote, its the English working men, they are so ignorant! half of them cannot read or write." But an ordeal lay before the leaders in England, and the difficulties soon commenced. I have spoken before of the threatening language which we had learned from our Whig schoolmasters. Although with them it was but the policy of words in the warmth of excitement, the multitude deal in facts. The whirlwind of popular passion had been unloosed, and those who raised it could not wield it. The combined opposition to it of every one of the Convention and other prominent leaders, had they been of one mind, would scarcely have changed the current at once.[185] Most likely it would have passed by them, carrying others in front. But they varied in opinion. The Convention being over had left no influence but vexation at its having failed to get the Charter at once. The more judicious felt they could do nothing but bide the time when events would open the eyes of the people, and as their own speeches were of the instructive and practical order they were always listened to with respect. But had they proceeded to attack the others as wrong and dangerous, then they would have been at once denounced as traitors in the camp.[186] O'Connor and his party knowing well those who disagreed with him, were ever on the watch to denounce them and to destroy their influence. In this they too often succeeded. For myself, from the first he knew that I was no O'Connor's man, yet as I never attacked him nor his party, but went steadily on propounding what I deemed true in doctrine and right in practice, leaving the people to infer the difference, I may not have been understood by him.

In describing the elements of the Convention and the extreme O'Connor's party in it, I have already stated the complaints made against O'Connor's speeches and those of his friends, which caused the Birmingham delegates and others to leave. It may now be asked, if the majority of the Convention was with O'Connor how did it complain of him? If it complained why not stop the language? The Convention was only a deliberative body, and its chief business was of a practical nature. Hence there was little temptation to utter hot language in the Convention, and even the extreme members were not violent in conversation, or when speaking apart from the crowd, nor yet was F. O'Connor. It was in the speeches outside of the Convention that they saw danger, but they had no power to stop this, and the majority would not have sanctioned an open condemnation of these speeches.

The authorities had never yet interfered, except in the dismissal of John Frost from the magistracy in Newport and in the imprisonment and trial of Henry Vincent, for libel[187]. But about this time the Government came down

---

[185] Compare Thomas Cooper: "the demagogue, or popular 'leader', is rather the people's instrument than their director", *Life*, p. 180; and O'Connor, "I don't lead; I am driven by the people", quoted in Asa Briggs (Ed.), *Chartist Studies* (1959), p. 10; cf. G. D. H. Cole, *Chartist Portraits* (1941), pp. 145, 203.

[186] Compare E. P. Thompson, *The Making of the English Working Class* (2nd edn. 1968), p. 176: "The Jacobin or Chartist, who implied the threat of overwhelming numbers but who held back from actual revolutionary preparation, was always exposed, at some critical moment, both to the loss of the confidence of his own supporters and the ridicule of his opponents."

[187] Frost had been deprived of his position as a magistrate in March 1839, after a vigorous personal correspondence with the Home Secretary, Lord John Russell. See G. D. H. Cole, *Chartist Portraits*, pp. 137 ff. Vincent was arrested—for attending a "riotous assemblage" in April—in London on 8 May 1839, but was released on bail until his trial.

as with a swoop, and numbers were arrested in different parts of the country, for sedition, &c., and held to bail until the assizes.

One night, after a meeting in Dundee, a person who had been a member in the Convention came up to me, stating he wished a few words in private.[188] But I must first state that during the autumn, shortly after the Convention dissolved, this person had called on me at Newcastle, and informed me that he had been at the supper given to Dr. Fletcher, at Bury, Lancashire (the Doctor had been member for Bury), and some of our leading men had been there, and that under cover of this supper some had met to concoct a rising, of which I would hear by-and-bye. I told him it would be madness to attempt such a thing. He dissented, and told me I did not know what he knew. I observed that I supposed it was F. O'Connor's scheme, and that he would leave them in the lurch. He answered, they had not let him into their secret, for they did not think he was to be trusted.

I had come to Dundee and seen little of this person, as he had never called on me, and I thought he had taken umbrage because I had been engaged to lecture instead of him, who had been member for the district, and was a resident. He now informed me that the affair he had informed me of was still intended, and that he had received a letter from Dr. John Taylor, that he had come into the Newcastle district, intending to give lectures on Chemistry, explaining the nature of explosive forces, but that he could make nothing of them, and he wished me to go up and try as I was popular there.[189] He knew that something was to take place soon in Wales. My answer was, "If Dr. Taylor makes bolts he may shoot them, but I am not such a fool as to try; but most likely he is at his usual lies, and this is a piece of his brag and mystery,—but it is too bad for such a fellow to send letters about at a time when we have every reason to suppose that the Post-office is tampered with, thus putting men's liberties in jeopardy, and I advise you instantly to write to Frost and inform him of the letter you have received from Dr. John and the danger of such letters.[190] I would save the midnight post at once, but mind be cautious in writing about it, put in no names, Frost will understand you without that."

Next morning's mail brought the news of the Welsh insurrection, which

---

[188] This was W. G. Burns, convention delegate for Dundee, who had taken a moderate line in the face of physical force demands, both at the Calton Hill meeting and in the 1839 convention.

[189] Alex Wilson "John Taylor, Esq., M.D. of Blackhouse", *Ayrshire Archaeological & Natural History Society Collections*, 2nd Ser., I (1947–9), p. 196 shows that Taylor, in his revolutionary conspiracy of late 1839, considered entrusting Lowery with control over the town and barracks at Newcastle. Lowery's account lends credibility to the view which G. D. H. Cole rejected in *Chartist Portraits* (p. 161) that "there may have been a national plan—of sorts—adumbrated during the last days of the Chartist Convention, but never fully worked out or agreed on".

[190] Lowery was correct in his fears. A warrant dated 3 August 1839 had placed the letters of Lowery, Fletcher, Carpenter and O'Brien under surveillance—F. C. Mather, *Public Order in the Age of the Chartists* (Manchester, 1959), p. 221.

came like a thunder clap on all Dundee. I had scarcely got the news when the person I have spoken of came breathless to my lodgings. "I am off directly," said he. "Off, why, where to?" "That letter, you know; they will open at Newport, and I shall be arrested." "But if you wrote it as I told you I cannot see they can get any proof of your connection with it." And on cross-questioning him I found that in despite of my injunctions he had put in my name and Dr. Taylor's, but *not his own!* Well, said I, I think it is me that should be off, you have put me in danger of an arrest and not yourself. However, he being evidently absorbed in self was soon off to some part where he imagined he would be safe. For myself, I at once saw that it was most likely that the letter would fall into the hands of the authorities and I should be chargeable with being an accomplice in the affair, but I determined to stand the matter out. I knew I was innocent, and to have run away would have looked ill, and perhaps directed attention to me, so I went on lecturing as usual, but for some weeks every strange knock startled me as if it would bring a warrant for my apprehension. However, none came, but it appeared strange that I had not heard of it in some way. The mystery was solved some time after, when Frost's trial came on before the Commission at Newport. I was then in London at a Convention, and as the person who wrote the letter was going to the trial I enjoined him to make every prudent enquiry at Newport about it that I might know whether it was in the hands of the authorities. On enquiry, he found, strange as it might appear, that although when it came, Frost was in the hills, and his outlawry had been declared, yet the Post-office delivered it at his house, Mrs. Frost was in, read it and at once put it in the fire.

In Dundee, and wherever I went, there was but one opinion—pity that a man so respected had been connected with such a mad and foolish affair. The more combative were annoyed to think that when they had risen they had made such a miserably poor job of it. "When they determined to start, what for did they no tak t' th' hills and stand it out like men?" was a common exclamation; but the general feeling was that the act was ill advised, and would put back the attainment of our objects. As is known, Frost, Williams, Jones, and others were arrested 4th November, 1839, and the insurrection quickly quelled, and a commission issued 6th January, 1840, to try the prisoners, who received their sentence on the 13th. A new danger arose from the state of mind among the people in England. The physical force feeling had not evaporated—it was aroused now on behalf of Frost. "Were they to let them hang Frost?" "No; never!" "What! would you not risk something to save Frost?" "The Chartists will show themselves base cowards if they do not rescue Frost," were common exclamations. They forgot that another insurrection was just the way to force the authorities to carry out the extreme power of the law. Feargus O'Connor was at once active in arranging for the best defence which could be obtained. Sir Fitzroy Kelly and Pollock were retained, and a defence fund was commenced, and O'Connor urged the people to elect another Convention. He was frequently but falsely accused afterwards by O'Brien and others by running away. But undoubtedly he knew what was soon to occur, and, through his newspaper and influence with the people, was the only man who could without much exposure have nipped the plot in the bud. This he should have done, or, if wishing it to succeed, and possessed of courage, he should have been at hand to assist. But, coward like, he ran off to Ireland, under pretence of business in Cork, as soon as he knew that the explosion was about to take place.[191] As it was he soon came back to address large meetings. He was in his glory when in the excitement of a large meeting, whatever that meeting was about. Although O'Connor had urged an immediate election of a convention, yet the country did not respond. They had not funds, and could not see any good a convention could do, beyond what the district committees could accomplish. However, some of the important towns notified their intention to send members. I urged the Committee of Dundee to send one, not that I agreed as to the propriety of holding a Convention, but knowing the state of the provinces of England I felt sure some of the more desperate men would be there full of the excitement of the moment, and if not counteracted by others who had seen through the folly of popular outbreaks, they would be concocting plots, and by them the cause would be thrown back many years, and the lives of Frost and his companions perhaps sacrificed.

I was elected for Dundee and Forfar and sailed direct for London. On arriving there I found that by the returns only ten delegates had been elected, and one of these was for London, a Polish major.[192] There was not one who had been in the former convention or who knew anything of the general state of the country. Full of the determination to save Frost at the risk of their lives, they were ready to sanction any desperate deed, not that they were men of naturally violent dispositions, but the contrary. We held our meetings in the Arundel coffee-house, in a room by ourselves. The room

[191] Gammage attributed to Lowery (one of his informants) in his *History of the Chartist Movement*, p. 267, the view that O'Connor "had nothing to do with getting up that movement [i.e. the Frost rising]; but he was perfectly cognizant of it, and was the only man that could have put a stop to it, had he been so disposed". Compare David Williams, *John Frost. A Study in Chartism* (Cardiff, 1939), pp. 200 ff. But Hovell, p. 176, says that Gammage's main informant on the Frost rising was William Ashton of Barnsley.

[192] This was Bartholomew Beniowski (c. 1801–67), an eccentric Polish refugee who fought on the Russian side in the early months of the 1830 Polish rising, but who went over to the Polish side. He was a member of the East London Democratic Association. His government pension of £3 a month, as trustee for a fund for the support of Polish refugees, was stopped by Lord John Russell in May 1839. Urquhart believed that Beniowski was a Russian agent, "mover and director of the whole plan" (to use Urquhart's own words) by which the Russians intended to embarrass the British government with a Chartist uprising at home; no evidence has ever confirmed Urquhart's belief. Lowery's account must be read in the light of his subsequent conversion to Urquhart's views, See Gertrude Robinson, *David Urquhart* (Oxford, 1920), pp. 89, 98; Henry G. Weisser, "Polonophilism and the British Working Class, 1830–1845", *Polish Review*, Spring 1967, pp. 92–3. Beniowski spent his later life trying to revolutionize the arts of spelling and printing, published his *Phrenotypics* (1842), and applied for printing patents in 1846, 1847 and 1849.

was not a public one, but if a person occasionally came in, the conversation was turned on general matters, and strangers soon saw they were intruding. All manner of plans and projects were spoken about evincing a desperate resolution that if Frost was to perish they would perish with him and involve the upper classes in the destruction. I contented myself with standing mostly by the fireside flinging in a word or two of objection and advice when I had an opportunity. I was frequently asked, would you really not be ready to risk your life to save Frost? I answered, yes, if it could do any good, but not to bring many others into the same danger uselessly. I know the country would not respond to any such projects as yours, and it would only end in more lives being sacrificed and many more being imprisoned. F. O'Connor was in London at first, and although he had urged the formation of this Convention he never attended it. Yet he knew its materials, and still took no steps to pacify it or the more desperate committees who had sent it up, except that he induced them to draw the £200 which the former body had left in the hands of Mr. Rogers, for the use of the next Convention, and to hand it over to him to be applied in Frost's defence. One day the conversation had entered on the most wild and dangerous topics as to what the people could do if roused to insurrection. Cutting off the gas, and exploding gaso-meters and such like was the theme, and the number of men some Lancashire towns would yield, and the force which the metropolis would furnish. I contented myself with an occasional exclamation of preposterous, absurd, or madness, but did not attempt to argue against them, for I felt it would be useless. The Pole depended a great deal on the *"torty tousand teives"* which were in London, which were sure to be with the people he asserted; "no doubt," I exclaimed, "but what to do?" Observing him taking notes I coolly stepped forward to the table and said, addressing the Chairman, "I have from the first told you I disagreed with you and objected to your projects. I know there is not a committee in Scotland would sanction your ideas or projects, yet wishing to do all I could to hinder you from doing harm to Frost and the cause, I remained along with you. I would be ready to run every risk to do good, but I am determined that if ever I have to be tried for opposing authority it shall be for something I can justify and feel proud of trying to do, and not stand at the bar with a fool's cap upon my head. You know that the police are on the watch and that spies are supposed to be in the house, yet here is a conversation going on, which, if known beyond our-selves, would subject us all to immediate imprisonment; yet I observe one has been taking notes of that conversation. I protest against any person being allowed to take notes of these proceedings. In an instant every eye was on the Polish major, and a general demand made why he was taking notes. He answered, to help his memory in the dispute, that he might reply to those he differed with.[193] I exclaimed no one shall do so while I am here; the

---

[193] In 1842 Beniowski was employed as a teacher of memory at the Royal Adelaide Gallery in the Strand.

others trust to their memories and you can do so equally as well as they. There was a general demand that he should put them on the fire or they would put him on, which he at once did.[194]

The trial of the Welsh prisoners was proceeding, and all the Chartist districts were more or less excited. We were informed that meetings of delegates were being held in Yorkshire, Lancashire, and Northumberland; and, although it was not stated explicitly, I could find that some in the Convention had expected a much larger attendance, so that they might have been able to arrange a rising of the people to save Frost. In the early part of the week on which the trial commenced a person was sent up from a meeting of delegates in the country to give the Convention notice to break up and get to their different districts, for that they had decided to wait no longer, and had arranged to commence an insurrection on the following Saturday evening. Had it not been for the fatal results that were pending it would have been laughable to have observed the selfish gladness of some of those who had been most urgent in the Convention to fix an insurrection. They were now glad that they had not done it, and that the responsibility rested on those in the districts who had arranged it. It was now found that few had funds to get home, and it was decided that one of them should be despatched down to Newport to demand as much as would pay the fare of each and settle for the room, and other expenses of our meetings. He went, and quickly returned with the necessary sum. He was a character in his way, and described humorously his interview with O'Connor, who at first demurred, as if the money was his own. Our messenger being pert and peremptory, O'Connor consented, saying, "Well, I think I will give you so and so," fixing a larger amount than had been requested. "Yes, better had," was the reply, "for if there's not mony on us we can dam the *Star* thou kens." All being arranged to depart, some begun to speculate how the insurrection should be conducted. They had the sense to perceive their inability to lead or command in such warfare. Some of them suggested to the Polish major that now was the time for him to be useful, and that he should take the command. The answer of the Pole was soon ready. He did not express unwillingness, but stated that before he could go he would need to be supplied with a sum of money to get things he must have before he could assume such an office. "He would need £50 to get a chronometer. He would want a number of maps and other things, besides." I had urged on them the evident madness and cruelty of such an attempt, entailing misery on those who attempted it. Yet they doggedly clung to the idea, while at a glance one might see that in their hearts they were convinced that the scheme was wrong and impracticable. In a very large

---

[194] This is the second point at which Lowery sheds new light on the conspiracies and plots of 1839–40. His is the only inside account we possess of the 1839–40 convention in London which opened on 19 December 1839. R. G. Gammage briefly refers to this convention in his *History of the Chartist Movement*, p. 165; see also M. Hovell, *Chartist Movement*, p. 183. Compare Lowery's contempt for London conventions by April 1840—below, p. 250.

number of the people at that time there was a sort of double-mindedness. The one mind, which was expressed, arose from the idea of the force of their numbers; the other, which was private, held convictions of the impracticability of such schemes. Fortunately, except in one or two places on a small scale, no rising took place. Each had wisely lain still until they heard how the others did. The Bradford leader, Peter Busy, wisely took to his bed, too ill to fight. Only some dozen issued forth at midnight, who were soon captured, though, unfortunately, a watchman was shot. The whole affair was calculated to excite contempt and ridicule.[195]

On arriving at Newcastle I found all quiet; the leading ones had seen in time the madness of attempting a rising. Some of them were off for America, as one desperate fellow, who was captured at Bradford, had threatened to inform of them to the authorities if they did not go on with their plot.[196]

---

[195] For events in Bradford, see A. J. Peacock, *Bradford Chartism 1838–1840* (York, 1969).

[196] Lowery nowhere mentions his *Address . . . on the System of Exclusive Dealing* (reprinted below, p. 195 & ff.) which must have been written in late 1839. The pamphlet advocates demonstrating the political and moral power of the people through exclusive dealing and co-operative retailing. "It is a measure that carries with it no principles of violence . . . It will unite us by a double tie—principle and self-interest: these will form a bond of union we have never had" (p. 200).

V

New Directions:
1839–1841

I was now seized with general illness, and had to refrain from going back to Scotland, where I was engaged to lecture in the districts of Edinburgh and Fife. I at last became bed-fast, and lay so over Christmas, getting weaker and weaker. From this time commenced a series of unexpected mercies, which, coming from utter strangers, rendered this period of my life to me most solemn and profitable. When cast down on a bed of sickness, surrounded by cares and difficulties, in pain and languor, my soul thrown back upon itself in inner thought, I first felt the nothingness of life here, unless conjoined to life eternal, and was led away from things of earth to commune with things heavenly. From that time forward my dear wife and I had a deep conviction that our duty was simply to live right each passing day, and not to fret for the future, which was in the hand of our Father in heaven, who ordereth all things for the best, and would provide for us.[197] When spring came I received a kind letter from Dr. Pearson, of Dumfries, whom I had seen for the first time on stopping at his house on the night I was at Dumfries, and spoke there at the torch-light meeting. I had left the next morning, and not seen him again; but having heard of my illness, he kindly invited me, if I could be removed, to come down to his house, where I should find a good garden, good air, and attendance, which he would feel a pleasure in giving me. I was removed. Week after week of the summer had passed away and I was no better. Then he thought it necessary for me to undergo an operation which, as he was not a surgeon, he felt that it would be more advisable for a skilled operator to execute. Although we were on the most intimate terms, and he knew my resources must be small, he did not know the scantiness of them. How my wife and children were fending [faring][198] I did not dare to ask. I

---

[197] Compare the situation of Henry Vincent at this time in the *Dictionary of Labour Biography*, I (1972), p. 329. See also B. Harrison & P. Hollis, *art. cit.* pp. 516–7. Compare A. R. Schoyen, *The Chartist Challenge* (1958), pp. 97, 116. Lowery's statement here echoes his sentiments in the *Weekly Record*, 23 October 1858, p. 366: "religion, obedience to the law of God, becoming godly or godlike, living righteously, is the only way in which men can be happy in this world." Lowery's letter (printed below, p. 249) dated 27 April 1840, refers to his recent "very ill health", but the vigour of his prose style suggests that by then he was recovering.

[198] Interpolation in the original, see fn. 68 above.

had left them in the book shop; the rent was large, and I was aware the profits of the business were not adequate to the expenditure, unless increased by my own labours. Not to distress me, my wife had not alluded to money matters in her letters. This I took as a proof that they were not prosperous, or she would have told me. I knew she could have food, but knew also she would in such circumstances deny herself to the utmost extent. I feared to ask her anything about these things. Had it not been for her and the children I would willingly have left this life. Day by day this world had seemed to fade from me. Weary and pained, I felt reconciled to die. Just at this time a working man who had been a delegate for London at the first Convention,[199] being on his way to attend a committee in Glasgow, called at Newcastle, expecting to find me at home. He was much grieved when informed where and how I was, and decided instantly to cross to Carlisle, and go to Glasgow by way of Dumfries that he might see me. I had taken much interest during the Convention in attending his meetings in Marylebone, and I being popular had thus conduced to sustain him in his position. This had produced on his part a kind feeling towards me. During my illness at Newcastle Mr. Urquhart,[200] the impeacher of Lord Palmerston's foreign policy, had been invited by the merchants of Newcastle to address them on our commercial treaties and relations. He had held conversational meetings with all classes and parties; and Mr. Charles Atwood[201] and other leading gentlemen of Newcastle had adopted them, as well as a large number of the working men. A gentleman from London[202] had called at my house and left me some of the

---

[199] Probably William Cardo, shoemaker and delegate for Marylebone at the general convention. Cardo had been active in the Grand National Consolidated Trades Union and in defending the victims of the Derby lockout in 1833–4. He was a close associate of Dr. Taylor during 1839, and advocated physical force in the convention, but was later converted by Urquhart. He brought several Chartist converts into Urquhart's camp, and was attacked by Chartists as a renegade. G. Robinson's *David Urquhart*, p. 92 says "none of the converted Chartists showed more enthusiasm, ability, and power of absorbing and reproducing the new ideas than William Cardo".

[200] David Urquhart (1805–77) took part in the Greek war of independence 1827–8. He was secretary of the British embassy at Constantinople 1835–7, but his involvement in disputes with Russia (see below, p. 183) ensured his recall, and on the death of William IV he lost his inside influence over government policy. He published many government documents in his *Portfolio* (1835–6), and converted several Chartist leaders to his belief that the Russian government was secretly fomenting physical force Chartism for its own purposes. Excluded from government circles, he turned to organizing popular support for his views and in the late 1830s and 1850s formed many foreign affairs committees (especially in the North-East) to inquire into government policy. Marx himself co-operated with Urquhart in campaigning against Russia, as the world's leading reactionary power. Urquhart believed that Frost was an unwitting victim of Beniowski (whom he labelled a Russian spy) and so did his best to defend Frost in 1839–40. Urquhart was M.P. for Stafford 1847–52 and published extensively. On his influence with the Chartists, see J. H. Gleason, *The Genesis of Russophobia in Great Britain* (Cambridge, USA, 1950), pp. 259 ff. See also R. Shannon, "The foreign affairs committees", in P. Hollis (ed.), *Pressure from Without* (1974); H. Weisser, *British Working Class Movements and Europe 1815–1848* (1975), pp. 99-107.

[201] Brother of Thomas Attwood, and one of Urquhart's earliest and keenest supporters.

[202] J. H. Gleason, *Genesis of Russophobia*, p. 259 says that a London barrister named Fyler introduced Urquhart's ideas to several Chartist leaders. But Gertrude Robinson, *David Urquhart*, p. 95 says of Lowery that "Cargill gained him to the cause in the April of 1840";

works on the subject to read, begging I would do so, and give him my opinion on them. The doctor informed my London friend what he considered necessary to be done for my recovery; and after spending a day with me, he passed on to attend the committee at Glasgow. In two days he returned in high spirits, stating that during the committee-meeting the London gentleman who had left the books with me at Newcastle asked where his friend was, and what I thought of the question? He answered, that I had been ill ever since, stating how he had left me in Dumfries, and the conversation went on about other matters. After the meeting was over another gentlemen present, whose name I had not previously heard, and who had never seen me, Robert Monteith, Esq., of Carstairs-house, Lanark,[203] called my friend to one side and asked him if he would write to me that he would gladly be at the expense of the best medical advice if I would go either to London or Edinburgh. Instead of writing my friend took coach to Dumfries and urged me at once to send my acceptance and thanks.

The answer was a most kind and gentlemanly letter, enclosing £10, desirous to remove all sense of inferiority or objections, by impressing upon me that, between such as he and I there should be no false feeling or delicacy in accepting at such a time what aid I needed, and which he felt honoured in being able to give. I at once informed my Dumfries friend, and asked the favour of his going with me to Edinburgh if he could arrange to leave his business for a couple of days and I would pay his coach fare; we proceeded thither next day, which was a Saturday. We took a lodgings near to Professor Lizars, and then waited on him. He advised an operation. "You'll be better directly, we'll operate to morrow," he observed. "Oh no," said I, "let Sunday be over." "Well, as you have had a journey perhaps it would be as well to defer it until Monday morning; I will come to you on Monday morning at eleven." My friend returned to Dumfries, and I remitted money to my wife, informing her I had come to Edinburgh and wished her to come to me by coach on the Monday without fail. I knew that the operation was sure to be most painful and might be dangerous. It would be over before she arrived and the distress she would endure if present would be spared her.

---

no doubt she was drawing upon the copy of Cargill's undated report to an unnamed correspondent of Lowery's conversion, in Balliol College, *Urquhart MSS*. I e 2; in this document, Cargill says "I have already arranged to send Lowery away as a preacher . . . A few days after you left Newcastle he came here. I saw him immediately in company with another. My interview was successful. He went to study and came back in a week better still—and I then saw him again. I then had a long serious conversation with him . . . In eloquence Lowry [*sic*] has always been the first man here".

[203] Robert Monteith of Carstairs (1811–84) was a member of the Cambridge "twelve apostles", from 1846 a Roman Catholic, and a lifelong friend of Urquhart. He was prominent in promoting Urquhart's cause in Glasgow. According to James Burn, he attempted a Tory-Radical alliance with the later Chartist Dr. John Taylor in 1837 as a way of splitting the liberal vote in Glasgow (*Autobiography*, 1978 ed., p. 146). See B. Aspinwall, "The Scottish Dimension: Robert Monteith and the Origins of Modern British Catholic Social Thought", *Downside Review*, Jan. 1979.

Everything went on favourably. She arrived about ten at night, just as the Professor's assistant, who had remained with me almost the whole time from my being dressed and put to bed, was retiring. She became my watchful nurse. I rested favourably all night and next day imminent danger was considered past. I sent word to Mr. Monteith that I had been operated on, and he kindly sent his servant man through to Edinburgh to see me with a letter enclosing me another £10, hoping I would not let myself want for anything. I recovered rapidly. I was able to sit up in a week—to go out in a fortnight, and in three weeks returned to Newcastle. Dr. Lizars, with his usual kindness, gave me his valuable services gratuitously. I felt as one just rescued from the grave by my sudden restoration to health and activity through the Divine blessing. And fervently frequently, did we implore Heaven's blessing on him whose kind liberality had been so instrumental to that restoration.

A few days later I was elected at a public meeting, at Sunderland, with Charles Attwood, Esq., as a member of a deputation[204] that was sent to Paris to assure the French that the English people did not sympathise with the acts of Lord Palmerston, then Foreign Secretary, who had formed an alliance with Russia and insulted France, and Mr. R. Monteith again sent me £10. In a few days I passed on to London, and was introduced to some gentlemen who took an interest in these deputations, fearing, from the umbrage which M. Thiers, Prime Minister to Louis Philippe, had taken at Lord Palmerston's quadruple treaty, that we might drift into a. war with France and retard liberal progress. A working-man, of the name of Thomas, was delegated from a London committee to proceed with me to France, it being deemed desirable that the working-men of Paris should be communicated with by working-men of England on the matter. He could speak French fluently, which I could not. Considering his small opportunities he was a marvel at languages. He was a shoemaker, and acquired them all when following his trade. He was a native of Cornwall, was apprenticed to a shoemaker at Falmouth, where he acquired his French from mixing with the French boatmen who came there. This he afterwards improved by books. He was thus frequently called in to interpret at the principal hotel. On the Duke of Palmella accompanying Donna Maria, of Portugal, to this country, before she had been acknowledged as Queen by our Government, they took up their residence at the principal hotel. The Duke wishing to study the English privately while staying there, Mr. Thomas was called in, and the Duke being able to speak French it became the medium between them, so while teaching the Duke English he learned Portuguese from the Duke. Afterwards a German ship with emigrants for America was wrecked near Falmouth in the autumn, and the Germans had to remain until the spring before they could proceed on their voyage, some of them lodged at his

---

[204] For this deputation, see J. H. Gleason, *loc. cit.*

164

mother's and he became very intimate with one of the young women; he got the rudiments of the German from her, which he followed up by books until he could read, write, and speak it fluently. During the war in Portugal with Don Miguel he was sent out with a vessel to trade on that coast. While thus engaged he acquired the Spanish and Italian languages perfectly. Although he had never been in France so perfect was his pronunciation that he was taken for a native. He delighted in the German, often saying that he deemed it of more worth than all the other languages which he knew. Yet, with all this knowledge of languages, he had turned it to no practical account in the way of elevating his position in life. He wanted energy and aspiration.

We took packet to Boulogne and stopped a day there to see it. On going to the market I was much struck with the similarity of the women's dress to those of Scotland, and I observed afterwards that in many things the Scotch appear to have been influenced more by French customs than by English ones. On arriving in Paris by diligence we put up at the Hotel Bristol, Rue St. Honoré, where we took apartments on the first floor that we might have a respectable address whence to date our letters; but being constantly engaged waiting on gentlemen to whom we had introductions we were rarely in the house until night. We were evidently a mystery to the people of the hotel; our expenditure, except paying for our apartments, was very frugal. We always dined out wherever we happened to be engaged, and so attracted little notice; but on the third day the Comte de Argout, then Governor of the Bank of France, called on us and left his card, and we evidently rose one hundred per cent. in estimation after that. Paris presented altogether a new phase of life to me, and from the mission in which I was engaged I was enabled to procure interviews with the leading characters of the country. Many of these I had read of but never expected to be in company with. I had interviews with Lamartine, Tocqueville, Odillon Barrot, Dupin, Ducos, Garnier Pages, General Bugeaud, afterwards Marshal of Isly, the Editor of the *Courier Francais*, Monsieur Cabat, the leader of the Icarians, and many others.[205]

There was a struggle in the Chamber of Deputies and a ministerial crisis, Thiers evidently wishing for war, while Guizot, who had been called in, was

---

[205] Alphonse Lamartine (1790–1869), earliest of the great French romantic poets, and at this time a deputy, who tried to persuade the conservatives to promote social justice. Alexis de Tocqueville (1805–59), the Liberal politician and political scientist, entered the Chamber of Deputies in 1839 and won a seat in the Académie Française in 1841. Odillon Barrot (1791–1856), Liberal monarchist under the July Monarchy, and leader of the left in the French chamber under the Thiers government. André Dupin (1783–1865), a lawyer and deputy who often opposed government measures, president of the Chamber 1832–9. Theodore Ducos (1801–55), a deputy from 1834, who almost always voted with the opposition. Étienne Garnier-Pagès, leader of the republican opposition in the Chamber from 1831 till his death in 1841. General Bugeaud (1784–1849) was prominent in subjugating Algeria. Étienne Cabet (1788–1856), utopian communist whose plans were formulated in his *Voyage en Icarie* (1842); Cabet arranged several interviews for Lowery with French working men.

struggling to maintain peace; yet all parties seemed to consider that Lord Palmerston had acted treacherously towards France and grossly insulted her. Among the people the war spirit was rising, and the songs of the street minstrels were chiefly about perfidious Albion.

The expositions of Thiers in the Chambers and in his dispatches showed that for some end Lord Palmerston had wheeled round and acted a double and inconsistent part. Without consulting France he had propounded a new treaty for pacification of the East and the defence of Turkey, which he had induced Russia and Austria to sign. M. Thiers naturally objected to it, showing that it was calculated to bring about the very results which England and France had been in alliance to prevent. The facts were these:—Becoming acquainted with the secret articles of a treaty between Russia and Turkey, wherein Russia had bound Turkey to agree to a treaty offensive and defensive with her, and in the event of a war between Russia and any other power Turkey was to close the Dardanelles against her enemies, but that if any power declared war with Turkey Russia was to aid Turkey with troops also to defend Constantinople. France and England had protested against this treaty—the Czar, however, had paid no attention to their protest. The alliance, therefore, between France and England had been, not to put Egypt's Pasha down, but to keep Russia from interfering and having a pretext to act upon this treaty. But by this quadruple treaty Lord Palmerston had sanctioned the very articles into which Russia had inveigled Turkey and against which they had protested; for it stipulated that while the Allies were to assist Turkey with ships, which were to remain without the Dardenelles, Russia alone was to assist Turkey with troops to help her to defend Constantinople! A child would have had the sense to perceive that if Russia once occupied Constantinople it would not be easy to get her out again.

I found all those I was introduced to extremely affable.[206] Knowing the excitement which affected the French public mind on the question, it seemed strange to me that there was no manner in which the people met to express their sentiments. On making observations on the contrasts between France and England on this matter to Monsieur Tocqueville, and others, the answer was, it would be well if they could do so, but that we were a cooler people, and would discuss and dispute in *words*, whilst the French populace were so excitable that once met to discuss and to decide they would at once proceed to carry out their decisions, and violence would be the result. I was much interested in the conversation of Garnier Pages; he appeared to me most intelligent, mild, and amicable, but firm in his ideas of needful progression. I inquired whether the French workmen, as a class, had studied the facts and principle essential to work out their elevation, or whether they were blindly impelled by the feeling that their position was not as it ought to be.

<hr />

[206] For Lowery's contemporaneous reports to the Chairman of the Committee for Investigating Foreign Affairs, dated 15 and 17 November 1840, see Gertrude Robinson, *David Urquhart*, pp. 108–11.

He answered that as a body they had not sufficiently studied facts and principles. I was astonished on my interview with General Bugeaud to find him enamoured with *Fourierism*, which he thought presented a panacea for our social evils. He talked about little else, and introduced me to a young gentleman, an editor of a Fourierist journal, who was in his house, and who presented me with some back numbers of the journal.[207]

I here met Mr. Urquhart for the first time, and was remarkably struck by his extraordinary powers, and his extensive knowledge of Eastern affairs. He did not look at the mere *forms* of government, but at the principles and spirit developed in its *action*. He would often show how, under liberal forms, the influence of the ruling power was to stop the progress of sound and liberal ideas, while, on the other hand, despotic States were sometimes linked with interests which advanced liberty.

There are some minds which you occasionally become acquainted with who at once lift you up beside them, and present to your vision a wider and clearer view than ever you had before; such seemed the effects of Mr. Urquhart's conversations on me.[208] There were points in his views which I could not see at first, but as time rolled on a further study of the subject, and the events which time brought forth, confirmed his views. Hitherto I had simply applied my mind to forms of government and popular rights, thinking that if these were attained improvement would be at once achieved. But he turned my mind to the fact that all law was dead unless its spirit was in the people, and that England was prostrate for want of great minds. That the hope of rousing the country from its lethargy lay in the working-men. Not that their minds were superior in knowledge to the other classes, but that they were more simple and unperverted, and thus in a better state to receive information, while the minds of the others were full of false notions, which had first to be removed before you could implant correct ideas.

One day I asked him if he did not think that the working-classes had a right to the Charter? He replied, You may as well ask me if they have a right to the air they breathe, but cannot you see that no institutional rights can give liberty unless the spirit is in the people. A nation may have these constitutional rights, and wanting that spirit be the slaves of faction. Greece and Rome did not fall because they had not the forms of liberty, but because the spirit of independence and patriotism had first died out. Then, although the forms remained, they were inoperative and lifeless. It is obvious, then, that if nations while they had these forms of liberty became enslaved

---

[207] For Fourier, see above fn. 43.

[208] According to his own account, Urquhart made a great impact even on Dr. Taylor. Gertrude Robinson, *David Urquhart*, p. 100 quotes Urquhart's own report: "I have had a conversation of nearly five hours with Dr. T[aylor]. I never so shook any man. He seemed tortured, struggling between responsibility, shame and failure brought home, and self-love and pride that linked him to a system, and the greater shame of sinking in the estimation of those he had led on." Unlike Lowery, however, Taylor did not join Urquhart's movement.

because they had lost the spirit, that a nation that is without them cannot exercise these rights until it first acquire the spirit which alone can create and sustain them. His idea of efficiently improving the national mind was not by at first appealing to the masses from platforms, but by men of mind communing with each other, and viewing the subject in all its aspects until they were agreed. Each would then proceed to impress the same facts and opinions on others in a similar manner till the basis of a public sentiment could be formed; when the masses could be addressed with that oneness of mind which rouses a nation. He would take any trouble to put himself in communication with men of superior intelligence, without reference to their station in life. In visiting a town his practice was to find these out, invite them to his hotel, and start some question for conversation on our commercial relations and treaties, or some social question, and urge everyone present to offer some remarks on the subject, and at last he would take a review of all that had been advanced, and cast a flood of light on the subject, drawn from the history of the past, and the varied circumstances of the present time, so that all would be struck with the convincing force of his views. His power of attaching men of different classes and opinions to his views on the questions he placed before them was amazing; minds discordant on other subjects became one, and in harmony with each other, under the influence of his conversations. The intelligent veteran Tory or Whig, men eminent for their knowledge of literature, and science, and commerce, Radicals, and most determined Chartists, men of the upper classes and working-men, all harmonised in admiration of and zeal for his views. During the month we were in Paris he held such conversations with the delegates and visitors, and much interesting information was elicited.

Everything was new and interesting to me in Paris in the manners and habits of the masses. I was at once struck with the obvious superiority of the working people to ours in courtesy and politeness. I saw very few people intoxicated during the four weeks I was there. What pleased me most was that the politeness was not mere deference to superiors, but the dignified courtesy of self-respect; where the working-man felt himself a gentleman, acted as such, and was treated as such in return. In England we have here and there working-men types of true gentlemanly bearing, but too often the hat is only grudgingly or sycophantly lifted to the superior in wealth, and never to each other, implying rather the sense of inferiority than the spontaneous courtesy of manhood. I visited the principal places of historical interest, especially those of the first revolution, where imagination would picture the views of terror and blood, of virtue and vice, of heroism and brutality, of nobility and fiendish ruffianism, which disgraced and adorned that eventful period. I have a peculiar pleasure in visiting places of historical interest and abstracting myself from the living present, re-peopling them with the scenes of past ages. I spent an afternoon thus entranced in Notre Dame, when all the memories of my readings of what had occurred in that venerable and majestic pile were called up with the vividness of reality. The general development of taste, elegance, and refinement seemed to me much more developed than in our English towns, and the ingenious and ornamental to furnish a much larger portion of their products. I at once saw a difference between the population and that of the English in their attendance on public worship. The first Sunday I was there I went out about eleven in the forenoon, and, to my surprise, found the shops open in the leading streets, in which the usual traffic of working-days was going on. I passed a new house which was being built, and the masons, joiners, and other workmen, were labouring. I observed no signs of leaving work until the afternoon. The bustle of the streets was the same as on an ordinary day, and there appeared no signs of a day of rest for man and beast. The scene appeared strange to me indeed. I felt at once the superiority of my own country on a Sunday, and missed its quiet calm which tends to create reflection and lift the soul above mere earthly and passing things, to fix it on that word of life which abideth for ever. During the week I was in a coffee-house, where I met with some English tailors, who had been in Paris for some length of time. They were evidently not religious men, but a sample of the average of their class. I expressed my astonishment at the Sunday working, and asked them how they liked it. "Its — — slavery," exclaimed one. "Customers come in quite regularly on a Saturday night and get measured for an article to be done on the Sunday, just as they would in England to be done on the Saturday, and you are forced to work or you lose your place, while work is that slack that we are doing nothing for the first three days of the week."[209] I found wages lower than in England. I am not bigoted as to particular forms, but the principle that God ordained a seventh day as a day of rest from temporal toil, and for the culture of head and heart in things divine, is obvious even from its adaptation to man's wants. It is but short-sightedness and "cant about cant" to call those enemies of the working-classes who would turn them from spending the day of rest in jaunting pleasures instead of cultivating their mental, moral, and religious powers to work out the changes needed to improve the condition of their class. 'Tis true they are overtasked with toil, working close during the week; living in narrow lanes, and streets, and confined dwellings. Yes, but there is a work to do before these things can be remedied. We want men to do that work—men of thought, men of action, and we need the day of rest to create these men. We would not curtail innocent pleasure nor debar the working-men from breathing the air of green fields, pure streams, flowery gardens, fruitful orchards, and sunny skies, but neglect not duty for pleasure. Labour to shorten the hours of toil—for half-holidays—for payment of wages on Fridays—jaunts on the Saturday afternoons instead of the Sunday afternoons—better dwellings and sanitary improvements.

[209] For working class attitudes to Sunday work, see Brian Harrison, "Religion and Recreation in Nineteenth-Century England", *Past and Present*, December 1967, pp. 103–6, 108–12.

The French appeared to me to have reached the highest material civilisation, and to possess in perfection those things which the senses would delight in and be proud of, but to lack the ennobling dignity and steadfastness of the Christian life.

After being a month in Paris the deputations returned to London, and, at Mr. Urquhart's request, I waited on him, when he kindly presented me with some valuable ancient classics. The "Portfolio"—a collection of most important State papers, besides his own, "Turkey and its Resources," "The Spirit of the East," and other books.[210] In a few days I returned to Newcastle. The committees which had been formed on the questions of foreign policy continued to seize any favourable opportunity to lay the facts of the question before the public through the press. After waiting until the spring to get strong, I prepared to fulfil an agreement I had made some time before to lecture for three months in the Edinburgh district to the Chartist Associations, and then wrote to Mr. R. Monteith, thanking him for his ever-to-be-remembered kindness, which had been so instrumental in restoring me to health; and as my station and path of life was different from his, and the Parisian Mission was over about which I had communicated with him, this closed our correspondence,[211] but frequently has his kindness been the theme of our conversations at home, and in our prayers have we invoked the blessings of Heaven to descend on him. I had received from the time of leaving Dumfries to my returning from Paris to Scotland £50[212]. Although I did not know his name before, and never saw him until near seven years after that—having then to lecture at the town of Lanark, I seized the opportunity to see him and thank him personally. His seat, Carstairs, being seven miles off, I took a gig and rode out, and passed him in his grounds, not knowing him. On riding up to the lodge gate and inquiring if he was at home, the good woman replied, "Oh, aye, Sir, yon's him pruning the trees, there." I turned round, introduced myself, thanked him, and in a few minutes, having to hurry back to catch

---

[210] The full titles are as follows: *The Portfolio* (Ed. David Urquhart) 1835–6; David Urquhart, *Turkey and its Resources, its Municipal Organisation and Free Trade* (1833); David Urquhart, *The Spirit of the East, Illustrated in a Journal of Travels through Roumelia during an Eventful Period* (2 Vols., 1838).

[211] The popular aspect of Urquhart's movement collapsed during 1841. Gertrude Robinson, *David Urquhart*, p. 117 shows Lowery writing in July 1841 from Kirkcaldy that he had waited till April in the hope that he would hear of the movement's further progress. When he heard nothing, and found Cargill desponding, he concluded that plans for further campaigning had been abandoned. Lowery is obscure here on his subsequent attitude to Urquhart's ideas, which recovered much of their popular following in the 1850s. This is surprising in an autobiography published so soon after the Crimean War. See John Salt, "Local Manifestations of the Urquhartite Movement", *International Review of Social History* XIII (1968); Asa Briggs, "David Urquhart and the West Riding Foreign Affairs Committees", *Bradford Antiquary*, N. S. Part XXXIX (1958); and R. Shannon, *op. cit.*

[212] Lowery is scrupulous about money: refusing to accept subscriptions from Cornish working people (see above, p. 131), and documenting the aid he received from the Urquhart circle.

the train, that I might reach Dumbarton, where I had to lecture that night, I passed on and saw him no more. Such incidents rise up as green spots in memory's wastes and strengthen the soul with faith and trust in God and humanity. By this time many of the leading men of the Chartists were in prison; they were generally indicted in batches, and the more sensible suffered from their connection with the violent and indiscreet. I have often been asked how I escaped prosecution and imprisonment, and I have answered, more by my good luck than by my good judgment, for men more mild and prudent were imprisoned, such as James Williams,[213] bookseller, of Sunderland, and others. As I have said, often a number were arrested at once in connection with some meeting, or with some illegal conduct, and although they, as individuals, were not guilty of violent utterances, they were, in the eye of the law, guilty as accomplices with those who had so spoken or acted. I never happened to be in the way when these onslaughts were made by the authorities. But even my wildest outbursts always had a semblance of reason, being based on a supposition of some illegal action which the authorities might commit, or some evil consequences most likely to ensue from their conduct to the people, so that it would have been difficult to separate the language from the illegal act supposed. About this time, 1841, Lovett and Collins had endured their term of imprisonment. On being freed, a pamphlet of 130 pages, which Mr. Lovett had written while they were in prison, was published in their joint names, entitled "Chartism, a New Organization of the People, Embracing a Plan for the Education and Improvement of the People, Politically and Socially." It is a well digested plan of progressive education from infant to adult schools, including evening classes and lectures on literature, art, and science. It presents one of the most comprehensive and practical plans for elevating the working men which has yet been offered to the public, and is especially calculated to enlist the working-classes in the work of their own improvement. Mr. Lovett sent a circular letter to the leading men of the body, requesting their recommendation of the plan if they approved of it, and a number sent him their signatures. I went to Edinburgh to fulfil my engagement to lecture in that district.

By this time Fergus O'Connor and his party had taken alarm at Lovett's plan of organization, perceiving that it would unite the sensible men in our ranks, and soon destroy the influence of mere noise and nonsense. O'Connor, through the *Northern Star*, at once denounced the plan as a "humbug," intended to lead the people from the organization for the charter to other

---

[213] James Williams was arrested in July 1839 for sedition, and imprisoned for six months. Gammage, *History of the Chartist Movement*, p. 32 says "he was what might be considered a good speaker, but almost entirely intellectual. Of soul, which gives force to the true orator, he possessed but little". But he was able, and influential in his district. He put up a stiff fight when misrepresented and attacked by O'Connor in 1842 for sympathising with the complete suffrage movement.

things.[214] He termed it the "New Move," and called on the honest men who had signed it without reflection to withdraw their names, and denounced those who refused to do so as traitors to the people's cause. In consequence, a number of those who were dependent on committees and his newspaper puffs immediately withdrew their names, giving as their reason, that the plan was already producing disunion. It was a melancholy exhibition of ignorance and subserviency to see these names published in the *Star*, headed "Rats Escaping from the Trap." Yet many of these were simply the victims of their position. Organization, while it has its benefits, has its vices. A number of men are urged into the movement in their neighbourhood and persuaded to fill certain offices in the public cause. These men are the best that can be had for the time being, but are afraid to differ with the dominant party, who, by denouncing them might cast them out of employment. An independent judgment can only be expected from those who, conscious of their own powers to keep the field by the force of their own energies, dare to speak what they think, even when they know many may not agree with certain of their sentiments. Yet they may be confident that in the end they will be understood and appreciated.

My first lecture was in Whitfield Chapel, High-street, which was crowded, and I endeavoured to direct the meeting to the comprehension of those fundamental principles essential to the elevation of the people. The audience was most attentive, and on the conclusion of my discourse, one of the committee, an admirer of O'Connor, rose and thanked me for the lecture, and stated that, as it must be obvious to me that the "New Move" was already producing a division in our ranks, and as many sensible men who had signed it had therefore withdrawn from it, he hoped that, for the good of the cause, I would withdraw my name. I perceived at once that if I was to continue free and independent in my expression of thought, then was the time to assert and at once establish it. I walked calmly to the front of the platform and said,—"Fellow-working men, if our friend, or any other man who has signed Mr. Lovett's document, has become convinced in his *own* mind that it is calculated to do harm, he has a right to retract his signature. But I am not so convinced, but on the contrary, that it will do good, and sooner than retract I would suffer that right hand to be cut off." The whole audience gave one simultaneous burst of applause which resounded in the neighbourhood. On its ceasing, I continued,—"Now, let us well understand each other. I came to speak freely my thoughts and opinions, expecting you will as freely object to, or adopt them as you may be convinced they are right or wrong."

---

[214] O'Connor insisted that all such new moves betrayed Chartism in two ways; ideologically, because they implied that working men must meet moral, religious or educational standards before they were fit for the vote; and tactically, because such moves were inevitably sectarian and would splinter Chartism. See the *Northern Star*, 3 April 1841 (reprinted in P. Hollis, *Class and Conflict*, pp. 264–5) and from 17 April 1841 on. On this whole episode, see M. Hovell, *Chartist Movement*, pp. 232–5.

From that day onwards I never was troubled publicly by any of the party.[215] My friend, A. Duncan, and I agreed to work together around Edinburgh and the principal places up to Stirling. We generally lectured five nights in each week, and preached twice, sometimes thrice, on the Sundays; and we were able to go round these districts once in three weeks. The mere excitement of getting the Charter immediately had passed away, and we now advocated its principles in connection with political and social economy. The literature and passing events of the day furnished us with topics. An article in a review, magazine, or newspaper, or speeches delivered in Parliament, would furnish the subject of a discourse. One of us occasionally took a tour into some other district for a fortnight. We had no fixed engagements, or claim on the committees for any distinct remuneration. The committees of a neighbour-hood arranged the meetings for each of us as we came one after the other.

On my second visit to Stirling I felt greatly interested. There was so much that was calculated to inspire those who struggle for the right with the faith, that, however dark the hour, there is still some star of hope above the horizon. Time, with his steady pace, carries forward the car of truth, tests the sound-ness of all prophecies, and surely, though often slowly, triumphs over wrong. I had wandered about the romantic heights of the Castle, surveying the adjacent field of "Bannockburn," and the more distant "Campsie Fells." The scenes of the past rose to view; barbarous violence first giving place to a semblance of law; industry, with her virtues, struggling amidst serfdom, at length succeeds in securing a standing-place, slowly strengthening and extend-ing her position even while subject to continual oppressions from the *nobles* whose rights were in their *swords*. Then, again, the national conscience, driven by persecution to the wilds, glens, and morasses, heroically suffering, fighting, and dying for truth foretold and ensured—the slow but steady progress of civil and religious liberty. I saw in all this chain of events the development of an eternal law of progress in men and nations. Although at times force and fraud had triumphed, yet in these very trials the advocates of truth and justice had attained wisdom and strength, and one by one many of the principalities of evil and fastnesses of injustice had fallen; onward and upward was evidently the destiny of our race. In the evening these convic-tions were vividly strengthened. During the afternoon I had stood by the

---

[215] Lowery fared better than C. H. Neesom, who tried to combine membership of Lovett's association with O'Connor's and "was threatened and entreated by turns; he was perse-cuted in the most outrageous manner by men professing to be Chartists, who often made a disturbance at his house between two and three in the morning, threatening to drag him out of bed and do for him . . .", *National Reformer*, 27 July 1861, p. 6. Lowery does not mention here the friction with O'Connor over payment for the reports of his Scottish tour —see *Northern Star*, 30 January 1841, p. 7; "I have no wish to detract from any favours Mr. O'Connor has done to the cause, or its advocates individually", wrote Lowery in the *Northern Star*, 13 February 1841, "but most assuredly I never received any from him; on the contrary, I have not been used even with the courtesy given to others of his agents". See also J. Epstein, "Feargus O'Connor and the Northern Star', *International Review of Social History*, 1976.

graves of Hardy and Baird[216] in the neighbouring churchyard, who had been executed for treason through Richmond, the spy and agent of the ministry of 1795. Yet that evening, by permission of the authorities, I stood on the bench of justice in the court-house, from which they received their sentences, and preached the same principles for which they had contended, and for which they were executed.

I passed on to the west, and up to Strathaven, the birthplace of Wilson, who was executed at the same period as these men, and as we had fears that the spy system might be again resorted to to lead the unwary into the meshes of the law, I endeavoured to glean what information I could regarding that spy system which *Tait's Magazine* had so ably exposed. [217] I found the niece of Wilson still alive. It is horried to think that a Government—men of rank and station—could deliberately plan the death of simple ignorant men through the instrumentality of spies. Wilson was represented by all who knew him as a simple honest enthusiast, who would have shrunk from injuring any one. Richmond and his agents got a few of them to hold secret meetings, in which they had assured them that changes were to be effected by men of influence, but they would need the demonstration of armed men, not for any violence, but to show the authorities the determination of the people. There was but a handful of these deluded victims. They set off for Glasgow, where they had been directed to go, and the authorities, informed of all by these spies, who had planned the trap, waylaid and seized them. Thus, examples were made, and poor Wilson suffered. After his body was cut down, the friends procured it to bury, and his sister sat with it all night alone in the room in which it had been put. She described to me her sensations during that night, but any words of mine could not convey them to others. Thank God, these days have passed away, and it is to be hoped such ministries—such spies—such witnesses and judges—have passed away for ever.

At this time the Melbourne Ministry was on its last legs. The attention given by the Tories to Peel's advice to "Register" had gradually increased their strength, while Lord John Russell's declaration of "Finality," and the resistance of the Ministry to the proposition of Joseph Hume for a fixed duty of 10s. a quarter on imported corn, with a provision for a gradual extinction of the bread tax, had so disgusted the Liberals that they were prepared to see them ejected from office. The working men considered that while some chance of their enfranchisement might turn up in the conflict of parties, they had none if the Whigs remained in. Lord Melbourne's commercial propositions were brought forward, but they came too late, for even the constituencies of the large towns had got beyond them, and were beginning to believe the

[216] James Wilson, John Baird and Andrew Hardie were among the 47 Scottish radicals arrested in 1820 for advocating violent tactics; all three were executed. For Richmond, see above, fn. 142.

[217] Lowery refers to articles on the spy system in *Tait's Edinburgh Magazine*, May & August 1833; Richmond instituted legal proceedings against the magazine—see *ibid.* March 1834, p. 77; April 1834, p. 152; and supplementary number (1834), pp. 785 & f., 805 & f.

"Corn-law Catechism." The leading Whigs of Edinburgh having received intimations from head quarters of the necessity for strengthening the hands of the Government, determined to hold a public meeting of the inhabitants of the city, and to carry resolutions in favour of the Ministry. But being aware that besides the Chartists there were many of the more liberal trades-men who thought the Whigs defaulters, they went to work very cautiously. They kept their intention secret from the general public until the meeting was announced, to give as little opportunity as possible for the arrangement of any opposition. They did not post the bills until very late on the Saturday night, and the meeting was to be held in the Assembly Rooms, George-street, at one o'clock on the Monday. The Working Man's Committee had held their usual Saturday evening meeting, and on coming out at eleven o'clock that night saw the bill-sticker putting up the bills. They saw the intent, returned to their room, and agreed to have a large placard ready for the printers to proceed with by one o'clock on Monday morning, to be posted through the city by five, so that the working men might see it on their way to work, calling on the people to attend the meeting and watch the resolu-tions, that the wishes of the Whigs might not go forth as from the inhabitants of Edinburgh. Volunteers were found to aid the bill-stickers, and one agreed to walk over to Dunfermline in the morning, fifteen miles, and invite me to come in by the early coach on Monday morning. It was arranged that the committee should meet on Monday morning at nine o'clock.

On the Monday morning when I came into Edinburgh the city was well placarded, and I found that numbers of the mechanics and masons had determined to drop work before twelve, that they might attend the meeting. It had been discovered that the guild of the trades were to meet at eleven, the Whigs feeling confident that that body would favour their views and support them at the public meeting.

A deputation was appointed to wait on the committee who had called the meeting in the Music Hall, to request to know whom they intended to nominate as chairman. Some half dozen were appointed, of whom I was one, and about twelve o'clock we proceeded to the Assembly Rooms and found the committee sitting upstairs. We introduced ourselves as a deputation from a political association composed chiefly of working men, who, as the meeting was to be a public meeting, wished to know whether the gentleman whom they intended to nominate as chairman would, in the event of any of the resolutions being objected to, put an amendment. Mr. Adam Black[218] was pointed out as the intended chairman, and he answered that he should decline doing so. We replied that such being his determination we did not

[218] Adam Black (1784–1874), politician and founder of the publishers Adam & Charles Black, Liberal advocate of burgh reform and member of Edinburgh's first town council. Black was twice Lord Provost, and later M.P. for Edinburgh, but declined a knighthood. See Alexander Nicolson, *Memoirs of Adam Black* (Edinburgh, 1885). For help with this and the two following footnotes, we are most grateful to W. H. Marwick, Esq.

consider him a proper person to occupy the chair, and would propose some other person. By this time it was past twelve o'clock. We had no time to ask any one of the middle class holding our principles to allow himself to be nominated in opposition, and decided at once to nominate a working man to be chairman. He was one of our deputation, a journeyman tailor, and he agreed to stand. We did not quit the room. The doors of the general entry were kept shut until one o'clock, the time for commencing the proceedings, but before they were opened some 400 who had met in the guild meeting and had come to support the Whigs were admitted by a back entrance. On the front doors being opened there was a continued flow of people, who in ten minutes filled the room, which would hold upwards of 1700 people. The audience were evidently the *élite* of those interested in politics in Edinburgh. It could be seen at a glance that they felt strongly interested in the subject on which they had met, and had thought on the matter before they came. On Mr. A. Black being proposed as chairman, one of our deputation very briefly stated our reasons for proposing Mr. Watson, a working man. This was received with cheers and hisses about equally blended. On the show of hands being taken it was fortunate for us that it was referred to Mr. James Ayton,[219] a gentleman of the Whig committee. The meeting appeared to me equally divided, and had I been asked I should have given the benefit of my uncertainty to our opponents. Mr. Ayton declared that Mr. Watson was elected. The volley of cheers and hisses again commenced, and the whole of the committee, except Lord Moncrief's son and another gentleman, quitted the platform and left the room. The confusion continued, and we were now in a dilemma. We had not arranged any plan of proceedings, intending simply to watch the resolutions and move an amendment to any that we deemed objectionable. Now it was necessary for us to take the initiative. I instantly drew up a short resolution, to the effect, "That, on account of their resistance to further reform, and disposition to maintain the corn laws and the unjust influence of the landed aristocracy, the Melbourne Ministry were unworthy of the confidence and support of reformers." But the confusion between the parties still continued. The chairman could not be heard, and whenever I attempted to read the resolution the hisses and cheers increased. I perceived that if the meeting broke up in that state the *Scotsman* and other Whig newspapers would be led to represent us as violent intruders, who had stopped the proceedings by uproar. So, as there were a number of reporters present, I determined to address an explanation to them, asking the favour that in justice to us it might go forth to the public. That moment the crowd, perceiving that I was not attempting to speak to the meeting, hushed their clamour, that they might hear what I was saying. On this a thought instantly struck me to take advantage of my opportunity. It was no *ruse*, but arose at the moment. I gradually raised my voice in this explanation,

---

[219] James Aytoun published several pamphlets on political and economic questions, sat on Edinburgh's first reformed town council, and was a prominent Anti-Corn Law Leaguer.

uttering sentiments which I knew none would disagree with, until my voice filled the room, and commanded the ear of both sides. I rapidly glanced over the history of the shortcomings of the Ministry. For upwards of an hour I was listened to with attention, and on the resolution being put, there were full two-thirds of the meeting in its favour. This meeting at once placed me before the Edinburgh public. Previous to this I had only spoken a few times in our own place of meeting, where the upper classes never came, and the proceedings at which the local press did not report. Being generally unknown, there were various conjectures who I was. This meeting opened the eyes even of the Whig clique, and Sir James Gibson Craig[220] did not hesitate to declare that the Government had lost the confidence of the people, and must advance in a more liberal spirit than hitherto if they would retain their position.

In my visits to so many places the different phases of society and peculiar individuals presented often a study. Being invited to Pennycuick, where the firm of "Cowan" has their extensive paper manufactories, I met with "Johnny Lawson."[221] Johnny was a "character" only to be found in Scotland, a shrewd, intelligent old man, who paid no attention to the forms of dress. In language and sentiment one of the old Covenanters, he was a warm Chartist and enthusiastic teetotaller, and an active local reformer. Having time and means, he was ever searching into old local laws and grants, and had given Sir J. Clark, a local "laird," some trouble, by discovering that his estate there had been a grant from the monarch in the feudal times, to which a condition of the grant had been that the holder should blow a horn at stated times round the boundary. Johnny was deemed "weel aff," and "weel liked." He had property, and was a good landlord, but lived by himself and had no one in the house with him. His common dress was an old coat of the old fashion, a long vest and knee breeches, and he mostly wore a red night-cap. When at home he might be seen every day on the turnpike road gathering manure, which he sold, and with the proceeds assisted his poorer neighbours.

Yet although thus humbly employed and very strangely clad Johnny was not ridiculed. Rich and poor would converse with him, always being interested by him. One day Sir J. Clark, on passing him when he was gathering up manure, observing that he was proceeding from the village, suggested to him that it would be easier to leave it lying, and pass on with the empty barrow

---

[220] Sir James Gibson Craig (1765–1850), a successful law agent, was a libertarian active in Whig reforming politics knighted in 1831. The *Dictionary of National Biography* describes him as "the natural leader of the Scotch Whigs".

[221] Lawson was an eccentric travelling packman who made enough money to retire early, and publicly promoted his advanced Liberal views at meetings which he summoned with a horn and addressed in strikingly coloured clothing. He died in 1849, but recollections of his wit and repartee were current in Penicuik for many years after. We are most grateful to Mrs. Helen Craig, of Midlothian County Library Headquarters, Musselburgh, for help on this point. See J. J. Wilson, *Annals of Penicuik* (Edinburgh, 1891).

until he got to the extent he intended to go, and then gather it up on his return. "Ah," responded Johnny, "but that would na dae, Sir James, there's compateetion amang us folk as well as amang ye in Parliament, if a' dinna tak it noo somebody else will, before I come back." Johnny would walk long journeys to attend what he deemed important public meetings, and his love of his principles often induced him to subscribe liberally, however penurious in regard to his own expenses. On such occasions, those who did not know him would be astonished towards the close of the Temperance meeting to see the strange old man, in his odd-looking garb, burst into energetic exhortations to be hearty in the cause, and tender his 10*l.* towards the subscription. His plain and direct language stood out in bold relief on the uniform level of social intercourse. The first time I met him was at breakfast at his daughter's, his only child, who was married. A friend who was with me not having been accustomed to grace at breakfast, was inadvertantly beginning the meal. "Sirs," said Johnny, "dinna let us eat our meat like cows at a woodie (hay rack), let us first ask a blessing." This daughter presented a contrast to her father. He had sent her to one of the best educational establishments, and she was highly cultivated, adding to her intelligence gentleness and refinement. While he lived in the humblest manner, he delighted to adorn and surround her with elegance.

My Pennycuick friends had procured the grant of the Town-Hall for me to lecture in at Peebles, fourteen miles off among the hills. On arriving, we found some had come sixteen miles over the neighbouring hills to attend the meeting. After the proceedings were over, and we were just about departing, a working man spoke to me, evidently delighted with the address. Grasping my hand warmly, he asked me if I would accept "a bit o' salmon frae him," for he would "like sae much to gie me something, and it would just tak twenty minutes for him to rin an get it." There was such an evident desire that I should accept the offer, that I saw it would wound him to refuse, so I answered I cannot wait twenty minutes, our friends are getting our conveyance ready, and we will be off directly, but you can send it in by the carrier. The parcel came in two or three days, a fine large salmon. I could not understand how he could spare such a gift; but afterwards I found that poaching in the Tweed was a general practice of the poor at Peebles, and that he had not required the twenty minutes to go home for it, but calculated that in that time he could go to some haunt of the fish, which he knew of, and catch one and bring it to me. We often joked about the gift of the salmon.

My next tour was to Aberdeen, where there were two societies of Chartists, one on Lovett's model, the other clinging to O'Connor. Yet the sense and caution of the citizens of the granite city was apparent. My visit was a hurried one; I delivered a course of lectures during the week, and took a run down to Peterhead to visit the scenes of my school-boy days, which imagination had so often dwelt on since I had left them when nine years old. All was changed

—the town looked less, the harbour smaller, and I looked in vain for the faces I had expected to recognize. I found some few old people whom I recollected, and they having heard of my lecturing I was asked to address them. I was kindly received, but evidently the older people were astonished "how that wild play-the-truant laddie had been transformed into a lecturer."

On returning to Aberdeen to proceed back to Edinburgh I found a tea-party had been arranged, to which I was invited, and a silver lever watch, which had been subscribed for during the three days I had been away, was presented to me. I was stopping at the Temperance Coffee-house, and there being a conference of the teetotallers then sitting in Aberdeen, a number of the delegates were lodging in the same house, and many of them knew me. As I have elsewhere said, from the first I had seen the obstructions which intemperance presented to popular elevation, and had often taunted the Chartists with the lavish expenditure in the public houses, and their niggardly subscriptions to their trades and political societies. And when speaking on the practicability of the national holiday, I had urged that if they were in earnest they would sacrifice their indulgence in strong drinks, and lay up a month's store of food in advance. Then a cessation of labour would derange the trade of the middle classes, and bring them to reason. If the body of the non-electors had not the virtue to sacrifice their sensual indulgences for such an object, it was nonsense to suppose that they would be ready to sacrifice their lives for it. Yet I had never perceived that the drinks in themselves were bad.[222]

One morning after breakfast a number of the delegates urged me to sign the pledge. My answer was the usual one of those who have not studied the whole question—that I was as good a teetotaller as any of them, for I had not drank any for a long time, seldom went into a public-house, and denounced the intemperance of the working men as much as they did. They properly pointed out to me the superior weight my example would have if I were a member of a society of abstainers for the sake of doing good to others. I have often smiled at the objections I have met with from others when pressing them to join, for they were precisely what I had offered myself in my ignorance of the subject—the miracle at the marriage of Cana, wine as an element of the Lord's Supper, Timothy's stomach case, and such like misunderstood passages of Scripture, which the researches of Temperance men have made plain since then. Although I had met numbers of teetotallers, and knew their organisation was extending, yet I had not read any work on the subject. This was not through bigotry or unwillingness to investigate its claims; but

[222] The teetotal movement had in fact been making rapid progress during the 1830s, but its relations with Chartism were always rather strained. See Brian Harrison, *Drink and the Victorians*, pp. 387–92. Relations were less strained in Scotland than elsewhere. L. C. Wright, *Scottish Chartism* (Edinburgh, 1953), p. 179 says of temperance coffee-houses "not only did they become the unofficial headquarters of the local Chartists but they became the common meeting-ground of the middle and working classes". See also B. Harrison, "Teetotal Chartism", *History*, 1973.

being constantly engaged in studying and advocating the political and trade questions I had but little time, and I had not become so interested in the subject as to lead me to set other things aside to study it. From my own experience I can perceive how ministers and professional men absorbed in their daily duties, when some hitherto neglected power has been brought forth into general society effecting a wonderful amount of good, may still remain in ignorance of its special properties, and pay no attention to it, while the unlearned masses, seeing its effects in their own circle, sooner believe it and understand it than they. Already prepared by observations on the evils of drunkenness, I was convinced it was my duty to pledge myself to abstain for the good of others, however unnecessary I might deem it for myself. I longed to see the working classes noble, enlightened, and free. I had become convinced that intemperance and consequent ignorance were the strongest links in the chain that bound them. A Dr. M'Millan was one of the most urgent on me to sign. The Doctor was an inveterate smoker, which had annoyed me much, for I felt interested in his company. "Well, Doctor, I am ready to sign," said I, "if you will promise me to abstain from smoking that abominable tobacco." The others enjoyed heartily the fix in which I had placed the Doctor, and called on him to set an example in flinging away the pipe, for it was a shame for a Temperance advocate to smoke. The Doctor agreed, and I signed the pledge.[223] Dr. M'Millan, I am sorry to say, did not keep his promise long to abstain from tobacco. His was one of those melancholy histories which our drinking customs so often furnish. A classical scholar, highly talented and eminently qualified to succeed in his profession, he had imbibed a passion for toddy, acquired in social intercourse with the middle classes; he became a drunkard and sunk from his position. The teetotallers succeeded in getting him to abstain, when the native vigour of his mind, freed from the incubus of intoxicants, again sprung forth, and he regained a respectable standing. Being a medical man he was able to bring his professional knowledge of physiology and organic chemistry to show that alcohol was injurious to men, and that the principles of the Temperance society were in harmony with science and experience. At that time this branch of the Temperance argument had been little studied, and his lectures did much good in Scotland. But after some years of abstinence he broke his pledge and sank deeper than he was before, being frequently seen wandering about Dollar, mad with drink, where he died in *delerium tremens*. Such is the sad history of too many who have injured the very structure of their brains by drink; unless watched and guarded and kept in continual activity in some good work, a slight temptation resuscitates the appetite, and their last state is worse than the first.

A general election being now announced, it was determined by the working-men to bring forward candidates to advocate our principles wher-

[223] For the temperance movement's attitudes to smoking, see Brian Harrison, *Drink and the Victorians*, pp. 158–9.

ever possible.[224] Two objects were to be gained by doing this—first, an opportunity to address the influential classes and electors on the question, which we could not accomplish at any other time or place so well; secondly, if we succeeded in the show of hands it would be a victory showing the candidates returned by the demand of a poll did not represent the people. The law in Scotland requiring no property qualification for Members of Parliament presented ready facilities for doing this. The day before I left Aberdeen some of the committee stated that they considered that if they had a candidate, a judicious exposition of our principles from the hustings would do more to bring them before all classes than the labour of twelve months by means of lectures. They urged me to come and stand when the city election took place. I answered that I could only promise conditionally. It had been arranged that Colonel Perronet Thompson[225] and I should be nominated for Edinburgh, and both the nominations might be fixed for one day, but if they were fixed for different days I would come to Aberdeen. This was agreed to, and I wrote an address to the electors that afternoon, announcing myself as a candidate, and left it with the committee to publish when the proper time arrived. When the time of the general election was announced, the plan of having popular candidates became general, and most of our leading speakers were engaged to stand. At the preceding election for Edinburgh, John Frazer, proprietor and editor of the *True Scotsman* newspaper, had been nominated, but did not get the "show of hands," so that there was the interest of uncertainty as well as the honour of standing side by side with the great essayist and orator Macaulay to rouse the mind. The idea of personal competition never was dreamt of. But we had a strong conviction that our claims were just and constitutional, and that therefore the refusal of the Whigs to admit them could not be justly defended. Our poet exclaims, "Thrice is he armed who has his quarrel just."[226] And when we are convinced our cause is right, and we are in earnest, all distinctions of individual strength and excellence vanish from our minds. Like the youthful shepherd of Israel, we feel our *small pebble* will give us the victory over any giant on the other side.[227]

The day for the nomination was announced, and, fortunately, that for the city of Aberdeen was fixed for the day after. The hustings were being erected on the High-street, and a question about them was being considered in the non-elector's committee, when up spoke "Jamie Grant,"—"Gie me twa mair to gang wi' me as a deputation to the Lord Provost, an' we'll soon get that settled to your satisfaction," "Jamie Grant!" What inhabitant of Edinburgh does not know Jamie Grant? His portraiture would have furnished Scott with three volumes equal to "Old Mortality." Grant and his colleagues

---

[224] Other Chartist candidates in 1841 included McDouall in Northampton.
[225] See above, fn. 72.
[226] Shakespeare, *King Henry VI*, Part II, I. ii. 232.
[227] *1 Samuel*, Ch. 17, v. 49.

proceeded to the Provost, to whom he was well known, for on many a deputation to the authorities had Jamie been. He at once proceeded: "My Lord,
we are a deputation from the Working men's Committee, who are determined
to bring forward two candidates to represent the city, for we dinna think
either Mr. Macaulay or Mr. Gibson Craig are fit, they are tied to the Whigs.
Now we have been looking at the Act, an it says the hustings are to be
erected on the Cross, in the High-street, and we find that the present
members have put up their hustings on the Cross. What are we to do, we
are no' gaun to put ours up behind theirs, or be driven one side, and to put
up ours in front of theirs would na' do for it might mak' confusion. Your
lordship is aware we have been accused of creating disturbances at meetings,
but we have no wish to mak' any disorder if allowed to bring forward our
candidates." His lordship courteously rejoined. You and your friends may
make yourselves quite easy, Mr. Grant, I will see that it is so arranged that
a certain number of tickets for the hustings erected are given to your committee, sufficient to accommodate those who wish to take part in the proceedings. They thanked his lordship and retired, and came back to the
Committee-room announcing the promise they had received. "Ye see
friens," said Grant, "there's naething like gaun about a thing the right way
—there's as gude as twenty pounds of the funds saved."

The day for the nomination turned out an exceedingly fine one. The
proceedings commenced at eleven o'clock. There was a very large crowd of
the citizens assembled, and the windows of the buildings in front of the
hustings were crowded with the upper classes of both sexes. I had not seen
Mr. Macaulay before, except from the gallery of the House of Commons. He
looked to me care-worn and out of health. His mind did not appear much
interested in the passing scene, but absent, musing, perhaps, on the speedy
end of their ministry. At such a time, undoubtedly, the election was of
secondary importance. He was certain of being returned, and seemed present
more from courtesy than choice. The movers and seconders were very good
speakers on both sides, and maintained their views with vigour. Mr.
Macaulay was questioned on the extension of the suffrage and other kindred
matters, and it was given forth that while proud of his talents and conscious
that he had aided reform, yet, however high their admiration for him, unless
he was prepared to advance with the spirit of the age, they deemed it their
duty to prepare from that day for the return of more liberal representatives
for the city. Mr. Macaulay seemed to feel that he could not enter into any
laudation of the finality position of the ministry, took some credit for its
earlier services in the retrenchments and reforms begun by Lord Grey, and
dwelt chiefly on their foreign policy, for which he gave them great credit.
Having to speak last was to my advantage, as it gave me the speeches of the
other candidates to comment upon. I appealed to first principles in confirmation of the just claims of the people to the franchise. Whatever was right was
practicable, and justice was the only secure basis on which a government

should proceed. There had been class discord, there was class division, and such would ever continue in our country until the enfranchised class admitted the non-electors to their electoral rights. Having shortly returned from France, and being thus fresh from the study of the untoward event of the battle of Navarino,[228] and the subsequent secret treaty, I was able at once to show that the foreign policy was negligent of England's rights, dignity, and interests. I dwelt at some length on the affair of the Vixen,[229] and showed the obvious policy of Russia in her acquisition of Georgia to open up a path to our East Indian possessions. Some of the gentlemen of the Whig party on the hustings, as I was stating this case of the Vixen, loudly interrupted me with cries of "No! no!" I turned to Mr. Macaulay, and said the honourable gentleman will not say "No! no!" to these facts. All their eyes were instantly fixed upon him, when he nodded his assent to my statement. This at once silenced their interruptions, for they evidently knew nothing of the questions themselves. Large as the assemblage was, my voice was clearly heard, as there were none of the unseemly interruptions which too often occur in English elections, and although it took me an hour and a-half to make my statements, no uneasiness was manifested to the end. On the Sheriff calling for a show of hands he declared the choice to have fallen on Colonel Perronet Thompson and myself. The others demanded a poll, and I in a few words appealed to the assembly, and protested against a poll as a sham, unless the whole people were allowed to poll. They had been called together to choose two persons, they had chosen them. Nothing was said to this by the Sheriff or the other side. Everything had been done in order, and our party had maintained a respectable position. Many of the gentlemen of the other side on the hustings shook hands with me and thanked me for my speech. It was half-past three when I got off the hustings; the perspiration was through my coat-back, and I had only until five o'clock to get changed and take refreshment and get to the mail coach office, where I was booked for the outside to proceed to Aberdeen during the night.

It was a fine summer evening, and I enjoyed the beautiful scenery through Fife to Perth. The conversation turned on the elections, and I found that a young lord and his brother were inside passengers; the former going down to stand in opposition to Sir Andrew Leith Hay. This I learned from his valet, who sat beside me. He informed me that his lordship was in the navy, and related some wonderful feats evincing the physical strength and hardiness of

[228] Battle of Navarino, October 1827, in which the combined French, Russian and British squadrons destroyed the Turkish and Egyptian fleets. For the diplomatic consequences, see E. L. Woodward, *The Age of Reform 1815–1870* (1938), pp. 209 & f.
[229] The affair of the *Vixen*. Urquhart, while secretary at the British embassy in Constantinople, doubted the Russian claim to sovereignty over Circassia. At his instigation, the *Vixen*, a British schooner, proceeded to Soudjauk Kale, where she was seized by a Russian warship on 26 November 1836. Urquhart thought he had acted in accordance with British policy, but the British government did not wish to press Russia too hard, and he was recalled on 10 March 1837. A motion to inquire into Palmerston's conduct in this incident was defeated in the House of Commons on 21 June 1838.

his master. When we changed at Perth his lordship and brother came outside to smoke, and I had an opportunity of observing them more closely. The younger brother was a slender young man, having the appearance of a collegian, and evidently not intended to "brave the battle and the breeze". His lordship was below the middle size, thickset and strong in person, his complexion and his voice were such as sea breezes and salt water alone can form, and altogether he appeared a real sailor. But as conversation proceeded it became evident that he was now attempting a sort of navigation he was totally unfit for. We arrived at Aberdeen between five and six in the morning, when I went to bed and enjoyed a sleep until ten o'clock. The nomination was to commence at eleven. After a hurried breakfast I proceeded with my friend to the Market-place Cross, where the hustings were erected. The day was a beautiful one, and there was a very large number of people in from the country, and all the citizens were a-stir. Mr. Bannerman, who had represented the city for some time, was much respected as a private man, an extensive merchant and manufacturer. He was supported from personal friendship by the Tories, although he himself was a Whig. He had met with severe losses, and latterly had been supposed merely to retain his seat in expectation that the Ministry would give him the Commissionership for Greenwich, or some other office. The Tories had brought forward a candidate, but while all thought they might poll a respectable minority, none thought he could get in. Neither of these gentlemen were speakers, so that there was not the same stimulus to exertion that there had been in Edinburgh. But the immense mass of people—the consciousness that so much depended in that quarter on our ability to give a commanding exposition of our principles, impressed me with a strong desire to win the convictions of that vast assemblage. It was a stirring sight. Union-street, which commenced a little in front of us, is one of the finest I have seen. The windows and house-tops were filled with people as far as the voice could reach, and a dense crowd extended far long the street. Yet the constituency for that large city and population under the Reform Bill was but some 1,200. I was forcibly struck with the farce of nominal representation by an arrangement the authorities had made for the convenience of the electors. In front of the hustings a space sufficient to hold them had been railed off. On looking down the smallness of their numbers stood in forcible contrast to the immense mass beyond. I pointed the attention of a friend beside me to this circumstance, observing, "That is my text." On it coming to my turn to address the people, after dwelling for a short time on the sacred duty they had met to perform, and the principles of civil and religious liberty taught in the Scriptures, and their responsibility as Christian men to try to remove falsehood and wrong wherever met with, I pointed down to the electors in the enclosure, and turned to the authorities, and then again to the mass, and asked them, Had that mighty mass of the citizens to elect a representative to serve them in Parliament, or only the small group within the railings?

Was there any gentleman who would dare to affirm that that small group—the electors—however good individually, contained a tithe of the intelligence and virtue, industry and wealth, that the mighty crowd around them possessed? The anomaly was so obvious, and I appealed to them so solemnly, that those in the enclosure hung their heads, while the mass beyond them made the air ring with applause. From this basis I reasoned against the class privileges and other monopolies. The enthusiasm was such, that when the Sheriff took the show of hands, not only the whole mass held up their hands for me, but also the electors within the rails. The other gentlemen demanded a poll, which was fixed to take place on the ensuing Monday, it then being Friday. In the evening the enthusiasm of the Chartist Association was high. The working-men felt as if for the moment they stood on an equality of public respect with the other political parties. It was urged that they should go to the poll, for, although they could not then succeed, it would prove to the Whigs their earnestness, and that at the next election, if they did not advance, they would lose the seat. It was finally agreed that it would confirm the impression that had been made if some were to poll, care being taken not to let in the Tory. The meeting adjourned until next evening. During the interval the shops were to be visited, to solicit funds for the electioneering expenses, and to enlist volunteer clerks for the polling. On meeting on the Saturday night it was stated that the necessary funds had been subscribed, —above £30—and that a full staff of polling clerks had volunteered.

At the commencement of the poll at one of the principal stations a humorous disappointment of the Whigs occurred. One of the brothers Hall, and Co., inventors of the clipper-built vessels, came up to poll, and being a Liberal he had always previously voted for Bannerman, by whose friends in the booth he was greeted with the usual blandness, as they had not a doubt but he came to vote for them. On the question being put, as a matter of form, to record his vote, Who do you vote for Mr. Hall, "I cannot in conscience vote for any but——," was his answer. Such scenes occurred frequently during the day, and although only some thirty odd votes were polled, some of them were men of influence and property, and as a whole they presented an average of society. Many had ridiculed the idea of the non-electors having candidates nominated, that they might get their claims brought before the electors, but the results in almost every instance were highly favourable to the extension of liberal views.

Thus Mr. Macaulay lost his seat at the next election, and Mr. Cowan, who succeeded him, was pledged to an extension of the franchise. Mr. Macaulay had to become more liberal before he could be returned again. Since Mr. Bannerman retired from Aberdeen the members have been Liberals pledged to a more complete suffrage. In the hands of richer parties the Edinburgh election might have furnished fine pickings for the legal profession. By wont and custom, when there is an opposition, and the Sheriff declares the choice to have fallen on certain parties, it is deemed a valid election until reversed by a poll, or till the withdrawal of those who have been so chosen. This appears to have been the practice of the old times before the modern electoral qualification became law. In our case there was no withdrawal, nor was there a reversal by any polling for Messrs. Macaulay and Craig. The Sheriff of Aberdeen told me that in his opinion the Sheriff of Edinburgh had not carried out the law. Mr. Roebuck was written to on the matter. His answer was, there was no doubt we might make out a case, but had we £2,000 to begin with?

VI

Temperance Lecturer:
1841

I passed at once from Aberdeen to Newcastle-on-Tyne, having determined to bring my family to Edinburgh and reside there as being most central for my labours in Scotland. My friend Duncan also came to reside in Edinburgh, and we continued to lecture in the Lothians, Edinburghshire, Stirling, and Fifeshire. I was now often invited to speak at Temperance tea parties, and to deliver lectures on Temperance, and the more I examined the principle the more convinced I became that it was necessary for the well-being of man's temporal and spiritual nature. I invariably found a number of the leading Chartists active as members of the Abstinence Societies, and mostly some on every committee. I met with many astonishing changes in individual families, which were most encouraging to the reflecting lover of humanity. Up to that time, being engaged constantly in politics, I had not seen so much of the good effects of the Temperance movement as private individuals do who are engaged in it in their own locality. In almost every place you hear of some persons whose history of degradation by strong drink shocks you with pain, and whom Temperance, with the blessing of God, has aided to struggle against the vice and to enjoy the blessings of sobriety. In the town of "——" there was related to me a most interesting account of the degradation and separation through drunkenness of a tradesman and his wife, and their reform and reunion by joining the Temperance Society. They had no family and had a prospect of doing well; they were intelligent and industrious, attended public worship and were respected by those who knew them. He, *to be like other people*, went occasionally to a public-house with a friend. He had no particular liking for strong drinks, *but could take them*, and enjoy a chat with a few friends when so met. He being often offered a *dram* out of the decanters of his friends and customers when he called on them felt that it would look mean and unneighbourly if he did not keep a bottle in his house. When he passed the evening at home he would take a glass of toddy and his pipe and urge his wife to join him. At first she would have preferred only to taste it, and not to have had a glass to herself. "Just a wee drap, a little will do you good," was his exclamation. She was prevailed on to comply. The desire for the drink was created. Their glasses eventually became larger,—their one glass soon became two. Sometimes, when he thought he needed it, during the day he would go to the closet and take a dram of raw spirits. She commenced to do the same, until both at last became inebriates. His duties engaging him more actively, he could not indulge his desire so much as she could in secrecy at home. In consequence she sunk faster than he did, and he frequently found her intoxicated on his return home. When she could not get money she began to pawn and sell their things. Men can sooner perceive the odiousness of vice in others than in themselves, especially in their wives. They feel its disgrace more in those they love than in their own persons. He would frequently be intoxicated, and afterwards, when sober, regret that he had "taken so much," and yet he did not feel disgraced by it, but now he felt humbled by the intoxication of his wife. Men claim the virtues of their wives as their own, and although conscious of doing wrong themselves feel a gratification that their partner does right. Man looks on woman as a purer being than himself, and overlooks and excuses in man what would disgrace a woman. So, while he saw the excesses of his wife, he forgot his own, and that he had trained her day by day until the appetite for strong drink which he now condemned was induced. He complained in angry irritating words, and continued still to go on in the same course as before. As she became more reckless he became so too. Work was neglected, custom was lost, clothes and furniture disappeared. And yet that husband and wife had some good points remaining, and there were occasionally signs in their hearts

"That God still lingered there."

When in her senses she would feel contrition and desire to be better, and she would shrink from meeting those respectable persons with whom she associated in her purer and happier days. She never blamed him for teaching her to be a drunkard. He in his anger never descended to violence. In his sober moments he would feel intensely when he saw their respectable neighbours going or returning from public worship in cheerful converse and in comfortable attire. Sunday always brought back more vividly the contrast between their present condition and the time when they enjoyed its privileges. Sometimes better aspirations would arise in his breast, and he would feel hopes of their happy days returning again. Pictures of prosperity and respectability would arise, but alas he took no steps to realise them. He wished to enjoy the rewards of wisdom, but he continued to walk in the paths of folly. He never obeyed the plain direction of the Scriptures he had so often heard: "Cease to do evil—learn to do well." Like too many he wanted to be good without ceasing to do evil, and hoped to be saved from the suffering without turning away from the sin. During some fresh excess of his wife despair began to fasten on his mind, and he would be contented to sink to the uttermost depths of disgrace. But the divine spark could not be utterly quenched. Again conscience would be touched, and wrestle with these feelings of despair. At last he thought his only chance was to leave the place, change his name, and seek some spot where he would find work, and not be known. He satisfied his conscience to abandon his wife, because he had tried every means to reclaim her, and the task was hopeless; and while he remained beside her it was impossible for him to become steady and recover his former position. These thoughts had been passing through his mind for some time, when one night he found his wife more intoxicated than usual. To procure the liquor she had sold some of the most essential articles of domestic comfort. This decided him. He sought not for sleep, but as she lay in the insensibility of drunkenness, he packed up his few remaining articles of clothing, and left the house before the dawn of day. He turned not to look on his still insensible wife. The dark spirit of the hour was too intense to allow any loving remembrance to struggle forth through his heart's bitterness. He closed the door and went forth without ever casting "one longing lingering look behind."

It was summer time, and he got to the outside of the town before daylight. He had decided to take a cross country road, and seek some place out of the common route of passengers. Day dawned, and the sun's rays gilded the mountain tops. The dewdrops clustered on the hawthorn, and on the way-side flowers. The lark's matin song swelled loud and sweetly from the sky; all without was beauty, order, and harmony. God's works, how fair, how lovely, how placidly calm! Man's spirit, apart from God, how gloomy, dark, and disordered! How different the spirit within that erring and suffering man and the spirit without. He walked brooding o'er his condition and blaming everyone but himself for his misfortunes. He had walked rapidly in excitement during the whole day, and was approaching a small hamlet which lay a little out of the road, surrounded by hills. It was a lovely summer eve— the "kye were coming hame," and the children were romping in the fields. As he approached he observed about six or seven persons looking along the road as if they expected some one, and when he came up to them they inquired if he was the lecturer. He answered he was not, but a traveller in search of work, and that he would feel much obliged if they could inform him of a decent lodging he could go to. One of them turned back with him to do so, and informed him that he and his friends were looking out for a gentleman who was a stranger to them, whom they expected to deliver a lecture on total abstinence that evening for their Temperance society, which they had lately established in that place. "There's na doubt Temperance is a very good thing," observed the traveller, "but I am not sure that teetotal can be right; its not in the Scripture. A man should be moderate, but he's not called on to do without any; a little will do him good," "It never did me any good, and I took it for many a long year," responded his companion, "and no doubt you are aware, sir, there are a large number of persons who cannot take a little and be moderate, and, you'll admit, we should be ready to give up our little drop for example's sake, it is the best means we can adopt to induce the drunkard to become sober." The traveller, even while his conscience told him that these drinks had never done him any good either, replied, nevertheless, "That sober men were not called on to give up their liberty because others abused theirs."

The villager, while not seeking to dictate, stated facts and principles with the firmness of settled conviction. He alluded to the history of some families in the neighbourhood, members of which had been ruined through the drinking customs. He showed that it was not only the duty and interest of their relatives to make sacrifices to set such captives free, but also of every Christian member of society to do so too. He described the ruin of some of these people. The traveller winced, for some of these cases resembled his own. They passed on to the lodgings, and as it still wanted some time to the hour of meeting, the villager said if he would go with him to hear the lecture he would come back and take him. He gave his consent, through a feeling of the other's kindness in having procured him lodgings. Afterwards, when the villager came, he had enjoyed a wash and refreshment, and felt quite disposed to go, as it would interest his mind and give rest to his body also; he wished to think about anything new to him rather than look back on what he had left behind. When they arrived at the school-room it was decently filled. The audience, like most of Scotch audiences, was sitting in expectant silence. The meeting was opened with a hymn invoking the blessing of God on their efforts to reclaim drunkards. The lecturer was one whose heart was in his subject; his eloquence was that of thought rather than manner. He described the delusions of the drinking custom, showing that good, kind, and generous-hearted people were the most likely to be deceived by its pretensions, and welcome it with open arms, until it wound its folds around them. He described the ruin of tradesmen and working-men, by its leading them to neglect their business and families, while they wasted their money and time in taverns. He appealed to them, if every one of them did not know of husbands, wives, sons, and daughters, in every class of life, who had lost their characters and position through these drinking customs. He called on them as men and Christians to join in banishing these evil customs from society. His words were as goads. His was the eloquence of faith. For a moment all difficulties were overlooked by the conviction of the truth. The audience was filled with fervour and zeal to remove evil and spread happiness. The force of habit, appetite, and interest was for a moment quieted. At the conclusion of the meeting a number signed the pledge. The traveller had sat deeply interested. The descriptions of the ensnaring and pernicious effects of strong drink came home forcibly to his own experience. He could not controvert one point of the lecture, yet he did not feel impelled to sign the pledge. Some new ideas had come to him, but only as passing lights seen in a mist. The villager had observed his serious air, and felt that interest in him which we often feel towards those who are labouring under concealed sorrow. With the delicacy of true sympathy he did not attempt to penetrate the causes of the evidently depressed spirits of the traveller, but showed his sympathy in kindly attentions. It fortunately happened that they were of the same trade. The villager wanted a journeyman, and the other gladly engaged with him. When questioned by the villager what he thought of the lecture, his answer was

that all his descriptions were "ower true," that none could gainsay his statements. "If so its your duty to join us." "I cannot see that; I think I can
command myself; I am not a drunkard." "Have you no friends or relatives
that are intemperate?" Here his conscience winced, and he felt that he had
been a drunkard. Yet pride resisted, and he replied, that he did not feel
called on to join. He once attempted to find solace in the tavern, and went to
spend an evening there, thinking he might thus banish thought. But his old
companions were not there, and with the two or three who were there he felt
no sympathy. Instead of banishing reflection the scene excited reflection. He
thought on his own follies, while repelled by the grossness of those present. He
remembered the wretched home and character he had aided to produce, and
when he thought for a moment upon the lower depths to which she whom he
still loved might sink, and the destitution she was in, he started with a convulsive pang from his seat, for he could sit no longer. His mind was racked
with conjectures about the condition of his wife, and he sought in vain for
rest to his troubled spirit. Fortunately for him he had come into a purer
moral atmosphere. His employer invited him to public worship, and, in his
lonely state, the truths he heard operated forcibly on his mind. He could
not banish them. When asked to tea on a Sunday, and he surveyed the family
circle, its happy faces beaming with affection, he thought of his absent wife
and her condition. When he put on the new garments he had procured, he
thought on the ragged condition he had left her in, and he could not be
happy. He felt she would not have abandoned him, but had borne with his
faults to the last, and tried to save him. When he attempted to pray he could
not implore the Divine blessing on what he was doing. He had not forgiven
or shown mercy; how could he expect his Heavenly Father to forgive him?
A continued wrestling went on in his mind. He could not long remain in
that state, for when truth comes men must welcome the light and go on
to perfection, or, if not, its spirit is quenched, and they become darker
than ever. A second lecture was given by the same gentleman who delivered
the first. This time he dwelt on our duty to others more fully—the father's
duty towards his erring son, the wife towards her husband, the husband
towards his wife, and the Christian towards his neighbours. He related some
touching cases where relations had, by self-denial and persevering kindness,
been instrumental in leading each other from habits of intemperance. He
impressively appealed to the consciences of his audience to come forward and
sign the pledge, that they might be instrumental in reforming their friends
and neighbours. At the close of the lecture the traveller signed the pledge. He
felt easier when he had done so; still he kept the same reserve as to his history;
but the desire to seek and rescue his wife became stronger. As he sat at the
fireside, imagination would transform it to his "ain fireside," and his wife
sitting beside him enjoying their Temperance home. Then doubt would
breathe a palsying suspicion that it would be impossible to reclaim her. Then
faith and hope would arise, and he felt he could not have peace of heart until

he tried to do so. He thought of various plans—of sending her money to clothe herself, informing her he had signed the pledge, and imploring her to sign it also, and to come and join him; but he was afraid that she might be tempted to take a *little*, become intoxicated, and so waste the money. He thought of going himself and appealing to her, but he could not muster courage to go back as yet to the scene of his disgrace. At last he unbosomed himself to his employer—told him of the tortures he had undergone and was enduring—and besought him to go and find out his wife, and if she would sign the pledge as he had done, clothe her respectably and bring her out to him; and he trusted God would enable them to continue sober and be happy together. His friend warmly grasped his hand, thanked him for his confidence, and proposed to start the next day. He said little, for he knew the heart, when in such a state, shrinks from the condolence of many words, but feels the sympathy of kindly acts. He gave his employer the necessary money to execute his mission, and the next morning, after a warm grasp of his hand, bade him a short good-bye and saw him off with the coach.

On arriving at ——, his friend went to the street where they had lived when he left his wife, and entering a neighbouring small shop, inquired what had become of them. "Ah! they went to rack and ruin through the drink" was the answer. "He was bad but she was worse, for if a woman takes to drinking it's awfu'. They were broken up and he lost a' heart, and went away and left her, and then she became worse and worse every day, and the few things left were sold for rent. I heard that she went to —— street to lodge, but I have never seen her since. It was a great pity, sir; they were a decent, respectable couple when they first lived in this street, and I think they might have prospered if it had na been for the weary drink. It is a pity people cannot content themselves with a little to do them good." The friend went to the street to which he was directed. He found it consisted of dilapidated houses, overcrowded with dirty and half-clothed people. The cause of this wretchedness was obvious on perceiving the number of whisky shops compared to those of provision shops which the population maintained, the former being fourteen, and the latter only three. While many of the women and children were but half-clad, the shelves of the "Wee Pawns" were filled with their clothes. On inquiry, he found her lodging in an attic, destitute of every article of comfort. Some broken chairs and a shake-down composed the furnishing. She was sober, and sitting alone; her countenance indicating deep, sad, and anxious reflection. He felt glad on observing these symptoms, and foresaw a happy issue to his mission. He introduced himself, stating that he knew her husband, and having business in the town had determined to call on them. She burst into tears, and answered that she could not tell how her husband was, for she had not seen him for some time, and did not know where he was, he having gone away without informing her of his intentions, but, wherever he is, I hope that he is doing well. On the friend's expressing to her his sorrow to hear that he had left her so, she replied that she could not blame him; that "the drink" had been their ruin, but although he was bad she was worse. "Oh, sir," she exclaimed, "the drink was my curse. I tried to be temperate, but could not. I felt I was going to ruin, and wished, yes, sir, prayed to escape, but I did not take the right way. When my husband left me I lost all hope and sunk into utter recklessness. But, thank God, his providence has opened a way for me to escape. He sent some good people who were kind to me and induced me to sign the pledge of total abstinence from these drinks, and I pray and trust that He will give me grace to abstain from them until I die. You see in what a destitute state I am, but, thank God, I am in my sober mind, and if I am granted health I hope soon to get decent clothing and a better dwelling, and be able to attend a place of worship. And oh, sir, if I could but learn that he has escaped from the snares of strong drink and become a sober man, I would feel happy. He was always kind to me, and I love him, and should he never return to me, I shall always pray for him." Her case shows the usefulness of visitations and tract delivery at the houses of the degraded. Two ladies were delivering tracts in the street, and having learned some portion of her history determined to watch an opportunity to try to induce her to sign the pledge. They always carried both religious and Temperance tracts with them in their visitations. They found her one day in a sober and rational state, and kindly inquiring into her circumstances, expressed their sorrow at finding her residing in such a place after having been used to the society of decent God-fearing people. At first, pride rebelled at their interference with her condition, but their gentle Christian spirit removed all resentment. They appealed to her womanhood— her sense of dignity—responsibility—her memory of the happy hours passed with the congregation assembled to worship God. These cords of the heart were touched, her spirit was softened, and the tears ran down her cheeks. "But, oh! what can I do? I cannot help getting drunk; I never intend doing so, but I cannot stop when I can get more after I have tasted." "Then why taste at all?" "That would look so odd. One does not like to be looked upon as an oddity among the people one mixes with." "But these people lead you wrong—why mix with them? Leave them and join the abstainers, and you will not be considered odd among them. We don't feel ourselves odd, and we never take intoxicating drink." "What, do you never take a glass of wine?" "No, nor any intoxicating liquors. We know they are not necessary for us, and can perceive they do much evil to others." "And have you signed the pledge?" "Yes." She mused in silence for a moment, and consented to take the pledge. God's blessing was asked on the deed, and they prayed for strength to keep that pledge. The selfish or the thoughtless, on seeing these sisters of mercy issuing from that wretched dwelling, might sneer or laugh at their labours, but a song of joy rang through heaven when that sinner repented; and who would not sooner have the glad sympathy of angels than the approbation of fools? The friend, while his countenance beamed with delight, informed her where her husband was, and the changes which his mind had undergone, and the mission with which he had entrusted him, expressing his gladness that the most important condition had been fulfilled before he came. The next day, after procuring respectable clothing, they departed on the coach. There are scenes and feelings which words cannot describe, therefore we leave to happy husbands and loving wives to conceive the delights of their reunion.

ADDRESS

TO THE

FATHERS AND MOTHERS, SONS AND DAUGHTERS,

OF THE

WORKING CLASSES,

ON THE SYSTEM OF

EXCLUSIVE DEALING,

AND THE FORMATION OF

JOINT STOCK PROVISION COMPANIES,

SHEWING HOW THE PEOPLE MAY FREE THEMSELVES FROM OPPRESSION.

BY ROBERT LOWERY,

MEMBER OF THE LATE CONVENTION, AND SHAREHOLDER IN THE
NEWCASTLE JOINT STOCK PROVISION COMPANY.

Newcastle-upon-Tyne:

PRINTED AT THE NORTHERN LIBERATOR OFFICE, 89, SIDE, BY JOHN BELL.

1839.

[PRICE ONE PENNY.]

Robert Lowery:
Address on the System of Exclusive Dealing

This eight-page pamphlet is not mentioned by Lowery in his autobiography, perhaps partly because it seems to have been produced only for local consumption in the Newcastle area. The sub-headings reproduced here are as in the original. The pamphlet must have been written in the autumn of 1839, and although at first sight it is vigorous and uncompromising, it is surreptitiously cautious, and marks the early stages of Lowery's change in political strategy. He has not yet forsaken the attempt to intimidate the middle class, for his tactics aim to hit their pockets. But he aims to show them how mutually dependent the two classes are. He was later to adopt more conciliatory methods in welding together a radical middle and working class alliance. A policy of exclusive dealing and co-operation would also have the advantage for Lowery of avoiding the situation which had arisen in summer 1839, where the Chartist leaders, in devising their strategy, were insufficiently informed on the extent of popular enthusiasm for their movement. The leadership would in future be able to gauge their real strength from the degree of popular support for exclusive dealing and co-operation. The pamphlet's message is very similar to that of the Newcastle speech in September 1839 (pp. 242-248), except that it does not stress the importance of concomitant electoral action.

Address

MEN AND WOMEN OF GREAT BRITAIN,

To you who are of the slave class, who have no part in the Constitution—to you who know and feel the miseries of the poor—who wish to be free in reality, and not in name only—who wish your homes to be comfortable, your wives happy, and your children educated—who wish to labour, and enjoy the fruits thereof,—I would point out a part of your duty you have too long neglected, and urge you to adopt it without delay, and overthrow the tyranny that oppresses you; and redeem your class from slavery, want, and woe.

As working men, what is your condition? Year after year, our toils have been increased; yet, as we increased our exertions, year after year, our wages have lowered, our privileges lessened, and our comforts departed, We build, and others inhabit—we spin and weave, and others wear—we sow, and others reap—we cultivate the orchard, and others eat the fruits—we adorn the pleasure ground, and others walk thereon—we fight the battles, but others wear the honours and pocket the rewards. The labourers of Britain are a despised, enslaved, and outlawed race, "hewers of wood and drawers of water" for their oppressors; they are starving amidst an abundance of their own creating—they are aliens in their fatherland—the brand of slavery is on their forehead—the honoured and ennobling name of freemen is denied them—their homes are dreary, and their hearths are desolate—the song of gladness has ceased there—the merry laugh is gone—the smiling face has disappeared—plenty and content, health and cheerfulness, have departed—want, care, sorrow, and sickness, sit bitterly remembering the past and brooding over the future. Their inheritance has been stolen—the gifts their God in his goodness gave them have been taken away; the earth and its loveliness is not theirs; their enslavers and oppressors have portioned its paradise among themselves. After eighteen hundred years have gone by since the establishment of Christianity, the misery and injustice which Christ lamented as the effects of error and wickedness are still supported and committed by men in power, professing his principles, and bearing his name. The unrighteous rule and the wicked sit in judgment; the poor, the widow, and the fatherless are oppressed; "the foxes have holes, and the birds of the air have nests, but the son of man has no where to lay his head." History informs us that our forefathers were free and happy; they enjoyed their lands, and had abundance of wholesome provisions. We work harder than they did; by the increase of machinery and an application of the discoveries in science and art to the production of food and wealth, political economists declare that we are able to produce ten times as much as our forefathers did. If so, how is it that so many of our countrymen are starving, sinking into an early grave from over-labour and want? If they produce ten times as much, they ought to be ten times as well-off as their ancestors were. They do produce ten times as much, but they have to pay twenty times as many taxes, forty times as many idlers, tax-gatherers, bankers, lawyers, placemen, pensioners, priests, and princes, who, like hungry locusts, are spread over the land, and devour the fruits of its industry, with a large standing army of troops of the line, and an army of unconstitutional bludgeon men and spies, called policemen, both of which our ancestors never knew; they were well governed, well paid for their labour, and the constable's staff and the sheriff's wand preserved the peace of every county.

After a long period of the most unexampled patience under these most galling wrongs and distressing privations, the working classes of England have at length been roused to a determination to endure them no longer; they have "taken their affairs into their own hands," they will trust Whig and Tory plundering quacks no more, but will do their own work. They have discovered that an exclusive possession of political power has enabled the wealthier classes to tax their labour, create monopolies, destroy the markets of industry, and reduce the wages of its reward to the starving point. They, therefore, are resolved to have their political rights, knowing that without them, their labour or comforts can never be protected. They have adopted a Charter of Freedom, not for a class, but for the whole people; they defy their bitterest enemies to point out one unreasonable, unjust, or impracticable clause; they wish all to enjoy their political freedom, rich and poor; they would deprive no man of his, they only wish to enjoy their own; they wish the master his fair profit, and the labourer his reward; they seek not to despoil or deprive any man of his property, but request to keep and enjoy their own—the fruits of their honest labour. They met in public meetings, in numbers exceeding four millions, and sent up a petition for this act of right and justice, signed by thirteen hundred thousand names, yet their rulers turned a deaf ear to their demands; their rights were denied; their cries for justice were called sedition, and remonstrances against oppression were deemed rebellion. They asked for freedom, and their tyrants treated them with scorn and contumely; for bread they gave them bayonets and bludgeons, and immured them in dungeons; the courts of law were turned into engines of tyranny, and political prejudice and class-animosity trampled on the justice seat and in the jury box.

The people are not dismayed. They have discovered the truth, and it will eventually make them free: they are extending their organization, disseminating their principles, and every obstacle they meet with will still urge them on to greater exertions. Their oppressors need not think that because they have not rushed unarmed into a struggle of violence and bloodshed with hired man-slayers and murderers, that they, the people, have deserted their banners, and left the oppressors triumphant. They are reposing in their strength; and they will proceed to action with the increased knowledge that experience has given them. They have adopted a series of ulterior measures which their Convention recommended; every one of which wounds the enemy in a vital part, and gives proof of the preparedness of those who act upon them to be fit for more severe and determined duty.

Whether we view it as a measure calculated to profit ourselves by enriching, inciting, and strengthening us; or as a means to weaken and destroy the power and pride of our unjust oppressors,—of the most prominently useful and less difficult of exercise, is—

EXCLUSIVE DEALING

The power that oppresses us is supported by the middle class shop keepers; if the Parliament is bad, it is they that send the members; they promised that if we assisted to get them the Reform Bill they would get us the vote; they have broken their pledge; they have arrayed themselves against us; they have persecuted us—calumniated our principles; they urged on the illegal attack of the self-constituted authorities; they have volunteered and armed themselves to put down our meetings when we were legally assembled; they have libelled us; they have unjustly accused us, and then passed into the jury box and condemned us, and perjured themselves through their prejudices; they have again and again declared we shall not have our political freedom; we are to continue their bondsmen; we are to be degraded slaves and serfs to them. There are greatly good men among them, but, as a class, the above is true to the letter. They are so ignorant and arrogant that they cannot see that if we were free it would be better for them; our food and clothing being untaxed, we would spend more in their shops, and their profits would be increased. They have turned against the hand that fed them; despised that poor whose spendings made them rich, and have leagued with the enemies of peace, just law, and social order to plunder the working men of their hard-earned wages by an infamous system of taxation. What is our remedy against this evil?—Exclusive dealing. We have made them and we can unmake them. Our pennies make their pounds; dealing at their shops made them middle class men and voters. If we cease to deal with them they will become poor, and lose their votes, and have to labour for their bread honestly. They will then feel the evils they now inflict on us, and be converted, and cry out for universal suffrage, and cheap government. Thus, while by ceasing to spend our money in the shops of our enemies, we have destroyed their power: by spending in shops of our own and our friends, we will have increased our own strength and added to our comfort. All those splendid shops we see in every town have been furnished by us; all those fine houses in which those gentry dwell, with their snug parlours, fine drawing rooms, and costly furniture, have been furnished by the profits on our labour; and if we have done so much for others, may we not do as much for ourselves? Some may question the LIBERALITY and JUSTICE of EXCLUSIVE DEALING, but the principle is decidedly just. A man has a right to have his opinions, but we are not bound to prefer the power that oppresses us, or forge the links that bind us. We can not be called on by any principle of morality to deal with our enemies and neglect our friends. If our custom enable men to be voters, and as voters they support an un-Christian, persecuting, and plundering system, if, by withdrawing that custom, we can relieve ourselves from oppression and keep them from the commission of political crimes, and we do not do so, we are as criminal as they. And who can deny the right of the working men to form joint stock companies, to increase their wealth by the profits on their own consumption, or any other project that combines the producer and consumer, or either of these alone? They have as much right to turn shop-keepers, employers, or merchants as the upper classes have. Do the Whigs or Tories deal with us or employ us when they can help it? Let the persecuted liberal voters and the labouring men who had been turned from their employment, because they went to Chartist meetings, answer. Our enemies, to prejudice our cause, have asserted that we were for using the torch and the pike to enforce our claims, rather than appeal to the principles of justice and reasoning.—They have cried, you took the wrong means; you frightened the peacably and honestly-disposed of the community by your talk of physical force. Well then they cannot complain.

THE MORAL POWER OF EXCLUSIVE DEALING

It is a measure that carries with it no principles of violence; it is simply using our own with discrimination; economising our means in the purchasing or supplying our food, and redeeming ourselves from slavery. It will unite us by a double tie—principle and self-interest: these will form a bond of union we have never had; and it will use us to habits of regularity in our plans; it will be a drilling for action that will indeed make our tyrants quake more than if it were the exercise of the musket and the bayonet, for they will be aware that the moral determination that can steadily pursue the one will as steadily keep the other in view. We need not resort to the weapons of our foes—bludgeons, cutlasses, muskets, bayonets, and sabres; we need not do as they do to their enemies—turn them out of their dwellings; we can stop the supplies and starve them out; we now have to put up with sneers and insults from them, and humbly ask for leave to toil for them; they will then have to become workmen with us; we can exterminate them as a class, morally; and one by one, as our just, liberal, and honest establishments succeed, one by one theirs will disappear, and they will become shopmen and shareholders with us on principles of equality and justice.

THE PLANS

I.—Wherever there are Radical shopkeepers, deal with them immediately in preference to those that are opposed to us.

II.—Immediately issue proposals for the people to form joint stock companies for opening stores or shops for the sale of provisions first; and, afterwards, when their capital enables them, all other articles that the working classes consume.

III.—The capital to be raised in shares of ten shillings each, to be paid by weekly instalments of one shilling per share, or quicker, if convenient, each person depositing one shilling each share on becoming a shareholder.

IV.—No shareholder to be allowed to hold more than fifty shares: each person holding one or more shares to have one vote and no more.

V.—When there are as many shares taken as the parties deem sufficient to commence business with, let the company be considered formed, and business commenced. The number requisite will vary, of course, according to the size of the places.

VI.—Let a meeting of the shareholders then be called for the purpose of electing directors, being shareholders, to manage the affairs of the company, their numbers to be seven, nine, or thirteen, to continue in office six months, being eligible to be re-elected.

VII.—Let the directors then elect a fit and eligible person to be store-keeper, salesmen, and others needed on the establishment, the store-keeper finding security to the amount deemed sufficient for protection, his duty being to keep an account of the quantity of goods received, and superintending the other men delivering the goods to the salesmen, and keeping an account thereof, that at any time stock may be taken and compared with goods and moneys received.

VIII.—Hold a meeting of the shareholders every six months to receive from the directors a statement of the affairs of the company, and declare a dividend of the profits arising from the sales.

IX.—Sell for ready money only; let the articles be of the best quality, and slightly below the market price: but if any member is sick, credit him to the amount of his shares, or to the amount of any other member's that will be answerable for him, but no more, as the success depends on a steady adherance to this principle.

X.—Let no shareholder dispose of his shares without first offering them to the company; pay interest of £5 per cent. on all shares above two each holder, and divide the profits among the rest.

XI.—To extend the principle by causing every consumer to purchase of you. Let each company, when they have been established a short period, or instantly on opening, if they can, inform the inhabitants of the surrounding districts that, by dealing at the joint stock provision store, they can get a better and cheaper article, and that when half of the profits on the goods they purchased amounts to ten shillings, they will be booked as shareholder, and be entitled to all its benefits.

THE BENEFITS

Will be a better and cheaper article than they can purchase elsewhere, with a dividend of profits on what they buy, which in every working man's family will amount to some pounds every year, which will pay his rent and increase his comforts; improve his health by living on good, unadultered provisions; unite him and his class in the firmest bond of brotherhood, and raise them from the destitute and degraded condition they are in. If properly supported and minded, it will change the face of society: we may become builders, cultivators, merchants, and producers for ourselves, and sit under our own vine and fig-tree, none making us afraid. We shall no longer be under the galling bondage we are under at present, with want continually before us, while we toil for profit-mongers who value neither men's bodies nor souls, except as materials to barter for gain; who hold us in political bondage, and arrogantly claim dominion over our minds, denying to us the right to think for ourselves, and to express our opinion. Let us to work then: for those who well consider the subject, cannot fail to see its beneficial tendency and be convinced of

ITS PRACTICABILITY

The mass of the people are of our principles; they are the consumers—the buyers; they can make or give the trade to any establishment they erect for this purpose. It is not as when during the Trades' Unions: the makers opened shops—they had buyers to seek; we are our own buyers—we can command a trade. Most of working men that are married lay out upwards of twelve shillings per week (I mean trades in towns); 1,000 shareholders, consuming to this amount, would purchase goods to the amount of £500 per week. This estimate is low, but it will enable you to judge. The whole of the working classes would join in it, if not immediately, progressively.

ITS PROGRESS ALREADY

The harpies of corruption are astounded at its advance in this town and neighbourhood, they are circulating all the calumny they can invent against the members, and even trying if there can be no old musty and forgotten law raked up to stop the thing. The shopkeepers, who a few weeks ago were armed as "specials" to destroy us, are now specially frightened that we shall destroy them in the most peaceable and constitutional manner.

In the Newcastle Joint Stock Company there are nearly three thousand shares taken. They have taken commodious premises, and will open in a few days. Wherever I have been in the neighbouring villages, the people are anxious that it should open as soon as possible, while, in many, they have clubbed together, and begun for themselves. At St. Peter's Quay, the workmen there were first in the field; and in that small place, the company are taking £70 a week. At Walker, a company was formed the other night, and nearly three hundred shares were taken on the spot. At Winlaton, they have opened one, and are proceeding rapidly. At South Shields, a great number of shares have been taken towards one; while, at Sunderland and its neighbourhood, the principle is progressing at an equal rate. The Newcastle directors have had letters from many parts of the kingdom for instructions how to proceed, stating that it is the unanimous wish of the people in their respective neighbourhoods to adopt the principle.

The above general rules may be varied to meet the circumstances under which they are adopted. Let the members be careful to elect as directors men of unimpeachable character and acquainted with business. Having chosen them, pay proper attention and see that they conduct it rightly, but have confidence in them until you discover wrong. It will be the object of the enemy's agents, through the press and in every other manner, to propagate lies and to blacken the characters of the managers, that they may excite the fears of the shareholders and cause dissensions amongst them, and break up the unanimity that is necessary for success. Remember it is a great work to distinguish between errors of judgment and dishonesty. Never condemn without proof, but chief of all, look to your own duty, and pay proper attention as shareholders, and you will secure order, regularity, and justice.

MEN OF BRITAIN!

Be firm—success is certain to crown your efforts to establish freedom, peace, law, and order. You have the materials among yourselves, if you will make use of them. If you will take the trouble you will be victorious; that trouble will be light and attended with no expense. The man who pretends to be a Radical Reformer, and will not adopt these principles if in his power, cannot be depended upon, there is no active faith in him. If he will not lay out one shilling a-week, or ten shillings for a share in such an establishment, or walk a little further to purchase his goods there, he will never lay out twenty shillings for a musket, and walk twenty miles to fight with it. We have a hundred modes to beat and destroy corruption and misgovernment if we would adopt them; this one requires no sacrifice. Oh! how the tyrants tremble when they see such moral force; they know that it will create and be able to bring forward a vast physical power if necessary. It was by such preparatory steps as these, that the glorious patriots of America harassed the tyrants of England, and gave assurance to their leaders that they were men who could be depended on, and were fit for any service that had freedom and justice for its end. Unite, then! Talk the question over in every workshop and every cottage. Begin! The time for words is gone by; we want deeds. Action! action! ought now to be every man's motto. Action in every way that will cripple the power of our tyrants. Already they are tottering in their fall. If ye will it, ye may be free—free from political slavery—free from social degradation, with happy homes, and altars free!

WOMEN OF BRITAIN!

On your co-operation much depends; without your aid we cannot be successful. You have the laying out of our wages; there is nothing so attractive about the present system of corruption, or its shop-keeping advocates, that you need hesitate to leave them, and purchase at a shop of your own. You suffer under the same evils under which your fathers, husbands, and brothers suffer; if their wages are low, and highly taxed, you have to provide for the house with them, and feel the difficulty where they will not do so. I know you wish to have your houses better furnished, your children better educated, clothed, and fed—unite, then, with us in this holy work of human enfranchisement. Purchase at your own establishment. Remember that no woman is worthy of the name of a working-man's wife, who will lay out his hard-earned wages in the shops of those who insult him and deny him his political rights. If we all go hand in hand in this just work, we shall succeed; and once more plenty and content will be inmates of the labourer's dwelling; once more the merry laugh will be heard; the children will again be taken from the dreary mine and factory hell; and from being stunted and decrepid, become smiling, active, and healthy; the green before the village school will again re-echo with the sounds of gladness; care, and want, and sorrow, and sadness, will be chased away: ourselves and our children will be happy and free!

Robert Lowery

Selected Letters, Poems and Speeches

(from newspaper reports)

Speech at the Public Meeting on Newcastle Town Moor, 14 April 1834

This was Lowery's third public speech and his first in the open air. His two preceding speeches had been on the Polish insurrection and the Irish Coercion Bill. The speech is on the motion "that this meeting had heard with indignation and surprise of the sentence on the Dorchester labourers having been put into execution, in defiance of the wishes and petitions of the people", and it is reported in Newcastle Chronicle, *19 April 1834. Lowery mentions this speech in his autobiography, at p. 80.*

Mr. LOWERY (from Shields) seconded the resolution, in doing which, he observed, that he had never felt such joy as he now felt at the numbers assembled that day; it was a proof that they were men of the same passions and the same dimensions as their oppressors; that they were fed on the same food and partook of the same air with them; if they were pricked would they not bleed, and if they were wronged should they not revenge themselves (cheers)? If ever there was a period when it behoved the working man to stand forward it was now; he urged them to put no confidence in an ostentatious aristocracy or the avaricious middlemen, who had no communion with, nor sympathy for, the people. Ever since they had wielded the destinies of the nation, they had wielded them not for the benefit of the people but for their injury and their disgrace. If the people would be free, their freedom must be gathered in conflict and reaped in storm, for never did tyranny relax her grasp till she was compelled by force (cheers). Could those things be permitted to continue?—(No, no). Look at the country; where was the agricultural labourer who blithely drove his team a-field? he was reduced to pauperism and starvation. Look at the towns, and they would see only one continued scene of misery; where was the industrious artizan? he was either walking the streets melancholy and cheerless, or he was ploughing his way across the Atlantic, an exile from his native land (hear, and cheers). And how did this arise?—there was no want of industry, for the sun in his course shone not on a more industrious race than the mechanics of England; how, then, came such misery? Alas! they had lived to learn that men might starve in the midst of plenty; they had experienced that in proportion as a man was useful, so was he held in contempt (hear). Should these things continue? No! they must, would, and should be altered. But how? By the Trades' Unions (cheers)! Their enemies had taught them the value of being united, and they (the people) would not fail to profit by the example. From the King upon his throne to the meanest turnkey, everything hinged upon self-protection. Let them, then, do their duty; and instil into the minds of their children a deep hatred of tyranny; and let those who maligned the people look at their own conduct. No object that ever was heard of was more just and wise than the object which the people now had in view (hear, and cries of "never"). It was some consolation, after all their sufferings, at length to see the mass of the people rousing from their lethargy, bursting their bonds asunder, and asserting the dignity of human nature (cheers). Who were they who were the enemies of the people? men who usurped the rights of others (loud cheering). In what a state of slavery did we live, when six men were transported from their country, for combining to protect their property. Tell it not in Moscow, publish it not in Warsaw, lest the serfs of Russia should think themselves better off than Englishmen. It was in vain for them to expect any amelioration from his Majesty's ministers; their duplicity had shown that they were leagued with the enemies of the people. Had the Dorchester labourers leagued together to massacre unoffending citizens, they would have been pardoned; but they met to protect their property, and they were condemned. And this was under the sanction of the law—law, indeed, it might be, but it was a desecration of justice. They knew what tyrants could effect by law; it was by law that Sidney perished at the block; it was by law that Emmet[1] died upon the scaffold; and it was by law that the field of Peterloo was strewn with unoffending men and women—law it might be called, but never justice (hear, and cheers). After some observations on the sanctity of oaths, the speaker went on to remark that every interest was leagued against that of the trades' unions—no pains would be spared to put them down—already did the base press exult in their distress—their enemies were in motion—and he did not know but they had their spies even on the hustings (hear); but of that he was regardless; never yet did his tongue utter that which his arm was not prepared to execute, and if they (the administration) did dare to pass an act for putting down the trades' unions, he for one would be ready to resist it to the death (cheers). Let them heap oppression on oppression—let them incarcerate thousands—thousands more would yet arise and beat them, and make them quail before them (cheers). The spirit which brought the first Charles to the block was not yet extinct, and let their enemies beware how they irritated it; the spirit of liberty was in their bosoms, and if they were but true to the unions all would be well (cheers). He would counsel them to obey the laws, but, at the same time, they had a right to remonstrate against the unjust portion of them; he would intreat them to commit no violence, but still to assert their just right to their own property. Let them remember that they were three millions in number, and that their cause was the cause of honesty and of truth. Let them assert their dignity and they would compel the respect of their enemies, who, be it not forgotten, climbed on their

---

[1] Robert Emmet (1778–1803), United Irishman hanged, after giving an eloquent speech from the scaffold, for leading an unsuccessful Irish rebellion in 1803. According to the *Dictionary of National Biography*, "the youth and ability of Emmet have cast a glamour of romance over his career".

shoulders to power, and then turned upon them and called them the "swinish multitude." But, better days were coming; the mists of error were about to be dispelled, and a knowledge of social order was coming, based on the equality of mankind (cheers). Let them strain all their energies to secure to the working man the free enjoyment of his labour and the protection of his property—to produce a state of society in which they would require but one altar, union—one God, reason—and one law, justice (cheers).

The resolution was then put and carried unanimously, with three cheers.

Speech at the Palace Yard Meeting on 17 September 1838

Reported in The Sun, *18 September 1838. This was the great meeting called by the London Working Men's Association to adopt the principles of the Charter. Lowery was elected as a Newcastle delegate, and this was his first visit to London. He describes the occasion in his autobiography at p. 108.*

Mr. LOWERY, of Newcastle, was the next Speaker. He had been delegated by the Radical masses of Newcastle, Sunderland, and Shields, to support the People's Charter, and to tell that meeting that they were willing to send them all the support in their power in their present agitation. Last Monday evening they had had a meeting, in order to resuscitate the Northern Political Union, which had done so much good in the time of the Reform Bill; but they had determined to give their support no more to this faction or that faction—they were determined to do no more except in the cause of the people.—(Cheers.) The men of the North were well organized. The men of Newcastle dared defend with their arms what they uttered with their tongues—(Cheers)—and that the military would have learned on the Coronation day had they made any attack upon the meeting. They were willing to try all moral means that were left. They were willing to try a throne, so long as it was conducive to the happiness of the people—they were willing to have an Aristocracy, so long as they behaved themselves civilly—(A laugh)—but they thought they had a right to have a reciprocity of rights, and if not, they were prepared to go against the throne and Aristocracy.—(Loud cheers.) The men of the Tyne and the Wear would not draw their swords against their enemies until their enemies drew upon them; but having once turned their hands to the plough they would never look back.—(Cheers.) The colliers there were organized, and prepared to demand Universal Suffrage, without which they could never be happy.—(Cheers.) They had found from experience that so far as a constituency was limited, so in proportion was it corrupt, unjust, and extravagant—they knew from experience that when the power was given to one section of the people, it would be used for the aggrandizement of that same section. History told them that all the evils they at present suffered under had arisen from their confiding political power to a section of the community. The spirit of the Tories, while they ruled the country, showed itself in their expensive wars, their shameful taxes, and their enmity to liberty both at home and abroad. The Whigs came into office, and they being a mere section of the community, was their conduct better? Why, with liberty in their mouths, they stabbed at it in Ireland.—(Loud cheers)—and he defied any man to show him a worse Act during any Tory Administration than the

Coercion Act. It was an Act that convinced with the bayonet and reasoned with a halter.—(Hear.) What had they got from the Whigs that they should bolster up and applaud my Lord Melbourne? Did they not consent to the transportation of the Dorchester labourers—to the passing of the Poor-law Bill; and did they not bolster up the Corn-laws?—(Hear, hear.) What hopes had the people if the Whigs were kept in office? They pleaded a want of power. However they once had too much of it, for they had an overwhelming majority in the House of Commons, and what use did they make of it? The Whigs were not to be relied on—they were only a mere section of the community, and the working men must have the Suffrage.—(Hear.) There must be no bit-by-bit Reform—they had suffered enough from that already. The working classes got the franchise for the £10 renters, and what gratitude had they shown? They must, therefore, exert themselves, and for themselves alone. He found the objection against them was, that there was a want of intelligence among the working classes, and that they were virtually represented already; that Universal Suffrage would be universal confusion, and that they were following a Will-o'-the-Wisp, because Universal Suffrage would not remove the poverty they laboured under. Now, as to virtual representation, they might be told the present constituency and the House of Commons represented them. He knew they would represent them, and would legislate for them, so far as their interests were united with the working-classes, but the moment they came into juxta-position, the working classes would be abandoned; therefore they had nothing to expect from virtual legislation. As to the confusion that would occur at elections, he denied *in toto* that any confusion would occur at all, on the part of the working classes. Who was it that feasted most and got drunk soonest at the present elections? Why, the middling classes.—(Hear, hear.) They had not the excuse that the labouring man had. They were daily in the habit of receiving good fare and of drinking the best liquids, while a working man, perhaps, did not get a good dinner once in six months.—(Cries of "Hear, hear.") As to Universal Suffrage not removing their poverty, he asserted it would in a great degree. Would any man tell him that if they had their taxes removed to a certain extent the wages of the working man would not go farther? and that if the national debt were removed and the Corn laws abolished, trade would not flourish? That man would be bordering on insanity who would assert that. As to intelligence, he held that God had given to every man a sufficiency of sense to manage his own affairs. He held, that as to the exercise of the franchise, integrity was the best guarantee; and if it came to a question of integrity, he asserted the working classes possessed it in the greatest abundance. It was not a want of intelligence they complained of in the present constituency and House of Commons, but a want of honesty. Did not history show that of all men the literary man had been the basest of apostates? No class had abandoned their principles more than literary men. For a proof of this let them look to the Press, and they would there see that principle was a marketable commodity, and sold to those who would pay the best for it.—(Cheers.) Could the people be worse than they were at present? If they were ignorant who had made them so? The Government and the aristocracy. They had enacted laws to keep the people in ignorance; and if they kept the people from their rights, on the plea of their being incapable of management, they were bound to remove that want of management. But hitherto they had not done so. Wherever there was a multitude of the people gathered together, so that a fair average could be ascertained of their integrity and sense, that multitude would be in favour of those principles—(Cheers)—and whatever had been great and glorious in the history of man, had been obtained by the assistance of the masses. Who flung the gauntlet to the despot of Europe in America, but the labouring men of America? Who dethroned Charles the Tenth of France? The labouring men. Who got the Reform Bill for England? Why, the labouring men of England. Who had bared their breasts in the breach, but the labouring men? To them we owed all that we possessed. If the structure was glorious, they had reared it, and were ready to defend it; and they might safely be trusted with that which they gave such assistance to produce. Could things be worse than they now were? The Throne was falling into contempt—the Aristocracy was held in disdain—the laws were considered as the medium of oppression for the rich on the poor, and the Church had dwindled into a political machine.—(Cheers.) Those who ought to preach humility and peace were the most greedy of wealth and the most tyrannical in power when they possessed it. They had seen in Ireland that the Ministers of the Gospel ever arrayed themselves with the sword in one hand and the Bible in the other. They had stript poverty of its last mite. In fact, wherever exertions had been made for the enfranchisement of the masses—or the amelioration of the people—the priests had always been found against them.—(Cheers.) In conclusion, he would exhort them to assert their own independence. They had a right to do it; and when they chose to do it, their rulers dared not refuse it.—(Cheers.)

Speech at a Meeting of Carlisle Radicals
on 29 September 1838

The speech is reported in Carlisle Journal, 6 October 1838; the paper says that about 2,000 were present at the meeting, which was held in front of the town hall, "although but a few hours' notice of the meeting was given." Lowery was sent to the meeting on his return from the meeting in London's Palace Yard. He says in his autobiography that this was the first visit he had paid to the Cumberland Chartists, and their poverty shocked him (p. 113). After he had spoken, Mr. Baird, seconding the motion of thanks, said that he "lamented that they had not in Carlisle such an eloquent advocate of their principles as Mr. Lowry."

Mr. Lowry then came forward and was received with much cheering. He spoke to the following effect:—I do not stand forward on the present occasion as the representative of the rich, but of a degraded class of my fellow men. I make it my boast that I am a working man, and as such, I claim to enjoy those privileges which are the legitimate rights of that class. It has long been our custom to trust the great and college-bred men, but I advise you to do so no longer, but to trust to yourselves, and if you are rightly banded together, where is the faction opposed to you that you cannot destroy? Mr. L. then alluded to the demonstrations in London and Manchester, and said that the press had belied them as to the number of persons attending them. He had himself witnessed the great demonstration in London, at which no less than 40,000 persons assembled,—at least that number passed to and fro during the meeting; and when they considered that London was the focus of corruption, that the shopkeepers and the working classes there lived by the aristocracy, however small the meeting might be considered, it was as large as could have reasonably been expected, and he defied the Whigs on any occasion to raise one third of the number, or the Tories one-eighth. The Lancashire meeting was perfectly astonishing; had he not been an eye witness he could not have believed it; the procession was three miles in length. Never was there such an immense assemblage of human beings, thousands of whom were armed, not for the purpose of creating riot or doing mischief, but for the purpose of defending themselves; and none who saw them could for a moment doubt that they could have overwhelmed every thing before them; but, like honest men, they were only armed for their own protection. The people ought to lose no opportunity to press their claims upon the government, and sure he was they would attain their object. I am called a demagogue (continued Mr. L.) and others are called so too, and it is said we go about to agitate. I have no interest in agitation, nor can any working man; our property is our labour, and it cannot be our interest to create riot, in which we would likely be the greatest sufferers; what we want is to be fairly represented. It is said that England is great and glorious; and so she is; but who made her so? The working classes; yet they are oppressed, and are more like slaves than free men. We are not in the position God intended us to be; look abroad in the country, and you will find extreme poverty on the one hand, and riches on the other. I ask, is this fair? Is it just, that the life-blood of the body politic should be in such a condition, as to baffle all description? Society is in an unnatural state. If you show me palaces, I will show you thousands of poor and wretched hovels. I do not want to pull down the rich, but to raise up the poor. God has showered his blessings upon us equally; how is it then that there is such a frightful mass of misery? I boldly assert that there is no cure for the manifold evils that afflict society until the government be placed on such a basis as will give equal rights to all men; until Members of Parliament have an interest in working out the good of the people. But both factions are our enemies; Whigs and Tories are much alike. Did we not assist the Whigs in gaining the Reform Bill? And what have the working classes gained by it? Nothing. The Reform Act has had too great a trial already. Why, the first act of the Whigs was an attempt to conciliate the Tories; they abandoned the working men; they passed the coercion bill for Ireland; they transported the Dorchester labourers and the Glasgow cotton spinners; and I would say anathema be on every man who supports a Whig, for they would reduce England to a manufacturing hell. They care not a straw for the morals of the people, if they can profit themselves. In 1801 only half the produce of the country was exported compared with what is exported now, and yet we only receive half the amount for our labour we did then. I demand that capital shall only have its due share of benefit. The working classes should have a due share of gain; they should be enabled to live well, and to instruct their children in those principles of morality which would be of service to them in after life. If I am compelled to take a low rate of wages, my employer is not the less dishonest for taking advantage of me. I can see no remedy for this state of things, until the people have a voice in making the laws; and then, if the people act as they ought to do, they will take care to secure the services of such men as will serve them honestly. I claim for the people those inalienable rights of which they ought never to have been deprived. He who rules the universe has declared all equal, the peer and the peasant should share alike. He has marked out no class to be superior to another. What have the working men had to do with making the bad laws? The corn law was enacted by force, and contrary to the will of the people. Then came the poor law, a most damning act; if ever there was injustice done to the working classes, it was in the passing of that measure, for by it the people have been completely robbed of their birth-right. Lord John Russell and Lord Brougham, will keep the title deeds of their estate, and yet they will barefacedly rob the poor of their rights. "What's sauce for the goose should be

214

sauce for the gander." Why not send the pensioned aristocracy to the poor house? If it be incumbent on the poor to keep their poor friends, surely the aristocracy are much more able to maintain theirs, and ought to be compelled to do so. It is said we are too ignorant to be entrusted with the franchise. I would ask those who make the accusation to come to our Mechanics' Institutions, and Working Men's Associations, and they will find that learning flourishes as much in the cottage as in the palace. The working men have set an example to the rich, and may fairly put them to the blush. Ignorance, forsooth! It is our intelligence they are afraid of; they know if we had the franchise, we would no longer allow them to rob us of our just rights. They know there is among the working classes a proper sense of what is right, and it is that which they dread. Many men of literature have been the basest sycophants and worst of characters, and who have not scrupled to write for money and otherwise prostitute their talents. Where are there so base a class of men as the conductors of the press? The *Times* had told all tales, and very few of its contemporaries were to be depended on; indeed with the exception of the *Northern Star*, the *Northern Liberator*, and the *London Dispatch*, there was not an honest paper in the kingdom; they did not give a fair stage and no favour. He would turn from the press to literary men generally. Southey, who resides somewhere in your own county, is a base apostate, and a dishonest man. He turned his coat and would have turned his skin. He entered life a liberal, and then for his own advantage forsook those principles. Then there was Scott, and Coleridge, and Brougham; but where was Brougham's eloquence, until he found it necessary to use it from private spleen towards the present ministry. If the rich are ignorant it is their own fault, for they have every advantage and opportunity to be wise. But if the poor are ignorant, whose fault is it? Did not the Tories put on the stamp tax? and did not the Whigs continue it, and in their turn became the greater persecutors of the press? Lord Denman condemned Hetherington, although he had before exclaimed that he would rather stab himself than put up with the indignity. If then they wish to see us informed, let them remove the tax which makes knowledge dear. The power of the press is almost wholly in favour of the aristocracy. If we had a free press, it would be exerted in favour of the people. I demand for them a regular system of education. It is not for want of wealth that we have not a national system of education. Thousands are expended on the Irish parsons, and no trifling sum to an old German lady; and we can give thousands for pictures and chairs, and other trifles, and yet we cannot spare anything for the improvement of the people. Ignorance is the choicest link in the chain of slavery. When men obtain knowledge they will not then sit down and endure wrong. The strength of our oppressors consists in the ignorance of the multitude. I deny that they need be afraid of the want of intelligence. The rich must retrench their extravagance, and allow the poor to drink at the stream which their own labour produces. If our country is great and glorious it is made so by the labouring classes. Who produces the various fabrics that clothe the people? Who built our villages? Who fight our battles? The labouring men of England. But instead of shooting foreigners, we should endeavour to secure equal rights for all; and instead of fighting for the liberty of others, we should now fight for justice for ourselves. For the nation to be free it was only necessary that she willed it and she might be so. I tell the middle class of people who flank our meetings, that if labour is not protected their tills will soon be empty. Everything they eat, and drink, and wear, is produced by labour. The middle classes then must join us; they are beginning to see that it will be to their advantage to do so, for their interests are identified with ours. It is said that we want a revolution, that we want what is not our own. No. We want justice for all, freedom for all, and protection for the poor and needy. I want no man's property, but I want my own to be protected. I want the law to be equally administered; and when I am told that it is the right of every Englishman to have trial by jury, I denounce such trials as those of the Dorchester labourers and the Glasgow cotton spinners; the juries who tried them were partly made up of their accusers. He next spoke of the Church. Religion placed on a proper footing does not mean £15,000 a-year to Bishops and large salaries to the parsons; religion is the outpouring of the heart to God, and an exercise of the principle of charity; and the prayers of the people are acceptable to Him whether offered up in the Chapel or in the Cathedral. We do not attack religion but the system, which is not that given by Christ. The church is made up of ostentation and pomp, and its ministers have lived with our oppressors and assisted in crushing the people. Instead of giving the people knowledge, they have banded themselves together with our worst enemies. We are the true practical christians; we can safely appeal to the consciousness of our own principles; we are not men of war but of peace; resistance to oppression is the God we seek; our rights are sacred and we will have them. If an attempt be made to put us down, we must resist; but we will not be the first to make the attack. We seek no combat but our own rights, and we are bound to get them and will get them, and that too, with moral force. Our enemies have besotted us and call us the swinish multitude; but we are now born again; we have cast off our foolish notions and prejudices, and put on the armour of truth and justice. Scotland with her heathy hills and green vales has buckled on her broad sword; but Lancashire and Yorkshire alone can secure all we want. Germany is clanking her chains; Poland is gasping for freedom; and France, twice cheated, is again standing forth in her National Guards; her people have petitioned the French tyrant and told him they will have freedom. Oh! there is a majesty in millions. I am glad that right principles are found in Carlisle, and that it promises fair to equal any town in zeal and spirit. Go on, neither swerving to the right nor to the left, and let not the corn law, or the poor law, or any other law draw you from the main object. If the corn laws were repealed tomorrow, what security have we that they will not be re-enacted. As for our immorality, I would ask the rich to show us their morals. I am afraid they are far from what they ought to be; but the vices of the poor are exposed, whilst those of the rich are concealed. The aristocrat can swill his wine and brandy and no one know it; but the poor man who drinks in the public house is immoral. For my own part, I hate a pot-house politician, who, to satisfy his own desires, robs his wife and family of those comforts he ought to administer to them; such are not the men on whom we must depend; no, we must rely on brave, honest, and sober men. Let not the principles we are seeking be placed in abeyance; let every man advocate them and we will eventually triumph. Remember the bonds of those who suffered captivity that we might be free, and let us no longer submit. We demand our rights, and we will have them. Mr. Lowry retired amidst much cheering.

Speech at the Newcastle Public Meeting on 8 October 1838

The speech was on the motion "that this meeting regards with deep indignation the baseness and treachery of the hireling portion of the press in labouring to perpetuate the slavery of the people, and that their resentment is especially directed against the Sun *London evening paper, and the* London Weekly Chronicle, *and* Weekly Dispatch*", reported in* Northern Liberator, 13 *October* 1838.

Mr. LOWERY then came forward, and was received with loud and oft repeated cheers. He said that when in London he had denounced the baseness of the hireling press, and in return he had the *Times* driving furiously at him the next morning.[2] In all the meetings he had subsequently attended, he had reiterated the assertion of its baseness, and as a proof of the truth of that assertion, he pointed to the *Times* itself. But he would not point to the *Times* alone; there were Southey, Coleridge, Scott, aye, and Harry Brougham, all evidences of the prostitution of literary talent. But it was honesty the people wanted; he denied that it was so much a question of intelligence as of integrity.—(Hear, hear.) The press was in the hands of the wealthy, and whether the wealthy were Whigs or Tories, they were, unfortunately for themselves, opposed to the rights of industry, and wanted to grasp to themselves the harvest of the labour of the country.—(Loud cheers.) They had a Journal in Newcastle, and did they think that John Hernaman[3] and the miserable wretches that were connected with him had that concern in their hands. No, the Duke of Northumberland and the Parsonocracy of Durham and Northumberland supported that sink of lies and infamy.—(Loud cheers.)—They had, on the other side, the Durham clique, who pretended to be their friends and yet used the people worse than those whom they called their worst enemies. They were both alike however, and that the people well knew, however

---

[2] *The Times*, 18 September 1838, p. 4 spoke of "the fretful, nay virulent, style in which several of the speakers of yesterday's meeting delivered themselves against educated men in general, and especially against the conductors of the periodical press". *The Times* went on "to use the very expression of one orator, 'of all men, the literary men had been the basest of apostates'. Surely this language was not very just to a power which has peacefully wrought what the pikes of whole provinces could never have accomplished: surely, we may add, it was not a language at all calculated to encourage the audience; for it informed them, in other words, that their cause was hopeless; that they would have to struggle for political power not only against the prejudices of the world, and the wealth of the upper classes, but against the whole array of cultivated intellect, throughout a population where opinion is almost omnipotent. We can tell these excited and inflated politicians that they would not have carried the Reform Bill against such odds".

[3] John Hernaman came to Newcastle from Leeds *c.* 1832, and became proprietor and editor of the Conservative *Newcastle Journal*, which in the 1830s was often very sarcastic towards local radicals. He died on 27 March 1875.

218

they might differ about the mode of going to work, and their only object was, to rob the labouring classes.—(Hear, hear.) It had been said by these worthies that the present agitation was got up by a few interested individuals; but whilst asserting this, they well knew that the history of all Reformers was a history of persecution and distress, and when a man threw himself into the gap, they might give him credit, and not malign him. He denied that the movement was got up by a few men—it was got up by the Whigs and Tories themselves. The people had long submitted to their nostrums, and when the Whigs passed the Reform Bill and excluded the people from elective right they laid the foundation of the present agitation.—(Loud cheers.) He had heard Earl Grey say, that the Reform Bill would ensure a true representation of the people, although that bill admitted less than 800,000 electors out of a population of 24,000,000. Every act that had characterized the Whigs was the product of selfishness, and of all Whigs breathing he denounced Earl Grey as the basest.—(cheers.) That immaculate statesman suppressed ten bishoprics, and yet he retained all their revenues for the use of the bishops or such as the bishops. He gave to his own brother-in-law a bishopric, which could have provided for one of the ten, who were saddled as a life charge upon the country. But the time was past when the labouring classes looked up to the Aristocracy as a race of superior beings. They now knew that when the Creator said "Man shall eat bread by the sweat of his brow," he did not mean an exemption to one class, but he applied it alike to all. (Loud cheers.) Some might wish to divert them from the movement by the ballot; he denounced the ballot under the present system of franchise, because, in that case, the electors could stab the cause of freedom without the people knowing who had done it. The interest of the middle classes were not different to that of the working classes—they were emphatically the same—but they thought they were different, and that was all the same so far as voting was concerned. The Whigs wanted to bring all the nobler feelings of man down to the vile standard of pounds, shillings, and pence—they wanted to reduce England to a manufacturing hell. (Loud cheers.) If he were compelled to a choice of evils, give him the old Aristocracy rather than moneyocracy which threatened, monsterlike, to swallow up the honesty, the virtue, and the independence of England. (Loud cheers.) The present movement was the people's own—emphatically their own—it had not arisen from the middle classes or the upper classes, and he would impress upon the vast assemblage around him that they could not now retrograde. (Loud cheers, and cries of "Never, never.") The unenfranchised millions were fairly pitted against the usurping government, and woe be to them if they turned back. (Loud and long continued cheers.) The tyrant and the hireling in his pay might sneer, but there was a might in millions that made them tremble. In Lancashire they had not taken up the question in a namby pamby manner. There it was seen that the strong hearts and arms of Englishmen was something more than was to be found amidst the sycophancy of courts. When that immense crowd assembled a trumpet could not be heard from the hustings to the outside, and only messengers were despatched to restrain the pressure, it would have carried hustings, and speakers, and all away before it. (Loud cheers.) It was no child's play when men lost their day's wages, which they could ill spare, and came, as many of them came, 15 or 20 miles to a meeting for the recovery of their birthright. The men of Manchester had not forgot the bloody day of Peterloo. There was a great outcry against the use of physical force, but on that day the peaceful people of Manchester saw their brothers and friends butchered by the sword of military despotism, but the men of Manchester had vowed that they would never again trust themselves to the mercy of military executioners. If the magistrates had not placed the borough police under the control of the meeting, and taken every means to prevent it from insult, two hundred thousand men would have met armed on Kersal Moor. (Loud cheers.) As it was, many thousands were armed, he saw the arms that they brought forward to defend themselves from aggression. What, though the London meeting was not so large, still there were never less present than 30,000 men; but London was a sink of corruption—the wealth of the Aristocracy was spent there—and the artizan lived by their extravagance, and, therefore, could hardly be expected to be so virtuous as the workmen in their own provincial towns. (Loud cheers.) Their case was that the country had been long misgoverned—that the land was fruitful—the clime genial—the resources immense—and yet that misery abounded where happiness should abound. He did not claim more than justice for labour; but he did assert, that whilst the capitalist went on realizing princely estates the happiness of the workman should progress in the same ratio. (Loud cheers.) This never could be so withcut the people got the franchise; at every step they were met by bad laws and bad institutions, and these laws must be removed. But he would not turn aside to attack any law till they got the franchise. Those laws, if repeated, could be easily re-enacted. (Hear, hear.) Could England be worse than she was at present? The large capitalists were swallowing up the small ones. The Aristocracy had sunk to a miserable pension-hunting crew, and the Squirearchy to a set of fox-hunters and gamblers, who thought that themselves only were to enjoy the fruits of the earth, whilst others laboured to produce them. Commerce had sunk into a system of gambling—one man failed and another realized £100,000 in a few years, and he must have realized it by robbery, under whatever name it might be disguised, as no honest trade could put it into his hands. The tyrants told the people they were ignorant, but it now was pretty well known that it was not the ignorance of the people that was feared but their intelligence. In 1832, the Tories said that the ten pound renters were ignorant; well, the people stood by them till the Tories were vanquished, and now those very men turned basely round and joined the Tories in the same senseless cry against the people.—(Loud cheers.) The vices and the ignorance of rich men were concealed from the public view, whilst those of the poor men were pointed to and exposed. The preamble that abolished Universal Suffrage declared that it was necessary to take that step, owing not to the faults of the people but to the disturbances that were created by the wealthy at elections. He appealed to benefit societies—trades societies —mechanics institutions, and he challenged the aristocracy to show him such an amount of talent and discernment as was to be found in the democracy of the country. Let him go to the House of Commons—by their own report there were upwards of 2,000,000 of human beings in Ireland in want of subsistence. There was land enough in Ireland, and the people only wanted to be allowed to labour to produce a superabundance of food. But the gentlemen of the House of Commons could find no employment—they could find nothing to cure the evil, but accommodation for 80,000 within poor law bastiles.—(Loud cheers.) Could the people possibly commit a greater blunder than this? They said that Englishmen were fond of riot and murder; if so, what prevented the 300,000 men of Manchester from overturning all before them? But it was the aristocracy, who had ever rioted in bloodshed when their system was put into jeopardy. When did they ever stop at laying a town in ruins, and filling the nations with the widow and the fatherless?—(Loud cheers.) They talked of the institutions of the country. He denied that any age or society had a right to barter the rights of coming ages, or lay down laws for their government. They talked of the constitution of England, but he asserted that England never had a constitution.—(Loud cheers.) Where was the constitution of England during the Manchester and Calthorpe-street massacres?[4] Where was it when Ireland was handed over to military execution by the infernal coercion bill?—Where was it when the constitution of Canada was broken? (Loud cheers.) Englishmen ever held what freedom they enjoyed, not in virtue of a constitution, but in virtue of the constitutional strength of their right arms. (Renewed cheering) As the people were apathetic they were oppressed, and as they aroused from their apathy the oppression was relaxed; their oppressors would now give them many things if they would only give up the suffrage, but as a working man he denounced all compromise.—(Loud cheers.) As to the question of their pitting themselves against the government, his opinion was, that in a free country every man had a right to be in possession of arms. England's best days were when they had no standing army, but when a nation of armed citizens were ready to spring forward in defence of their country. But now the government was afraid to reduce their standing army lest the people should rise up against oppression. The people were in chains—the government was an usurpation. He denied its right—he looked on their laws as based on injustice, their taxes a robbery, and their application of physical

---

[4] The government forbade a meeting of the political unions planned for Coldbath Fields, London, on 13 May 1833. The meeting was held regardless, and when the police dispersed the crowd, Policeman Culley was killed in Calthorpe Street. At the inquest, the jury decided that the stabbing was justifiable, and were much praised by radicals for doing so. See Gavin Thurston, *The Clerkenwell Riot* (1967).

force in support of the atrocious system, as a murder, both in the eyes of God and man. (Tremendous cheers.) If the people had a right to arm, were they justified in trusting themselves to the sabres of an aristocratic government? It did not follow that the people would tilt a muck with each other, but the time was fast approaching when the government must grant them their demands, or put them down.—(Tremendous cheers.) If the government granted their just demands, they asked no more; but if they did not, it remained to be seen whether a few thousand aristocrats, and twenty or thirty thousand of a standing army were in a condition to put down the mighty and incensed millions of England.—(Loud cheers.) Resistance to oppression was obedience to the laws of God. Had America trusted to moral force, where had been her republic? The Americans calmly discussed the matter, and when they came to the conclusion that tyranny was to be resisted, they set about it with heart and hand.—(Loud cheers.) It was the duty of Englishmen to prepare for the worst. Already the system tottered; the press, that abject tool of oppression, had lost its moral influence; the tremendous "WE" had now sunk into nothingness. Let them press forward for the last time; perseverance was necessary to success; by perseverance they wrung from the tyrant Whigs the reluctant admission that they had expatriated the Dorchester Labourers unjustly; they had brought those men once more to England; they had placed them in comfortable homes; and there was an ear of wheat (displaying it to the meeting) of the first year's crop of the Dorchester Labourers' farms.—(Immense cheering.) He would call upon every man around him, of whatever sect, to join with the movement. The philanthropist who was endeavouring to alleviate human misery, would find that bad laws would be able to create more misery than he would ever be able to remove. In London, it was known, that 10,000 rose daily without knowing how to get their subsistence; similar destitution was to be found in every great town; and whilst these things were permitted, how could the philanthropist expect to benefit the human race. The religion of God had been desecrated by a crew of imposters; but intelligence was progressing, and would soon tear down the veil and expose the money changers that defiled the temple.—(Loud cheers.) The throne must become the throne of justice, and the temple the temple of peace. However the aristocracy scoff, they must accommodate themselves to the times that were approaching; men would no longer allow their minds to be shackled, or their body to be enchained at the dictates of a few insolent tyrants; that day had gone by for ever, and a better day was about to dawn on England and the world.— (Loud and repeated cheers.)

The Chairman then put the resolution, which was carried unanimously.

Speech at Carlisle, October 1838

The speech was on the motion "that it is the opinion of this meeting, that the National Petition just read be adopted, and signed without delay", reported in Carlisle Journal, *27 October 1838, p.3.*

Mr. LOWREY, of Newcastle, seconded the motion. He did not stand there as a member of the aristocracy, of the moneyocracy, or of the shopocracy; but as a labouring man, who with his own hands had toiled for his bread since he was ten years of age; and as a labouring man he wanted to know if those whom he saw before him would continue any longer to do as they had done—if they would any longer suffer others to waste what God had provided for them—whether they would any longer continue to be worse fed than the dogs and horses of the rich. ("No, no", and cheers.) It was from the labours of the poor that all riches flowed—it was the poor who cultivated the deserts,—who built their cities, who wove the cloth with which the rich were covered; it was the poor who had borne arms in triumph to the ends of the earth, and chastized every tyrant but their own. (Cheers.) Therefore it was that he demanded that the labouring man should share in the benefits to be derived from his toil. It had been said that it was a bread and cheese question. It was so. He cared not so much for it as an abstract right. What he wanted was to see the people well fed, with happy and comfortable homes. These were what they had in the olden time, and these were what were worth contending for. He wished to ask those assembled if for these they were prepared to contend at all hazards. ("Yes yes," and cheers.) The time might come when we shall have to fight for them. ("We are ready now.") They might talk of moral force till doomsday—it was not that which the rogues wanted. The only thing was to bring on the issue, and God uphold the right. (Cheers.) He contended that Governments existed but for human happiness—that it was a benefit society for that purpose, to secure the greatest happiness to the greatest multitude. If Government would assert that the multitude could not be happy—if it was shown that happiness could not be secured with a queen, an aristocracy, with a law-established church, and with a commercial system such as now existed, then he would say, perish the queen, perish the aristocracy, perish the church, perish commerce, perish society itself, and let them return to the woods and forests as in a state of nature, where they would at least have the free air and the fresh fruits which God provided for them. (Cheers.) They were bound by no laws but such as were founded on the principle of the greatest happiness to the greatest number. It was time the present system should end, and a new system be established which should give the working man the benefit of his labour. They wanted not to bring any one down, but to support their own rights, to build up what had been destroyed, to clothe the naked and feed the hungry. It was said, in answer to their demands, that they were not educated—that they were ignorant. He replied that not much education was needed. Magna Charta was wrested from John by barons most of whom could not write their own names. (Cheers.) They had the common sense to know friends from foes, and the honesty to act upon that knowledge. He contended that when the suffrage was confided to classes it was exercised for selfish purposes, but that if given to the whole body of the people that selfishness would be for the general benefit, for that the nation could have no interest in robbing itself. Mark the history of the past, and they would find that learning gave them no guarantee for honesty. Where could be shown a greater villain or apostate to his principles than Earl Grey? or where could they find a baser renegade than Brougham? Yet these men ranked high for learning and political wisdom; and what had been their history? They had been continually pandering to the classes which could promote their own selfish ends. There was scarcely a principle on which they had set out in life that they had not set aside or renounced. One of the old Whig principles was that every country had a right to chuse its own form of government; yet in Canada they had murdered the people, burned their villages, and destroyed their property for attempting to act upon this principle. And these were the scoundrels who talked of using only "moral force". Their whole history was a history of bloodshed. If justice were done, those men now in the gaols of Canada ought to be set free, and Lords Melbourne and Glenelg hung by the head in their places. (Cheers.) Both factions had contrived to live by setting the people against each other—by raising the cry of "God save the King," and "God save the Church." But the people had at last found out that kings were an expensive thing. The little girl now on the throne he had no wish to see hurt or injured; but he wished to see her in her proper employment— that of knitting stockings. (Cheers and laughter.) She had been drawn from her proper place; and the Whig Ministry had given to her an income sufficient to keep the families of 18,000 labouring men—(shame)—yet they who had granted such an income as this were the men who were now trying how little they could force the poor man to live on. He took the Queen as an instance to show that learning was not necessary for taking part in political affairs. She had no education—he did not mean book learning, but that education which was derived from practical experience of life. More than this, they were all aware that this country had been ruled for half a century by the moon struck madman, George the third; and during his reign the country had been saddled with a debt of eight hundred millions. If the factions had a right to place that madman upon the throne, and to keep him there, he would say that the men of England had a still more legal right to elect members to sit in the Commons' House of Parliament. He proceeded to say that he was certain to be one of the delegates appointed to meet in London; and he wanted to have the opinions of men not only in his own neighbourhood but in other parts of the country as to what should be his proceedings. At present the brand of slavery was on their foreheads, and it was their duty to have that removed. No government was a just government that did not admit the whole people within the pale of the constitution. He, therefore, denounced the present constitution of the House of Commons as an usurpation. He did not think that he and others who were excluded from a share in its election were bound by its laws; they were not amenable to its authority; it was with him a mere question of expediency—he submitted to it only when he could not help it. He held himself at perfect liberty to fling it off whenever he could, and to refuse to obey its laws until he was admitted to a share of the representation. Was that the opinion of that meeting? ("Yes, yes," and cheers.) The men of Newcastle sided with him in his opinion: they say there should be no government of which they did not form a part, and they will overthrow every government that will not admit them. (Cheers.) This was the old constitution of England, which gave a vote to every man twenty-one years of age. The very word used in their polling booths was proof of this. He would tell them the origin of the word poll. It was this—the Sheriff of the County called all the men together to elect a representative. They met as the people had met that day, and they divided by show of hands—by universal suffrage. If a division was required, the Sheriff divided them, and counted the votes by laying his hand upon each man's head. This was the poll. Now, they were told by those who had usurped the power, that the poll means freeholders. This was said by the men who had robbed the people of the land. The men of Newcastle said they wanted that universal suffrage restored; and they were determined to throw off what the rascally Whigs had established in its place. They wanted to have the old constitution restored, when the Sheriff's wand and the constable's staff were sufficient to preserve the peace and enforce the law—when no garrisons and no bayonets were required; when no men with blue coats and bludgeons in their hands were necessary to preserve the peace. Wherever the law had to be enforced by the bayonet and the bludgeon, that law ought to be put down. (Cheers.) Would the Whigs dare to call out the militia—the ancient constitutional force of the country? He would like to see them place a gun and a bayonet in every man's hand. By law every man was entitled to be in possession of a weapon of defence; and their fathers used to meet on their village greens to practice games of defence. He believed it was not for the mere purpose of preserving a few hares that the Game Laws were enacted. The villains knew that the hand that could shoot a hare could also shoot a man; and that they who were expert at such work would be chosen as leaders. He hoped that every man who had the means, and who had not already a firelock, would with all speed provide himself with one to hang over his chimney-piece. It was the best piece of furniture he could have, for it would protect the other furniture. The villains would scarcely venture to enter his doors for taxes if they saw this. (Cheers.) "The is the law; and therefore we will arm." In truth, they were armed, and he hoped Scotland would follow the example, for their Petition must be carried. (Cheers.) He wanted to face the House of Commons. If they allowed the delegates to plead at the bar of the House, they should be kept pretty hot for six weeks at least. By all means in their power the delegates would bring the House into contempt, and set its laws at defiance. If the House should reject the Petition, the Convention would be justified in sitting as the real Parliament; and he for one, on the day the Petition should be rejected, would be ready to sign a proclamation calling on the people to refuse all obedience to the House of Commons, and let the delegates only be obeyed. (Cheers.) If the House of Commons would have their own constitution let them fight for it; if they will have their own constitution let them pay for it. If they did this, the people would not quarrel with them. ("That's right" and Cheers.) They would then see how the mills would look without hands to work them; and how the ploughs would answer their purpose without hands to guide them. After proceeding in this strain for some time, and repeating several of the doctrines laid down in the earlier part of his speech, he again animadverted on the Poor Laws. It was singular, he said, that those who had been foremost in passing that law to deprive the people of support, were the holders of lands belonging to the poor, which had been granted to their ancestors. As they had raised the question of the maintenance of the poor, another question arose out of that which would not be over-pleasant to them; and that was, to whom did the soil belong? The land of England was the people's—it was all held directly or indirectly from the Crown: the Crown was the people; and, therefore, the land belonged to the people. (Cheers.) When the holders of the land got it—not by trade or industry, but by sinful grants and villainous plunder—it was on the condition that they should pay the taxes, support the poor, and maintain the army in time of war. That was the proviso on which they got the land. Now, the poor were refused support, and the burthen of the taxes was thrown upon their shoulders. What was sauce for the goose was sauce for the gander —if the holders of the land would break the contract, the people must take the soil into their own hands again; and let those who had broken faith be answerable for the consequences. Having dwelt on this topic for some time, he proceeded to ask were the meeting prepared at all hazards to force their way, by their representatives, to the floor of the House of Commons? ("We are"). He would give five years of the hardest labour to meet the villains face to face. They boasted of their learning, and of their classical knowledge: he knew nothing of the classics, but, on his soul, he believed he could beat them. (Cheers.) He called on them to be up and doing. Scotland should stand with the petition in one hand, and the broad sword in the other; England could sit and sign the petition, pointing to the musket over the chimney-piece; and as Ireland was poorer, she might prepare herself with the pike—

at the use of which she used to be a very good hand; they would then be ready for both moral and physical force. (Cheers.) "Gird on your arms, then, and to your tents oh! Israel." They could not be wrong, for they were but following the advice of that Book which they were told was a sufficient guide for all. He concluded by calling on the meeting to resolve that man should be as free as his immortal maker intended him, and that he should sit under his own vine and fig tree, and worship God as his heart dictated. (Great cheering.)

The resolution was then put and carried unanimously.

Lowery's Report to the Northern Political Union on his Scottish lecture tour in *Northern Liberator* 3 November 1838

The report is headed "Progress of Mr. Lowery. To the Council of the Northern Political Union". It is unsigned, and although the report on Dumfries is clearly by Lowery, it is possible that the reports on Wigton and Dalston were contributed by another correspondent. Lowery mentions this trip in his autobiography (p. 115) and says that it impressed him with the intelligence of Scottish audiences.

GENTLEMEN—The agitation is going on swingeingly here. In all parts the Whigs are dumbfoundered, and gnash their teeth in vengeance; the Tories are completely out of their reasoning, and cannot tell what to make of the peoples' spirit and notions. They are like the old Austrian Generals when opposed to Napoleon, they never were used to such a mode of fighting, it is out of all former rule and method; poor souls they thought they were the only state physicians in the nation, and that if the sick and suffering people left one shop, they must, perforce, come to the other. The people, however, will not have any more bleeding, they have turned doctors themselves, and prescribe good food, warm clothing, comfortable houses, fresh air, and gentle exercise. The old rival quacks may shut up shop. After the Carlisle meeting was over, being strongly pressed to go to Dumfries with Mr. Duncan, we started in a gig with Mr. Arthur, bookseller, after breakfast, and enjoyed a delightful journey. As we approached the border we passed the beautiful domain of Sir James Graham, whose apostacy ought to be pondered on by those that prate about learning and education being necessary for the voter,[5] and was struck with the present aspect of the country, as compared with its history of other times—the times of aristocratic barbarism. Now all shows the aspect of peace, and the people freed from the shackles of prejudice, acting and thinking for themselves. We crossed the rubicon of border strife, and soon were at that dread of ambitious fathers and guardians, the far famed Gretna Green; we drove up to Mr. Linton's, the Bishop, that confirms the vows of love's faithful votaries. He was exceedingly kind to us, and favoured us with a view of the state chambers and the register, where I remarked many names whose follies had made a noise in the world, among

[5] Sir James Graham (1792–1861), First Lord of the Admiralty and at that time an advanced reformer, resigned in 1834 when the Whigs proposed to meddle with Irish Church revenue; henceforward Graham was a prominent supporter of Peel's Conservative Party. Arthur the bookseller came from Carlisle, but Lowery says in his autobiography (p. 115) that he accompanied the Chartist lecturers on their tour of Scotland.

the rest Edward Gibbon Wakefield[6] and that of his Neapolitan Majesty. We pushed on to Annan, where we found they were at the good work. We left them some of the peoples' paper, and dashed on through a fine open country, full of literary recollections. On the left was the Solway with Scotland's hills before us, where Meg Merrillies wandered, and where Redgauntlet urged another effort for a falling dynasty.[7] We approached Dumfries, there was the last resting place of Burns; there was the river Nith; here he had wandered, felt the cold world's neglect, and solaced himself with the enjoyment poverty and persecution could not take away. The first thing we did was to visit his monument, it is worthy of those who erected it, and better than a thousand essays on the equality of man; there stands the true nobleman of nature, Scotland's brightest genius and greatest honour, though born in the lowly cottage and cradled amid poverty and toil.

MEETING IN DUMFRIES.—We sought the leading Rads out, got leave of the mayor for the meeting, and I was astonished at the muster they made, but I need not, for go where you will the workies are all Democrats. The Drummer gaed through the town, and when we entered the market there were full 3000 people, although only two hours notice had been given. The place was well lighted up with torches, and there were many of the middle classes in the crowd, and numbers of respectable females. A working man was called to the chair and opened the meeting with some excellent observations on the duties of working men at this crisis, and introduced Mr. Duncan, who, in an able speech, pointed out the sophistry of all Whig and Tory claims on the peoples' confidence. He was very happy in his sarcasms upon Sir Robert Peel and his party, and showed the impossibility of him or any Tory stopping the progress of the present movement. He dealt some hard blows at Wallace, the M.P. for Greenock, at Joseph Hume,[8] and Dan O'Connell. It is astonishing how Hume has fallen in the opinion of the labouring classes here. Mr. D. was very happy in his exposure of the Church Endowment scheme. It was nothing but a plan to hoodwink, and under a pretence of taking care of their souls to take from them what should feed their bodies. (Cries of "Aye, aye, that's just it" and cheers.) It was establishing a Government Agent to gull them and keep them quiet. When there were disturbances in the North, and the authorities wanted to send soldiers to keep the people quiet, "No, no," says the Magistrate, "I want na sogers, send ma a parish priest." (Roars of laughter.) Mr. D. then called on them to come forward and sign the National

---

[6] Edward Gibbon Wakefield (1796–1862) carried off Ellen Turner, daughter of a wealthy Cheshire manufacturer, to Gretna Green for a marriage ceremony in 1826. He was imprisoned, and the marriage was cancelled by special act of parliament. Wakefield is now remembered as a prominent colonial statesman.

[7] Meg Merrilies, gipsy character in Walter Scott's *Guy Mannering* (1815). For Redgauntlet, see Scott's *Redgauntlet* (1824).

[8] Joseph Hume (1777–1855), prominent radical M.P., keen advocate of cheap government, and active committee-man in the House of Commons. Though sympathetic to Chartism, his relations with Chartist leaders were often strained.

Petition, and be ready to defend it. (Cheers.) They must not be refused, but demand it. Universal Suffrage was theirs, and they must have it at any price. Mr. D. concluded an able speech amid loud cheers. Your humble servant was then introduced and kindly received—I told them I was your delegate, and had just slipped ower the border to know if they were ready for action, and pointed out the folly of trusting to anything but our right in the Legislature to ameliorate our condition, and urged them to denounce any man as an enemy who wished them to turn aside for repeal of Corn Laws, Ballot, or Household Suffrage. Then showed that a crisis had arrived, when the people would have to stand or fall by their principles. It ought, if rejected, to be their last petition, and the question would soon be a one of acting not talking, of deeds not words. Were they prepared, having calmly weighed the justice of the thing they were bound to, to have it at any hazard. (Cheers, and cries of "We will.") Never let them think they would get their rights from a sense of justice in the Governing power; liberty could not spring from the courts of tyranny, but must be forced upon it. The general opinion of the working men of the nation was that they ought to be prepared for the worst, and for fear a tyrannical Government should attack them, and persist in wronging them, they ought to have the means of self-defence. Was this their opinion, if so, show it by their hands? (One dense mass of hands, cheering, and waving of bonnets.) They knew resistence to oppression was natural to the hearts of men, and that the men of Scotland inherited the spirit of their forefathers, and hoping that when the struggle came they would be found at their posts, and that when next they met they would be able to greet each other as free men. I bid them good night.

MEETING AT WIGTON.—Mr. Lowery having signified his willingness to attend a public meeting at Wigton, one was called for at eight o'clock on Monday evening last, at the Market Hill. About seven o'clock the procession commenced; it was very numerous and brilliantly lighted by torches. There were a number of banners, which had a beautiful appearance amid the strong glare of light; when the procession reached the hustings there were near 3,000 people on the ground, out of a population of 6,000. Every man and woman appeared to have come out. There is not a more determined set of Radicals than those in this district; their sufferings are such that they are determined to die rather than let them continue. Every patriotic resolve is greeted with enthusiastic cheering, and the firing of muskets. The following resolutions were ably moved and seconded by the several speakers:—

1st. That this meeting is of opinion that under the present system of representation, there can be no permanent remedy for the distress that exists in this country, until our representative system is founded on a basis more in accordance with principles of justice and right, and with the increasing knowledge of the people.

2nd. That this meeting is of opinion that the principles as contained in the Peoples' Charter are just and reasonable, embracing namely, Universal

Suffrage, Vote by Ballot, Annual Parliaments, no Property Qualification for Members of Parliament and that they be paid for their Services, and that those principles, if put in practice, would be the only means of securing honest representatives in the House of Commons.

3rd. That the people be called on speedily to sign the National Petition, to join the Political Union, and to stand by and support the Delegates to the National Convention.

MEETING AT DALSTON.—On Tuesday evening last a meeting was held in the commodious long room of the Blue Bell. It was densely crowded; Mr. Lowery adressed them on the necessity of carrying out the work they had begun, and entered into the rights of labour and capital, and showed the spoliation of the rich upon the poor in robbing them of their common lands and their share in the tithes, and exposed the injustice of the Poor Law Amendment Act and its evil tendencies on labour. There was no protection without they had the suffrage. The people of Dalston are like those of Wigton most determined men, and having demanded the suffrage, knowing their right for it, if need be will fight for it.

Report from Lowery and Duncan from Cornwall to the Convention, Dated 12 March 1839

(British Library, Add. MSS. 34,245A, ff. 120-1.)

At the end of February 1839, the Convention sent out fifteen delegates as missionaries for one month to agitate the apathetic districts and to collect signatures for the National Petition. Lowery and Duncan were sent to Cornwall. The local magistrates' shocked reaction is vividly described in the three magistrates' letters which Dorothy Thompson publishes in her Early Chartists, *pp. 187-90; clearly the missionaries made a great impact, and when the Convention recalled them they pleaded to be allowed to remain longer so as to consolidate their work. On behalf of local radicals, John Carne wrote from the Chartist gathering at Gwennap Pit (B.L. Add Mss. 34245A f.178) on 1 April, praising their efforts amidst much local intimidation, and arguing that if the Convention's commands were obeyed, "they would have furnished our Enemies with a triumph and have thrown a damp over the new born ardour of the people". This document, whose punctuation and spelling have not been corrected, captures well the jaunty mood of the Chartist delegates as they travelled through unknown territory, though as has been pointed out above (fn. 149 p. 130) full justice is not done to the delegates' local Chartist predecessors. Duncan's appreciation of the Cornish women is reported in somewhat muted form in Lowery's autobiography, whose account accords well with what was said in the letters of the time.*

Cambourne Sunday

Gentlemen

We arrived at Falmouth on Monday Evening, and after circulating some of our copies of the Pettition, and giving an advertisement of our arrival and the objects of our visit we proceeded on Tueasday to Truro, and instantly sent the Town Crier round to call a meeting, in an open square beside St Mary's Church at 7 o clock in the evening above 2000 people attended the meeting and listened with marked attention some attempts to interupt us were made but we soon silenced them.—On Wednesday we proceeded to Redruth and called a Meeting for 6 that Evening here every attempt was made to baffle us, and a message was sent by one of the Magistrates to say that we would be taken up if there was any disturbance, I sent our compliments and said he was welcome to do so if he liked altho a Cold night & Short notice the Meeting was well attended we procured a number of names to the pettition, and left some sheets for signature,—On Thursday Night we returned to Truro and held a Meeting in The *Town Hall* before 6 o clock it was crowded to excess down to the bottom of the Stairs, hundred going away for want of admittance, we got a Working man Mr Heath to take the Chair. Mr Spurr & Mr Rowe moved and seconded the first resolution adopting the National Pettition &c the second & third pledging support to the National Convention, and requesting their Members to support the Charter, we got 4 responsible persons appointed as Treasurer to receive Rent. In our absense the Whigs had been trying to get up an opposition, but had not the pluck to face us tho we dared them to discussion, all the resolutions were passed unanimously. On Friday evening we held a Meeting at a villidge Called Chesswater of about 700 people who Adopted the Pettition &c we left them sheets to sign. Last Night Saturdy we held a Meeting at Cambourne in the open air the Enemy had bribed the Crier, he would not call it, we got Bills printed and dispatched notice to the neighbouring mines and altho it snowed the whole time we had a numerous meeting, many signed the Pettition, and I think we we will be able to form the nucleous of a Charter Association. We find that to do good we will have to go over each place twice for the People have never heard of the agitation, and know nothing of Political principles, it is all up hill work were we not going to it neck or nothing we would never get a meeting. the trades people are afraid to move, and the working men want drilling before entering the ranks but they are poor and oppressed, and that is a gaurrante that they will join their fellow opearatives and if properly managed I can see Cornwall contains a rich mine of Radical ore which if skilfull miners bring it forth may be fashioned into weapons that will do dreadfull execution, on the host of misgovernment. At first when they come to hear us, they listen to Duncans withering denunciations and satire against the Government and the Aristocracy like men who are just awakend to a knowledge of a cause of their wrongs long felt, but appear thunder struck, at anyone talking so boldly of authority they have thought unassailable, but when We afterwards appeal to them for sympathy for the starving poor and ask them if they are are content with their condition and when I attack the Atrocious Poor law Bill it is evident the cord of sympathy is struck and their hearts go with us, our desire increasing has caused us to think on trying a County meeting to terminate our labours on Easter Monday at a place[9] wher Wesley used to hold his central gatherings, it will depend on how we succeed elswhere, hoping that you are receiving assurances of increasing strenth and support Gentlemen we

Remain yours

Robt Lowery   A. Duncan

[P.S.] Dear Lovett

If any Letters have arrived for Me or Duncan get them Franked and Direct them Care of Mr. Uren Painter Truro. Also anything that may have arrived at Cleaves, send us Petition sheets for 10-000 names with copies of

---

[9] Gwennap Pit.

Pettition, some copies of the Charter, and 1000 Copies of Stephens sermon at 1d 1 doz. copies Marcus[10] tell Cleave to send me the sermons, direct the parcels by steam to Falmouth Care of Mr Hartwell Cutler Cornwall is a wild place any one coming here 6 month after would find every thing easy after we have gone over it. Give our respects to Miss Mathew, & Mrs. L., Duncan says the Cornwall Girls have almost tempted him to marry would the Convention allow any thing for a Woman [. . .]

Adieu

Robt Lowery   [postmarked 12 March]

---

[10] Marcus was the pseudonym for the writer who bitterly parodied Malthus on population; he recommended infanticide and a gas chamber as means of population control.

Report from Lowery and Duncan from Cornwall to the Convention, Dated 22 March 1839 (British Library, *Add. MSS.* 34,245A, f. 148)

Penzance March 22nd '39

Gentleman

Since we last wrote we have succeeded in rousing the people beyond our expectations altho we have not been able to hold meetings so rapidly as at first, our difficulties have been many every open and underhand annoyance has been resorted to by the Whigs & Tories, and from the Authorities, in fact it appear to us that the Mayors in Cornwall have nothing to do but look after the Bellmen, The People here have never heard Politics nor had any agitation on that Question when we enter a place we know no one, and if we ask if there are any Radicals they dont seem to know, or when they answer in the affirmative it turns out the persons are mere Whigs or Anti Corn Law men, yet our meetings are well attended, they come from curiosity they are Radicals and do not know it they are poor and oppressed and that moment they hear our expositions, they adopt them. Thus you will see that we are obliged to go over the places twice, for we have concluded it best to cultivate one district well and now that we are going the round again the sensation is tremendeous. On Monday the 12th we held a meeting at Hayle Upwards of 1500 attended and altho every inducemen had been used to hinder the work-People from attending, we were listened to with marked attention, and the People continued signing the Pettition untill 10 at Night On Tueasday at 6 o'clock we held a meeting in the open air at St Ives, near 2000 stood in the rain an Hour and a half untill we were first to give over being drenched to the skin, round the tops of the very walls the People were sitting with their Umbrellas. On Wednesday night we held a meeting at Penzance in the large Room at the Hotel it was crowded to excess, a long Consultation had been held amoug the Mayor & Councell men whether to allow the Town Crier to give the Notice, they decided he should not. On Monday the 18th we held a meeting in the open air at Falmouth when an immense number of People attended every manuevere was resorted to by the enemy to annoy us one Whig gave the Boys 5/- worth of fire works it would not do, the People felt we and them had a common interest. On Tueasday we we had a meeting at the famous Penryn[11] of rotten

[11] In 1828 two boroughs, Penryn and East Retford in Nottinghamshire, were found to be

noteriety near 3000 reechoed our sentiments, to Night we again adressed the people of Penzance it had to be in the open air upwards of 7000 of People were in readiness but at the appointed time it commenced torrents of rain and we had to hold it in doors, there was a great sensation in the Town. The Authorities had written to Lord John[12] for instructions about arresting us, (for we are producing excitement and disorder say they) what answer they got we cannot learn, but the Police were all ordered to be in attendance an hour before we commenced, and the Coast gaurd were ready we expressed our willingness to suffer under any law that punished instructing the People as a Crime, dared our Enemies to discussion, and claimed the rights of the People, had we had twice as many of Stephen's sermons they would have sold, the feeling was powerfull in our favour. Thus far we have gone every meeting has adopted the Petition unanimously the spirit is raised in the People, but they want Leaders to organize them deputations are coming urging us to visit them but every Night is arranged for, the Middle Class and the Priests are moving Heaven and Earth against, the Teetotalers and the Methodists[13] have monopolised the speakers and their Leaders are against us, Yet Cornwall though it may not yeild the immediate fruit, that other places may that have had a previous Political Feeling yet I am sure it will eventually be a stronghold of Democracy if looked after. We have determined on holding a Demonstration for the County at Gwannap Pit on Easter Monday after which we shall set out for London via Plymouth Gentleman congratulating you on the firmness of your present course and trusting our triumph will be speedy.

we remain
Your obedient servts.

Robt Lowery   Abram Duncan

---

highly corrupt. The Canningite Tories urged that their seats should be transferred to unrepresented Manchester and Birmingham, and when this was refused, they resigned *en bloc* from Wellington's cabinet. Penryn was united with Falmouth in 1832, but only by enlarging the area and thus merely increasing the cost of corruption.

[12] Lord John Russell, Whig Home Secretary.

[13] See the hostile comments of the local vicar and magistrate, reprinted in D. Thompson, *The Early Chartists*, p. 189: "I cannot close without adding my very sincere approbation of the conduct of the Wesleyans of the Parish on the occasion—the leaders consulted with me and cooperated with me in the most effectual manner to prevent any outbreak and also to discourage the intruders . . ."

Report from Lowery and Duncan from Cornwall to the Convention, dated 26 March 1839 (British Library, *Add. MSS.* 34,245A. ff. 169–70.)

Friddarnn [*?Fraddam*] *March 26th 1839*
[postmarked Hayle, addressed to Lovett]

Gentlemen

We received yesterday the Letter of the Lectr. containing the Resolution of Messrs. O Connor & Nesom reminding the Missionaries to be in the Convention on the 25th our interpretation of the vote for the time of the Mission was that it was one Month, ending Ap. 1st and we made our arrangements accordingly, by this time you will see by our last Letter that we have arranged and issued the notice of a County meeting on Ester Monday it being a Holyday we knew this would cause us to stay a week longer than our time but hoped that you would acquiesce in our arrangement, for it's expected advantage. Now we are constrained to request your leave for a fortnight longer, that is untill Ap. 8th as it will take us untill that time for fullfill our engagements, in fact 2 months would be too little to agitate this County the people being so scattered we might have left on the receipt of yours but deem it advisable to stay. Since we last wrote we held a Meeting at St. Just when at least 1500 people attended and adopted the Pettition. on Saturday we held an open air meeting at Goldsinthney the centre of a mining district above 1700 people were on the ground who took the greatest interest in our proceedings. last Night we should have been at Camborne but having sore throat an having spit blood frequently Mr. Duncan went alone. to Night I address the People of Hayle and Mr. D those of Redruth. to Morrow St.Ives If the weather is fine we expect a large attendence at Gwenapp Pit, after which we proceed home.

> Gentlemen
> I remain yours
> Robt. Lowery

PS Dear Pit

I hope you have sent the Sermons , I'll take all risk they are working wonders here if you have not I will abuse you when I come back

> respects to all

I see you are doing well very well very the little Kings are all in an uproar here we have invaded and overturned their dominion, but Lord John has told them to let us alone.

Speech at a Public Meeting on Newcastle Town Moor, May 1839

This speech was given during the adjournment of the Convention. Delegates were attempting to establish how much support there was in the country as a whole for "ulterior measures" if the petition should be rejected. Here Lowery is performing his delicate balancing-act, involving simultaneous encouragement and restraint of his followers, together with an attempt to impress the authorities with their impatience. His experiences in Cornwall have not yet convinced him of the need for longer and more sustained preparation. The speech is reported in Northern Liberator, *25 May 1839.*

Mr. Chairman and fellow working men, months had rolled on since they last met together, and the movements since that time, had been such as to give them all gratification. It was not these who were the quickest at the start that always succeeded in winning the race, and the reliance of the people was not so much on the rapidity of their movements, as upon the calm eye, the steady hand and the firm heart, that would enable them to strike the blow of freedom. The Convention had not been rapid in its movements, it had put off the presentation of the petition, but in doing so, it had doubled the numbers of its signatures, since he last stood before them he had stood upon the seashore at the Land's End, in Cornwall, and preached the doctrine of Universal Suffrage to those who had never heard of Universal Suffrage before. The men of Cornwall were like the men around him—a primitive race. Like themselves, they had believed that all which was told them by the Whigs and Tories must be gospel, but the delusion was over, and the magistrates, coast-guards, and all the petty authorities of the place, did all in their power to keep the people from meeting to discuss their grievances; but the men of Cornwall were not to be deterred from their duty, and he could tell them that, when the struggle came, the men of Cornwall would not be the last in the race. (Loud cheers.) They (the Delegates) were here from the Convention on a commission of inquiry, what would they (the meeting) do? Would they run on the banks? (cries of "we will.") It was true, many of the working men had no money in the banks, but their benefit societies had money in them, let them draw out that money immediately, if they did not they would not get it at all. (Loud cheers.) These were times to try men's souls. If the property men said, they would not give them their rights, would they come out from their property and leave it to themselves? Would they make a general strike? (Cheers and cries of "we will.") Never was there a better time for a general strike, than the time that was approaching. Within three months the crops, which God sent for their use, would be upon the ground and when men asked them to reap it, and offered them wages for doing so, let them reject the offer—let them say of what use is your wages, when after we have earned it three-quarters of it will be taken from us in taxes. Then, when the crops were rotting on the ground, and when trade was stagnated, the property-men would say to the Government, for God's sake give the men their rights. One of his friends said, that was physical force. Why, so it was, but they lived in strange times, and could not do as was done by the men of the Union in 1832. He knew he would be liable to transportation did he advise the people to arm,—he knew it would implicate the Chairman and all the men who got up the meeting, if he said anything of the kind; but surely there could be no harm in asking them were they armed? (Loud cries of "yes, yes," "we are, we are.") It was no harm for one neighbour to ask another whether he had a good musket, as he was ordered to have by the constitution—the law and the Bible. (Loud cheers.) When a man went to ill-use Moses, he turned round and knocked his brains out; and Nehemiah, when he found the city in jeopardy, called upon them to get arms and defend their city. It was their duty to tell the Queen that, if her throne was in danger from either Whigs or Tories, there were one million of armed men ready to protect her and the Charter. If she would protect it, they were the men to protect her from every kind of danger. The people had been plundered of all their honest earnings, and now it was said that they were poor, that they had nothing to lose in a commotion. If that were so, there was the con-clusive proof that they had been plundered, as how else could it happen, that those who produced everything had nothing; whilst those who produced nothing had everything. (Tremendous cheers.) He remembered once the *Newcastle Chronicle* published a black list of Tory villains, and the *Journal*, in return, published a grey list of Whig scoundrels, both lists were true to the letter; for both comprised nothing but damned thieves. (Loud laughter and cheers.) They were now threatened with a Bourbon police, and armed middle class, "national guard;" but he trusted that there was yet too much virtue remaining to throw down their arms and submit to such a system of coercion. (Never, never.) No, on the contrary, he knew that if driven to it by uncon-stitutional acts of the Government, they would take up their arms, and never lay them down till justice was done them, or till the members of a treasonable Government had their heads fixed on Temple Bar. (Loud cheers.) They talked about order—there was no order in giving one man £10,000 a year and another man 10s a week—there was no order in it, let them have their constitutional rights in their eye, go right on to their object, and he had no doubt the next time they met in a mass, they would meet to celebrate the triumph of their cause. (Loud and long continued cheers.)

Poem Entitled *The Collier Boy*, Signed "R. Lowery" Printed in *The Charter*, 23 June 1839

The Collier Boy.

Oh! mark yon child, with cheeks so pale,
As if they never felt the gale
That breathes of health and lights the smile;
It tells of nought but lengthened toil.
Its twisted frame and actions rude
Speak mind and form's decrepitude,
And show that boyhood's hours of joy
Were never known to the Collier Boy.

'Tis night, when youth with pleasure dreams
Of meads and woods and gurgling streams—
Soft cooling baths, in sunny hours
Whose banks are blooming with gay flowers;—
Of birds and beasts, and all the play
Fancy forms for the coming day:
The Collier's lonely calls destroy
Those dreams of bliss to the Collier Boy.

Bright morn has come, each young heart hies
To chase the gaudy butterflies,
Or to follow the flight of the humming bee
Amid the wild wood's minstrelsy;
Entomb'd in earth, far, far, away
From all the light of glorious day,
Hard toil and danger doth employ
For the dreary mine, the Collier Boy.

'Tis eve—the cattle seek their fold,
The western sky's a flood of gold;
The old men sit, and tell the tale
Of youthful deeds, and quaff their ale,
And looking round them, smile to see
The urchins playing merrily;—
He wants, yet cannot it enjoy,
So toil-worn is the Collier Boy.

Oh! curse upon that love of gold
For which the young heart now is sold,
With care and sickness withering
The sunshine of its early spring.
Oh! shame upon that barbarous state
That toil for infant years create,
Whose accursed influences destroy
The mind and form of the Collier Boy.

Speech at a Public Meeting at the Lecture Room, Nelson Street, Newcastle "On the State and Prospects of Radicalism" on 30 September 1839.

The speech is printed in Northern Star, *5 October 1839, p. 1. Mr. Charleton was in the chair; after Lowery's speech Mr. J. Ayre reported on his journey to the South, and three cheers were then given for Lowery. After the meeting, the class leaders met in the committee room "and steps were taken to renew the agitation with vigour". The speech is still vigorous in tone but—like Lowery's pamphlet on Exclusive Dealing which he wrote about this time—cautious in strategy* (cf. p. 196 above).

Mr. LOWRY then rose. Before he entered on the principal part of his address, he deemed it to be his duty to advert to some part of the history of the late Convention. He stood there ready to defend his acts in that body, having to the best of his judgment conscientiously done his duty to them and the cause. He likewise believed that under all circumstances the Convention had produced all the good for the people their power enabled them to do up to the moment of the fatal error of the vote for the 12th of August. It had committed few errors indeed, circumstanced and composed of the materials which it was. It found the National Petition with 600,000 names, and presented it with 1,300,000. It sent its missionaries into the northern counties, and in many places where the Charter had never been heard of and there established a feeling in its favour that will never die. But it was urged into premature action by the impatience of some districts that had been long organised, while it ought to have been allowed to wait until the other parts of the country were up to the same mark of intelligence and determination. Many parts were urgent for the strike, but many others were averse to the measure; they could not see the practicability of the measure. They were not less ardent in the cause. They had no thoughts of retreating, but wished themselves and the country to be better prepared. I might mention Rochdale and Bury as examples. There are few better Radical places; their associations were numerous, they contributed largely to the rent and the expenses of their delegates and their local organization, but they were not willing to leave their employment, and enter on a project injurious to themselves and impracticable to the whole people. While thus situated, the Convention had been urged on by the people's impatience in some parts, and threatened with a loss of confidence if they did not proceed, while they were conscious at the same time such a step was premature. There had been a misconception on both sides; the people expected the Convention to do what they could do themselves only, and the Convention expected the people to do that they were not as a body prepared for. To have called on the people to have entered on a strike that would have been the destruction of our best men, and most efficient organization, would have been a wanton sacrifice of the cause; but I am persuaded that the difficulties consequent on that act, was a necessary ordeal for us to pass through to give us experience in our future movements. We have learned much; we must no longer rely on the boasted equality of our laws, and our right of public meeting being secure. We have found them to be a farce—we are now convinced beyond doubt that there is one law for the rich and another for the poor—that it is maintained to support the aggrandizement and protection of the wealthy and the subjection of poor. Our personal liberty has been trampled on, our right of meeting violated, and we cannot but be aware that we will be ruled by a despotism if we will let them; remember that on your own determination to defend your freedom, rests its only security. (Loud cheers.) Every fraction of the liberty we possess has been wrung from the fears of our tyrants, and not granted by the justice of our rulers. Why have the Chartists been so persecuted? Because an unjust and dishonest system was shaking to its centre by their attacks upon it? (Cheers.) Was there ought new in this agitation, except the honesty of its intentions? Our principles were the principles of the constitution and our doctrines the doctrines of honesty. This movement arose not out of committees or cabals—it was not fostered into existence by high and weighty names—it had no sinister purpose—the enthronement in power of a faction was not its aim. The people, the whole people was its author—the cry for it came from myriads of desolate hearths and ruined homes. They had drank the oppressors' cup of misery to the dregs, and could bear it no longer—they were indignant at the base tyranny, the heartless treachery, and infamous hypocrisy of the Whigs. They talked about it at the corners of their streets—they met together in hundreds in their Rooms, and vowed to struggle for a just and free Government; and afterwards, in the open air, they assembled in hundreds of thousands, and ratified the engagement. Contrast their agitation with that for the Reform Bill. You all remember when large meetings were held on that subject, the workmen were asked if they were for the measure, or were going to the meeting. The orders were, "Close the shop"—"Shut the factory up;" and, thus compelled to cease labour , animal curiosity led many to view the raree-show. But when a large meeting was held for the National Petition, the masters threatened to turn them out of their employment if they went: the factories were open, and every engine of persecution tyrannical employers could invent was sent to work to deter the men from advocating their own cause. Yet, in defiance of all these, our meetings were always more numerously attended than the Reform Bill ones were. Above 4,000,000 of people met in public meetings, and sent a petition for justice signed by 1,300,000 signatures; and not one

breach of the public peace occurred—not one molestation was offered, either
to the persons or property of our enemies, libellous and insulting as their
conduct was (Loud cheers.) Whence, then, originates the unjust persecution
of the Whigs? They had a favourite project to carry that they had long been
intent on doing. When the fears and political conduct of the middle classes
were high against us, they thought it a fit time to introduce their rural
police force; their spies were sent among the people, to excite them to
violence and insurrection; false rumours of riots and sedition were propagated by them; they attacked the people while legally assembled, and
arrested their leaders on trumpery and false charges, that they might make
a case of insecurity out, and introduce their Bourbon standing army, and
crush the agitation for equal laws and personal right. Then commenced the
Whig reign of terror: to be accused as a friend of popular freedom, was to
be condemned. We had slanderous and libellous charges from political
Judges, charging the Charter as a plan to overthrow order, and seize on the
property of individuals. We had packed and prejudiced middle-class jurors,
panting for the destruction of the prisoners, who had just laid aside the
carbine and cutlass, with which they hoped to butcher them, and thence
entered the jury-box , to use the very evangelists as instruments of hatred and
oppression. There were the Attorney-Generals, armed with acute knowledge
of the subterfuges of the law, and the Treasury gold to secure the conviction
of the prisoner: there were the suborned and perjured *non mi recordo* witnesses,
who, after a period of six months, could recollect every letter of six lines of a
speech, and could not remember one word or line of any other part of it.
Did not all this show previous design? Where did the 5,000 muskets come
from that were seized on their way to Chester? Why was Mr. Stephens not
tried on the first indictments that were prepared against him—indictments
for acts both he and Oastler had dared the Government to try them? Why
was he tried and convicted on a false, a paltry, twaddling shuffling affair,
that any unprejudiced man in his senses knew that Mr. Stephens never
entertained an idea of, nor was so foolish as to utter. If it was the bugbear—
physical force language—they wished to stifle, why was Lovett, Collins,
Williams, of Sunderland, and many others that had always deprecated
allusion to such a subject punished with the most inveterate malice—
(cheers)—anything, everything served them for accusation, and they found
willing tools to do their dirty work every where. Here you were accused of
bringing the magistrates into contempt. God save the mark. I can tell them
the Radicals of Newcastle are not such fools as to do that they knew was
already done; the magistrates had long since brought themselves into
contempt. Most consistent men! None of them had never talked of leading
the people to the death in defence of their rights. None of them had declared
himself a Republican under compact, nor spoke at an open air meeting in
support of a resolution denouncing the base Whigs for their Coercion Bill,
and for employing the infamous Spy Popay, and justifying—aye justifying—

the man Furzey for stabbing the policeman when that force attacked the people in Calthorpe-street.[14] He had never condemned them for it, or the Manchester massacre, or called for justice on the authors of those illegal assaults on the populace. If any of them have done these things, and we know they have , how dare they blame any man for bringing them into contempt. (Loud cheers.) Ha! ha! they have always venerated the throne, and revered the altar, and been ever ready with their blood to protect them. Republicans, infidels, and levellers, they are no upstart gentry, no mushroom quality; their fathers age after age have been the pillars and supporters of the institution, and have lived on their own patrimony, and sleep in their own ancestral halls. (Loud cheers.) I now would direct your thoughts to the future. You ask me what our agitation has done. It has roused the people to a sense of their wrong, and pointed out the only path to attain national justice, a moral organization and determination to be free, a firmness of purpose, a perseverance that will shew our enemies the physical power such moral determination must contain. If you would be free, you must earn it. We have done much. Let any rational man survey the state of the country now and eight months ago, and he will see our organisation farther in advance than we could have expected, where political agitation had never been heard of. Chartist associations formed in the South are advancing fast, Scotland has set to the work in earnest. Shall Newcastle on the first rebuff grow apathetic? (No, no.) Will you on the first attack retreat? (No, no.) No I tell the Whigs; no magisterial cabal shall suppress the movement for popular liberty in this district. We have not forgot ourselves yet, we are not content with slavery. Men of Newcastle, begin afresh from this night. Let our difficulties spur us on to increased exertion. Have all your resolutions come to nought? Were all your meetings idle show? Have all the speeches been forgotten or passed away like the whisperings of the passing breeze? Was all bravado? Has all vanished in thin air? (No, no.) Will you leave your brave brethren in this district, your friends and neighbours, to linger deserted in the gaols of tyranny? (No, no.) I for one will not. I will go from village to village to rouse an indignation against their wrongs and our own. I will denounce their oppressors, preach for them, pray for them, beg for them, or do ought that can be useful to them. (Loud cheers.) Let the leaders of the classes meet to-night, after I have done here. Let us again call our energies into action. The people only want leaders. Come forward and volunteer. (We will, and cheers.) We have the ulterior measures to work out; first stands exclusive dealing, the best means of converting our enemies, and consolidating our organization. Our earnings reared the palaces in Grey-street, and stocked the splendid shops and mansions in this town. Exclusive dealing has taken safe root here, and is spreading to every town and village in our neighbourhood. There are now 2000 shares taken in the Joint Stock Provision

[14] See above, fn. 4 (p. 221).

Store of this town alone; keep up the cry "Run for gold", the bank cannot pay, the Government is fast for money, the system totters in its fall, apply the battering ram of agitation. The one pound notes must soon come; combine to refuse them; turn which way they will they will soon be fast, and we'll be free. Let each one ask himself—Am I prepared to defend my country in these eventful times, when domestic treachery and treason stalk abroad in open day. We must work out our freedom, a day may bring it forth. Every turn of the wheel is for our advantage; and these progressive steps give a guarantee of our fitness for firmer action. The man that will not go the length of the street to spend his money in the shop of a friend or the store, the profits of which he may share, will never walk ten miles with the musket on his shoulder to fight for freedom. If landlords are to lose their licences for allowing meetings to petition for Universal Suffrage to be held in their houses, let such meetings be held elsewhere. Let every class of the Union become election committees—let us have Colonel Thompson and another as candidates for this town. We can canvass the electors, and note down who are for or against us. We can solicit them for subscriptions to defray the expenses. We can hold meetings in every parish; one candidate can agitate the district, with another to assist him. We can rouse the people— we can run our enemies into expense. Mr. Ord will have to give away one thousand five shilling tickets for refreshments. We will have the opportunity of telling our enemies on the hustings truths they have not the courage to come here and hear. Added to the ordinary excitement at elections, such an election would be tremendous. The declared members by the sheriff, from the show of hands, would protest against polling ten pound renters only as an abrogation of the people's rights—demand their seats—if refused sit somewhere else. If the people would not protect them, they are not worth their thoughts. (Cheers.) Aye, and could we do nought else, we could repeal the Reform Bill. We made an agreement with them when we joined them for that measure; they have been treacherous deceivers—we will punish them if they will not give us the vote. We will take theirs from them. Send fifty more Tories and they will soon do it. It is only the people that protect them from the Tories. They are powerless in the Lords—they have a petticoat Ministry, and a paltry majority in the Commons. They may call us Tories if they like; but I use the tiger to destroy the hyena, and yet admire neither. The Tories were milder despots than the Whigs. They boast of descent they wished not to tarnish—they claimed the right to govern the rest of their fellow-men—they asserted that God had given one portion of men the right to lord it over the other portion—(hear, hear,)—they had a character to lose, they did not like to be thought mean or ungentlemanly: they were no traffickers in petty speculation. But your Whigs are the *fungi* of society, sprung from the lees and dregs—the things of yesterday, sprung from God knows whom, and come from God knows where—(cheers)—capable of any dirty act, fit for any lie or wickedness. When in the House of Commons, on the night of Attwood's motion, my blood boiled with indignation to hear the foul-mouthed slanders and libellous assertions of Lord John Russell against us. There he sat, protected by his situation, uttering what he had not the courage to do towards those who were privileged to defend themselves. He charged the people with wishing to plunder the property of the rich, and produce anarchy. He talk of plunder whose family is revelling in the wealth of estates plundered from the people—whose ancestors were the great plunderers of their age: he who uses the little talent he has got to support an infamous system, that deprives the poor of their rights, and robs them of their wages. He charges men with eking out an existence by deceiving the people, while he receives ten times as much as he is worth for advocating the most knavish system of jugglery that ever was practised. I looked in vain for one mark or line of nobleness or generosity; all the higher feelings of the heart appeared to have been long suppressed, and the hard unblushing front of the factious advocate only remained. After him came Fox Maule: he said the people of Scotland were not Chartists; yet, a few days before, the whole population of the West and North of Scotland had met to advocate the Charter. What did he know of the people of Scotland? He had proceeded from London to Perth, and back again, in a carriage, and been in a few inns, where every waiter would bow and cry "All hail" for a shilling. What else could be expected, when you view his calf's head and idiotic countenance, which common sense would involuntarily pass, exclaiming "There is no abode for me". These are samples of the persecutors of Chartists, and the vindicators of the law. If my Lord Russell is so anxious to vindicate the law, why did he let the synod of Scotch Priests break it with impunity? Why were they not punished as well as Chartists? Why was the Duke of Cumberland not punished for his treasons, when certain individuals in Ireland called for his impeachment, and offered evidence of treasonable conspiracy, for which he ought to have been brought to the block? I ask my Lord John Russell, why letters were written to those men begging them not to bring it forward, but to hush the matter up? All is well; the last card of tyranny is played; I can tell them they shall not succeed (Cheers.) The speaker here gave an account of his mission to Ireland, and showed how the agents of O'Connell had taken possession of two meetings by brute force, and denied him the privilege of stating his sentiments; he also rebutted the slanderous charge of O'Connell, that the Radicals of England are against the freedom of Ireland, and showed them how both countries suffered by the union, and called on his fellow working men to assist the Irish in securing their personal and legislative independence, during which, he was frequently cheered. For my own part, my choice is made for the movement. I will work with all my energies. When I set my hand to the plough I had no thought of turning back. I will not act the bravado, nor will I shrink from danger. Still my motto is:—"If there has been no comfort in the cottage, there shall be none in the palace—if there has been no freedom in the workshop , there shall be none in the palace—if I am not admitted in the Constitution, it shall be no Constitution for me, no vote, no taxes—I will use every method to destroy their unjust power—I will smile, and be determined when I smile". (Cheers.) Every act of coercion still binds the advocates of justice more firmly together. The spirit of freedom cannot be immured within the walls of a dungeon: she laughs at bolts and bars: she scorns the gaoler's controul—and shrinks not from the tyrant's power. She cannot be destroyed—she is the gift of God to man, and never dies. For a time, her onward march may be retarded; but it is as when the course of a mighty river is dammed up by the rotten trunks and branches of the once stately trees that adorned its banks, and the lees and impurities of its own stream. Every hour it is stopped, increases its strength—anon with a mighty force it bursts the barrier of its confinement, and scatters the rubbish far and wide. The martyrs of liberty never die. Hampden and Sydney still walk the earth. The murdered Emmet and Fitzgerald still live, and are communed with on every mountain and in every dell. Though in a dungeon, the suffering champions of liberty still are free: there is a cord that binds and links them to the martyred many. Though absent in body at our meetings, they are more emphatically present in spirit. Every one that looks on their dungeon walls—those land-marks of oppression and arguments of tyranny the thought of abandoning the contest never enters his head. He vows fresh allegiance to the holy cause; and swears to be revenged on his oppressors. From this night, let us go forward. I am at your service wherever I can be useful. (Loud cheers.)

Letter Dated 27 April 1840 "To the men of Bath and the Radical Reformers of Great-Britain"

Lowery's plea for Chartist unity was published in Northern Star, *2 May 1840, but is not mentioned in the autobiography. His Chartist missionary work of 1839 had convinced him that major propagandist effort throughout the country was needed before Chartism could move forward, and his message is again being repeated here. He is recovering from his serious illness, and no doubt this reinforced his feeling that he was not the man to give the Chartist movement the lead it needed at this point. When Lovett produced his "new move" in 1841, Lowery courageously followed; he was never more than a Chartist leader of the second rank. At the 1841 general election he also practised what he preached as regards electoral candidatures, but the exclusive dealing and co-operative schemes recommended in his Newcastle speech of 30 September 1839 seem now to have fallen into the background.*

To the Men of Bath and the Radical Reformers of Great Britain.

Fellow-citizens,—Owing to very ill health I have to apologise for not having sooner answered your kind invitation to visit your good city. I am glad to see the spirit still reigneth among you to never cease agitating until you get your rights.

Having been asked by many places for my opinions on what should be done, I address them thus publicly to you that they may be more generally known. I have waited anxiously for this last four months, hoping that some one of those, who from the position of their circumstances, public and private, ought to have given a plan for a fresh and vigorous agitation, and nothing new has appeared—no effort has been made to communicate with those who might have united for that object, with the exception of Mr. O'Brien bringing again before the country his election plan, which he brought before the Convention, and which was embodied in the Manifesto. Now, that all, or nearly all of my late companions are suffering in the dungeons of tyranny for truth's sake, no man, who has acted as a servant of the people, should from diffidence hesitate to give his advice and his labour to advance the cause.

As a party, we have reason to be proud of our position. It is much superior to what it was twelve months ago. The virtues and powers of a country are not [to] be judged of by its sayings and resolutions when it first declares war with a formidable enemy. It is after they have met on the battle field, when the first campaign is over, that you can estimate its prowess and patriotism. Now that the inflations of vanity, and braggart valour subside, and if she still remain true to her own honour, and firm in her strength to face the foe, she has all but achieved a victory, Now, our first campaign is over; we have stood the onslaught of Whig and Tory persecution, of class hatred, of hireling malice, of assassin spies, of prejudiced juries, political judges, and perjured witnesses. Have we retreated, asked for quarter, or struck our colours? No. We have still possession of the field, our standard is still flying, and of all who have fallen prisoners to the enemy, I know not one that has offered to compromise his principles, or desert our cause, to secure his personal safety; and of those who are still on the field, I know none who owe their liberty to shrinking from their battle, or their duty. In our career, we had desertions before the struggle commenced; they were to be commenced; they were to be expected. Many men will wear liberal colours, and give a little time and money to forward its principle in time of peace, because it gets them esteem, but when the tug of war comes, when it [is] no longer a little, but a risk of all, those men will abandon the cause. We are better without them; the fault was not in them so much as in the people choosing such as they ought to have known could not, from their position, remain true and active.

We have thus nobly encountered our greatest difficulties. In every large town we are triumphant; our opponents at first denied our existence; we drove them to an acknowledgment of our numbers and power; and now they are disposed to treat with us for our assistance to carry their prospects. All these prove our strength and importance. The late meetings throughout the country shew the immense numbers still in our ranks. All that is wanted is to appoint officers, agree to a plan for the campaign, and unite our forces for action.

We must struggle for an uniform object with uniform action; it is of no use one place petitioning for one thing, and another passing resolutions about another thing; nor yet overthrowing an anti-Corn Law agitation, unless we go on united in a superior agitation, because if we do not intend to do something better than those we oppose, we have no right to oppose them. The people will soon tire of merely obstructing the middle-class schemers, if they have nothing to do themselves. What must we do then! Agitate for the Charter, and, while doing so, for the enlargement of those suffering imprisonment on land and ocean for the truth's sake.

The quarrels of the factions at home, the anarchy in the affairs of the Whig Government here and abroad, the wide-spreading distress among the poorer order of the shopkeepers—to say nothing of the miseries of the people—all conspire to engender hatred and dissatisfaction to the Whig rule, and produce fear and alarm in the minds of the public plunderers, and cause routs, riots, and rebellion against those who are endangering the happiness of the people, and their mother—the Queen, their rights, and their dignity.

What plans have we, and which should we adopt in our present position? A Convention sitting in London or any town is worse than useless. What we want is men deputed to agitate and combine our party together. If the district can pay a man to sit in a Convention, it can pay him to agitate; and he will do the cause ten times as much good; and unless he is fit for an agitator he is of no use. We are not in the position of a party having legislative power, merely requiring heads to plan; we require hands to execute.

Mr. Bronterre O'Brien's plan is good—nay admirable—for bringing things to an issue, but will need others conjoined with it to ensure its success. First, an election may come soon, or it may be long. After this, if so, what are we to do in the mean time? Secondly, we cannot expect to get men to stand for every borough and county. Thirdly, we must have something prepared for that body to do when elected. The plan is most useful as an ulterior object, and as such should be wrought. I would recommend, then, every district to be organized to fix on the places to be contested; to have, for form's sake, an election committee in their union or association. Under it they can hold meetings in any public house without the authorities daring to suspend the licence, and they may ask for subscriptions for the candidates' expenses anywhere, if in a proper manner. This, with petitioning, protesting, and carrying out the ulterior measures of the late Convention, must be our first steps in uniting and agitating as our organization proceeds: we can make more bold and energetic movements, and always be firm, uncompromising, but prudent. Yet, added to the local organizations, we must have a general one to unite the whole, or the districts will sink in apathy, thinking nothing is going to be done, and even wait for general agitation; any adventurer may visit them, and to suit his purposes may give a colouring that he will flatter their hopes and wishes, instead of the promulgation of truth and the advance-ment of steady organization. The agitation never can be properly conducted without we have a portion set apart who can give their whole time to it. That body should be as efficient and as light of expense as possible. I would divide England, Scotland, and Wales into ten divisions, where the Radical strength lies, and let them each elect a man as lecturer, agitator, candidate, delegate, or what you will; they should be the best fitted for agitators that can be had, men known in the movement, having laboured in it. Their duty should be to contest one place in the district, and agitate in the rest, by holding meetings, and extending the organization, and helping the election of others. They would thus become thoroughly acquainted with the people, and they with them, at the end of two months. I would have them to meet altogether, and transact general business; then separate, changing their districts, and so on, until the districts agreed the time was come for another push, when more men could be elected to join them, and they would thus be a body perfectly in the confidence of the people, with a full knowledge of their powers. If the election came on in the mean time, let it be the push. These men would be in weekly communication with the Committees; their reports, published in the newspapers, would keep the attention of the public concentrated on their movements. I would propose the division of districts to be somewhat as follows:—

Bath, Bristol, and Wales; (1 member.)
London, Brighton, and the South; (1.)
Birmingham and the Midlands, &c.; (1.)
Yorkshire and Lancashire; (3.)
Northumberland, Durham, and Cumberland; (1.)
Glasgow, and the West of Scotland; (1.)
Edinburgh, Midland, and Borders; (1.)
Fifeshire, Forfarshire, and Aberdeen; (1.)
In all ten.

If there is not power to do this, there is no power; without an assemblage of the kind, I am afraid we will retrograde. I hope the different districts that are organized, will declare their opinion on it by adopting it, suggesting amendments, or proposing a better plan. To call a Convention at present without it, or on some acknowledged plan, would be a failure. I hope those that have influence will use their exertions to establish it. Had I the means, I would have taken the circuits of the districts, and urged its adoption; as it is, I trust those that are better able will do so, or that the Association will find them the means. We have a weighty responsibility upon us in the generous confidence the people have placed in us; their wrongs and sufferings demand our sympathy. All our imprisoned companions, with our widowed wives and families, look to us for support and redress; and it is only by keeping our party united and extending its power, that that support and redress for them can be had.

Trusting soon to hear the bugle sound "the gathering," and hoping soon to meet you in the ranks,

Fellow-Citizens,

I remain, yours,

ROBT. LOWERY.

Newcastle-upon-Tyne, April 27, 1840.

Speech to a Leeds Parliamentary Reform Association Meeting, January 1841

The Leeds Parliamentary Reform Association aimed to unite members of the middle and working classes behind a joint radical programme. It was founded in autumn 1840, and was supported by prominent Leeds supporters of the Anti-Corn Law League. Its overall strategy anticipates the class collaboration encouraged two years later by the Complete Suffrage Union, but the strains involved in such an alliance are well brought out in Lowery's speech (reported in Leeds Times, *23 January 1841, p. 8). Even after his illness and contact with Urquhart, Lowery remained a resolute champion of the dignity of his class. For the background to this meeting, see Lucy Brown, "The Chartists and the Anti-Corn Law League", in Asa Briggs (Ed.),* Chartist Studies *(1959), pp. 357-8.*

Fellow countrymen and fellow workmen, for it is to you I come to speak— if ever there was a day that we have a right to be proud of, this is the day (hear, hear). This is a day that I have longed for—it is a day that we all have wished for—it is a day which the middle and working men could meet and could discuss their grievances, and then which had been in error. I stand here as a working man, I stand here as a Chartist; as a man bred and born in the lap of poverty; as a man who claims nought from his riches; but from his existence as a man, who scorns that agitation which refers men back to musty parchments for the rights of the people. I stand here as a man who says that his rights of citizenship are written in Heaven and not in the Courts of Kings and of Parliaments (cheers). Now, gentlemen, what do I, and all who are of my class say to you—I use no menace to you; but I say it to you as a fact that you and I must sink together, and if we sink, you sink also along with us (hear, hear). I have wished for the day in which you would come to discuss grievances with us, and to seek for a remedy. I know you will tell me that as Chartists, we have been violent, that we have uttered language that no honest man could ever assent to—but middle men, I ask you, have you ever stepped into the huts of poverty? Have you seen your wives in rags, and your children without food? If you have not, then I ask you to bear in mind the causes why those of whom you complain have been violent, to keep in mind that those who have been violent have drained degradation to its bitterest dregs, and for them I ask you, in the charity of human nature, to allow them to give expression to their agony (hear). I pass from that and I come to the question before the meeting—namely, what is the extent of representation that will truly represent the people, and secure to them their rights? I say no representation short of that which admits every man arrived

253

at a mature age to a vote—that is to say Universal Suffrage (hear). Why then talk to me about expediency. If expediency is right, then Universal Suffrage is right; and any thing short of Universal Suffrage is not expedient. We all remember before now to have heard of expediency (hear). There was a man who ought to be here to night, who talked of expediency (cries of— Hear, hear, and shame). I say shame upon that man (cheers from the Chartists, and groans from others in the meeting). I cry cowardice upon that man for not being here (renewed cheers from the Chartists, and loud groans and hisses for the speaker, from others in the hall).[15] I expected that it was arguments I was to hear—I expected gentlemen would listen to reason. I expected that the classes who are clad so bravely would have listened to me; but I am sorry that I have been mistaken in them. But I say, where is your security, if you enter into the traffic of expediency, that you will not be sacrificed? It was found expedient to sacrifice the 40s. freeholders (hisses and cheers). It was found expedient to give up the principles of civil and religious liberty (hisses and cheers). And what is this of which we are complaining? Are we not here to complain of Lord Melbourne's government? Are you Whigs satisfied with it, or are you not? Why seek for further Reform if you are satisfied with it? (Hisses and cheers.) Now, once for all, I say that I will stand here until morning, but I shall be heard (cheers from the Chartists). I have a right to be heard, and I have a right to address to you these sentiments, and to discuss such sentiments, and to give expression to such opinions. The Whigs are men of expediency, and they have ruined their own cause by it. If they had been honest, we never should have complained of them. They have taught us a lesson, and we know from them, that he who trusts to expediency, trusts to a broken stick (hear). Then what Suffrage should we have? should it be an individual's right, or should it be property. That is the question which we have met to discuss. The individual right is the only test of the Suffrage for the people. Every man amenable to the law has a right to be a maker of the laws. When you get Universal Suffrage, you get all the intelligence of the nation; and by Household Suffrage you shut out a large portion of the intelligence of the people. Middle men, I put to you a question —it is a solemn one. You cannot deny our right to the Suffrage. It never has been denied even by the most rabid Tory. They have always said you have the right, but you are not wise enough to exercise it. Now I ask you—have

---

15 *Leeds Mercury*, 23 January 1841 reports that this meeting received apologies for non-attendance from Edward Baines, Sen., and William Molesworth, both M.P.s for Leeds. Baines was probably too Whiggish in outlook to be the man Lowery condemns, but Molesworth, who at this time was recommending franchise extension only in accordance with the progress of public opinion, was close enough to the Chartists in general outlook to evoke bitterness by adopting such a standpoint. The *Leeds Mercury* gave very little space to Lowery's speech: "he ridiculed expediency, and claimed Universal Suffrage as a right. When Hissed, he replied with great anger, and set his opponents at defiance, telling them they should have war if they wanted it". We are most grateful to Dr. R. J. Morris, of the Department of Economic History, Edinburgh University for this reference, and for help on this point.

you not admitted in your own churches and chapels young persons of fifteen years of age to choose their own ministers and their own communions? Why? it is because they are old enough; and then if they are wise enough to choose their own religion, surely they are wise enough to choose their own members of Parliament (cheers from the Chartists, followed by cries of "oh! oh!") I am sorry for this class-feeling, and to see dislike so strongly marked; and as a Chartist, I tell the Chartists, if they are afraid to hear the arguments of their opponents—if they seek to cloak these arguments by brawling and clamour; then I say that I am ashamed of them, and I wash my hands of them (cheers). I would give every man a fair hearing. I claim the Suffrage for myself, for my fellow workmen, and for the aristocracy themselves. I say for the aristocracy, because I know they have stood our friends, as well as other classes, and that good men are to be found amongst them. When, then, I say the people, I mean the whole classes of the empire. It is strange—it is passing strange, that men, who till the land, who ply the loom, who build your cities, who fight your battles, who have borne the British standard across the waters, and chastised every tyrant but their own; it is strange that you will not give them the privileges that they require (hear, hear). Is it to be right and might, and which is to be prepared to exclude its neighbours? Then those who are prepared to act on their might, must also be prepared to come in collision with their fellow countrymen. This is the feeling that has roused up society. This it is which has made them angry; for a man, who will bear poverty patiently, will not bear insult—if he is a man he will not do so (hear.) And the man who is not privileged is insulted, and he is a renegade to human nature, if he does not attempt to remove it. Are you then, I ask, prepared for the continuance of agitation in this country?—to have that state of feeling in this country—to see it dropping into ruin, while faction hinders all classes from coming together. I expect that this night will be the foundation of good feeling for the redemption of our common country. I expect that those who hitherto stood aloof will now join us; and those who were supposed to be opposed to us, will now be friendly to us. I impress then upon you the necessity that whatever the movement be made by you, it will be one admitting the whole of the population within the bounds of the constitution (cheers and hisses). What am I to learn from this? I will not mince matters with you (hisses). If it is war you want, you shall have it. If it is opposition you desire—you shall have it also (hisses). When I see men pluming themselves upon their station in society and yet acting in this way, I want to know and to understand what it means (hisses). Am I to understand that we are to be gammoned (cries of oh! oh!) Now I tell you and all who call you respectable, that there is nothing in the cut of your coat, nor in the quality of your cloth, to give you that title. The man, who fulfils his political duties in his station, and who has done all he can to forward the happiness of the community, then I say that man gives the best guarantee that he is fitter for citizenship. If you are prepared to scout such an idea, then the sooner we cease to come together the better. I am afraid that prejudice prevails so far with you, that you cannot forget and forgive; and I beg therefore of you not to think of me as one individual; but to think of our common country. I am willing to bear every insult; but when I do bear it, I hope you too will also shew your patience; and as you do plume yourselves upon your superiority, I shall sit down expecting to hear your better wisdom (cheers and hisses).

Further Reading

The best general introductions to the period are to be found in Asa Briggs, *The Age of Improvement, 1783-1867* (1959) and J. F. C. Harrison, *The Early Victorians, 1832-1851* (1971), but for more detailed accounts of events during Lowery's lifetime, see E. Halévy, *The Triumph of Reform (1830-1841)* (first ed. in English, 1927) and E. L. Woodward, *The Age of Reform, 1815-1870* (1938).

There is abundant literature on Chartism, for which see J. F. C. Harrison & Dorothy Thompson, *Bibliography of the Chartist Movement, 1837-1976* (Hassocks, 1978). For a concise introduction, see F. C. Mather, *Chartism* (Historical Association pamphlet, 1965) and the essay by Asa Briggs, "Chartism Reconsidered" in *Historical Studies, III. Papers Read Before the Third Conference of Irish Historians* (1959). The standard textbook on the Chartist movement has long been Mark Hovell's *The Chartist Movement* (Ed. T. F. Tout, 1918), but J. T. Ward's *Chartism* (1973) provides a general introduction based on more recent research, and David Jones's *Chartism and the Chartists* (1975) is an admirable survey of the issues and preoccupations of the Chartists. The best way to recapture the flavour of Chartism is to read some of its documents; for these, see Y. V. Kovalev's *Anthology of Chartist Literature* (Moscow, 1956), Patricia Hollis's *Class and Conflict 1815-1850* (1973) and Dorothy Thompson's *The Early Chartists* (1971), which also includes a valuable bibliography. Further bibliographical information on Chartism has been collected by W. H. Maehl in *Journal of Modern History*, September 1969.

No biography of Robert Lowery himself has so far been published, though several aspects of his career are covered in our article, "Chartism, Liberalism and the Life of Robert Lowery", *English Historical Review*, July 1967 and in our memoir published in *Dictionary of Labour Biography* (Ed. J. Saville and J. Bellamy) IV (1977), pp. 112-7. As a Chartist who spent most of his life outside London, Lowery needs to be seen in a provincial context. Asa Briggs's important collection, *Chartist Studies* (1959) studies Chartism in several provincial districts, but contains no essay on Chartism in Ireland, Scotland or the North-East of England where Lowery was active. For the

North-East it is therefore necessary to consult W. H. Maehl, "Chartist Disturbances in Northeastern England: 1839", *International Review of Social History*, 1963, and D. J. Rowe, "Some Aspects of Chartism on Tyneside", *ibid*. 1971. Lowery was particularly active in areas outside England. There is no good study of Chartism in Devon and Cornwall, but see Alexander Wilson's *The Chartist Movement in Scotland* (Manchester, 1970), and two articles on Irish Chartism—J. H. Treble, "O'Connor, O'Connell and the attitudes of Irish Immigrants towards Chartism in the North of England, 1838-1848", in J. Butt (Ed.), *The Victorians and Social Protest* (Newton Abbot, 1973), and R. O'Higgins, "The Irish Influence on the Chartist Movement", *Past and Present*, No. 20 (1961). Chartism's London background has been outlined in three recent articles—D. J. Rowe, "The London Working Men's Association and the People's Charter", *Past and Present*, No. 36 (April 1967): D. J. Rowe, "The Failure of London Chartism", *Historical Journal*, 1968: and I Protheroe, "Chartism in London", *Past and Present*, No. 44 (August 1969).

Lowery's autobiography richly portrays the many influences which helped to make him a Chartist. For the history of pre-Chartist radical and working class movements, see E. P. Thompson's paperback, *The Making of the English Working Class* (2nd ed. Pelican, 1968) and G. S. Veitch, *The Genesis of Parliamentary Reform* (1913). For an impressive, though controversial, study of the growth of class-consciousness in the first half of the nineteenth century, see John Foster's *Class Struggle and the Industrial Revolution. Early Industrial Capitalism in Three English Towns* (1974). The economic and social background of the period can be studied in S. G. Checkland, *The Rise of Industrial Society in England 1815-1885* (1964). Chartism originated largely in the disappointment of working men with the results of the 1832 Reform Act, analysed most recently in M. G. Brock's *The Great Reform Act* (1973). Lowery also discusses the resentment inspired by the reformed poor law, which can be followed up in M. E. Rose's essay, "The Anti-Poor Law Agitation", in J. T. Ward (Ed.), *Popular Movements c.1830-1850* (1970) and in Derek Fraser (Ed.), *The New Poor Law in the Nineteenth Century* (1976). Another major influence on Lowery was Robert Owen: G. D. H. Cole's *The Life of Robert Owen* (1925) should now be supplemented by J. F. C. Harrison, *Robert Owen and the Owenites in Britain and America* (1969).

Several secondary works illuminate the various phases of Lowery's Chartist career. For the unstamped press of the 1830s, see Patricia Hollis, *The Pauper Press* (1970) and Joel H. Wiener, *The War of the Unstamped* (Cornell University Press, 1969). Lowery's youthful enthusiasm for liberal causes overseas can be set in context through consulting Henry Weisser, "Polonophilism and the British Working-Class, 1830-1845", *Polish Review*, Spring 1967 and his *British Working Class Movements and Europe 1815-1848* (1975). Perhaps Lowery's most interesting comments on Chartism relate to the plots and conspiracies of 1839-40. These are more fully discussed in David Williams,

John Frost (Cardiff, 1939) and A. J. Peacock, *Bradford Chartism 1838-1840* (York, 1969). For valuable accounts based on government documents, see F. C. Mather, "The Government and the Chartists" in Asa Briggs (Ed.), *Chartist Studies* (1959) and Mather's *Public Order in the Age of the Chartists* (Manchester, 1959). For Urquhartism, see Asa Briggs, "David Urquhart and the West Riding Foreign Affairs Committees", *Bradford Antiquary*, n.s., Part 39 (1958) and R. T. Shannon, "Urquhart and the Foreign Affairs Committees", in Patricia Hollis (Ed.), *Pressure from Without* (1974). There is no good study of the relationship between Chartism and religious movements, but see H. U. Faulkner, *Chartism and the Churches* (first published 1916, Frank Cass ed. 1970). The Complete Suffrage Union is best studied through the biographies of Joseph Sturge by Henry Richard (1864) and Stephen Hobhouse (1919); but see also T. R. Tholfsen, "The Chartist Crisis in Birmingham", *International Review of Social History*, 1958 and (for a Chartist who followed a course very similar to Lowery's) Brian Harrison's memoir of Henry Vincent, in Joyce M. Bellamy & John Saville (Eds.) *Dictionary of Labour Biography*, I (1972). The relationship between Chartism and teetotalism is analysed in Brian Harrison's "Teetotal Chartism", *History*, June 1973, and the temperance movement in which Lowery spent his later years is discussed in Brian Harrison's *Drink and the Victorians* (1971).

Lowery's autobiography should be seen in the context of autobiographies written by other working men in the nineteenth century. The best is Thomas Cooper's *Life of Thomas Cooper* (1972), but William Lovett's *Life and Struggles* (1876), though overloaded with formal manifestos, is at times a moving document, and was republished in 1920 with a useful introduction by R. H. Tawney. David Vincent has edited the autobiographies of Thomas Hardy, James Watson, Thomas Dunning, James Bezer and Benjamin Wilson in his *Testaments of Radicalism* (1977); see also his edition of James Burn, *The Autobiography of a Beggar Boy* (1978); both are in this series. For a study of working class literature in the nineteenth century, see Martha Vicinus, *The Industrial Muse* (1974). Other major influences on the evolution of the working man's autobiography were Samuel Bamford, *Passages in the Life of a Radical* (Ed. W. H. Chaloner, Frank Cass reprint, 1967) and Joseph Arch's *The Story of his Life* (Ed. the Countess of Warwick, 1898). Francis Place's *Autobiography* has recently been published for the first time (Ed. Mary Thale Cambridge, 1972) and George Howell's rich autobiographical material has been drawn upon in F. M. Leventhal's *Respectable Radical: George Howell and Victorian Working Class Politics* (1971).

As for the secondary comment on major Chartist figures, there is an excellent collection of memoirs in G. D. H. Cole's *Chartist Portraits* (1941). There are also several studies of individual Chartists whom Lowery mentions in his narrative. See A. R. Schoyen, *Chartist Challenge* (1958) for Harney, and J. T. Ward's "Revolutionary Tory: J. R. Stephens", *Transactions of the Lancashire and Cheshire Antiquarian Society*, Vol. 68 (1958). Two Chartists who receive special attention from Lowery are Augustus Beaumont and Dr. John Taylor, who can be studied further in W. H. Maehl, "Augustus Hardin Beaumont: Anglo-American Radical (1798-1838)", *International Review of Social History*, 1969 and in A. Wilson, "John Taylor, Esq. M.D. of Blackhouse, Ayrshire (1805-42)", *Ayrshire Archaeological and Natural History Collection*, 2nd series, I (1947-9). For two biographies which illuminate the later evolution of Chartism, see F. B. Smith, *Radical Artisan. William James Linton 1812-97* (Manchester, 1973) and John Saville, *Ernest Jones, Chartist* (1952). The best accounts of the labour movement in the mid-nineteenth century are F. E. Gillespie, *Labor and Politics in England 1850-1867* (Durham, U.S.A. 1927) and Royden Harrison, *Before the Socialists. Studies in Labour and Politics, 1861-1881* (1964). But by this time Lowery was moving away from the mainstream of British working class movements.

Index

A text which is likely to be consulted for many purposes is in special need of an adequate index. Every effort has been made to meet this requirement here. Where several entries appear under one heading, the most important of them feature in heavy type. Apart from names and places, the index includes subject-headings, of which the most important are listed below for convenience: